# BRITAIN'S
# AIRLINES

PART TWO: 1951-1964

# BRITAIN'S AIRLINES

## VOLUME TWO: 1951-1964

GUY HALFORD-MacLEOD

TEMPUS

This book is dedicated to the late Deboorne Piggot
*Thanks, Buzz*

First published 2007

Tempus Publishing
Cirencester Road, Chalford,
Stroud, Gloucestershire, GL6 8PE
www.tempus-publishing.com

Tempus Publishing is an imprint of NPI Media Group

British Library Cataloguing in Publication Data.
A catalogue record for this book is available from the British Library.

ISBN 978 0 7524 4276 1

Typesetting and origination by NPI Media Group
Printed in Great Britain

# CONTENTS

# PREFACE and ACKNOWLEDGMENTS

This is the second volume in my history of Britain's post-war airlines, and it covers the thirteen years – 1951 to 1964 – when the Conservative Party was in power, beginning with the return of Sir Winston Churchill as Prime Minister after six years in opposition. Churchill was succeeded by Sir Anthony Eden, followed in turn by Harold Macmillan – who was Prime Minister from 1957 to 1963 – during a time of growing prosperity. Finally Sir Alec Douglas-Home led the nation for a year before calling an election in October 1964, which saw the return of a Labour government. When the book starts, Britain's airline industry was dominated by the two state-owned, loss-making corporations – BOAC and BEA. There were a number of vigorous independent airlines too, getting by on government contracts, car-ferry flights across the English Channel, holiday flights, and third-level scheduled services; as this volume ends, the situation had not changed very much.

The library at the National Air and Space Museum in Washington, D.C., provided me with much invaluable research material, as did the National Archives at Kew, and I am very grateful to both institutions and their staff for their help. It is also a pleasure to acknowledge my debt to those who have gone before, and to those who so painstakingly collected the information that I have used: Air-Britain (Historians), Ron Davies; Tony Eastwood; Tony Merton Jones; Mike Ramsden; John Stroud; Maurice Wickstead and the many others who have recorded the passage of events. I acknowledge the rights of the Crown and the waiver of copyright; I have tried to contact all possible copyright holders and if I have failed in this, please accept my apologies in advance and contact me.

The publishers of *Flight International*, Reed Business Information, unhesitatingly allowed me to quote from the magazine and to use photographs from the Flight Collection; I am grateful to Paul Gladman for taking the time to go through the images with me. IPC Media were equally helpful in permitting me to quote from *The Aeroplane* and John Donaldson helped me find images from the magazine's archive. My thanks go to Air-Britain (Historians), Richard Riding and the late Roger Jackson for allowing me to use photographs from their respective collections and, as ever, to Brian Pickering for providing me with the bulk of my photographic material. Martin Senn helped prepare them for publication.

Finally, thank you to my wife, Johanna, to my support group at the National Air and Space Museum, and at the Washington Airline Society, and to my former colleagues who worked – or still work – with Britain's airlines.

# INTRODUCTION

'Civil aviation is such a restless subject,' and, Lord Brabazon of Tara might have added, 'difficult and rebellious'. The first English pilot to fly in England, in 1909, and holder of the Royal Aero Club's first pilot certificate, Brabazon's influence continued throughout the Second World War and long after; his thoughts here on civil aviation were delivered in a debate in the House of Lords in December 1951. Winston Churchill had just won the election and been returned as Prime Minister after six gruelling years of Labour government under Clement Attlee, during which Britain had experienced the introduction of the Welfare State, but had also suffered years of austerity as it lurched from one economic crisis to another. The new government faced the unnerving task of coming to terms with all the changes that the previous Labour administration had wrought, from the introduction of a free heath service to the large-scale nationalisation of much of the nation's industry – particularly the energy and transport sectors.

Why restless? There is no perfect formula for civil aviation, and the previous fifty years had shown how precarious the nascent industry was. It may have opened up the world and drawn it closer, but the one thing civil aviation did not do was make money. The British were mercantilists, manufacturers, traders, exporters – they needed links with their markets and their countrymen around the world; but the shipping lines and railway companies that made this possible had to pay their way. The same was expected of air transport; 'civil aviation must fly by itself', said Churchill after the First World War:

> ...but the Government's response to the challenge of imperial flight was fumbling and unimaginative... Deference to laissez-faire and free-market principles made ministers and civil servants extremely reluctant to invest public funds in air transport at a time when the government was short of money.[1]

The early entrepreneurs had to be helped nevertheless and in 1924 the pioneering airlines were brought together to form Imperial Airways. Although a publicly owned company, it was now the government's 'chosen instrument', and received a subsidy of £1 million spread over ten years to develop commercial air transport under the robust leadership of its long-serving general manager – Colonel George Woods Humphery.

Imperial Airways' routes were the threads in the fabric of Britain's early air services, reaching out through India to the Far East and Australia, and across Africa as far south as the Cape. A major innovation was the introduction of the Empire Air Mail Scheme, inaugurated with a new fleet of flying boats, which transmitted all first-class mail within the Empire and Commonwealth by air. Other parts of the globe did not fare as well; it was not until 1937 that the first survey flights across the North Atlantic were attempted and European routes were sparse — aside from the prestigious London to Paris route, which continued on to Zurich, and another line to Brussels and Cologne. Most long-haul services in fact started at a railway station in Paris, to continue down to Brindisi in Italy and a connection by flying boat to Cairo. That left two main areas open to development by the many that had also been called but, unlike Imperial Airways, had not been chosen.

The first area was within the United Kingdom itself. The weather, shorter distances and an excellent network of railways did not suggest air travel as an obvious choice, but the pioneers persevered, and discovered that services were viable if they crossed water, so those that did best were those that connected the mainland with islands offshore: the Channel Islands and the Isle of Man, the Isle of Wight, the Scillies, Lundy, Ireland and the many small islands off the coast of Scotland. Less successful were the trunk routes between big cities, although that was not for want of trying. Worried by the possible competition, but rightly seeing the benefits of air service, the railway companies came to dominate the domestic market as they bought out, or entered into partnership agreements with, the growing number of small internal airlines; by the time domestic services came to be rationalised during the Second World War, the railway companies controlled all but one of the airlines offering scheduled services within the United Kingdom. Of course, there were rebels. Eric Gandar Dower was one, stubbornly flying from Aberdeen to the Northern Isles throughout the war outside the railway companies' grasp. There were others, like North Eastern Airways, which tried before the war to develop trunk routes in competition with the railways and was severely punished by them as a result. The railways imposed a booking ban at travel agencies on North Eastern's flights, which was only lifted in 1938.

Another airline affected by the railway companies' boycott was the first British Airways. This company was an amalgamation of various airlines, all of them owned by Lord Cowdray's Whitehall Securities, which ran both European and domestic services and thus filled the other hole in the British airline route map; for Imperial Airways chose not to interest itself in European services, except for those which connected with its own long-haul routes, like Paris and the eastern Mediterranean. British Airways had powerful backers — the Hon. Clive Pearson, second son of Lord Cowdray, and the merchant bank Erlangers, one of whose scions, Gerard d'Erlanger, was an early board member and who reappears later — and the airline managed to rewrite some of the rules. For a start it was not obliged to fly British-built aircraft, whereas it was understood that the chosen instrument would only fly aircraft manufactured in Britain. So British Airways bought sturdy German Junkers and speedy American Lockheeds for their routes to Germany, Scandinavia and Eastern Europe; it also competed against Imperial Airways on the route to Paris. Then the company persuaded the Government to subsidise its services too, so that Imperial Airways now had to share the bounty with someone else. Finally, it saw off the railway boycott after Pearson joined the board of the Southern Railway.

Spacious and comfortable, the Handley Page 42 airliners of Imperial Airways were brought into service in 1931, and continued in service until the outbreak of war. Here G-AAXC *Heracles* is seen at Croydon. (MAP)

British Airways bought Lockheeds in the late 1930s. Lockheed 14 G-AFMO at Heston, ready for its next flight to Frankfurt and Budapest. (Flight)

There were other independent airlines: Western Airways was owned by Whitney Straight, an early protagonist and establishment figure, and flew high-frequency services across the Severn between Cardiff and Weston-super-Mare; and there were a number of charter airlines. The latter did not serve routes to a schedule but were available for hire; aircraft were smaller then, a de Havilland Rapide carried between six and nine passengers, so the services they offered were more akin to taxi flights, whereas scheduled flights were, and are, more like a bus or train service. Later, as aircraft grew in size, charter flights became more specialised; third parties would charter the capacity of an aircraft for resale to the public, very often as part of a 'package' that included hotel accommodation, which led to the birth of package-tour holidays or Inclusive Tours (IT), a major source of business for charter airlines in the years after the war. For now, charter airlines met a steady demand, maybe carrying passengers on urgent business, or the newspapers to France, or the post in Scotland. Others did good business abroad; Airwork, a company based at London's fashionable Heston Airport, not only serviced aircraft there but helped run air services in Egypt and the Middle East. The doyen of air charter was the adventurous Captain Gordon Olley, who had worked for Imperial

Airways before starting his own company, Olley Air Service, in 1934. He collaborated with the railway companies in a number of joint ventures, but also undertook charter flying out of Croydon, London's main airport and the base for Imperial Airways. One of his flights had notable repercussions; he sent Captain Bebb down to the Canaries in 1936 to take General Franco to Tétuan in Spanish Morocco, who, once there, would raise the Spanish army to fight against the Republican government at the start of the Spanish Civil War.

As the Second World War loomed, charter airlines did increasingly good business with the army, attempting to train its searchlight operators to find aircraft at altitude at night. The coming war had other repercussions. Uneasy with a public company that received subsidies, the government restructured Imperial Airways and, for good measure, fired its general manager, Woods Humphery. Lord Brabazon had some comment to make on that too: 'He is the best airline operator this country has ever had, which is why I suppose he got the sack.'[2] The Conservative government then went further – possibly because it felt the need to secure the services of its two major airlines in the event of war – and bought out the shareholders of Imperial Airways and British Airways, amalgamating them into the British Overseas Airways Corporation (BOAC), which was established on 1 April 1940, just before the fall of France. Britain's international airlines had been taken into state ownership; in other words, they had been nationalised.

When war broke out, all internal services were suspended for a while, but services in Scotland, to the Scillies and Ireland were resumed; the charter operators were allowed to go on flying for the Royal Air Force (RAF) until the government thought that it was paying too much for the privilege of keeping them in business. Therefore, it bought their aircraft from them and they stopped flying; many continued to give sterling service as commercial repair organisations. The railways were allowed to take over all but one of the internal routes under an umbrella organisation, the Associated Airways Joint Committee, and then bought out Captain Olley's various companies. BOAC depended on its many overseas bases in Canada, Africa and the Middle East to maintain its air links with the rest of the world and was called on to perform many vital air support duties, not least during the siege of Malta, in the operation of high-speed flights to neutral Sweden and the Return Ferry Service – carrying pilots to North America to collect aircraft for delivery to Britain. BOAC had a chequered start to life, reflected in constant changes to its top management, but by 1945 was emerging as a global flag-carrier, more concerned with prestige than costs, and increasingly carrying a heavy load of responsibility alongside the few 'Priority' passengers who managed to get a seat on its flights.

With the coming of peace, and the election of a Labour government in July 1945, the words nationalisation and monopoly were commonplace. Competition was deemed wasteful, rationalisation of industry – through amalgamation into bigger units – was more efficient, but that in turn could lead to monopoly suppliers. Better to let the state run these corporations to ensure that they did not abuse their monopoly positions; that was the political theory that lay behind Labour policy to take control of the transport industry. Civil airlines, the road hauliers and the railway companies were the first to be put into the bag; the bus companies came later, but the shipping companies never succumbed. When the shipping companies later came to invest in the post-war airlines, they found the transition from the unregulated freedom of the seas to the closely circumscribed so-called 'freedom of the skies' difficult to manage and incomprehensible. The government already owned BOAC, but now

BEA Vickers Viking G-AJBN *Vindictive* shows the corporation's logo, the 'key' to Europe. (MAP)

created two more state-owned corporations, one to operate – as a monopoly – all scheduled services within the United Kingdom and to Europe, the other to pioneer services to South America, a market the British had not yet got around to developing, despite their extensive interests there. The first of the new corporations, British European Airways (BEA) took over the routes and the equipment of the erstwhile Associated Airways Joint Committee; as the railway companies were also to be taken over, their protests were muted. Conversely, the Channel Islanders fought a hard rearguard action, even though their airline, Channel Islands Airways, was in fact owned by two British railway companies – the Great Western and the Southern. They were joined in battle by Eric Gandar Dower, but the government forced the issue and by April 1947 BEA had taken over all legitimate scheduled services within its sphere of influence. The corporation was given a fleet of new British-built Vickers Viking transports to fly alongside its ex-wartime Douglas Dakotas and the many de Havilland Rapides it had taken over from the railway companies. The other corporation, British South American Airways (BSAA), launched services to South America under the command of former Bomber Command 'Pathfinder' Air Vice Marshal Bennett.

To achieve all this, the government passed the 1946 Civil Aviation Act. As well as confirming the monopoly powers for the three corporations and prudently securing provision for deficit grants to wipe out their probable losses, the government tried but failed to close the door on private-enterprise airlines. The government doubtless thought that if other airlines were prohibited from flying scheduled services, that would be that – any airline entrepreneurs would soon get bored with playing at air-taxi services on the sidelines. But things did not quite work out as planned.

For a start, there was a short interregnum, before the government had passed the new legislation, when there were no legal restrictions on starting air services and, as there was an acute shortage of seats on commercial airlines, there was huge demand for them. Passengers without sufficiently high priority might have to wait weeks, if not months, to book a flight and the situation with shipping was not much better, as most liners were needed to repatriate the forces; personal travel was difficult, yet many people wanted to resume contacts, both business and private, after more than five years of war. There was a pool of former wartime pilots, a surplus of aircraft that could be easily converted to civil use, and a lot of people who wanted to fly with them. By the end of 1947 there were over eighty airlines, flying more than 450 aircraft, on services that ranged from long-haul flights to South Africa, the Far East and Australia, to short trips across the Channel for a holiday in Jersey; although many of the aircraft were still quite small, an increasing number were multi-engine transports. Almost every flight to Europe was guaranteed a return load of fresh fruit, for the British were now allowed to import long-forgotten delicacies from Italian and other Mediterranean growers. When the government's new legislation came into effect, it was supposed to put a stop to all this free market enterprise. However, business went on much as before and the independent airlines either ignored – or found ways around – the new restrictions. Government attempts to enforce their new measures met with a largely unsympathetic hearing from magistrates, who did not seem to understand what the fuss was about and were inclined to rule that the airlines were performing a useful public service. By 1948, however, demand for these extra services had diminished as the state airlines improved their services, by which time the remaining independent charter airlines had evolved into a number of different species.

There were the big contract carriers, like Airwork, Hunting, Skyways, Scottish Airlines and Silver City, which flew regular services on behalf of corporate or government clients. Airwork got an early break when it contracted with the government of the Sudan to fly special staff-leave flights back to the United Kingdom. Hunting contracted with all manner of organisations, like the British Legion, to carry large groups of people around Europe in its fleet of new Vikings. Skyways signed contracts with British oil firms in the Middle East – Iraq Petroleum and Anglo-Iranian Oil – to support their sizeable operations; Anglo-Iranian had 4,500 expatriate staff based at its huge refinery in Abadan, which needed extensive logistical support from the United Kingdom. Silver City flew its Lancastrians, converted Lancaster bombers, on behalf of its owners, the Zinc Corporation (later Rio Tinto-Zinc) and the Imperial Smelting Corporation, carrying staff to-and-from their facilities in South Africa, Burma and Australia. Scottish Airlines undertook contract flying for other airlines, including BEA; its parent, Scottish Aviation, developed an expertise in refurbishing wartime Douglas Dakotas for civil use at its Scottish base – the wartime airport of Prestwick.

Other airlines did different things. In Kent, Wing Commander Kennard started his airline – Air Kruise – flying charters from Lympne to France and quickly establishing a relationship with a local tour operator to offer holidays on the continent. In Derby a wartime reserve flying school stayed in business by continuing flying training after the war, supported by the occasional charter flight; by 1949 Derby Aviation was flying its Rapide on holiday flights to Jersey. At Southend, Squadron Leader Jones relied on pleasure flying at first, but then began to look for business elsewhere for his East Anglian Flying Services company. In Wales, Cambrian Air Services acquired some kudos by putting on a special flight on 1 January 1946, the first day that commercial charter flying was resumed after the war. Further north, Eric Rylands established the Lancashire Aircraft Corporation at Blackpool and, when opportunity beckoned, he flew converted Halifax freighters from a base nearer London, at Bovingdon in Hertfordshire. At Croydon, Captain Olley was somewhat miffed when his chief pilot, 'Sammy' Morton, left to start his own company, leaving the two competing with each other for much the same business, with much the same equipment, from the same airport. Olley

Skyways's Avro Lancastrian G-AKFI, *Sky Consort*, used for services to the Middle East. (Riding T. Riding)

was in an anomalous position, as his company was now owned by the nationalised railway board, although his airline and his aircraft had not been taken over by BEA. He still had Captain Bebb and, soon, a new neighbour, Gerald Freeman, who started Transair as a contract flyer – delivering newspapers and the post to the continent and the Channel Islands – using specially converted twin-engine Avro Ansons. Another anomaly: Whitney Straight, by now a senior figure in the BOAC hierarchy, still owned Western Airways in a personal capacity.

Talking of BOAC, things were not going well at any of the corporations. 'Another dismal and disheartening chapter to an already depressing story,' wrote John Longhurst in *Aeronautics* magazine,[3] referring to the combined losses of £11 million that the three corporations had amassed in 1948. He returned to the subject: 'Our state corporations seem to make such heavy weather over everything they do, and they lose an awful lot of money in the process.'[4] BOAC was finding it hard to adjust after the war – it was overstaffed, with engineering bases spread far and wide, and a motley collection of aircraft only recently enhanced by the purchase of a small number of American-built Constellations for its transatlantic services. BEA was having trouble both digesting its component parts and launching new European services. As for BSAA, it had a poor safety record. Matters came to a head after two of its new Avro Tudors disappeared over the Atlantic Ocean in relatively short order, leading to the grounding of this fleet and the firing of its managing director. BOAC had to take the airline over in 1949; but by this stage, BOAC's fortunes were improving, for the corporation had a new chairman, Sir Miles Thomas, a hard-headed businessman, who, shocked by what he found, determined to trim staff numbers and to procure some decent aircraft. When he joined BOAC there were over 21,000 staff; by the end of 1951, that figure was down to 16,000. He also persuaded the government to buy more stop-gap aircraft from North America in anticipation of the British types that were further down the line. BOAC bought Stratocruisers and Canadian built 'Argonauts', and waited for the British manufacturers to deliver the all-new jet Comets and turbo-prop Britannias that promised to boost both the airline and the aircraft industry. At this point, Lord Brabazon reappears.

The post-war development of Britain's aircraft-manufacturing industry is dealt with more fully in Appendix One, but suffice it to say here that in 1942 Lord Brabazon had been asked to recommend what types of civil aeroplanes should be built when the war was over. Accepting that a certain number of interim types, mainly bomber conversions like the Avro Lancastrian and York, would have to be used initially, Brabazon went on to specify seven major design proposals: a huge transatlantic airliner, the Bristol Brabazon, of which only one example ever flew; a Dakota replacement for European routes, which was met by the turbine-engine Vickers Viscount and the piston-engine Airspeed Ambassador; a four-engine airliner for empire and commonwealth routes, the unhappy Avro Tudor, and eventually the Bristol Britannia; a jet-propelled mailplane for the North Atlantic, the de Havilland Comet; and two small feederliners for British and colonial services, the very successful de Havilland Dove and the quite unsuccessful Miles Marathon. There were further additions to the list, but by and large the future success of the country's twenty-seven different aircraft manufacturers and eight aero-engine builders was to depend on how correct Lord Brabazon had been in his assessment; both BOAC and BEA were to learn that much was expected of them in terms of supporting Britain's manufacturers, both by buying their aircraft and developing them in service.

BEA, meanwhile, was ramping up its staff levels, firing any managers with experience and imposing its inflated costs and standards on an impoverished nation. The government had transferred d'Erlanger from the board of BOAC to become BEA's chairman, but he was really not up to the task. Salvation came from an unlikely source. In yet another reshuffle – the third in as many years – a new Minister of Civil Aviation had been appointed in June 1948, the erudite Lord Pakenham, later the Earl of Longford. He asked his friend Lord Douglas – the two had worked together in Germany – to look into BEA and make recommendations. The catalyst had been a bizarre reversal of policy; dismayed by BEA's losses and lack of progress, the government – barely two years after it had introduced the new legislation – decided to backtrack and allow the independents to take over a few services, those that BEA really could not ever see its way to operating profitably. Whitney Straight's Western Airways was soon back on the Cardiff-Weston run in 1948, teaching his colleagues at BEA, as *The Aeroplane* puts it elegantly, 'how to suck eggs';[5] a few other stalwarts also launched limited services. Seeing that BEA still held the monopoly, these services had to be flown under 'associate agreements'; BEA was nominally the provider of services, the independents flying in association with the corporation. In practice BEA just pocketed a fee and let the independents operate the services, which they had to market and sell themselves; they also had to bear the losses but kept any profits. Profits, however, could attract the attention of the corporation, which was quite entitled to take back any services at any time, especially after the traffic had built up and profits had been made. Lord Douglas was ostensibly asked to look at the workings of the 'associate agreements', which he did, but he was much more interested in the workings of BEA. He was appalled:

> There appears to be a lack of drive in the management of the Corporation. Instead of pursuing an aggressive policy and going out looking for business, they seem content to undertake the minimum services required of them and find excuses for avoiding new work.[6]

There was more criticism in that vein, so much so that Lord Pakenham fired d'Erlanger and asked Douglas to take on the job of running the corporation as chairman. Another new star, Peter Masefield, joined BEA as its chief executive, primarily to give the corporation a good grounding in economics. Together, Douglas and Masefield did manage to turn

BEA around, cutting some costs, ordering the world's first turbine airliner – the Vickers Viscount – and even learning to co-habit with the independents.

The independents now learned that they were allowed to apply for associate agreements on a regular basis and decisions about them would be made by a nominally more independent body, the Air Transport Advisory Council (ATAC) – not by BEA nor the Ministry. Its chairman, Lord Terrington, an experienced and shrewd lawyer, learned how to push the system to its limits, but never bucking it, nevertheless giving the independents far more in the way of new opportunities than they ever thought they would have realised. An early beneficiary was Silver City, which switched from long-haul charters to ultra-short haul cross-Channel hops and inaugurated a car-ferry service between Lympne and Le Touquet in France. Carrying just two cars (and their drivers and passengers) in its Bristol Freighters and with marketing help from the motoring organisations, Silver City offered a reasonable alternative to the British Railways' ferry services. Other airlines seized similar opportunities: Cambrian began to develop routes out of Cardiff; Lancashire, Scottish and others were awarded routes to the Isle of Man and the Channel Islands; there were new services to the Isle of Wight and one enterprising newcomer, Aquila Airways, launched services to Madeira from Southampton, using converted Short Sunderland flying boats. The Channel Islands regained their own airline, as did the Isle of Man. In 1949, Maldwyn Thomas started charter operations with Rapides in the Channel Islands; unable to use the name Jersey Airlines – it was too similar to the now nationalised Jersey Airways – he registered the company as Airlines (Jersey) and painted Jersey Airlines on his aircraft anyway. He was soon applying for associate agreements out of the Channel Islands; in a parallel development, Manx Airlines transformed itself from a charter airline to a scheduled airline, flying its Dakotas under associate agreements to the mainland. For the smaller independents, flying as associates gave them a start, an entry ticket into the commercial world of aviation. It was a break.

The independents were about to get another break. After the surrender of Germany in 1945, the country was divided into four zones, each administered by one of the occupying powers, the United States, the Soviet Union, Britain and France. In the middle of the Russian zone – linked precariously with the western zones by autobahns, canals and railway lines – lay the former German capital, Berlin. This was also divided into four sectors; the Western Allies had to rely on surface transport to keep the population of over 2 million Berliners in their sectors fed and warm, something that became increasingly difficult as the former allies turned against each other and the Iron Curtain descended on Europe. As the Western Allies and the Russians diverged, the Russians began to restrict and disrupt road, rail and barge traffic carrying coal and food to the West Berliners. There was no formal agreement guaranteeing access to West Berlin with one exception; the Russians had agreed to allow allied aircraft to fly along three air 'corridors' into Berlin, an unexpected concession with far-reaching consequences. Meanwhile, the Western Allies encouraged their zones to rebuild the German economy and part of the process was the replacement of the old Reichsmark currency with the new Deutsche Mark in June 1948. When this happened, the Russians blockaded Berlin, cutting electricity supplies, closing the autobahns and stopping rail and barge traffic. The Allies realised that the only way to continue to supply West Berlin was by air – a daunting task. The city needed at least 4,000 tons of supplies a day; a Dakota could carry two and a half tons. The Americans took the lead in organising the airlift, using C-54 transports – the military version of the Douglas DC-4

Skymaster – which could carry around eight tons. Around two hundred of these aircraft flew a continuous pattern, flying up the southern-most corridor and back along the middle corridor. The British did their best flying along the northern corridor, but they could not muster a transport fleet that matched the Americans in size or uniformity. The RAF flew Yorks, which could also carry around eight tons, and the much smaller Dakotas, but the service became severely stretched despite help from Commonwealth aircrew. The British Government looked around for further help and eventually, with many misgivings, decided to contract the independents, who then contributed a varied assortment of equipment – Lancastrians, converted Handley Page Halifax bombers, Tudors, Yorks, Dakotas, the occasional Viking and Bristol Freighter, even Aquila's flying boats. Homogenous it was not. Despite facing many organisational challenges, the British contribution of the RAF and the independents – helped administratively by BEA – worked alongside each other tolerably well. The independents contributed over ninety aircraft in all, flying intensive and repetitious operations which demanded good organisation and engineering support. Although they carried less aid in total numbers than the Americans and the RAF, their share was nevertheless important, for they were responsible for bringing in all of the liquid fuel for Berlin's power stations and vehicles. The airlift went on for over a year and by the end the allies were flying in more than 5,000 tons a day. The Russians lifted the blockade in May 1949, but the allies continued the airlift until sufficient stockpiles had been built up.

When the airlift was stood down at the end of September, the British charter airlines had to adjust from feast to famine. Many of them had prospered during the airlift, not least two young entrepreneurs, Freddie Laker and Harold Bamberg. Laker ran his own aircraft-engineering company, Aviation Traders, and had opportunistically bought a number of Halifaxes from BOAC just before the start of the airlift; he then leased them to Captain Treen of Bond Air Services, a typically canny move by a man who was later to make more such deals. Bamberg's Eagle Aviation had started flying Halifaxes on fruit flights from Italy that summer and became a reliable contributor to the airlift, as did Lancashire Aircraft Corporation, Skyways, Alan Cobham's Flight Refuelling company, Air Vice Marshal Bennett and his former employers – BSAA – and many others. Readjustment was painful. Skyways more or less collapsed and its shell was bought by Rylands to join his Lancashire Aircraft Corporation. Laker and Bamberg both went on to greater glory and they will reappear in later chapters.

Well-established carriers like Airwork and Hunting found continuing work, but the return to a hand to mouth existence was painful for the others. There were just fewer opportunities now; even fruit was being carried on trains again. Two developments, however, changed the situation. One was a providential lifeline thrown to the independents by the Labour government, when it decided to start using charter airlines to carry military personnel to their bases around the world; the other was a short series of flights to Calvi in Corsica in 1950, when a Russian-born journalist, Vladimir Raitz, organised a series of holidays by air for nurses and teachers and launched the inclusive-tour industry.

The British had military bases around the world – they were especially dense in the eastern Mediterranean, the Middle East and along the Suez Canal – but there were garrisons in all the colonies from the islands of the Caribbean to Malaya, Singapore and outposts in the Pacific. To get to and from their bases, troops travelled by sea; it took a long time, not just the journey, but also the endless waiting for a passage. After the successful conclusion of the Berlin Airlift, the military authorities in Britain looked a little more kindly on the independent

Harold Bamberg's Handley Page Halifax G-AIAP which flew 390 sorties during the Berlin Airlift for Eagle Aviation. (MAP)

airlines; cooperation had been made to work, they got the job done, lines of communication were short and direct, there was little bureaucracy, they seemed to get by on a small amount of money. Perhaps they could ferry troops around the world, too? It would be less expensive than using the RAF, which was reluctant to spend money on air transport; with the advent of the Cold War, Britain was busy re-arming and money saved on transport could go to building more fighters and bombers. The Air Ministry suggested to the other service ministries, and the Ministry of Civil Aviation, that a committee be established to investigate trooping by air. Over a period of almost two years, under the chairmanship of Ronald Melville, the committee finally agreed to issue formal tenders for trooping – to Gibraltar, Malta and the Canal Zone. It took an inordinate amount of time for there was a battle of wills between two clever and determined civil servants and their equally clever and determined ministers. On the military side, Sir James Barnes was the civil servant in charge and his minister was 'Manny' Shinwell; they wanted to give the business to the independents because they could be more easily controlled and would be much less expensive. Facing them across the divide was Sir George Cribbett of the Ministry of Civil Aviation, a formidable foe, backed to the hilt by his boss, Lord Pakenham. They wanted the business to be given to BOAC and BEA on ideological grounds; the state-owned carriers should have the right to control all regular flying. They lost out in the end to the service ministries, because when push came to shove, the corporations were unable to submit tenders that were even remotely competitive, but that did not stop the civil ministry fighting a long rearguard action. Hunting, well used to organising large passenger movements, won the first tenders late in 1951, using its Vikings to fly around forty to fifty flights a month to Malta and Gibraltar. Airwork was successful in bidding for the more complicated tender for the Canal Zone, which involved taking over some of BOAC's unwanted Handley Page Hermes four-engine transports; it was galling for the corporation to have to accept that another company could operate its own aircraft less expensively. Lancashire also helped out, flying its Yorks on the long thirteen-hour flight to Fayid in the Canal Zone. Trooping became a major source of business for the independents, although not always a very profitable one.

In the long run, inclusive-tour charters became an even more important source of business. Raitz started something with his cheap fourteen-day holidays in tented accommodation in the Mediterranean sunshine. Nothing was wasted. Because Raitz could guarantee that the accommodation would be used, he got better rates from his suppliers, quickly moving on to hotels in Corsica and then to Palma in Majorca. The aircraft that brought one load of holiday-makers in took the previous, now suntanned, load home. He could keep his rates low – unbelievably low – and his company, Horizon, was always in the forefront, discovering and developing new holiday resorts in the Mediterranean. Others quickly joined him. The only obstacle was that the tour operators could not charge less than the equivalent round-trip air fare for their inclusive-tour holidays; but there were ways around that problem too. The law said that an associate agreement was needed for journeys that amounted to a 'systematic service operated in such a manner that the benefits thereof are available to members of the public.' Operators quickly learned that they did not need a licence if the journey was not 'systematic' or was not made generally available to 'members of the public.' Closed groups flourished; Hunting flew many charters for the East African Club, offering cheap flights from Kenya and Uganda. Even Raitz had started his business by just offering the holidays to nurses and school teachers. Ironically, one of the biggest closed groups, or affinity groups as they came to be called, was Britain's civil service whose members did not scruple to avail themselves of cheap flights and inexpensive holidays.

As 1951 drew to a close, and with it the prospect of the return of a Conservative government, the participants in Lord Brabazon's restless industry faced mixed fortunes. The corporations were definitely on the mend – BOAC was looking forward to introducing the Comet, which would surely give it a competitive edge. Its sister corporation, BEA, was carrying over 1 million passengers a year and awaited the delivery of its first Viscount aircraft. Both corporations were still losing money, but not so much now; in any case losses were wiped out by the Treasury's deficit grants. Some of the independents faced a small revival in their fortunes too. Trooping helped, as did other government contracts. After Dr Mossadeq nationalised Anglo-Iranian's refinery at Abadan in May 1951, the British Government was forced to charter all manner of aircraft from a wide variety of airlines to evacuate its personnel; there was a further crisis in Egypt which demanded the use of chartered aircraft to fly in reinforcements. The war in Korea raised demand for the independents' services, but it also helped those that wanted to quit the business as prices for modern American-built aircraft soared; a number of airlines decided to sell up advantageously rather than continue in uncertainty. The Russians were making trouble in Berlin again, so the government based a Tudor there to provide cargo lift. Silver City enjoyed real growth as it cut fares on its increasingly popular cross-Channel car-ferry services; Silver City and other airlines, benefited from being awarded longer associate agreements, for five years and more. But the independents were increasingly dependent on the government for favours. *Flight* magazine had said in 1948:

> In these days of government monopolies, which mainly appear to mean the sole privilege of losing the taxpayer's money, the charter companies must, presumably, be grateful for any crumbs which may fall from the boards of the corporations. [7]

The independents had moved on a little from that position, but not much.

# ONE

# UNDER CONSERVATIVE GOVERNMENT
## 1951-1953

### THE CONSERVATIVES IN POWER

The results of the election on 25 October 1951 gave the Conservative Party an overall majority in the House of Commons of seventeen, although the Labour Party had won the popular vote. Attlee resigned and Winston Churchill, now aged seventy-seven, was asked to form the next government. He appointed Anthony Eden as his Foreign Secretary and the Hon. John Maclay as Minister of Transport and Civil Aviation, combining the two posts, although for a time the actual ministries remained separate and finally amalgamated in October 1953. The Tories inherited a balance of payments crisis caused in part by the loss of invisible earnings from the Abadan oil refineries and the cost of the escalating war in Korea. The government's priorities were to be rearmament and the rebuilding of Britain's battered economy and housing stock. Such a small majority was not compatible with controversial legislation; the new government accepted and even promoted the welfare state and denationalisation was limited to steel and the road-haulage industry. As *The Aeroplane* noted:

> Compared with the two main lines of thought, the financial crisis and rearmament, which are currently occupying the minds of MPs, aviation is extremely small fry and scarcely worth parliamentary time for debate when related to the gravity of other subjects which Parliament will need all its time and wisdom to resolve.[1]

Nevertheless, the House of Lords did manage to debate civil aviation at an early opportunity in December, although more concern was expressed over the fate of the Ministry of Civil Aviation than that of the independents. Lord Leathers – previously Churchill's Minister of War Transport and now the new government's spokesman – pointed out that the private operators were happier now because of the growth of charter work and recent contracts; also they had been allowed a small foothold in the field of scheduled services. He hoped to give them more opportunities 'without in any way impairing the competitive strength of the international services'. The only change that Lord Leathers did announce was that no new or existing associate agreements would be extended beyond March 1953, in order to give the government breathing space for working out future plans. Britain's new Chancellor, 'Rab' Butler, cut the currency allowance for tourist travel to £50 in November and reduced it further to £25 the following January. He then imposed a passenger service charge at all state-owned airports: five shillings for all international departures, excluding the Channel Islands and the Isle of Man. It was to be the first of many punitive taxes imposed on air travellers and hit the short-haul operators like Silver City hardest.

## BRITAIN AND EGYPT

In October 1951 trouble had erupted in Egypt. There had been a British military presence in Egypt since 1882, even though Egypt was never part of the Empire. The country was strategically important, especially following the building of the Suez Canal in 1869, which provided a vital link with the Empire; Britain was able to exercise considerable political and commercial influence, having also bought out the Egyptian share of the Suez Canal Company. Following General Gordon's exploits at Khartoum and the eventual recapture of the Sudan, Britain and Egypt together governed Sudan as a condominium, although the governor-general was always British and most of the civil servants were British too; hence Airwork's contract for the leave flights. In 1936 the British and Egyptians had signed the Anglo-Egyptian Treaty, which ended the military occupation of Egypt, but allowed the British to station 10,000 troops in the Canal Zone. It also gave the British the right of re-occupation in the event of war, with unrestricted use of Egyptian ports, airports and roads; extremely useful, as it turned out, when the Second World War broke out three years later. At the end of the war the British took some persuading to respect the 1936 treaty, but eventually retired back to the Canal Zone, albeit with over 70,000 troops stationed there.

The rise of Egyptian nationalism – with its demands that British forces leave Egypt and that Sudan become part of Egypt – led to many clashes which became particularly violent in October 1951. Just as Prime Minister Attlee was calling the election, the Egyptians abrogated the 1936 treaty and withdrew a large proportion of the Egyptian workforce on which the Canal Zone depended. Almost the last act of the outgoing Labour Prime Minister, still smarting from the final eviction of Anglo-Iranian Oil from Abadan only a few days previously, was to reinforce the British garrison in the zone, boosting the numbers to over 80,000 and importing East African soldiers to replace the now departed Egyptian workers. The RAF was up to the task of reinforcing the garrison, having by now taken delivery of new Handley Page Hastings transports, which were used to shuttle troops in from neighbouring Cyprus as well as from the United Kingdom. Civil aircraft also flew in reinforcements, BOAC and Lancashire provided Yorks and Airwork contributed its Vikings. The new British Government rejected the Egyptian abrogation of the Anglo-Egyptian Treaty on 6 November and placed the Canal Zone under military control. More riots and acts of sabotage followed, which became particularly violent after the death of forty-six Egyptian policemen during a shoot-out at their headquarters in Ismailia. Civil unrest did not just affect the British military, by now reinforced and well dug in along the Suez Canal; the Egyptian King Farouk abdicated in July 1952 following a coup by the army which eventually brought Colonel Nasser to power.

The Egyptians were sensitive about the use by civilian aircraft of Fayid, the main military airfield in the Canal Zone. There were strict limitations on the British force's personnel entitled to enter the Canal Zone via Fayid, and those who could enter through Fayid were supposed to arrive in military aircraft; all others had to enter through the normal ports of entry and undergo Egyptian immigration and quarantine checks. Whilst permission was given for civil flights in some instances (mainly leave flights to Cyprus), the British Government did not want to force the issue and, after much discussion with the Embassy in Cairo, agreed only to allow forces based in the Canal Zone – together with their families and NAAFI[2] employees – to use the new civilian-trooping services. When matters had calmed down a little and regular trooping flights by civilian aircraft to the Canal Zone began to be implemented in 1952, some care was taken to ensure that those aircraft had at least the appearance of RAF transports, being assigned RAF serial numbers and in many cases carrying RAF roundels. The roundels and serial numbers usually appeared alongside the civil registration markings, giving the airline liveries a curious hybrid look. Crews were given military commissions; air hostesses were left behind at Malta. There followed a period of intense activity for British charter airlines which became responsible for trooping flights from the United Kingdom into Fayid and also for troop movements within the Mediterranean area; many troops based in the Canal Zone spent their leave in Cyprus – a British colony and military base – and the Canal Zone remained the headquarters of the British Middle East Office for the time being, controlling Britain's considerable military infrastructure within the area. Eventually the British agreed to start talking to the new Egyptian government about quitting the Canal Zone; the withdrawal started in 1954 and was phased over the next two years.

## THE GOVERNMENT HAS CHANGED; THE POLICY, IT SEEMS, HAS NOT.

Back at home, the independents were excited that a Conservative government was back in power. Had not the chairman of the Conservative Party's Civil Aviation Committee, Alan Lennox-Boyd, stated his party's intended policy quite clearly?

> We are determined, when the opportunity comes again, to restore a wide measure of private enterprise in the air, to throw the lines open to private competition under proper regulation, and to have some system analogous to the Civil Aeronautics Board in the United States, which has given the benefit of coordination and the benefit of competition as well.[3]

But, with only a small majority, the new government was not about to become embroiled in possibly contentious issues involving the loss-making corporations. The conventional economic wisdom of the time, propagated by the Treasury, was that competition was wasteful, that it would divert traffic away from the established carriers, reducing their market and increasing their losses; the size of the cake was fixed and each slice cut for the independent airlines was a slice taken away from the corporations. When the new Conservative government found itself holding the corporations' purse-strings, it too was reluctant to allow anything that might spoil things, whatever it might have said whilst in opposition. Nor was it anxious to introduce new legislation with a full and complex programme to push through; it wanted to avoid a head-on conflict with the Labour Party.

In his foreword to the annual report of the Air Transport Advisory Council, the new Minister tried to sound encouraging: 'The review of civil air service policy which I am now undertaking has among its objectives increased opportunities for independent companies.' Despite this optimistic tone, the minutes of the Home Affairs Committee of 29 February 1952 show how little room there was to manoeuvre:

> The Minister (of Transport and Civil Aviation) recalled that the policy pursued by the previous Government of using BOAC and BEA as 'chosen instruments' for scheduled international services was similar to that adopted by other countries and he proposed no radical alteration to it. But he did not think that existing policy for air transport within the United Kingdom had been successful. A number of scheduled services had been operated by private companies as 'associates' of the two corporations. But it had been difficult to develop these satisfactorily, since the operators had no guarantee of continuity. The Air Transport Advisory Committee, which examined applications to introduce services, operated under instructions that no service should be authorised where the corporation already had a service or contemplated that they might introduce one. His view therefore was that so far as international services were concerned, little alteration in the present position was practicable except for the possible introduction of a lower class of travel within the colonial empire. Within the United Kingdom he hoped that it would be possible to hand over to free enterprise some of the services of BEA who were losing about £1,000,000 a year on them. Very few freight services were at present being provided either internally or internationally and the corporations and private companies should be given equal opportunity in this field, where there was room for considerable expansion.[4]

Maclay resigned as Minister of Transport and Civil Aviation due to ill health and it fell to his successor, Alan Lennox-Boyd – he of the pre-election promises – to finally announce the government's new policy to the House of Commons on 27 May 1952. The independents would be allowed to start new international services, he said, but not to compete on existing routes; inclusive-tour-charter services could be developed, provided there was 'no material diversion' from the corporations; they could introduce a new C-Class, or Colonial Coach, low-fare service to points in overseas colonies; they could start new all-freight services (albeit with some restrictions), vehicle ferry and helicopter services. The Minister also said that, henceforth, the corporations would not maintain aircraft specifically for charter work, an important concession in view of forthcoming government contracts. The government was equivocal on the matter of domestic services; it would have been humiliating to Lord Douglas to have to hand over any routes to the independents, most especially the trunk services out of London, so he fought another successful rearguard action and the status quo prevailed.

To avoid making any changes to the existing Civil Aviation Act, the Minister chose to enhance the role of the Air Transport Advisory Council (ATAC), which would continue to make recommendations to the Minister on routes under new terms of reference. ATAC was given the task of recommending the new licences to the Minister and instituted a more formal application system, requiring proper notice (four months for international services, only three for domestic), application forms, a hearing process and publication of applications and decisions. Once approved, an operator could operate the route for seven years, and in special circumstances for ten years. Nobody seemed to question that the new government was using existing legislation – which had been introduced by the previous Labour administration in pursuit of its own doctrinal objective of greater state control – in order to pursue quite a different policy. The same laws that had barred the independents from competing against the corporations were now being used to promote greater competition.

The independents were said to be 'profoundly disappointed' in this and the other concessions in the government's statement, although diplomatically, the British Independent Air Transport Association (BIATA) – their trade association – went on to say that it was 'grateful for the assurance that the door has not been entirely closed'.

'We do not want to share their cake; we ask no more than permission to go into the kitchen and bake our own,'[5] wrote Eric Rylands, managing director of Lancashire Aircraft Corporation and, at the time, chairman of BIATA. He later expressed himself more forcibly, criticising the government for continuing the 'socialist policy of wet-nursing the corporations' and observing:

> The independent operators are invited to raise private capital, at double the interest paid by the corporations, whose capital is government guaranteed; the independent operators are invited to operate international freight services on those routes which the corporations have not considered sufficiently profitable to justify putting on services themselves; the independent operators are invited to operate on colonial routes third-class services on which corporation participation will not be denied.[6]

For all its imperfections, the 'New Deal' did allow the independents to go into the kitchen and bake their own 'low-cost, low-fare' cake. They found that the ATAC would take a robust stance on 'material diversion' and under its guidance inclusive-tour flying became firmly established as an important element in the charter airlines' business plans; the development of long-haul services through trooping contracts and Colonial Coach Class brought much needed year-round revenue and utilisation to their aircraft fleets. Within days the first of the C-Class services had been licensed and were ready to start.

## THE START OF COLONIAL COACH CLASS

The concept of Colonial Coach Class services did not suddenly emerge from thin air, nor as a result of brainstorming sessions. Airwork and Hunting were already carrying passengers at low fares between the United Kingdom and colonial Africa under the guise of closed groups; existing contracts had allowed them to offer cheaper fares on a fill-up basis, out of which developed a healthy low-fare market. The granting of Colonial Coach Class licences legitimised the flights in the eyes of the Ministry and brought them within the regulatory net. In his deliberations Maclay made a distinction between international services, served by first- and second-class travel, and the possibility of a lower class of travel within the colonial empire which, 'might be termed coach class. There is, however, practically no scope for this lower class of service on routes serving foreign territories owing to restrictions imposed by bilateral agreements and international fares control.'[7]

The Minister specified that these services were to be a 'lower class of service than that of normal scheduled services, e.g. as regards type of aircraft, short stage lengths, passenger amenities, baggage allowance'. The first of the new services was licensed to Airwork and Hunting jointly between London and Nairobi, Kenya. Each carrier was allowed to operate a fortnightly 'Safari Service', which took two and a half days to get to Nairobi and the same amount of time to return. Two night stops in each direction were planned; meals and hotel accommodation were included in the price of the ticket, which cost £98 one way, as opposed to £140 on the normal service; return fares were £180 and £252 respectively. Both airlines were licensed to use their twenty-seven-seat Vikings which were to compete against BOAC's speedier Comets, Argonauts and Hermes. Aviation writer John Stroud was on the inaugural Airwork flight from Blackbushe on 14 June 1952:

> The feature of the 'Safari Service' which has allowed its operation parallel to BOAC at lower fares is its scheduling. Southbound flights leave London on Saturdays in the morning and arrive at Nairobi on Monday afternoons. The return flights leave Kenya on Wednesday mornings and arrive in London on Friday afternoons. Night stops are made at Malta and in the Sudan in each direction and hotel accommodation together with all meals and road transport is included in the fare.
>
> I flew on the inaugural 'Safari Service' to Nairobi with Airwork, and back on the inaugural northbound flight with Hunting and can therefore vouch for the high standard of operation of the service and the first-class cabin service. The flights were extremely interesting with landings at Nice, Malta, El Adem, Wadi Halfa, Khartoum, Juba and Entebbe. The sectors were not too long and the height at which the flights were made offered good views of most parts of the route. The only disadvantages that I could see were those associated with turbulence over the desert which must on occasion be encountered by unpressurised aircraft flying at about 10,000ft. This was however never excessive on the flights I made. Personally I think the interest of the flight more than outweighs this possible disadvantage.
>
> (After First class and Tourist class) Airwork and Hunting have introduced a third type of service which is best described as first class slow. In this third category high-density seating has not been resorted to and cabin service is of the highest standard only the schedules place the 'C' rate in a special group.[8]

The London-Nairobi route at this time was a cabotage route. Traditionally, cabotage – a shipping term – had meant the right to carry goods and passengers between ports both of which were located in the same geographical entity, for example, between Portsmouth and the Isle of Wight. However, in aviation use its meaning had been extended to cover services between airports both of which were in the same political entity; that meant not just within the United Kingdom but also to and from its colonies and overseas possessions. At the time Kenya was a colony and the British Government had merely to stipulate the types of service it was prepared to authorise without invoking any international relations or agreements; generally speaking, cabotage rates were lower than similar international fares. The early development of the tourism industry on the southern coast of Spain owed much to the availability of cheaper cabotage fares between London and Gibraltar. Cabotage routes were

Hunting Air Transport's Vickers Viking G-AGRW landing at the airline's Bovingdon base. This aircraft went on to serve with Overseas and Autair. (Flight)

reserved to the carriers of the relevant political entity; British carriers had right of access between the United Kingdom and British colonies, but the same privileges did not extend to the self-governing dominions of Canada, South Africa, Australia and New Zealand.

## COLONIAL SKIRMISHING

The services were soon booked to capacity, and both carriers achieved load factors over 80 per cent – in other words, over 80 per cent of the seats were taken – in the first six months of operation, indeed between June and September load factors were in the low to mid nineties. At such high levels of occupancy most scheduled airlines would have increased the frequency as a matter of course; Airwork and Hunting had to be mindful of diverting traffic from BOAC but nevertheless they successfully applied to increase their respective frequencies from one every two weeks to once a week, and at the same time each obtained a seven-year licence. All was not entirely plain sailing, however; a certain level of sniping from the incumbent corporation was only to be expected. At an early stage, BOAC was complaining to the Ministry of Civil Aviation that Airwork was carrying passengers on its service who were not covered by the terms of its licence, provoking a spirited response from Airwork's managing director, Sir Archibald Hope:

> We know of course perfectly well that BOAC dislike our service intensely. It is awkward for them that we are operating at fares nearly 40 per cent below theirs and making a profit when they need a vast subsidy. They are doing everything they can to embarrass us and make our service fail. In my view it is high time that somebody hit them over the head and told them

to stop being stupid and try to cooperate. There is plenty of room for both them and us on the East African route and we are not taking any traffic that could afford to go by BOAC or that would go by BOAC. They themselves have admitted that fact.[9]

The limited frequencies ensured that demand for these services was never properly met; they were operated at a very high load factor, with long waiting lists. In later years when BOAC found itself with more capacity, it began to look somewhat enviously at the low-fare market and started to lay claim to it. But its attitude towards the low-fare market was ambivalent; when it could it always preferred to court the higher-fare passenger, and its interest in developing cheaper travel facilities tended to wax and wane depending on its surplus capacity. Whenever BOAC was introducing a new fleet type and thus bolstered by large deliveries, it suddenly took an interest in 'new' markets, usually those that had been developed at some cost by independent airlines. This was especially true in the late 1950s, when BOAC, inundated with new aircraft – DC-7Cs, Britannias, Comets and Boeing 707s – scrabbled around to try and find work for them and seized on the colonial coach-class market as a source of business. The government then forced the independents to surrender a large proportion of their share of the traffic to BOAC. The pattern repeated itself in the late 1960s when transatlantic charters were perceived as a new market to be targeted by the scheduled carriers, particularly BOAC and Pan American, as they faced up to the challenge of finding work for their newly ordered jumbo jets, the Boeing 747. At other times, however, BOAC (and its successor airline) preferred not to trouble itself with the low-fare market, for which its higher costs in any event made it ill-suited.


## REALITY CHECK


With the granting of a seven-year associate agreement licence, Airwork and Hunting were able to plan their marketing strategy on a more permanent basis; Colonial Coach Class became an accepted low-fare service, albeit tightly circumscribed as to service standards, frequency and equipment. Although the Colonial Coach Class services made the headlines, the reality was that these services represented but a tiny proportion of the output of the independent airlines. BOAC was largely successful in its attempts to thwart their development; fortnightly services with Vikings and Yorks hardly made a dent on demand, and of the twenty-five applications for Colonial Coach Class in 1953, eighteen were rejected following objections from BOAC and BEA.

Thereafter, limited route expansion followed when Hunting and Airwork were granted a further coach-class licence in June 1953 to Central Africa, serving N'Dola, Lusaka and Salisbury. This time the reciprocal operator, Central African Airways (CAA), was also granted a licence. As the service was limited to one flight a week, Hunting and Airwork operated in practice only once a month, with CAA operating the other two services. Hunting flew the first flight out of its London base at Bovingdon on 26 June 1953.

Another new entrant in the Colonial Coach Class market was Skyways, which was awarded a fortnightly licence from Stansted to Nicosia via Malta. The service started on 11 November 1953 and was dubbed 'Crusader Class'. Skyways also held rights between Malta and Nicosia, though not between London and Malta. The Stansted-Nicosia flight took over fourteen hours in a York and left most passengers somewhat deaf, but Cyprus was in the sterling zone so there were no currency restrictions, the fare was only £75 for the round-trip, and there were high hopes that this attractive island would start to welcome more tourists. Skyways was no stranger to flying tourists into Nicosia. Together with Cyprus Airways it operated the Cyprus Leave Service flights for troops stationed in the Canal Zone, and had Yorks based at Nicosia for that purpose, flying around 13,000 troops during the six-month leave period between May and October for rest and recreation in the Troodos Mountains.

## IATA AND TOURIST AIR FARES

Colonial Coach Class was just one manifestation of a growing trend towards cheaper air fares. As new, more efficient airliners entered service, and the demand for travel began to reassert itself after the early post-war years, some airlines sought to make air travel less exclusive; international long-haul flights were still sold at so-called standard rates, equivalent to first class. Led by the American carriers, transatlantic airlines came under pressure to offer lower fares for the summer season of 1952. Fares had to be agreed unanimously by the airlines under the auspices of IATA, the International Air Transport Association, the cartel to which most flag-carriers belonged; governments for their part merely approved the fares set by IATA. So during the later months of 1951, IATA thrashed out an agreement between its members, leading to fare cuts of around 30 per cent for tourist travel. The ordinary single fare from London to New York was £141 2s, whilst the new tourist rate was set at £96 9s, a saving of over 31 per cent. The savings for off-season round-trip fares were lower, at around 20 per cent. Changes in service standards will be familiar to modern readers; meals had to be paid for, there was no bar service, and seats were narrower and set at a closer pitch. By 1953, BOAC was reconfiguring its aircraft to carry more tourist-class passengers, and extending service to its other destinations in Africa and the Far East, whilst BEA in turn introduced tourist class on its European services.

## LOW COSTS, LOW FARES

Colonial Coach Class may not have transformed the commercial mix of the independent airlines, but they did highlight the main ingredient: low fares. Almost by stealth the independents had come to be the suppliers of low-cost products: inclusive tours, trooping contracts, Colonial Coach, closed groups. Low fares require low costs and these can be achieved through such time-honoured methods as buying aircraft less expensively second-hand, using fewer staff and paying them less, eschewing grand office accommodation, operating from smaller and less costly airfields. Many airlines, mainly the smaller operators, pursued this formula successfully and reaped the benefits in their chosen fields.

Others adapted the formula: Hunting and Airwork bought new Vikings and went on to buy new Viscounts, indeed Hunting and it successors almost always bought new; Eagle came to be based at Heathrow and paid its engineering staff on a par with those from the corporations; Silver City bought brand new Bristol Freighters and even went so far as to build its own airfield in Kent; Skyways bought second-hand but in large and extravagant quantities. These, the major independents, did not rely solely on low-capital costs to make them competitive; they also had to deploy their aircraft more efficiently if they were to offer a cheaper alternative. Putting in more seats spread the cost over more people, so individual passengers paid less; aircraft bought from the corporations invariably had their seating capacities increased, even aircraft bought new were configured for more passengers. One airline, Channel Airways, became a past master at squeezing in more seats, ruthlessly stretching capacity to its limits.

> If you fit sixty passenger seats into an air liner normally fitted by the scheduled air-line operators with forty seats, obviously the fares can be considerably reduced. The comfort is also reduced, but while there are many people who will always prefer to pay extra and travel in comfort, there is a very much larger number of people who would prefer to travel squashed and without first class service rather than not make the journey at all.[10]

Charter flying allowed high load factors to be achieved; not only were there more seats on the aircraft, there were fewer empty ones. Leisure travellers are less time-sensitive than business travellers; if a flight is full, the holiday passenger may well elect to travel on a different day, rather than abandon the holiday altogether or fly with another airline. Staff were paid less, and more was expected of them; pilots flew longer hours in the air, fewer staff were around to handle departing and arriving aircraft. The aircraft were also expected to fly intensively, easier over long distances, more of a challenge for short cross-Channel hops. Commercially the airlines had to be nimble, finding business where they could, changing plans at the last moment when an unexpected 'rush' job was required, flying off-route, carrying freight outbound and maybe returning with a load of passengers, minimising dead sectors, always trying to keep the aircraft in the air.

Two further observations on low fares and low costs. Personal spenders are attracted to lower fares: inclusive-tour holidays became items of household expenditure; visiting friends and relatives in America and the Commonwealth would have been beyond the reach of many people had there not been a cheaper charter alternative. Over time personal travel has fuelled the greatest demand, and the independents unwittingly discovered, then developed this market. Doubtless they would have preferred to fly more scheduled services, but these were denied them, and in the process they stumbled into a bigger market. When, however, they did operate scheduled services, they did so from a lower cost base. This gave them two advantages; a marginal or loss-making service of the corporations' might make a profit for a private airline, and fares set artificially high by IATA[11] allowed increased profits over the norm when charged by low-cost independents. The perceived security and prestige of a scheduled service network remained the holy grail for most charter operators, long after the advantages of specialisation had uncovered a more profitable alternative.

## 1952 ACTIVITIES

Be that as it may, there was still plenty of work for the charter airlines on their own turf. Ships' crews needed to change, ships' spares had to be sent out in a hurry, people went on holiday, they attended special events like car racing. Early in the new year, Airwork was re-awarded the Sudan Government leave contract, this time for two years, and stated that it would use its newly acquired Hermes aircraft to supplement the Vikings on the service. The previous year the airline operated 150 round trips, carrying over 4,000 passengers and providing year-round utilisation for at least two aircraft.

In the new year Eagle was finding more competition now in the big four-engine aircraft market, with Lancashire released from its Air Ministry contracts, but that did not stop Eagle from securing a worthwhile contract from the United Africa Company to fly textiles to Kano and then continue with more flying within Nigeria during the railway strike there. In the meantime, Air Ministry work provided plenty of utilisation for Eagle's Yorks with four flights a month to the Far East; and on 7 January the airline was awarded a two-year contract to fly RAF personnel and their families between Rhodesia and the United Kingdom – around forty flights a year. In April 1952 Hunting lost the West African trooping contract that it had held for almost two years; it was awarded to Crewsair, giving the Southend-based airline eighty flights a year, worth around £250,000. The Air Ministry were not the only organisation moving people and freight about; the NAAFI – purveyors of goods, stores and services to the military – frequently had to make its own transport arrangements for its staff, using Crewsair for its weekly flights to Fayid, and Scottish Airlines to Cyprus.

1952 saw an unusual long-range flight by another four-engine aircraft when the Falkland Islands Company chartered an Aquila Sunderland flying boat to carry mail out of Southampton to Port Stanley and back, as part of its centenary celebrations. The flight left Southampton on 21 April and travelled by Madeira, Sal, Natal, Rio de Janeiro and Montevideo, arriving at Port Stanley on 28 April. The charter was a thoughtful publicity stunt but expensive, at a time when sea-travel was the accepted norm, and it was never repeated. Another special flight occurred when BOAC's Argonaut *Atalanta* brought back the new Queen, Elizabeth II, from Kenya, where she had been visiting, after her father, King George VI, died in his sleep on 6 February 1952.

To ease the shortage of aircraft, the Air Ministry decided to release on to the market about thirty C-47s, the military designation of the Dakota, which were stored at the RAF bases at Silloth and Kirkbride. There were restrictions on the resale of these aircraft, they could not be sold abroad for example, but they would boost capacity and provide competition for the existing operators. Over the next two years the Air Ministry released sixty Dakotas, thirteen Yorks, four Proctors and one Dominie (Rapide) for sale to independent airlines: a welcome addition to their inventory. There were some name changes: Hunting Air Travel became Hunting Air Transport and Aero Charter added its joint owners' initials to its title, becoming BKS Aero Charter.[12] Skyways had sold out to Lancashire, but in this case the name stayed the same; Lancashire preferred to use the Skyways name for its long-haul charter activities and retained the Lancashire name for its domestic scheduled services. At the time of the takeover Skyways had just sold its remaining two Dakotas under charter in Kuwait, but retained its maintenance division at Stansted in Essex, having moved there from Dunsfold in 1951. Stansted would be the new base for Skyways's trooping flights and an important engineering facility. Blackbushe was also developing as an important base for the independents. Britavia, the parent company of Silver City, bought a maintenance organisation, Aviation Servicing, based at Blackbushe; it soon gained another new customer when Crewsair shifted its base of operations from

Southend in order to run its trooping flights to West Africa more conveniently. Eagle and Airwork had already moved their trooping operations to Blackbushe. After Crewsair ceased flying, Eagle bought Aviation Servicing from Britavia in November 1952, renaming it Eagle Aircraft Services in July 1953. On a sadder note, Hunting suffered its first fatal crash on 16 February when a Viking – en route from Bovingdon to Nairobi – crashed into a mountain in Sicily with the loss of all thirty-one passengers and crew on board.

## AIRWORK, BOAC AND THE HERMES

Airwork, meanwhile, was waiting to accept the first of its four Hermes from the manufacturer. The aircraft had initially been returned by BOAC in order for them to be modified for the trooping flights. The aircraft were fitted with sixty-eight rearward facing seats for trooping, but a more spacious layout was used for the Sudan leave service flights. These were new aircraft which had never entered service with BOAC and they are significant as the first modern, pressurised four-engine aircraft to enter service with an independent airline. Because of the lack of 115-octane fuel at some of the airports Airwork used, the engines were modified to use 100-octane fuel and the type designation for this modification is Hermes 4A. Later, as 115-octane fuel became more widely available, the engines were converted back to the original standard. The first aircraft for the Fayid Task were delivered in a very austere all-metal finish, with RAF roundels and serial numbers, but all aircraft were eventually painted in Airwork's green and white scheme.

Their entry into service was little short of disastrous. Airwork operated the first flight to Fayid on 17 June, using G-ALDC/RAF serial WZ840.[13] By the end of July it had three Hermes in service – however, on 23 July Hermes G-ALDB was written off after a forced landing in the dark near Pithiviers in France whilst outward bound from Blackbushe. The starboard outer propeller broke off and was thrown onto the starboard inner engine which partly broke from its mountings; its propeller could not then be feathered. A loss of hydraulic power allowed the undercarriage to become unlocked and to fall into a down position. Faced with a loss of power, excess drag and a windmilling propeller, Captain Lovelock elected to make a forced landing, skilfully missing high-tension wires and telegraph poles as he did so. There were no injuries amongst the seventy soldiers and crew on board. Just over a month later, on 25 August, Hermes G-ALDF, operating to Khartoum on the Sudan Government leave service with fifty-one passengers and a crew of six, suffered a double engine failure and had to ditch off Trapani in Sicily. The sea was fairly calm and the aircraft stayed afloat for about ten minutes, but five passengers and one of the stewardesses drowned. Inevitably there were calls for the Hermes to be grounded but the Ministry resisted. Both accidents were later attributed to fatigue fracture of a crankshaft web in the engine. Airwork now only had one Hermes available for trooping; to cover the shortage in 1952, an additional aircraft was leased from BOAC, as the fourth on order would not be delivered until October, and a further aircraft was acquired in February of the following year. Judging from Sir Miles Thomas' remarks, BOAC was happy to see them go:

In 1950 there was introduced into service another converted war-time aircraft, the Handley Page Hermes. Although it stood on a tricycle undercarriage instead of – like its precursor the

Handley Page Hermes G-ALDC about to depart on its first trooping flight to Fayid in the Canal Zone on 17 June 1952. (Flight)

> Hastings – drooping its tail on the ground, it was not an economic aeroplane. For one thing it flew wearily with its tail down, which induced an appalling amount of drag, and we had a whole sheaf of troubles to eliminate before it was route-worthy.[14]

By October 1953, three years after first entering service, all the Hermes had been withdrawn by BOAC, their places taken by the Argonauts, and were offered for sale at around £200,000 apiece.

## NEW EQUIPMENT

Airwork had at last introduced new four-engine Hermes airliners, but there was nevertheless a growing investment gap. BOAC and BEA were both bringing on line large new aircraft, financed advantageously by the government. Comets, Britannias, Viscounts and Ambassadors were about to, or were already gracing, the front-line fleets of the corporations. The armoury of the independents was pitiful by contrast; the two Hermes, themselves rejects from BOAC, were the most modern aircraft. Otherwise long-haul flying depended largely on Yorks, Vikings and Dakotas, none of which came with a youthful pedigree. British manufacturers were more interested in producing warplanes for the services, and most charter airlines could only dream about buying Viscounts and Britannias. Even good second-hand equipment was hard to obtain and expensive – prices having been driven up by the Korean War. A DC-4 Skymaster now cost between £175,000 and £200,000 and that was for an unpressurised aircraft. The Air Ministry was only awarding one- or two-year contracts, hardly long enough to enthuse a serious backer or City investor. By contrast, the operator of the two newly ordered troopships was given a ten-year contract to manage them.

For the time being the charter airlines would have to muddle through. Air Commodore Powell, chairman of BIATA, cautioned as he introduced the annual report for 1952-53:

> Most of our progress must be considered in relation to our earlier precarious existence, and although conditions are better we are by no means sailing in sheltered waters. Some of our forward financing and new fleet problems are relatively worse than the earlier struggles for survival. [15]

The Ministry of Civil Aviation still had ten surplus Tudors to dispose of, left over from the Berlin Airlift, but even at give-away prices, down to £10,000 apiece, and with the added inducement of their passenger-carrying certificates being restored, there were as yet no takers. The aircraft had been built as freighters, so a great deal of work would have to be done to bring them up to passenger-carrying standard. More promising was the decision of BEA to start disposing of its Viking fleet to join the supply of Yorks and Dakotas still being released by the Air Ministry; Eagle was an early buyer of the surplus Vikings.

Hunting decided to tackle the problem head-on. With renewed confidence, and a major network of services about to be launched from Newcastle, the airline announced an order for three Viscounts, costing some £900,000, for delivery in 1955. It was a bold move, serving notice on the other charter airlines, and even the corporations, that at least one independent had faith in the future and was prepared to invest in it.

In October the Cayzer shipping group, through its Clan Line Steamers subsidiary, purchased an interest in Hunting Air Transport and Field Aircraft Services, and the airline subsequently changed its name to Hunting-Clan Air Transport. Hunting, also a ship owner (at the time the Hunting group had major interests in the oil industry and owned sixteen tankers) and Clan Line each held 50 per cent of a new parent group, Hunting-Clan Air Holdings. The Clan Line maintained a schedule of shipping services from the United Kingdom and continental ports to India, Pakistan, Ceylon, South and East Africa and Australia. The other parts of the Hunting Group, Hunting Aerosurveys, Aerofilms and the aircraft manufacturer Percival Aircraft, were not affected by the change.

## CHARTER MATTERS

In July 1952 Laker amalgamated all his charter airline flying activities under the name of Air Charter. He also took on George Forster as his commercial manager and towards the end of the year ordered two Bristol Freighters. The South African airline Tropic Airways acquired an ex-RAF Dakota; it needed a British airline to operate the latter under the terms of sale, and so registered a British company, Meredith Air Transport, using the name of one of its British directors. When it lost one of its other Dakotas on 27 July, after a successful ditching off Malta, Tropic had to sub-charter a number of flights to British charter operators. The Olympic Games in Helsinki that summer also provided good business for the charter airlines; Skyways operated twenty-two flights between the United Kingdom and Helsinki, mainly carrying equestrian teams and their horses, but Eagle and Silver City were also visitors to Helsinki in August. In September, Eagle was acquiring both medium- and long-range aircraft; four Dakotas were bought from the RAF, of which two were sold on to BOAC's East African subsidiary and two Yorks were bought from BOAC, bringing Eagle's long-haul fleet up to six.

With Airwork still faltering on its Canal Zone flights, Skyways was heavily committed to trooping to Fayid, but found time to secure a contract from KLM for a twice-monthly freight service between Amsterdam and Bangkok using two of its Yorks. Scottish Airlines still had its valuable contract from Iraq Petroleum for regular freight and passenger flights to the Persian Gulf, mainly to Dukhan, and Silver City, which sent its Freighters far and wide during the winter months, was an occasional visitor to Dukhan too.

The end of October 1952 was a bad time for charter airlines with the bleak winter months ahead of them; now it was Crewsair's turn to cease operations. Crewsair was notable for its immaculate fleet and for being the progenitor of BKS. Its four Vikings went to Eagle which went on to build up the second biggest Viking fleet after BEA; the West African trooping contract was re-let to Airwork in the New Year. Next, Air Transport (Charter) (CI), a prototypical charter airline, announced it would cease flying, bringing to an end a career which had embodied all the main elements of charter activity in the early post-war years: ad hoc freight and passenger work, both long and short haul; participation in the Berlin Airlift; pioneering inclusive-tour flights, both domestic – to the Channel Islands – and international – to Corsica; sub-charters for the corporations; even some occasional flights for the Air Ministry, although the airline was never a significant trooping contractor. A study of Air Transport (Charter) (CI) reveals the British charter airline industry in microcosm; even the fact of its demise was somehow typical.

*The Aeroplane* marked the passing of Air Transport (Charter) (CI) with a round-up of the survivors:

> This leaves eleven operators with medium- and long-range equipment. They have between them forty Yorks, twenty-one Dakotas, twenty Vikings, nine Bristol 170s, four flying boats, two Hermes and two Tudors. By companies the fleets are as follows: Air Charter, eight Yorks, one Dakota, one Tudor; Airwork, eight Vikings, one Dakota, two Hermes; Aquila, three Hythes, one Solent (Four Hythes in reserve); BKS, four Dakotas; William Dempster, one Tudor; Eagle, five Yorks, four Vikings, three Dakotas; Hunting, eight Vikings, one Dakota; Lancashire,[16] 24 Yorks, two Dakotas; Scottish, two Dakotas, three Yorks; Silver City, nine Bristol 170s; and Starways, seven Dakotas.[17]

There were also a number of vigorous domestic airlines, Morton, Olley and the rising stars Jersey Airlines and Cambrian, which operated smaller equipment such as Rapides and Doves mainly under associate agreements.

## SILVER CITY

Silver City, meanwhile, was looking further afield, and worrying about its short-sector economics:

As we reviewed our results for 1951 we had anxious thoughts about where we were heading. We had proved that we had a good and attractive product. The twenty-minute flight and the quick unloading time put the cars in the Customs at the same time as their owners so it was perfectly possible for them to be on the road again within ten minutes of arrival. We were offering a good timetable with four flights a day in the winter, rising to twelve at Easter, twenty-four at Whitsun and thirty-six or more by mid-July. From the latter part of July in 1951 we had actually operated forty-two round-trips daily between Lympne and Le Touquet which, allowing for essential maintenance, was about the limit in daylight hours for our fleet of six aircraft. We had therefore wound up our fleet of six to very nearly their maximum output.

There seemed to be two possible solutions. Firstly, we could fly another route; preferably one slightly longer so that the work output of the aircraft could be increased in terms of revenue hours. With only the short route in operation the aircraft were locked at 800 to 900 hours a year in spite of the buzz-saw operations in the summer months. An improvement to 1,200 or even 1,500 hours was what we were after. Secondly, we might be able to improve the carrying capacity of our aircraft by getting longer models built. If for instance we could carry three cars at a time we would be able to carry more traffic in fewer flights and also increase our hourly revenue rate.

Every sort of poor economic result showed up in the operating costs of such a short route. Three take-offs an hour meant high petrol consumption and engine wear. The three landings an hour also meant high landing fees and a high instance of total terminal and ground handling costs. In fact these terminal costs came to 27 per cent of our operating costs, closely followed by maintenance and engineering at 22 per cent. Take for instance (the) maintenance and engineering at 22 per cent. This figure was nearly twice that achieved by contemporary operations of Viking aircraft, which had normal stage lengths. The Vickers Viking of BEA had the same engines but instead of three landings an hour was only down every two and a half hours in most cases. Some difference in wear and tear. If our stage length had been 247 miles instead of 47 terminal and landing costs would have dropped from 27 per cent to 15 per cent; nearly a half.

Of course there was enough jam on the other side to make it all worthwhile. We had a very high load factor that stayed above 90 per cent for weeks on end. We had low promotion and selling costs because the two motoring organisations carried our message direct to the continental traveller.[18]

Silver City decided to open up a new route, Southampton to Cherbourg, which was less intense than the short cross-Channel run, but at eighty-eight miles somewhat longer, allowing a thirty-five-minute sector. The route did so well that Silver City pioneered a third route, from Southend to Ostend; however, instead of basing aircraft at Southend, they were detached from Lympne, which involved a certain amount of dead flying between stations. Silver City pulled off that route at the end of the first 1952 season, a decision it came to regret when Laker and his Air Charter company started a regular vehicle-ferry service from Southend to Calais in April 1955. Silver City also persuaded Bristol Aeroplane to build a longer version of the Freighter, which could carry three cars and up to twenty passengers. Six were ordered, at a cost of £500,000, at the time the largest ever order for new equipment by an independent, and they were introduced in 1953:

Bustling scene at Lympne in Kent, with two of Silver City's Bristol Freighters ready for their next load of cars for the short flight to Le Touquet in France. (Flight)

The year 1952 put our cars-carried total over 40,000 and the passenger figure to 130,000 so we were now an accepted and substantial element in the total cross-Channel traffic. We also had a notable victory in the course of the season – we got permission to carry unaccompanied passengers. There were not many seats available for them – two or three in each Mark 21 – but a few hundred each week made a satisfactory increase in revenue for no extra effort.[19]

The success of Silver City was all the more remarkable for the many obstacles that the government and its agencies threw up in its path. This was not due so much to malevolence, rather to carelessness and neglect. Silver City, with its ultra-short-haul routes, was particularly affected by the passenger service charge imposed in February 1952. A passenger on the fifty-seven-mile route from Lympne to Le Touquet paid his or her five shillings in the same way that a passenger flying from London to Athens did, and in the case of the Ministry-owned airfield at Lympne, the concept of a passenger service charge was surely misplaced. Despite the considerable income that the Ministry derived from both Silver City and Air Kruise in landing fees and now with the new tax, no money was actually spent on passenger services. The Customs building had been enlarged, but departing passengers still had to wait out in the open. Furthermore, nothing had been done about the state of the grass runway which was poorly drained.

One area of activity that Silver City actively pursued was that of passenger and cargo charters. The occasional long-haul flight would be undertaken[20] during the winter months when the crews and the aircraft could be spared, but the airline was just as ready to fly extra sections on its short-haul routes. The winter of 1951/52 found Silver City flying 1,800 head of cattle across the Channel, en route from Ireland to Italy, carrying on average eight 11 cwt. bullocks on each flight. Sometimes the opportunity was taken to carry French cheeses in bulk on the return flights, exchanging one set of smells for another.

## BRITAVIA'S COMPANIES

Silver City pursued a policy of lowering fares whenever possible, and for 1953 announced rates that were in some cases 50 per cent below the previous year's rates. Doubtless helped by a small increase in the foreign exchange allowance, the results of this policy were little short of sensational. In 1953, 38,973 cars were carried, up from 10,910 in 1952. A new service from Gatwick to Le Touquet was introduced, with two flights a day connecting with the frequent train service to Victoria; cars were carried but the main purpose was to provide a low-cost passenger service. Gatwick had been expanded during the war when the racecourse and other adjoining lands had been requisitioned to create a much larger airfield. At various times after the war the government would periodically announce its intention to derequisition Gatwick, which would have meant the racecourse reverting to its owners and so prevented the development of the airport. But the government never carried this out. Prodded by Peter Masefield – long an enthusiast for Gatwick who saw it as a useful diversionary airport for London – the government announced its intention in July 1952 to develop Gatwick as an alternative to London Airport.

Gatwick was not the only airport that Silver City was interested in developing.

> By the beginning of this 1953 season it was evident that we were being handicapped in our Lympne operations by the ground facilities and the restricted and not very flat grass surface. Lympne was the property of the Ministry of Civil Aviation and was only just big enough. When it was wet we had braking and skidding problems. Another disadvantage was that it was perched on a ridge over 300ft above the coast at Hythe, which put it much nearer the cloud base and sometimes in it. The Ministry was not inclined to spend money on hard runways, which could not have been extended beyond the existing boundaries but which would have cured our braking problems in the wet and muddy winter months.[21]

When conditions got too bad at Lympne the operation had to be transferred to Southend, at some cost to the company. In contrast the Municipality of Le Touquet was only too eager to accommodate Silver City, enlarging and lengthening the concrete runway left by the Germans and eventually laying down a cross runway as well as rebuilding the terminal to suit the airline's needs. Silver City decided to go ahead and build its own 'Ferryfield' at a site near Dungeness on the Romney marshes. The design was optimised for the vehicle-ferry services and the company was even able to run its own airway control out of Ferryfield, which opened in 1954. It cost the company around £400,000 to build the basic airport and took about six months.

Aquila also had to deal with curmudgeonly British officialdom at its 'airport'. Aquila had a unique problem in that it had to maintain, at its own cost, full airfield facilities at Southampton Water; Barry Aikman, its managing director, explained the consequences:

> Madeira is perhaps exceptional and it is only because we use parallel facilities to the shipping and because the Portuguese charge us no landing fee that we can keep our costs down.

The other end of the route shows a very different picture. At Southampton we require more facilities because of the congestion in Southampton Water and because we operate at night. Notwithstanding the fact that we provide and man our own facilities, the Harbour Board charge us a landing fee, the Docks and Inland Waterways Executive charge us a docking fee and we have to use the port stevedores to handle the luggage. All this is very costly indeed. We use two control launches with radio, one of which is stationed at the upwind end of the alighting area and the other at the downwind end. At night we use five or more flare dinghies to mark the alighting area between them.

In addition to this, the Ministry of Civil Aviation insists that we provide a fire-float although there is no case on record of a flying boat catching fire on take-off or landing. Furthermore, if such a disaster did occur, it is doubtful if it could offer any assistance. There is enough water around as it is. The only fire we have experienced at Southampton was when our fire-float burst into flames and became a total loss.[22]

The flying boats landed in the Atlantic off Funchal harbour; in order to minimise the effects of the ocean swell, flights were scheduled to arrive at dawn when the sea was usually at its calmest. That entailed a night-time departure from Southampton at eleven o'clock, and arrival back at Southampton also in the dark. Aquila went through a bad patch at the beginning of 1953, losing two of its Sunderlands in accidents, fortunately with no fatalities. That left only the one remaining Sunderland airworthy which operated alongside a Solent for the rest of the year.

In March 1953, the company sold out to Britavia, parent company of Silver City. Britavia then continued its acquisitions by buying Wing Commander Kennard's airline, Air Kruise, also based at Lympne, operating Dakotas and Rapides across the Channel and further afield to Switzerland.

## ASSOCIATE AGREEMENTS: NEW SCHEDULED SERVICES

In August 1952 the ATAC published details of the first applications it had received under the new scheme of things; they appeared rather conveniently in the weekly aeronautical journals thus ensuring a wide distribution. The first application, No.1, was from Flightways for an internal service from Southampton to Alderney in the Channel Islands using Rapides. Nos.2 and 3 were from Airwork for a Colonial Coach service to Aden, using Vikings, and a normal scheduled service to Aden, using Hermes, respectively. Airwork was nothing if not quick off the mark; it also applied for scheduled freight licences to New York and Montreal.

By the middle of March 1953 the ATAC had awarded a number of seven- and ten-year licences. Hunting-Clan received approval for a network of international services out of Newcastle, and Airwork was granted an all-freight service to Canada and the United States. Cambrian consolidated its position in Cardiff and took over the Bristol services of Morton; the airline also moved into Gloucester's Staverton Airport after it bought out the previous incumbent, Murray Chown Aviation. Jersey Airlines was becoming a major player in the Channel Islands and at Southampton, and introduced the de Havilland Heron onto its services in May 1953. On the shorter cross-Channel routes Air Kruise now had a

Jersey Airlines was an early user of the DH 114 Heron. G-AMYU *Duchess of Jersey* was delivered in 1953 for the airline's scheduled services out of the Channel Islands and Southampton. (MAP)

seven-year licence for its Lympne-Le Touquet and Lympne-Ostend service; East Anglian was licensed for a small network out of Ipswich, Rochester and Southend to Ostend, Jersey and Paris. It was to be the start of the legendary summer-only Southend-Ostend services, which were to carry many hundreds of thousands of British holidaymakers on the first leg of their journeys to the sun. Summer weekend services from London to the Channel Islands were licensed to Transair, Morton and Olley. BKS, as the airline was now known, picked up the Horizon charter contract now that Air Transport (Charter) (CI) had stopped flying and was awarded IT licences from Southend to Corsica and Palma, Majorca. The Chancellor even increased the foreign exchange allowance from £25 to £40, and later in the year it went up to £50. BKS was also awarded scheduled-service licences from Newcastle to Jersey and the Isle of Man, more holiday routes.

Hunting-Clan launched its ambitious Newcastle network on 15 May 1953 with a twice-daily service to London, followed by a daily Newcastle-Glasgow summer service and international routes to Paris, Luxembourg, Basle, Amsterdam and Dusseldorf. Fares were set at a 10 per cent discount, but following objections from SAS, the Scandinavian airline, fares could not be agreed by IATA and so flights to Scandinavia were not launched. Negotiations at IATA had been conducted on behalf of Hunting-Clan by the corporations as Hunting-Clan was not a member; following this experience, Hunting-Clan joined IATA in its own right. This was the era when IATA exercised almost total control over the setting of international tariffs; governments merely rubber-stamped fares which the Association had agreed amongst its members.

The 'new era' in associate agreements was marked by *Aeronautics'* roving reporter, Squadron Leader David West, who set out on a round-Britain aerial tour to sample a number of the services, new and old. He gallantly admits that it was a new experience for him and on the whole an enjoyable one. An abridged account of his trip, *Everybody's Airlines*, which appeared in *Aeronautics* in September 1953, is reprinted in Appendix Four.


## THE CORPORATIONS

Under Sir Miles Thomas's astute chairmanship the tide had begun to turn in the affairs of BOAC. Finally, more than ten years after it had been established, BOAC had its first profitable year.[23] For the year ended March 1952 a profit of £275,000 was achieved, helped along by a further Treasury grant of £1,500,000. Productivity was up, staff numbers down and the front-line fleet consisted of ten Stratocruisers, ten Constellations and twenty-two Argonauts, with the twenty recently delivered Hermes – the only product of British manufacturers – already being prepared for disposal. BEA meanwhile continued to chalk up handsome losses, £1.4 million for the same period. The BEA results were particularly disappointing as the yearly deficit had been decreasing; now it was starting to rise again. BEA blamed various factors, such as industrial disputes, a steep rise in wages and prices and late delivery of the new Ambassadors for the increased losses, which were covered by a Treasury grant of £1.4 million. BEA's losses continued into the next year. Commentators glossed over the fact that BEA's employee numbers were actually increasing; capacity ton-miles per employee decreased from 7,511 in 1950-51 to 7,107 in 1951-52, reflecting a loss of productivity at the same time as wage costs were increasing significantly.

Both airlines were about to take the lead in introducing new transports: BOAC with the Comet in 1952, BEA and the Viscount in 1953. As a foretaste of what was to come BEA had at last been able to put the first of its Airspeed Ambassadors into regular operation during March 1952, a year later than originally planned. For a year the elegant Ambassador, named 'Elizabethan Class' by BEA, was the corporation's flagship aircraft, introducing pressurised comfort and higher speeds to its passengers.

1953 started unpromisingly for the corporations, with long spells of foggy weather affecting operations. BEA suffered its first fatal accident in over two years when a Viking crashed on final approach to Nutt's Corner at Belfast, killing twenty-seven passengers and crew. However, the Viscount entered service at last, when flights to Rome, Athens and Istanbul were inaugurated on 18 April, and during the year more and more routes were to be operated by the newly delivered Viscounts and Ambassadors.

On 2 May, on the first anniversary of its introduction into service, BOAC's Comet G-ALYV suffered structural failure in a severe storm and crashed near Calcutta, killing forty-three. It was the start of eighteen long months for BOAC. There followed two more Comet crashes, on 10 January 1954 and 8 April 1954, which eventually led to the withdrawal of the type's Certificate of Airworthiness: the loss of a Constellation at Singapore on 13 March 1954, killing thirty-three; on Christmas Eve, a Stratocruiser crashed at Prestwick with the loss of twenty-eight lives. As Sir Miles Thomas described it, 1954 was a swine of a year. BOAC lost aircraft in both the following years; an Argonaut crashed at Tripoli on 21 September 1955, with the loss of fourteen lives and another Argonaut crashed at Kano on 24 June 1956, killing thirty-two.

## THE SECOND, OR MINOR, BERLIN AIRLIFT

Laker now held the contract with the Foreign Office to carry manufactured goods out of Berlin with his big Tudor, which he acquired when he took over Bennett's airline, Fairflight. The business had ebbed and flowed the previous year, depending on the mood of the Russians, but during 1952 this second airlift became a major source of business for the charter airlines, in particular Air Charter and Silver City; the latter used up to five Freighters during the otherwise lean winter months. At the same time BEA, faced with an increasing need for additional flights to cope with refugees, brought in Air Charter to operate Yorks on its behalf between Berlin and Hamburg, as many as five passenger flights a day being operated. These were for refugees from the Russian Zone who had made it as far as the western sectors of Berlin, and then had to be transported by air to the western zone of Germany in order to avoid border checks whilst travelling through the rail corridor in the eastern Zone. The airlift's significance is apparent in this report from *Flight* which gives in detail a typical week's activities:

> One of the most urgent charters was a dash to Marseilles, by a Dakota of Eagle Aviation, carrying a new ship's boiler to a disabled vessel. An Eagle Dakota flew to Geneva and returned with twenty-four passengers and a York returned from its helicopter delivery trip to Khartoum. That city was the destination of forty-two passengers flown out from England in Dakota aircraft of Air Transport (Charter) (CI), manned by Airwork crews and under sub-contract to Airwork.
>
> Bristol 170s on the 'minor airlift' completed thirty-five round trips Berlin to Hamburg, Hanover and Dusseldorf; about ten of these were passenger flights. Other Silver City work included two freight trips to North Africa and a return horse flight between Le Bourget and Blackbushe. The usual load of eleven tons of cheese was ferried across the channel from Lympne to Le Touquet *(sic)*, as were seven tons of periodicals. Air Charter's Yorks also completed thirty-five round trips from Berlin, many of these being passenger flights.
>
> Scottish Airlines completed one return Dakota trip to Dukhan (Qatar) with freight for the Iraq Petroleum Company and took twenty-eight passengers to and from Innsbruck and Salzburg.
>
> A Skyways York returned with freight from Bangkok but heavy trooping work prevented this company from undertaking commercial work. BKS Aero Charter brought back a Dakota from Johannesburg with a load of freight and sent out a similar aircraft to the same destination, with twenty-nine passengers, for Tropic Airways. There may be a falling-off of normal business in the next few days, but this should be counter-balanced by a very substantial rise in the amount of passenger flying from Berlin.[24]

Airwork needed to subcharter its Sudan services because of the loss of two of its Hermes, and Tropic Airways was still suffering from the loss of its Dakota in July. This is one of the last references to Air Transport (Charter) (CI), which closed down its flying operations at the end of October, although the company itself stayed in business in Slough overhauling and repairing radio and navigational aids. Silver City had by October completed a year on the minor Airlift, operating over 1,000 flights and carrying more than 5,000 tons of goods out of Berlin. Air Charter bought additional Yorks, and by the end of the year between them Air Charter and Silver City were operating more than 100 flights a week, carrying over 1,000 passengers and around 500 tons of cargo out of Berlin. Occasionally the big Tudor, now with seventy-eight seats, was used to carry the refugees[25] but additional leased capacity arrived in the shape of two of BKS's Dakotas.

By early 1953 the flood of refugees into Berlin had reached such proportions that it was estimated between 700 and 1,000 would need to be airlifted out of Berlin every day in order to clear the backlog. BEA was responsible for issuing the tickets and documentation, but it asked Air Charter to coordinate the arrangements to ensure there were sufficient aircraft to provide the uplift. In March more aircraft joined the airlift, six Dakotas coming from BKS, Eagle, Scottish and Hunting-Clan. For a while BEA contributed five of its Pionairs. Air Charter had its Yorks, and used the Tudor and its Bristol Freighters for freight. Flights operated out of Berlin Tempelhof to either Hamburg or Hanover. Depending on availability, most charter airlines participated at some stage; Dan-Air's first commercial operations in June 1953 were on the Airlift. By the end of the year 50,000 refugees had been flown out of Berlin, as well as 34,000 tons of freight. The Airlift continued into 1954; although the flow of refugees stopped, the export of goods out of Berlin carried on unabated for several more years.

British carriers were able to benefit from the unique status of Berlin, to which German airlines did not have access as Berlin was controlled by the Four Powers, and they continued to carry freight between Berlin and airports in the British Zone of Germany, Hamburg and Hanover, and between Berlin and other points in Europe – like Amsterdam, important for the Dutch flower trade. In later years British charter airlines went on to develop the holiday market out of Berlin.

British airlines also benefited from the strengthening German market in other ways. In the new Federal Republic, previously the three western zones, the reformed German airline Lufthansa was not permitted to take to the air again until 1955 and, during this interim period, only non-German airlines were able to do business there. A network of travel agencies, shippers and freight-forwarders developed close ties with British airlines; Air Charter, Skyways and Eagle found it worth their while to base aircraft at Hamburg for charter freight-flying, much of it for Aero Express, a freight-forwarder which was also an early but short-lived participant in the holiday market. Even in the latter half of the decade British charter airlines still remained active in the German market, switching from freight in order to capture a share of the burgeoning German inclusive-tour holiday traffic, mainly to Spain; some airlines went further and helped establish new German carriers. Skyways based three Dakotas in Germany during 1954 and 1955, and participated in the start-up of *Deutsche Lufttransport*, whilst Airwork was the initial operator of services for *Deutsche Flugdienst*, maintaining its aircraft and training its crews. Eagle was involved in Bavaria, when *Bayerischer Flugdienst* started operations in 1955 using Eagle's Vikings. Further north, two British entrepreneurs – Bernard Dromgoole and Ronald Myhill – and their German partners, founded *Lufttransport Union* (LTU), drawing on the resources of their former employer, BKS, to prepare and operate a small fleet of Vikings. Neither *Deutsche Lufttransport* nor *Bayerischer Flugdienst* made it beyond the first fence, but *Deutsche Flugdienst* – in which Lufthansa, the West German railways and two major shipping lines participated – eventually became better known as Condor, a major German charter airline. LTU has also endured as a successful charter airline, but Myhill and Dromgoole later gained notoriety through their involvement with the

Flugdienst's Vickers Viking D-BONE saw service later with Lufthansa and its charter subsidiary, Condor. Condor used the same tail-marking, a modified version of Lufthansa's famous Flying Crane. (MAP)

ill-fated Overseas Aviation, a British airline that they had started, which drew much of its early custom from the German market.

## TROOPING

In August 1952 a whole raft of new trooping contracts to the Far East was awarded by the Air Ministry, after initial opposition from the Indian Government over transit rights at Indian airports had been overcome. These contracts were short term but welcome nevertheless. Eagle obtained ten flights to Singapore for its Yorks, Airwork was awarded six Hermes flights and Aquila, which routed its flying boats via Portuguese Goa, was also awarded six flights. The latter's big Solent took five days in each direction, with night stops at Beirut, Bahrain, Karachi and Trincomalee in Ceylon. By the end of 1952 British charter airlines had been undertaking trooping flights under the government's new policy for just over a year. More than 120,000 passengers had been carried in that year, around 100,000 of which by the independents; the main destination was the Canal Zone. Skyways had up to twenty-eight Yorks equipped with forty-three rear-facing seats dedicated to trooping, and had emerged as the main government contractor, carrying some 40,000 passengers. In addition to operating over fifty flights a month to the Canal Zone, Skyways also flew three or four flights a month to Jamaica. Skyways had taken over most of the Fayid contract from Airwork which had found itself seriously short of suitable aircraft; as already recounted delays in the delivery of Hermes were merely aggravated by the loss of the two aircraft earlier in the year. Whilst in theory Airwork remained the prime contractor to Fayid, and still managed to carry 9,000 passengers on the route, Skyways had been awarded some very significant supplemental contracts. Next largest contractor was Hunting-Clan, flying 30,000 passengers a year to Malta and Gibraltar, followed by Airwork with its Medair contract, shuttling 20,000 service personnel around the bases in the Mediterranean area. Eagle was another important contractor, carrying 3,000 passengers a year to Singapore and Livingstone, Rhodesia in its fleet of five dedicated Yorks; Singapore flights averaged three to four a month, Livingstone around six a month. Of the main contractors Crewsair had been the other significant operator, with around seven flights a month to Nigeria operated by its Vikings. Aquila operated occasional services to Singapore and elsewhere, and both Scottish Airlines and BKS picked up additional flying including the NAAFI flights to Cyprus and Fayid. Scottish Airlines went on to gain the contract for the Canadian trooping flights carrying air cadets to Montreal.

Early in 1953, the Air Ministry awarded two further one-year trooping contracts to Airwork using its Hermes; the first to West Africa, for between 1,500 and 2,000 passengers, and the second to East Africa, for up to a maximum of 1,850 passengers. On 2 February the first civil trooping fatalities occurred when a Skyways York was lost over the Atlantic, en route from the Azores to Gander, Newfoundland, with the loss of all on board, six crew, ten soldiers, ten wives of soldiers and thirteen children. There was some dismay over the loss of the York; Skyways voluntarily stopped its services to the Caribbean until these doubts were resolved.

Meanwhile the trooping net was being cast wider. Air Charter was awarded a contract to carry service personnel to Singapore, the aircraft then operated a further shuttle between Singapore and Fiji carrying Fijian servicemen to and from their jungle warfare training in Malaya. Over twelve months the airline operated seventeen such flights. Trouble in Kenya allowed the charter airlines to participate in the way that the Air Ministry had hoped; reinforcements were flown out in RAF Hastings and around twenty flights by Air Charter and Skyways Yorks; at last the 'merchant fleet' was backing up the RAF in the way that the Chief of the Air Staff had intended.

Just how important, and widespread, the trooping contracts had become is shown by the activities of Scottish Airlines in 1953. Scottish had recently acquired three Yorks fitted with fifty rearward-facing seats and only held one of the major contracts, or Tasks, that to Montreal. Yet in the year its aircraft operated supplementary trooping flights to Australia, Canada, Southern Rhodesia, Cairo, Sudan, Aden, Singapore and Nairobi. When Hunting-Clan was re-awarded the West Med contract to Gibraltar and Malta for another two years from November 1953, it transpired that the airline was operating around 500 flights a year to Malta, with another 100 flights a year to Gibraltar; the round-trip flying time between Bovingdon and Malta, with a refuelling stop at Nice in each direction, was fifteen hours, so that part of the contract alone was worth over 7,500 hours annual utilisation, year-round work for three Vikings.

To put the figures into perspective, between them the major charter operators – Airwork, Eagle, Hunting-Clan, Lancashire/Skyways, Silver City – carried 207,000 passengers, both charter and scheduled, in 1952, of which around 100,000 were under trooping contracts. In addition, another 68,000 passengers were carried on scheduled services by smaller operators. Airlines like Air Charter were carrying over 1,000 refugees a week out of Berlin by the end of the year, and this together with other passenger-charter work possibly accounted for a further 27,000 passengers, making an estimated total of

302,000 passengers carried by the independents. For comparison, in the same period, BOAC carried around 290,000 passengers, and BEA 1,630,000 passengers.

Trooping accounted for just over a third of passengers carried, although in terms of production the proportion was even higher as the trooping flights covered much greater stage lengths than, for example, domestic scheduled services and the Berlin Minor Airlift. Passenger figures at this juncture should be treated with some caution; there are few reliable statistics, and such figures that emerged tended to be either airlines' own statistics or figures published in the BIATA annual report. The latter covered the year from 1 July, and furthermore, some significant airlines, like Airwork and Aquila, were not yet members of BIATA.

## EAGLE

Following the closure of Crewsair and Air Transport (Charter) (CI), and frustrated by the lack of opportunities for independent airlines such as Eagle, Harold Bamberg thought seriously about closing down his airline. A veteran of the Berlin Airlift, Eagle had specialised more recently in long-haul charters, gaining government contracts to the Far East and Rhodesia as well as continuing to obtain numerous ad hoc passenger and freight charters. It came as a surprise to the aviation community when Bamberg announced in November 1952 that he was selling his fleet of Yorks to Skyways together with the Air Ministry contract to Rhodesia; Skyways paid around £160,000 for the five Yorks, boosting its fleet of these aircraft to twenty-nine. Bamberg then leased three of his recently acquired Vikings to Airwork.

He then had second thoughts; Eagle still owned a fleet of Dakotas and these aircraft were active in the charter market, indeed, they were busier than ever after the Yorks were sold. Bamberg soon overcame whatever doubts he may have had; Eagle now changed its focus but lost none of its energy. In early 1953 he started buying BEA's surplus Vikings, many of which entered service still bearing their BEA 'Admiral Class' names. By fitting thirty-six rearward facing 'Payloader' seats the aircraft could be used for trooping flights, normal passenger services and freight; the seats could be folded flat against the side of the fuselage. They were used to operate the first of Eagle's new international scheduled services, from Blackbushe to Belgrade, with a refuelling stop in Munich, which started on 6 June. Five months later Eagle inaugurated scheduled service to Aalborg, Denmark and Gothenburg, Sweden, a service that it had abandoned by July of the following year. The Belgrade service operated throughout the first winter, but then became a summer only service. Average load factors down to 18 per cent showed how difficult it was for a small airline to develop such thin routes, although in any scheduled operation there are inevitably initial losses until the route becomes established and accepted.

Such risks were part of the 'New Deal' too. Trooping, Colonial Coach and inclusive tours all offered smaller margins with less risk. New international scheduled routes might offer higher margins in the long run, but in a much more strenuous environment. Was this what the Conservatives had in mind when they had expressed their determination to restore a wide measure of private enterprise in the air and to throw the lines open to private competition?

# TWO

# LIVING WITH THE NEW DEAL
## 1953-1956

### DAN-AIR SERVICES

Meredith Air Transport operated a single Dakota, G-AMSU, in association with its South African counterpart Tropic Airways, but found itself in trouble over Christmas 1952. The aircraft had been operating an aerial cruise around the Mediterranean; the aircraft stayed with its group of passengers and flew them from location to location. On Christmas Eve the Dakota over-ran the 3,900ft runway at Jerusalem and damaged the tail wheel. Meredith had to charter a Dakota from BKS to fly engineers out there to repair the damage and continue the tour with the group. With only one aircraft in its fleet the airline was vulnerable; furthermore, Tropic had suffered a difficult and expensive year after it lost a Dakota the previous summer and had to hire in replacement aircraft. Meredith's brokers, Davies and Newman, took a debenture on the Dakota in order to help the struggling airline and the aircraft eventually returned to service six weeks later. Further ad hoc flying followed, including trips to Johannesburg and more air cruises; *The Aeroplane* noted that on 21 May 1953 it left with a full load of NAAFI personnel for Nicosia and collected a three-ton load of cinematographic equipment from Malta on the return flight. But the airline was in serious difficulties by this time; as they held a lien on the Dakota, Davies and Newman took over control of the aircraft, having first registered their new company Dan-Air Services Limited. Meredith was contracted to manage the airline for six months and the aircraft was dispatched from Southend to Hamburg in June to join the Second Berlin Airlift bringing refugees out of Berlin.

So Dan-Air London was born, without fanfare, without fuss and wholly typical of its nigh-on forty years of existence. The name, incidentally, had nothing to do with Denmark; it used the initials of the two founders' surnames. The airline acquired a second Dakota, G-AMSS, early in 1954 and former RAF Yorks began to join the fleet in 1955, by which time the company had settled into a typical pattern of charter activity, flying ad hoc passenger and freight flights, as well as some trooping and Inclusive Tour Service. *Flight* reported on one charter that was rather more spectacular:

Meredith's Dakota G-AMSU, or 'Sugar Uncle' when identified by the last two letters of its registration. (A.J. Jackson Collection)

Dakota G-AMSU, operated by Dan-Air Services Ltd, recently took the leading part in what is believed to be the first operation of its kind – an emergency air-drop of spare parts to a ship in the Atlantic. The spares – pistons and rings of 11in diameter – were required by the SS *Capetan Ilias,* disabled and drifting some 200 n.m. W.S.W. of Fastnet.

Commanded by Captain Watson, the Dakota left Blackbushe Airport in the early hours of 13 April for Shannon, where it was refuelled. The met. office at Shannon reported poor visibility and low cloud in the area of the ship, and take-off from Shannon was therefore delayed until contact with the ship could be made through Valencia marine radio station, and a weather actual obtained.

The aircraft left Shannon at 0930 and made immediate visual contact with the ship two hours later. As the aircraft approached and Captain Watson circled the ship to make positive identification, a dinghy was seen pulling away to a position some 100 yd from the ship. After one dummy run Captain Watson flew at reduced airspeed past the dinghy with wheels and flaps lowered, and dropped the package at low level some 50 yd from the dinghy. Consisting of a sealed drum containing the spare parts, with an outer-protective padding of cork, the package was pushed out by a crew member through the passenger entrance, the door of which had been removed before take-off. As the aircraft left the area the master of the ship signalled that the spares were safely on board and undamaged.[1]

The original partners in Tropic Airways – Captains Meredith and Creed – went their separate ways. The name of Tropic Airways was resurrected in 1955 by Captain Creed. Captain Meredith transferred his attentions elsewhere, forming a new South African airline – Trek Airways – which was soon operating three Vikings on the Johannesburg–Europe charter route.

Looking pristine a decade later, Dakota G-AMSU, Dan-Air's first aircraft, is accompanied on the ramp at Gatwick by a British United Airways Britannia and a Luxair Super Constellation. (MAP)

## SILVER CITY

Silver City seemed unable to put a foot wrong; it carried more passengers than any other independent airline and, just for good measure, it also carried the most cargo. In 1952 Silver City had carried 28,836 passengers and 6,896 cars; the following year, after the introduction of the bigger Bristol Super Freighter, the airline carried 95,287 passengers and 24,011 cars, an increase of between 330 and 340 per cent. There were further price cuts for 1954 and Calais was added as another destination. By now it was substantially cheaper to travel with a car than it had been when the service first started. In 1948, it would have cost the owner of a Morris Minor £54 for the return trip; in 1954 the same journey cost £21 3s. Silver City had captured about 25 per cent of the cross-Channel vehicle market, although British Railways' shipping service was beginning to respond by introducing new tonnage such as the *Lord Warden*, which Air Commodore Powell always described as 'huge'. At over 3,300 tons gross and able to carry 120 cars and just under 1,000 passengers, this car-ferry allowed cars to be driven on and off through a stern door rather than being craned on and off at the dockside. She was a sign of things to come.

Competition from a different source materialised on 1 September 1954 when Air Charter started car-ferry flights between Southend and Calais, using standard Bristol Freighters which the airline had been using on the second Berlin Airlift and other charter work. The airline introduced long-nosed Bristol Super Freighters during the summer of 1955, by which time frequencies were up to a peak of thirty-two round-trips a day, and added a second destination, Ostend, in October of that year. By 1957 the car-ferry services were being marketed as the 'Channel Air Bridge' and the Ostend route was jointly operated with Sabena, the Belgian airline.

Air Charter's Bristol Super Freighter, G-ANVR, shows its elongated nose and larger tail.
(Richard T. Riding)

Silver City now cast its net wider, introducing vehicle-ferry services to Belfast from Stranraer and Liverpool, and from Southampton to Cherbourg and Deauville. None of these new services could match the efficiency of the core Ferryfield-Le Touquet route and the proliferation of new stations added considerably to the airline's costs and overheads; they did tap into new markets, however, and improved the fleet's utilisation.

## FREDDIE LAKER AND THE TUDOR

The Ministry of Transport and Civil Aviation found a buyer for its stock of new and used Tudors when Air Charter bought most of the remaining aircraft in storage, intending to convert at least ten[2] for passenger work. Laker needed a replacement for the Yorks currently being flown by Air Charter and calculated that a rebuilt Tudor, many of which were brand new and had hardly flown, would be somewhat less expensive than either the Hermes or DC-4 Skymaster. Although the bigger Tudor 2 could carry up to seventy-eight passengers it was range limited, unable to carry a worthwhile payload over 1,200 miles; but the smaller Tudor 1 and 4 could carry forty-five passengers over sectors of around 2,000–2,500 miles non-stop. Stansted-Fayid was 2,100 nautical miles, Nairobi-Malta 2,610 n.m., and both sectors were flown successfully non-stop on test with a 12,000lb payload. For a total investment of around £400,000 after all the modifications had been carried out, Laker acquired a fleet of ten reasonably modern, long-range aircraft; at this time a single DC-4 with 15,000 hours cost nearly £180,000. He went ahead and converted the first of the Tudors for passenger services, intending to use it on trooping flights. Despite new Certificates of Airworthiness, the War Office resolutely refused to allow these Tudors to be used for military passengers and their families, although they were used extensively to carry service freight:

Air Charter's Avro Tudor G-AHNM converted into a Super Trader by the addition of a large cargo door on the port side. Here it is being loaded at Fayid in 1955. (MAP)

> This policy was based upon a Ministerial decision by the First Sea Lord and the Secretaries of State for War and Air in March 1954, on the grounds that, with the past bad history of the type, the Service Departments would find themselves in an indefensible position if a Tudor were to be lost on a trooping flight when aircraft of other types had been available for charter.[3]

Characteristically, Laker determined to make the best of a deal that had not quite turned out as planned. He bought DC-4 Skymasters instead for passenger work, bidding successfully for trooping contracts to West Africa and received a well-deserved endorsement from the Service Ministers:

> We consider that the DC4 would be an admirable aircraft for the Cyprus task. It is basically the same aircraft as the Argonaut used by BOAC and, although not pressurised, the standard of passenger comfort is acceptable. Our experience of the operations of Air Charter Ltd are very favourable and they have been both reliable and efficient.
>
> The withdrawal of York aircraft from air trooping has given the owners of Hermes aircraft a monopoly in the field of long-range air trooping and considerably reduced the number of long-range aircraft available in the charter market. The introduction of the D.C.4 would both revive the competitive element in long-term charter contracting, and make a most useful addition to the number of aircraft available for strategic moves.[4]

He converted six of the remaining Tudors into freighters – renamed Super Traders – with a large freight door cut into the aft port side. Augmented with beefed up Merlin engines, they were able to carry a ten-ton payload. The first one was used on the Miniature Berlin Airlift, releasing the Bristol Freighters for the growing vehicle-ferry services from

Southend. Then from March 1955 Air Charter gained a major government contract to supply the Commonwealth weapons and rocket-testing establishment at Woomera in South Australia, a contract that was to be held by British independents for nigh on twenty years.

## THE SHIPPING COMPANIES START TO INVEST

Clan Line had become the first major shipping line to invest in one of the independents when it had bought a half share in Hunting Air Transport in October 1953. Now, encouraged by the government, other shipping lines followed suit. First, Furness Withy acquired a majority interest in Airwork, over 60 per cent, early in February 1954; in June Airwork announced that the Blue Star Line had also acquired a large shareholding in the airline. Then, on 15 February, P&O Steam Navigation announced that through its subsidiary company, General Steam Navigation, it had purchased a majority shareholding in Britavia, the parent company of Silver City and Aquila. Suddenly the ownership of the major charter airlines was transformed, with substantial stakes now being held by large shipping concerns.

British shipping had enjoyed a post-war boom despite heavy losses incurred during the war; they exuded respectability, solidity and prosperity. Many of the shipping companies had expressed an interest in aviation during and immediately after the war, only to be set back by the Labour Government's nationalisation of air transport: the Booth Line had been one of the main backers of British Latin American Airways, the forerunner of British South American Airways, and the Hunting Group already owned a fleet of tankers. Now with a Conservative Government back in power the time was surely right to explore once again the synergies that might evolve from a partnership between shipping and aviation. Both sides stood to benefit from a closer relationship. Charter airlines, managed and operated on very tight budgets, now had access to increased capital and London's financial institutions thus releasing a new source of funds with which to start re-equipping their fleets. Airwork – having bought Hermes from BOAC for the trooping contracts – was about to embark on an ambitious North Atlantic scheduled freight service for which specialised aircraft, Douglas DC-6As, were needed. Hunting-Clan had ordered Viscounts hoping to use them on Colonial Coach Class services to Singapore and Hong Kong, for which the airline had recently applied for. The government, now that it recognised the value of an independent strategic reserve, was glad to see the independent airlines on a sounder financial footing.

For the shipping companies, a stake in aviation seemed to promise a stake in the future. Though it was not immediately apparent, the British merchant navy was already declining as a world force; other countries were building up their fleets, increasing competition and denying traditional trades to British ship-owners; poor investment decisions led to the wrong type of ships being built, unsuited to the modern bulk trades. There were also labour problems at British ports and on British ships. Some of the ship owners were prescient enough to recognise that aviation offered a respite. Ship owners already benefited from air services to speed the exchange of crews and urgent spare parts for ships that had broken down; now the ability to send urgent cargo at a premium by air was an obvious additional service that could be offered to shippers. Both airlines and shipping companies would benefit from stronger overseas representation; it was hoped that the airlines would gain from the established sales offices that the shipping companies had in their particular ports. Furness Withy operated to North America; its acquisition of an interest in Airwork was timed to coincide with the launch of the airline's North American all-freight service. Blue Star Line covered South America, South Africa and the North Pacific coast of the USA and Canada. P&O was the main operator of passenger and freight services to India, the Far East and Australia and had observed how Silver City had successfully operated passenger services to Australia in its early days; parallel development of air services to its existing shipping services seemed one way of backing a winner either way. Britavia and Aquila applied almost immediately for all-freight licences to Australia, services that theoretically were open to the independents.

## DISAPPOINTMENTS

It was a shock to the powerful shipping companies to enter a world that was so tightly regulated. The freedom of the seas meant just that; owners could start sailing between ports carrying passengers and cargo, with little interference from government agencies aside from health and safety concerns. (There were other issues, of course, not least the system of conferences, arising from this *laissez faire* approach.) The freedom of the air was much more complex and circumscribed, and despite their undoubted clout even the British ship owners were unable either to persuade their own government, or those overseas, to ease the constraints of very limited route access. P&O ran hard aground when it tried to take on the Australians, who resolutely refused to countenance the appearance of a second British airline operating schedules into Australia. The Australian Government was even more protective towards its airline Qantas (QEA) than the British Government was towards BOAC, and the issue was taken up to the very highest level, as the following extract from the official history of the airline suggests:

> The introduction of an independent cargo service would undoubtedly lead to the development of independent services demanding the carriage of passengers and mails, which would mean the eventual disintegration of the partnership (between BOAC and QEA). The matter was before Cabinet and 'we were fighting it on the basis that it was a direct attack on the existing partnership agreement between the UK and Australia.'[5]

There is something about civil aviation that brings out the most ardent protectionism in governments, possibly because many of them also own the world's major airlines and see them as 'ambassadors' for their countries.

On the whole, the shipping companies were disappointed by their various forays into aviation; they were up against other governments with their own powerful vested interests and were unable to prevail. A feeling of frustration soon became apparent, affecting the independent airlines and their owners. New aircraft were becoming available, but were expensive, and the means of financing them, or rather to persuade investors to finance them, were hampered by the apparent lack of opportunity afforded to the independents.

No airline could afford to buy them on the back of uncertain ministry contracts; the War Office and the Treasury favoured the lowest tenders and returns on trooping flights were meagre. The business was year-round, was guaranteed and airlines were even paid eventually, but the economics favoured the use of older aircraft which were cheaper to buy; rates were defined by costs at the margin, so that whilst trooping contracts covered short-run marginal costs they did not produce enough revenue to cover replacement costs. Trooping contracts were awarded for one or two years, not long enough to convince a banker to lend the money for a new Vickers Viscount which would have to be written off over a much longer period, say eight or even twelve years.

Other business was slow in developing; inclusive tours, though a growing market, were still in their infancy; Colonial Coach Class licences prohibited the use of more modern equipment and were granted sparingly (the ATAC duly refused Hunting-Clan's applications to fly to Singapore and Hong Kong, using Viscounts); and other scheduled services were frankly too thin to allow for the use of modern, larger aircraft. Cargo services were an option, but Airwork was soon to learn that dedicated cargo services were at an economic disadvantage when set against the joint costs of the passenger and freight services of the other transatlantic airlines. The foreword to the 1953-54 BIATA Annual Report was deeply pessimistic:

> This is a 'frustration' Report. By 1955 the independent operators should have been bringing modern new aircraft into operation; procurement plans should have been made for years ahead; commercially sound operations should have been under way which held out clear long-term prospects of future progress. Instead, only a small number of new aircraft have been ordered; the independent operators are still mainly confined to insecure and financially doubtful operations; and they are finding it increasingly difficult to assess where their future prospects – if any – lie. A deep feeling of 'frustration' is an inevitable result.

## AIRWORK

One casualty of this frustration was Sir Archibald Hope who stepped down as joint-managing director of Airwork in 1956, leaving Myles Wyatt as sole managing director and chairman. Sir Archibald said he was leaving because of 'continuing restrictions on the activities of private airlines.'

When faced with difficulties at home, British companies often looked abroad for growth opportunities, and airlines were no different. Airwork had always had extensive interests abroad; before the war the company had helped form Misr-Airwork in Egypt and Indian National Airways, and the bedrock of its business after the war had been its long-running involvement with the Sudan. The company had then gained the concession to operate Straits Air Freight Express in New Zealand, using Bristol Freighters to carry freight between North and South Island in conjunction with New Zealand Railways; by the mid 1950s a fleet of six Freighters carried over 30,000 tons of freight a year across the Straits. Airwork still had a number of operating contracts for oil companies in the Middle East throughout the years, and tourist and aviation interests in East Africa. In the last chapter we learned how Airwork had helped the fledgling German airline industry re-establish itself. As well as looking abroad for new opportunities Airwork sought another way out of its problems by beginning to buy out rival airline operators. In August 1956 Transair was taken over, but the two airlines continued to function as separate units. Transair had taken over the development of newspaper and Post Office flying after the war, using specially converted Ansons, but had since entered the inclusive-tour market and upgraded its fleet with Dakotas. Both airlines now ordered Viscounts.

Airwork did not depend solely on airline activities either and was buttressed to a certain extent by the activities of its various subsidiaries, not least of which were Airwork General Trading. They maintained Airwork's fleet and held government contracts for the overhaul of RAF and Royal Navy aircraft. The Airwork School of Aviation, later known as Air Services Training based at Perth, provided conversion training and other technical instruction for Service pilots.

## ESTABLISHMENT AIRLINES

Hunting-Clan moved the London terminus of its new Northern Network from Bovingdon to the less remote Northolt on 1 April 1954; when Northolt reverted solely to military use at the end of October that year, Hunting-Clan moved again – this time to London Airport, now better known as Heathrow, to which it also transferred its engineering base and the remaining services from Bovingdon. In July 1955 Airwork joined Hunting-Clan at London Airport.

By April 1954 Hunting-Clan had boosted its Northern Network, adding Glasgow and Manchester and finally launching services to Scandinavia. Enterprisingly, and against considerable hostility from IATA, fares were set at a discount of 10 per cent to the normal IATA through fares. Thirty-five schedules were flown out of Newcastle (Woolsington) on Dakotas every week that summer: thirteen to London, seven each to Manchester and Glasgow, two to Oslo and on to Stockholm (later the Stockholm section was dropped and an additional stop was made at Stavanger), two to Hamburg and on to Copenhagen, two to Paris, two to Amsterdam and then on to Dusseldorf. Later, speedier Vikings replaced the Dakotas. Viscounts were briefly introduced in 1955 before Hunting-Clan concluded that the time and the conditions were not right for them to operate modern turbo-prop aircraft, and the aircraft were leased out instead to Middle East Airlines.

Under the circumstances it was a brave and professional attempt to develop a new range of services. Independent airlines were barred from developing a worthwhile network from London as the corporations had been given that as a monopoly: above all there was to be no material diversion from the corporations. If the independents were to expand they would have to innovate: regional or provincial scheduled services were one answer, inclusive tours were another and freight services a third possibility. Both Airwork and Hunting-Clan were establishment airlines and played according to the rules of the game. Rather than fight the government, these two airlines accommodated themselves to the government's wishes as best they could. The Conservative Government had said that some new opportunities would be allowed for the independents: Colonial Coach Class low-fare services, all cargo services and new 'unused' international routes. Obediently Airwork and Hunting-Clan launched new Colonial Coach services to East and Central Africa, to which a weekly service to

West Africa, as far as Accra, was added in June 1954. Although Colonial Coach Class was an attractive service in many ways, it was intended to be a 'hard class', taking longer than the normal schedule and flown on older equipment. In 1957 services were still being flown by old Vikings, despite attempts by both Hunting-Clan and Airwork to introduce Viscounts. As for cargo services, Airwork applied successfully for an all-freight-service licence to North America; later Hunting-Clan was to start its Africargo all-freight service.

When denied access to a London network, Hunting-Clan made a courageous attempt to develop a regional network of international passenger services. In time Airwork and Hunting-Clan were to chafe at the bit and protest the lack of opportunity for the independents, but at this stage both seemed resigned to earning a living from the crumbs that fell from the table. Rather than try and occupy the main hall, they built an annex, as the government allowed them to do. Owners of lean-to sheds can become quite as possessive as home-owners, and one of the marks of an establishment undertaking is the need to stake out a patch that is undeniably reserved to that particular enterprise. When Hunting-Clan and Airwork finally merged and formed British United Airways, and later when the merged airline was taken over by Caledonian, the resulting airline tended to behave like a little corporation, developing a niche at Gatwick and demanding 'Spheres of Influence', route swaps and other preferential treatment. Not all independents behaved in this way, though: Bamberg and Laker both tried to break the mould – at the risk of labouring the metaphor, they wanted to live in some of the rooms in the main house and were not satisfied simply with the annex.

## BOAC AND SKYWAYS

Even the ultimate establishment airline, BOAC, was frustrated with the status quo. The Conservative Government had pledged that the corporations would not be allowed to maintain surplus aircraft for use in the charter market, which ruled out participation in any long-term charter contracts, most pertinently the trooping contracts. As we have seen the Service Chiefs were reluctant to allow the corporations to take over these contracts, fearing any long-term dependence on a state monopoly. BOAC could of course tender for one-off and short-term contracts with the Air Ministry, but it was understood that regular trooping was reserved for the charter airlines. This was not a situation that its chairman, Sir Miles Thomas, could accept submissively and he sportingly tried to expand the opportunities for BOAC whenever he could, even if it meant cooperating with the independents. He was clear in his mind which airline he wanted to work with:

> At the other end of the scale there were the negotiations with the independent air operators. Half of them took the view that the Airways Corporations were a blundering, inefficient and wholly anti-social excrescence. The other half showed themselves willing to work with us. Among the latter was an enterprising operator, Mr Eric Rylands. He and his colleagues in Skyways realised that if they helped in forming a pattern whereby such work as was not compatible for an airline that ran regular schedules – work like carrying troops and service personnel from one part of the world to another – were to be undertaken by the 'independents', it made good commercial sense.

In my view there is room in the sky for both independent and nationalised air companies, but this situation cannot be rationalised by forcing the independents to run cut-price charters with outmoded aircraft, while the nationalised airways are made the proving grounds and their passengers the guinea-pigs for new designs.[6]

For his part, Rylands, having seen three of his competitors come under new and somewhat heftier ownership in the last six months, determined to meet the challenge. But instead of knocking on a few doors in the City, he sent his boss, Sir Wavell Wakefield, MP, to talk to Thomas at BOAC on 2 March 1954.[7] Together they hatched a plot whereby BOAC would sell its remaining nineteen Hermes to Skyways for £90,000 each, payable over seven years, and in return take a 25 per cent shareholding in Skyways. The sale of Hermes to Skyways – and their use on freight services to the Far East – would have allowed both BOAC and the government to persuade themselves that no further competition on freight, or other services, to the Far East was required. BOAC would have been able to tender for trooping contracts, albeit through a proxy, and sidestep the few remaining restrictions that the government had imposed on the corporation. It was a smart deal, conceived by two clever men.

Thomas regarded the transaction with Skyways as a 'key stone' in the bridge between BOAC and the independent companies. He had to submit the proposal to the Minister, of course, but Lennox-Boyd was sympathetic towards it and raised no objections; the Minister merely asked for a little time to consider its implications. On 19 March Lennox-Boyd approved the agreement and confirmed it to the chairman of BOAC on 22 March. But later that day he had second thoughts and asked Thomas to defer signing the agreement.

## 'THEN THE STORM BROKE'[8]

There were some minor complications to deal with first. In February BOAC had already offered to sell up to six of the Hermes to Silver City's parent company, Britavia, for £100,000 each. But when Air Commodore Powell, the managing director, followed Wakefield eight days later to BOAC headquarters to sign the deal, he was told that the original agreement had only been verbal, and now no options were being granted; instead, he could have four of the aircraft if he agreed to pay cash, and also covenant to use the aircraft only on trooping flights (other services would require the consent of BOAC and a substantial adjustment to the price of each aircraft). As rumours of the impending sale grew, trade union opposition to the sale of these Hermes was initiated, an unwelcome factor in the equation; the aircraft were parked at London Airport, cocooned in plastic and would need engineering support from BOAC to prepare them for service. Powell went back to BOAC on 15 March with a cheque for £40,000 as deposit on the four aircraft and initialed a new agreement. Four days later, BOAC then sold another three Hermes to Airwork – for £90,000 each – reducing the number available to Skyways to twelve. The corporation also told the unions of the proposed investment in Skyways, news of which reached the ears of Powell.

Then the storm broke. He was furious, both at the terms of the deal, which were much more favourable than the tough conditions BOAC had imposed on Britavia, and at the prospect of BOAC controlling a large charter airline equipped with the most modern aircraft available. As John Profumo, the Minister's parliamentary secretary later summed it up:

> He understood that the aircraft now to be sold to the other independents would be sold for cash and subject to a covenant restricting the purposes for which they might be used, while in the case of the aircraft to be sold to Skyways payments would be spread over seven years and there would be no restrictive covenant.

Worse was to come: when Powell complained about the uneven treatment at a meeting with the Minister and Thomas and proposed a standstill on the Hermes deals, to his chagrin BOAC returned the deposit cheque the very next day and told him the deal was cancelled.

But Powell no longer had to fight alone; a veritable flotilla of irate ship-owning lords and knights called on the Minister and made their views known to him regarding the BOAC deal with Skyways:

> Their fears were the same but if anything they were more outspoken, stating that if this project went ahead, they would have been misled on the field open to independent air operators and their money would have been obtained under false pretences.[9]

Airwork went even further, and threatened to pull out of aviation altogether and return the Hermes that it already operated to BOAC. Meanwhile the trade unions put their collective boot in by laying down their own conditions for the dispersal of the Hermes fleet, a contribution that can only have aggravated the feelings of an already extremely irritated Minister.

As *Aeroplane* records laconically, on Friday 26 March Lennox-Boyd withdrew his approval, saying that he thought the proposed agreement would discriminate against other independent operators.[10] Privately, he reprimanded Thomas:

> I am glad to see … that you told the Trade Union Members that negotiations were under way with Britavia. I have no doubt that you said this. But is it not rather remarkable that you told them at the same meeting that the Britavia deal was off, that the very same day you wrote to Britavia telling them this and returning their deposit, and that the Press published all this? I suppose it is hardly surprising that your letter makes no reference to the standstill agreement reached in the Parliamentary secretary's room on the Britavia contract – not even to the BOAC version of it.
>
> I certainly have no objection to your circulating copies of this letter to Board Members. I am always ready that you should do this. It is very reasonable and indeed I should have thought only usual, to keep your Board informed of all important developments; but I must confess that some doubts as to whether this was the practice in BOAC crept into my mind when I received your Deputy Chairman's[11] telegram which he sent when I considered asking him to return from France to handle the Hermes situation during your absence in Singapore. I quote the telegram below:- 'Will of course return if you instruct but I have no knowledge of and no responsibility for Hermes negotiations which Chairman has conducted personally. Am therefore absolutely unable make any useful contribution on this matter. Suggest must wait Chairman's return.'[12]

## IT WOULD BE A DRAG ON BOAC TO HAVE TO RETAIN THE HERMES[13]

Britavia was then able to negotiate for its six Hermes again and on more favourable terms. Getting them was another matter. The surplus aircraft were still at London Airport but, as we have seen, the corporation met unexpected opposition from its workforce as the aircraft were about to be prepared for transfer, with the trade union members of the BOAC Joint Panel Committee instructing its members not to undertake any work 'until satisfactory assurances have been obtained that they will not be engaged on work which could be undertaken by BOAC'. [14] The chairman of BOAC had already expressed his relief that the corporation was no longer operating the 'weary' Hermes and he still wanted them off his books, even if his plans for their disposal had to be altered. Nor was this the first time – and certainly not the last – that the corporations were to sell obsolete equipment to the independent airlines for possible use in competition against them. BEA had just sold nineteen Vikings to Eagle and BOAC had disposed of most of its Yorks to Skyways. So the action of the trade union was a blow to the corporation as well as to the independents. *Flight* commented severely:

> The corporation itself has no wish to operate the Hermes on its network of scheduled services. And there is no possibility of their being retained - as the BOAC engineers demand - purely for charter or trooping services; the Government decided otherwise nearly two years ago. This sudden attempt by one small section of the aviation community to alter a policy laid down by a democratically elected Government has been rightly condemned as irresponsible and anti-social.[15]

The dispute dragged on for a number of weeks. Thomas attempted to placate his staff by assuring them that the aircraft would only be used for trooping and other work which the corporation did not wish to undertake. He pointed out:

> In selling the aircraft we are trying to get the best price and terms obtainable in the interests of the corporation and all who work for it. It has not been an easy task. Although the aircraft have been offered for sale throughout the world for more than six months…we have in fact received no firm offer from foreign buyers.[16]

Other obstacles, such as the demand that the engines should be overhauled at BOAC's facility at Treforest, were also met and overcome. By the beginning of June 1954, four of the Hermes had been delivered to Britavia, and Skyways obtained its first in September; by early 1955 Skyways had taken delivery of a further seven and the rest followed in ones and twos, Airwork acquiring its final example in July 1957.

Thwarted in its deal with BOAC, Skyways turned to the Bibby Line, which in March 1955 bought a substantial interest in the airline. Bibby Line was the main government contractor for trooping services by sea and had recently taken over the two new troopships under a management contract; nevertheless the company could see that more and more trooping contracts were being awarded to the airlines. Skyways, with its long and substantial record of government work, must have seemed another safe each-way

Britavia's Handley Page Hermes G-ALDP shows off its handsome lines at Blackbushe. (MAP)

bet. However, BOAC and Skyways maintained a close relationship for the rest of the decade. Skyways bought ten of the surplus Hermes, a substantial investment on its part, and from 1956 flew BOAC's freighter services to the Far East using Hermes and, later, Constellations, which it also bought from BOAC.

## JOHN BOYD-CARPENTER

Thomas never stopped trying! Fortunately for him, in view of his recent contretemps with Lennox-Boyd, he soon had a new Minister of Transport and Civil Aviation to deal with – John Boyd-Carpenter, transferred from the Treasury and promoted to the Cabinet in July 1954. On his first day, as Boyd-Carpenter recounts in his memoirs, he received a courtesy call from Thomas and recounts what happened next:

> In my predecessor's time it had become established policy, as a means of keeping the private airlines in business, to reserve trooping, i.e. the carrying of troops when they travelled by air to and from our then numerous garrisons all over the world, to the private airlines. On my first day…Miles Thomas came in on what he described as a courtesy call. We chatted for a minute or two, and then as he was leaving he said with apparent casualness 'I take it it will be all right if we do trooping'. I did not need the audible drop of my Private Secretary's jaw to respond to the effect that he really ought not to try this on my first day. Utterly unabashed he grinned pleasantly and said it had been well worth trying.[17]

Boyd-Carpenter remained in office for just under eighteen months and enjoyed running his unwieldy ministry. By the middle of the following year, he was giving some thought as to how he might make good on those pledges which the Tories had made to the independents. His ideas included establishing a proper licensing authority and allowing the private airlines access to certain scheduled routes: South America (recently abandoned by BOAC); New York and some domestic trunk routes. European and other intercontinental routes were not deemed practical because any route awards would have to come out of the corporations' share, but domestic routes and North American routes, already served by two American carriers, were not so constrained. In return, the corporations might be allowed to bid for some of the trooping contracts. His ideas, forwarded to the Treasury for advice, quickly became mired in more than just red tape:

> Whether a special committee of the Cabinet need be appointed depends on how far it is possible to digest the subject: so far it has not been digested at all.
>
> The Minister suggests that the subject should be remitted straight away to a Committee of Ministers. If this is done, the right procedure would be for him to circulate to the Cabinet a short paper setting out the main issues very briefly, without arguing them, and asking for a Committee to be appointed…
>
> But all this seems very elaborate; is not the Minister putting his functions into commission too soon? This will be his bill; had he not better instruct his officials to discuss all these questions in the normal way with the other departments concerned? When this has been done he can circulate a paper to his colleagues, containing the product of digestion.[18]

So wrote an official from the Treasury on 12 July 1955; it reads better, and makes more sense, if you substitute the word 'bull' for 'bill'.

It fell to Boyd–Carpenter's successor, Harold Watkinson – appointed at the end of 1955 – to try and push the ideas forward. He had different ideas, however, which are discussed in the next chapter.

## BIATA

BIATA began to produce some more usable statistics from 1954 onwards, reflecting its wider membership now that both Airwork and Aquila had finally joined the Association. The Association worked hard to represent its members' interests, organising frequent meetings and social gatherings attended by government officials, and producing reports and statistical tables that fleshed out what otherwise was a desert of information. Being private companies most of the charter and other independent airlines were under no obligation to publish any financial information about themselves – so they did not. The Ministry failed to require the reporting of traffic and other statistical information, although the ATAC as the licensing authority produced in its annual report details of scheduled-service carryings, and for their part the aviation magazines also elicited rather more information.

As we have seen, BIATA's annual reports around this time reflect the increasing frustration of its members, locked into low-revenue trooping contracts with the government, unable to make any progress on any other front and faced with an increasing need to re-equip with more modern and economical aircraft. Their sources of business were unbalanced, with too much reliance on government contracts. The Annual Report for 1954-55 noted:

The conditions applicable to this category of operation have not, however, improved in any way during the past twelve months and air trooping contracts are both short-term and low-revenue earning. It is an unhealthy feature of independent air transport that such a large proportion of its operations is represented by air trooping which does not provide any satisfactory basis for investment in new aircraft.

By 1955 trooping accounted for 67 per cent, or two thirds, of BIATA's output measured in passenger-miles; the independents actually carried many more passengers on their limited scheduled services, 376,489, compared with only 214,594 on trooping flights. The apparent discrepancy arises from the different ways of measuring airline output. A single passenger remains statistically one passenger, whether he or she flies from London to Australia or from Ferryfield to Le Touquet. In terms of production, however, the passenger to Australia flies many more miles and pays rather more for the airline ticket than does the cross-Channel passenger. In an attempt to reconcile these disparities airline economists and statisticians add up the total number of miles actually flown by each passenger for each flight; a passenger to Australia clearly has more weighting than the cross-Channel passenger, and hence produces more 'passenger-miles'. Cargo is similarly dealt with. Sometimes, a weight is imputed to each passenger, aggregating both passengers and cargo – an unconvincing figure. Both passenger figures and passenger-miles have their place and it is true that passenger-miles reflect distance and hence productive effort, but sheer weight of passenger numbers should not be ignored either.

# RESULTS

Despite all the difficulties BOAC faced in 1953 and 1954, the corporation still managed to produce a net operating profit of over £2 million in the year to end March 1954. The operating surplus was large enough to pay interest and still leave enough to show an overall profit. After the loss of the Comet off Elba in January 1954, the corporation was able to redeploy aircraft and fly others more intensively; no aircraft had to be sub-chartered from other airlines and the Comet was re-introduced into service on 23 March. But after another Comet disappeared near Naples just over two weeks later, the jet fleet was withdrawn and grounded; services to South America were abandoned; additional Stratocruisers and Constellations were bought to strengthen the other schedules and even the unloved Hermes were temporarily reinstated. BOAC was also able to hedge its bets against the late delivery of Britannias when it was allowed to order long-range Douglas DC-7C aircraft for delivery in 1956. In March 1955 BOAC placed an order for the larger Comet 4, reconfirming its faith in the jet airliner, although Thomas was to be frustrated in his attempts to launch the long-range Comet powered by Rolls-Royce Conway engines, an aircraft which would have had true transatlantic range. In his autobiography, *Out on a Wing*, Thomas wrote about the proposed Conway Comet, known as the de Havilland DH 118:

> For the technical, we were proposing to retain all the parts on the Comet Is and IIs that would have soaked up man-hours on drawing boards to redesign- parts like the control systems, the flight-deck instrumentation and similar features which had been tried, tested

and found highly satisfactory in service. The fuselage, with its thicker skin, would have been widened by the simple and well-tried device of putting a gusset from stem to stern some nine inches wide, so that five seats abreast could be accommodated... Items like the galley and toilets, the doors and windows, the ventilation and pressurisation systems, would not have needed drastic alteration. The engine mountings in the wings could without difficulty have been modified to take Rolls-Royce Conway engines and at the same time the sweep-back of the wings would have been increased to conform with the higher maximum speed.

Thomas's years at BOAC – years of growing profits and gathering confidence – surely point up the positive advantages of great leadership; if the corporation's first ten years had been messy, they were as nothing compared to the accumulation of disasters that were to follow Thomas's departure. He left to join Monsanto Chemicals in May 1956 – before his term was up – uneasy in his relationship with Watkinson, the new Minister:

> So I kept on badgering and pressing for a decision on the Conway Comet. It was not forthcoming. I personally felt more and more frustrated. In other spheres, too, a feeling of dictatorship, of assuming authority without accepting responsibility, spread arrogantly from the Ministry buildings in Berkeley Square right down to London Airport and beyond.[19]

BOAC lost its two men at the top in short order; Whitney Straight had also just left to become executive vice-chairman of Rolls-Royce in October 1955. The government recalled Gerald d'Erlanger to be part-time unpaid chairman; he had previously been chairman of BEA. His appointment was sharply criticised;[20] not only did he have a poor track record, it was felt that the job merited a full-time chairman. He had as his deputy Sir George Cribbett, who was transferred from the Ministry of Transport and Civil Aviation – in joining BOAC Cribbett was acting no differently from his former boss, Sir Arnold Overton, who had joined the board of BEA in 1953. The corporations' boards were well connected, of course, but this appointment suggested that the government wanted to tighten its grip on BOAC, indeed the government had proposed Cribbett as chief executive; it had backed down when the Board of BOAC, led by Basil Smallpeice, deputy chief executive and Financial Comptroller, protested. Instead the post of managing director was filled internally by promoting Smallpeice. He managed to shunt Cribbett into the sidings, consigning him to running international relations and the associated companies. In his autobiography Smallpeice paints an unsympathetic portrait of the man he successfully beat to the top job:

> I was much more worried about Cribbett. He had the arrogance of a man who, when you went to see him in his office at the Ministry, would lean back in his swivel chair, put both his feet on his desk, and talk at you as though you were no better than the furniture... The civil service is often the worst field from which to recruit people to be heads of industry. With too few exceptions, the civil servant has never managed anything in his life, and has little or no idea of how to handle people. His job does not require that quality, and tends to stifle creativity. He comments, criticises and reports from his ivory tower in some Ministry building, far removed from the world. And he is never held to account for the result of his recommendations, nor held responsible for making ends meet financially.

We had arrived at an arrangement with Harold Watkinson under which Cribbett would not be allowed to interfere in any way with the management of BOAC itself.[21]

## CHANGES AT BEA

BEA meanwhile was still ringing up losses and still drawing down massive exchequer grants; for the two financial years 1953 and 1954 £2,750,000 was paid out in grants, reducing but not eliminating the net losses. It was not until 1955 that the corporation recorded its first annual profit, some eight years after nationalisation. Having at last gone into profit BEA was about to lose its chief executive. In 1955 Peter Masefield was asked by the government to take over as managing director of Bristol Aircraft. Bristol was privately owned but was to a large extent dependent on government contracts and finances; the company was having some difficulty putting the Britannia into service and the government thought it needed firmer direction. It was a bad move for Masefield whose career reached its apogee during his time with BEA. Bristol Aircraft proved resistant to change – not helped by its 'West Country work ethic' – and even more frustratingly Masefield was subsequently forced to pass up on the top job at BOAC after Thomas quit. Ironically, Masefield's previous employer BEA ordered the Vickers Vanguard, of similar layout and size to the Britannia but optimised for short-haul routes. Britain was now launching two very similar four-engine aircraft which were to enter service within three years of each other. Masefield's replacement at BEA was Anthony Milward.

At the end of October 1954 the Viking was withdrawn from regular service; the aircraft it was designed to replace, the Dakota, however continued in BEA service as the Pionair class. BEA took a further step in rationalising its fleet early in 1956 when it came to an agreement with Jersey Airlines that allowed the latter to take over all BEA's Channel Islands inter-island routes which were still operated by the corporation's Rapides. Jersey Airlines also took over the Guernsey-Southampton route and substituted Herons on many of the former BEA routes. As part of the deal, BEA bought a 25 per cent shareholding in Jersey Airlines. Later that year BEA signed a similar agreement with Cambrian, allowing the Welsh carrier to take over its services from Liverpool to the Channel Islands. Cambrian bought three Herons, its first new aircraft. Neither of these deals provoked anything like the controversy that accompanied the BOAC/Skyways link.

## INDEPENDENT NOTES

By 1954 East Anglian Flying Services was operating under the name by which it became so well known, Channel Airways, reflecting its network of routes from Ipswich, Southend, Rochester and Shoreham across the channel to the Channel Islands, Paris and Ostend. Derby Aviation began re-equipping with Dakotas; registered G-ANTD, the first flew its inaugural service between Derby and Jersey via Wolverhampton and Birmingham, on 6 May 1955. A year later, Derby introduced two Marathons bought from West African Airways Corporation on the growing scheduled-service network, freeing up the expanding fleet of Dakotas for charter and IT work. The Marathons had neither heaters nor auto-pilots; passengers were kept warm by constant infusions of hot tea and coffee, although the aircraft did not have toilets either. BKS acquired Vikings to add to its fleet of Dakotas and was developing a worthwhile network of scheduled services out of Leeds/ Bradford, including a new service to London Airport.

Air Kruise, BKS and Transair were becoming significant inclusive-tour charter airlines, although licence applications still drew continual objections from BEA on the grounds of 'material diversion'. A further boost came in October 1954 when the British Treasury increased tourist allowances from £50 to £100. Destinations served included Jersey, Ostend, Lourdes, Perpignan, Basel, Klagenfurt, Corsica, Majorca, Pisa and Venice. Many of the destinations on the continent involved long coach rides to the final resort or hotel. Transair, which had recently recruited Captain Bebb as its operations manager, had by now re-equipped with Dakotas and although still heavily involved in newspaper flying, found the size and range of the Dakota allowed for some worthwhile daytime flying on inclusive tours and soon built up a good relationship with Horizon Holidays, with whom the company formed Pilgrim Tours to jointly promote pilgrimage flights to Lourdes.

Meanwhile, Vladimir Raitz's company, Horizon, was facing increased competition from both old and new tour operators. Increasing prosperity, after the rigours of the early post-war years, led to a steady and perceptible increase in the demand for holidays by air abroad; it was to be some time before the corporations, especially BEA, realised just how significant the market for overseas holidays had become. The independents reaped the harvest as many of them made the transition from all-purpose freight airline to the more specialised role of low-cost, holiday-passenger airline. Airwork, with its long-standing connection with the Ski Club of Great Britain and the Polytechnic Touring Association, remained a major inclusive-tour operator, as well as providing the air transportation for George Wenger's Whitehall Travel representing one of the largest closed groups, the British Civil Service. Eagle Aviation had linked up with Sir Henry Lunn, an old established name in the holiday business, but was also flying for Wenger Airtours, the inclusive-tour component of George Wenger's business. Air Kruise, now part of the Britavia group, had started its long association with Blue Cars which – as its name suggests – offered coach tours and coach connections on the Continent; in 1955 they ordered six of the new Handley Page Herald forty-four-seat feederliners for its cross-Channel services to supplement its fleet of Dakotas and forty-four-seat Bristol Wayfarers. Blue Cars had been started by another important figure in the inclusive-tour business, Captain Langton, and after he had sold out, he started another tour operator, Sky Tours – much to the annoyance of the buyers of Blue Cars. Sky Tours concentrated on low-cost holidays to Majorca and the Costa Brava; to secure allocations of rooms Langton started paying hotel owners large deposits, much to the annoyance of the other tour operators. By 1956 Dan-Air was flying for Arrowsmith and Mercury Travel, operated out of Blackbushe. Inclusive tours were not solely confined to the south of England. Starways at Liverpool had long been associated with tours and pilgrimages organised by the Catholic Church and, together with the Cathedral Touring Agency, developed inclusive tours to France and Italy.

Now that Aquila had put into service its second Solent, named *City of Funchal*, and had reinstated two more of its older Sunderlands, it was in a position to expand its network, adding the Isle of Capri as a summer-only destination in June 1954, served by

Transair's Dakota G-ANEG previously saw service with the RAF at the very end of the war. (Richard T. Riding)

a once-weekly flight via Marseilles. The Solent was luxuriously fitted out for forty-two passengers, looked after by two stewardesses and two stewards in three spacious cabins over two decks, with a separate bar as well as dressing rooms and toilets. *The Aeroplane* described some of the special attributes of flying-boat operations:

> Because of the depth of hull necessary in a boat, there is real roominess and the possibility of walking about and even climbing stairs. Because there is no pressurisation the windows can be big and numerous, each one of them an emergency exit. And because of the need for watertight half-bulkheads there is none of this coach-tube, sardine-packed business.
>
> The Solent has two normal lower-floor passenger compartments with, aft of them, a promenade and bar from which a spiral staircase goes to the upper deck, which runs aft. This compartment is probably the most comfortable from the vibration and noise point of view, though the promenade area is good and there is nothing to complain about in the forward ground-floor compartments. These become temporarily submarine while the Solent is building up speed in the early part of the take-off run and until the aircraft gets on its step. Take-offs and landings are very great fun... I had long forgotten that slight feeling of helplessness as the engines are run-up and propellers exercised with no chocks or brakes to hold the aircraft. All the warming-up and running-up can usually be done while taxiing out.[22]

The take-off, with the Hercules engines at full power, usually took forty-five to fifty seconds; once at cruising speed, the aircraft flew along at 190 mph. During 1955 the airline introduced a once-weekly, summer-only service to Genoa. By 1956 the airline was operating four Solents and by removing the cocktail bar and the ladies' powder room, were able to increase the seating capacity to fifty-eight to allow for more tourist-class passengers. Ten flights a week were operated, to Lisbon, Madeira, Las Palmas, Genoa,

Aquila's Short Solent G-ANAJ creates a bow-wave as it taxis in after landing on Southampton Water. (Richard T. Riding)

Santa Margherita and Marseilles. It remained a costly operation, though: Aquila still had to provide all the facilities of an airport at Southampton Water, with flare floats, control launches, fire pinnaces and so on, while the aircraft needed constant maintenance and anti-corrosion treatment. The average utilisation for each aircraft was around 800 hours a year, low by prevailing standards; nor was it all obvious how Aquila would replace their existing fleet.

A new name appeared in January 1954, Dragon Airways – which as its name suggests had a Welsh connection – pleasure flying from Pwllheli where there was a Butlin's Holiday Camp. Its managing director was Captain Maurice Guinane, formerly a pilot with Eagle and indeed one of the first directors was Bamberg; they were to continue their partnership at Eagle later. Dragon ordered Herons but events overtook its planned expansion in the Liverpool area when Hunting-Clan bought the airline late in 1955, and used Dragon to take over its by now struggling Northern Network. Hunting-Clan in turn sold Dragon and the Northern Network to Britavia early in 1957, which absorbed them into Silver City's northern division. In 1956 Rylands had sold Lancashire Aircraft Corporation, his Blackpool-based domestic airline, to the acquisitive Britavia group, which had earlier bought Manx Airlines from its original owners; both these airlines were now also incorporated into the northern division of Silver City, flying Dakotas and Bristol Wayfarers, although they continued trading under their own names until the start of the 1958 season. Further south, Silver City opened the new Ferryfield Airfield at Dungeness on 13 July 1954, gradually transferring its services there and those of sister company Air Kruise from Lympne, from which it flew its last flight on 3 October 1954. The Ministry, owners of the old airport, tried to sell it, failed, and instead closed it down. That was not the end of the story for Lympne, which was to enjoy a successful renaissance just one year later.

The driver of the Jaguar roadster has his pick of four Silver City Bristol Super Freighters, waiting for the morning's flying to start at Ferryfield Airport, on the Romney marshes in Kent. (Flight)

## SKYWAYS COACH-AIR

Rylands had long been a proponent of the linked coach-air service, gathering passengers from all over the country by coach and taking them to a seaside airport for the short hop across the water, to join another coach for the ride to the final destination. During the early 1950s Lancashire Aircraft Corporation had flown a high-frequency service, up to twenty-five flights a day, between its base at Blackpool and the Isle of Man, drawing on the whole of the north of England as a catchment area by integrating the flights with the schedules of the local coach companies. Passengers avoided the sea journey but had to travel fairly long distances overland. For a passenger from Leeds it was cheaper to travel on the coach-air service to the Isle of Man, although not as fast as a direct Leeds-Isle of Man flight, but it was quicker than going by coach or train to catch the Isle of Man Steam Packet from Liverpool Docks or Fleetwood and not much more expensive.

Rylands took the concept a stage further; Skyways, which he part owned with the Bibby Line, began operating scheduled services between London and Paris on 30 September 1955, using two Dakotas taken initially from the Lancashire fleet. East Kent Road Car provided one of its magnificent maroon and cream thity-two-seat coaches for the three-hour journey from Victoria Coach Station to Lympne, now reopened, where the passengers transferred to a thirty-two-seat Dakota for the fifty-minute flight to Beauvais, north of Paris. From Beauvais it was a one-hour coach ride to the Place de la République in north Paris. The total journey time was around seven hours, not much faster than the rail-ferry-rail services but considerably cheaper. The Coach-Air return fare was £7 14s (£8 15s at weekends) which compared well with the return rail fare, via Newhaven and Dieppe, of

£12. The return tourist air fare on the normal BEA and Air France services from London Airport was £15 9s and took four hours. Both Lympne and Beauvais were well sited as airports for the service, Lympne being somewhat closer to London than Ferryfield and served by better roads; Beauvais is only one hour away from central Paris

Air Kruise offered a connection between Ferryfield and Le Touquet, on the coast and further north than Beauvais, which involved a three-hour train journey to Paris; its service to Ostend linked up with Belgian coach companies for the long transfer to holiday destinations in southern Europe. There was another service, the 'Blue Arrow', which made onward rail connections from Lyons to the south of France and Italian Riviera. Air Kruise ran its cross-Channel services, branded as Trans Channel Airways, mainly as a link in its extensive continental coach programmes and inclusive tours, operating over seventy-five flights a week; independent travellers who used public transport found they were not well catered for. Silver City, like Air Kruise part of the Britavia Group, decided to step up the Group's competitive response to Skyways the following year, 1956, by introducing the 'Silver Arrow' in May; this was a makeover of the original Air Kruise service with better connections for independent travellers. Passengers traveled by coach from Victoria to Ferryfield, where they boarded a Bristol Wayfarer for the twenty-minute flight to Le Touquet. At Le Touquet a dedicated de Dietrich 'Autorail' diesel-railcar took the passengers to the Gare du Nord in Paris; there was also a coach link with Brussels. Le Touquet was at the end of a branch line and although French Railways invested heavily in improving the links, eventually building an extension into the airport itself, the connections always suffered from the need to operate special trains to connect with the flights. Gatwick is different, having been built near a main line; there was no need for special trains as there were always fast connections to London and other destinations.

Eagle introduced a similar concept in 1957 with its Swiss Eagle air and rail service to Basle; passengers were flown to Luxembourg and then transferred by rail to Basle. In 1958 Laker joined the competition, by introducing a Coach-Air service from Southend, using spare capacity on the existing car-ferry services to Calais, Ostend and Rotterdam.

## TROOPING

On the trooping side it was all change again, as old contracts expired, new contracts were let and Laker's Air Charter emerged as the favoured carrier for 1954. Airwork was pulled off the Canal Zone contract and starting in August 1954, Air Charter operated a daily York flight from Stansted to Fayid. Air Charter had already taken over the West African contract from Airwork in May. Britavia, the parent company of Silver City and Aquila, launched itself as a long-haul charter airline under its own name, using its recently acquired Hermes. It was awarded the Cyprus and East Africa trooping contracts, taking over from Airwork in July 1955. The following year Air Charter also successfully bid for the Cyprus contract using Skymasters, somewhat to the annoyance of the MTCA. It thought the service ministries were somewhat cavalier in taking the contract away from an airline operating the British-built Hermes and lobbied hard for Air Charter to be debarred from offering its Skymasters for trooping work. The service ministries thought otherwise, as usual, and were not about to discourage competition for the establishment charter airlines by another operator of reasonable long-range aircraft.

However, if Airwork seemed to be losing out on the contracts, they were more than amply compensated in September 1954 when they were awarded the biggest trooping contract to date, to carry up to 10,000 forces personnel a year to Singapore. The contract, worth at least £1.25 million, was for two and a half years and marked a further change in government trooping policy, as the last major long-haul trooping service switched from sea to air. Instead of four weeks at sea, journey time in the Hermes was a mere three days, with a night stop at Karachi. Even so, the journey must have seemed interminable. The Hermes was short on range and had been designed to carry a maximum of fifty-four passengers in BOAC use. On trooping flights up to sixty-eight passengers were carried, and the air conditioning and ventilation struggled to cope; an RAF officer once described the atmosphere inside a Hermes on arrival at Singapore as foetid and unhealthy. This was somewhat improved by removing one row, reducing the number of seats to sixty-three. There were also other more delicate issues:

> We have been considering ways and means of segregating Far East air trooping passengers by rank categories…To satisfy Indian political susceptibilities, all personnel travelling on this route have to wear plain clothes and in spite of genuine efforts by the contractors to follow normal Service procedure, it is impossible to segregate officers and OR's (Other Ranks) at meals in hotels and airport restaurants on the route and embarrassing incidents still occur. As a result of human error or through lack of adequate facilities, Service air passengers are expected to share sleeping accommodation not appropriate to their respective ranks and sometimes with other travellers of quite inappropriate categories.[23]

This matter was never satisfactorily resolved, although some flights were classified for officers only, allowing the airline to offer upgraded accommodation for these flights. In 1955 Airwork was awarded a further contract for twenty-four flights between Singapore and Calcutta to carry Ghurka troops to and from jungle training in Malaya, considerably reducing the transit time from Nepal where the Ghurkas are recruited. The contracts were extended to cover both spring and autumn movements, and by the following year Airwork and Skyways between them were operating an intense pattern of fifty-eight round-trip flights to move 4,500 troops and their families.

Hunting-Clan still had the Malta and Gibraltar contracts and early in 1955 seemed to strengthen its position on the Gibraltar route by starting Colonial Coach Class services, initially on a once-a-month frequency. In 1954 Eagle had taken over the Cyprus leave scheme flights from Skyways; during the six months from May to October inclusive Eagle had four to five Vikings based at Nicosia shuttling back and forth to the Canal Zone, carrying 16,000 men to and from their leaves. Then Eagle consolidated its firm hold on trooping contracts by taking over the West Med operation (to Gibraltar, Malta and Libya) from Hunting-Clan in 1955 and in the following year won the West African contract, involving a weekly Viking flight. Eagle also secured a two-year extension to its Medair contract, using its Nicosia based Vikings to operate shuttle flights around the various British bases in the Mediterranean, North Africa, Iraq, Jordan, the Persian Gulf, Aden and Kenya. The Yorks of Dan-Air and Scottish Airlines were increasingly used on freight services; Dan-Air won its first major Ministry contract in 1956, to carry freight to and from the Far East.

Of the major charter airlines only Skyways was now without any major trooping contracts, although its aircraft were still used extensively by the Air Ministry for ad hoc charters. However Skyways' prospects improved in 1955 when in turn it was awarded the Cyprus contract for twelve months, and also started sharing the Singapore contract with Airwork, thus providing some work for its large fleet of Hermes. The joint operation with Airwork continued until 1959; aircraft and crews were shared between the two airlines, so it was quite possible, for example, for an Airwork crew to fly a Skyways aircraft. Between 30 April and 3 May 1957 a team of RAF Transport Command officers from the Examining Unit (TCEU) flew down to Singapore in a Hermes trooper, thereafter submitting a report back to their superiors. The Examining Unit was established to check RAF Transport Command pilots so they had no official remit to check or comment on civilian airline flying or procedures, but their report is a readable description of a very long flight in a piston-engined aircraft. It also illustrates the dangers of awarding contracts to the lowest bidder; it is clear that the examiners felt that items like meals were skimped on, and there is some anguish over the refusal of the airline to use mobile air conditioners when the aircraft was on the ground due to the additional cost of renting the units. The report ruffled feathers at the Air Ministry and some correspondence ensued between the Air Member for Supply and Organisation on the one hand and the AOC-in-C Transport Command on the other. Attached at Appendix Five is the report from the TCEU, together with the Passengers Flight Report and comments on the TCEU report by the Air Ministry.

RAF Transport Command was still involved in regular trooping and other government contract flights; Comet 2s, taken over from the Ministry of Supply order following the grounding of the Comet 1s, were used to transport personnel to and from the rapidly expanding Commonwealth rocket range at Woomera in Australia, in parallel with the existing freight services flown by RAF Hastings, now also supported by Air Charter's Super Traders. The Comet 2s were also increasingly used to support British military interests in the Middle East, rather than commercial contract carriers.

There were other changes, too. On 27 July 1954 the British and Egyptian Governments had signed an agreement covering the progressive withdrawal of all British troops from the Canal Zone over the following two years. Henceforth the Canal Zone's importance as a destination for trooping flights declined and dwindled as the evacuation got underway; the last British forces left by sea on 31 March 1956. There were changes in the Sudan as well. The British outmanoeuvred the Egyptians by siding with Sudanese nationalists; the Sudan never became part of Egypt, and on 1 January 1956 was proclaimed independent.


## TROOPING BRITANNIAS

In 1956 Scottish Airlines lost two Yorks whilst carrying out trooping contracts to the Canal Zone; the first, at RAF Luqa in Malta on 18 February, the second at Stansted on 30 April. Following the second crash there were calls for more modern equipment to be used by the Air Ministry on its contracts. The Ministry suspended any further passenger flights by York aircraft although the type continued to be used for freight services. The Ministry was now dependent on Hermes and Air Charter's Skymasters for medium and long-haul flights; Eagle's Vikings performed most of the short-haul Mediterranean tasks.

There was no mistaking the operator of Avro York G-AMUN. Scottish Airlines' military style livery seems suitable for a trooper. (MAP)

Britannias were the obvious choice; the type was about to enter service with BOAC and had been ordered for the RAF. Recognising the difficulties that the independents faced in obtaining finance for such relatively large and expensive aircraft, and in order to help the economy in Northern Ireland, the Ministry of Supply took the unusual step of ordering three Britannias. They would be built in Belfast by Shorts on the same production line as those for the RAF, and the plan was to make them available to the independents for use on trooping contracts. But the various ministries involved could not agree amongst themselves how to release the aircraft to the charter airlines. The Civil Aviation Ministry favoured long-term contracts, five to seven years, which would have allowed the charter carriers to buy the aircraft and operate them on a long-term basis, as happened with the British shipping companies which had bought ships against long-term trooping contracts. The Service Ministries were uncertain as to what their overseas commitments would be in the future, as the United Kingdom divested itself of its overseas possessions and ran down its military commitments elsewhere, especially in the Middle East, so they preferred short-term contracts. Nor did the Air Ministry want to be tied to long-term contracts, preferring the flexibility of shorter-term contracts that permitted it to benefit in full from competitive tendering. There was even talk of the aircraft being offered to Howard Hughes and TWA. The Ministry of Supply, which had to buy the aircraft, just wanted someone to make up their minds about the aircraft so they could get on and specify them for the manufacturer. The wrangling was interminable: 'The only firm decision is that they are not to be taken over by Transport Command.'[24]

Then Hunting-Clan ordered two aircraft of its own at the end of 1956 for delivery in 1958, but it was not to be the first independent operator of the Britannia; that distinction fell to Laker, who spotted an opportunity when the American airline Northeast cancelled its order for five, and took over two of them for Air Charter in 1958.

## AIRWORK AND THE NORTH ATLANTIC FREIGHT SERVICE

On 1 March 1955 Airwork inaugurated its transatlantic freight service from London, Manchester and Prestwick to New York. All-freight services were amongst those that the Minister had indicated might be operated by the independents, although BOAC had been dismayed when Airwork applied for and received a licence for North American flights. Typically, Airwork set about developing the route in a thoroughly professional manner, ordering three new Douglas DC-6As and chartering in Skymasters from the American airline Trans-Ocean Air Lines (TALOA) and a DC-6A from Slick Airways until the new freighters were delivered. It also began to build up feeder services from Europe, starting first with Frankfurt, using a Viking freighter converted for it by Eagle Engineering. The TALOA aircraft operated twice-weekly services initially and the Slick aircraft flew a weekend service that continued on to Chicago and Los Angeles, giving the British carrier transcontinental connections. One prestige load was Donald Campbell's *Bluebird* which brought the airline much publicity as newsreel and television crews filmed the craft being loaded on to a DC-6A. But despite the publicity, the service was short-lived; Airwork closed it down on 18 December of that year after only nine months, selling the DC-6As on the production line to Slick Airways. All-freight services are difficult to operate profitably; they work better if the airline can also carry passengers, but that was denied to Airwork. Government inertia did not help either; HM Customs refused to provide a duty-free trans-shipment zone at London Airport and the Board of Trade dragged its feet over granting import-duty exemption to the freighter DC-6As on order. Airwork also faced severe competitive pressures from the other transatlantic carriers like KLM and Pan American which were able to offer both passenger and freight services to points in Europe as well as London; Airwork had problems establishing its European feeder services because the British Government would not, or could not, obtain the necessary permissions. BOAC was relieved to see its competitor depart but faced the same problems itself when it came to launch its own freight services.

## HUNTING-CLAN AND THE AFRICAN CONNECTION

Hunting-Clan, however, had an altogether happier experience when it went down a similar path shortly afterwards, starting its 'Africargo' all-freight service to East Africa on 23 July 1955, using Yorks. The weekly service was soon boosted to twice a week with traffic stops at Malta, Khartoum, Entebbe and Nairobi. The Yorks could carry up to seven and a half tons and the flying time was around thirty hours. The advantages of speed were more apparent in the service to East Africa (the alternative was a long sea voyage through the Suez Canal to Dar-es-Salaam), and it was a market with which Hunting-Clan was already familiar. Indeed, Hunting-Clan was well entrenched in the African market, having extensive aerial-survey interests in Kenya and Rhodesia and was keen to develop airline services; its collaborator, Airwork, had aerial-spraying and tourism interests in Kenya and its long-standing connection with the Sudan.

Frustrated in its attempts to upgrade the Colonial Coach Class services and hoping to find other work for its Viscount and Britannia aircraft, Hunting-Clan tried to buy control of the loss-making Central African Airways Corporation (CAA) from the colonial

Airwork used this Douglas DC-4 of TALOA, an American charter airline, to start its North Atlantic freight service from London Airport. (Flight)

governments of the Federation of Rhodesia and Nyasaland. The shrieks of protest from BOAC must have been heard from the Cape to Whitehall, but there was nothing to stop a British entity buying or establishing an airline in one of the colonies. Provided they were properly licensed by their relevant authorities such airlines could not only operate domestically but on cabotage and international routes as well. Hunting-Clan clearly had in mind to use its modern turboprop aircraft on CAA's existing services to London, thus neatly circumventing the ban imposed by the British Government. As Maurice Curtis, Hunting-Clan's managing director, said: 'It is extraordinary to suggest that you must never replace your aircraft with more up-to-date ones.'[25] He was able to upgrade the Africargo service with Douglas DC-6As, but had to sell two of the Viscounts to Icelandair when it became obvious that the government was not prepared to allow them to be used on Colonial Coach Class services. Nor was he successful in his attempt to gain control of CAA. BOAC simply outflanked him and took over all CAA's long-haul services for ten years in return for a royalty payment, coyly described as a revenue-sharing formula, which guaranteed CAA £175,000 a year. Similarly, his attempts to establish Hunting-Clan African Airways in Rhodesia met with considerable opposition from the Central African Air Authority which said that licensing another carrier would lead to 'uneconomical overlapping' with Central African Airways and denied Hunting-Clan a licence to operate low-fare flights between Bulawayo and Salisbury, although other services were approved. Dakotas and Rapides were used on some schedules within Central Africa and for charter flights to South Africa and

One of the last of its kind to be built, Hunting-Clan's Douglas DC-6A/C G-APNO unloads at Uganda's Entebbe Airport on the Africargo service. (Flight)

Mozambique; more importantly they connected with the Africargo service at Nairobi, collecting and distributing freight within Rhodesia and Nyasaland.

## HELICOPTERS

Commercial use of helicopters was the subject of much interest to both operators and commentators alike after the war. As early as 1948 BEA was using Sikorsky S-51s on various experimental services carrying Royal Mail; in 1950 a short-lived passenger service was inaugurated between Liverpool and Cardiff. In 1951 another passenger service was introduced between London Airport, Northolt and Birmingham, the last served by the delightfully named 'Rotorstation' at Haymills. When this failed the routing was changed to Southampton and the larger Sikorsky S-55 introduced late in 1954; S-55s were also used to launch another short-lived service, between London Airport and the South Bank heliport near Waterloo station in London. BEA abandoned scheduled-service helicopter operations early in 1957 but retained the unit for charter and experimental work. Sabena, the Belgian airline, introduced the first international helicopter service to London in 1953, when veteran pilot Anselme Vernieuwe flew a Sikorsky S-55 from Brussels to the South Bank heliport.

Independent operators were also keen to explore the helicopter's possibilities. Lord Beaverbrook had a S-51 painted in the colours of the *Evening Standard* and their use as

Autair's Westland Sikorsky S-51 G-AJOV on the deck of the *Oluf Sven*, expedition ship for the 1955-57 Falkland Islands and Dependencies Aerial Survey Expedition, undertaken by Hunting Aerosurveys. (Royal Aeronautical Society Library)

flying billboards was appreciated by other concerns, like Silver City, which also saw the helicopter as a possible replacement for its fleet of Bristol Freighters. BEA sold three of its S-51s to a new helicopter charter operator in 1954, Autair, an offshoot of Ronald Myhill's Overseas Motors, which he formed with another former RAF colleague, William 'Bill' Armstrong. They were used initially on the Continent for advertising purposes and based in Dusseldorf, but one was sent to the Antarctic in 1955 to help with a surveying project in Grahamland; others were deployed in Africa and the Far East. Fisons Pest Control was an early user of helicopters and in May 1955 the firm linked up with Airwork to form Fison Airwork to develop the business beyond the agricultural and forestry work that Fisons had initiated, by participating in oil exploration work in the Persian Gulf and Nigeria.

Then there was Alan Bristow. Formerly a chief test pilot with Westland Aircraft, which had secured the licence to build Sikorsky designs in Great Britain, Bristow had worked with a French company, Helicop-Air, before starting his own firm, Air Whaling, which spotted for the Onassis whaling fleet in the Antarctic for three seasons up until 1953-54. When the whaling industry was hit by depression, he changed the name of the company to Bristow Helicopters and looked for work elsewhere. He found it in the oil industry, ferrying men and equipment between shore bases and off-shore rigs and secured his first major contract with Shell in 1955 which involved him ferrying out two nine-seat Westland Whirlwinds from Southampton to Doha. This expedition took eight days to cover the 3,400 miles.

## WORLD EVENTS

On 30 November 1954 Britain's Prime Minister Sir Winston Churchill reached his eightieth birthday. Typically, he paid gracious tribute to his fellow countrymen and their kinsmen throughout the world:

> I have never accepted what many have kindly said, namely that I inspired the nation.... it was the nation and the race dwelling all round the globe that had the lion's heart. I had the luck to be called on to give the roar.

Just over four months later he resigned, to be succeeded as Prime Minister by Sir Anthony Eden, the former Foreign Secretary and heir apparent for many years. Eden almost immediately called a General Election on 26 May 1955 from which the Conservative Party emerged with an increased majority of fifty-eight.

The new Prime Minister – for so long intimately involved in foreign policy issues – looked out over a world that was increasingly hostile, especially towards British interests. The Greek community in Cyprus[26] had for long championed the cause of *Enosis*, or union with Greece: it was not a prospect that recommended itself to the Turkish minority on the island. Recognising the island's strategic location in the increasingly volatile world of Middle Eastern politics the British were not prepared to quit. In 1955 a campaign of terror was launched against British forces and their families in Cyprus, led by a former Greek army officer General Grivas; the British garrison was strengthened to some 30,000 men and a new military airfield built at Akrotiri. Skyways was an early casualty when its Hermes G-ALDW was blown up and totally destroyed by saboteurs at Nicosia on 4 March 1956, fortunately with no loss of life. The importance of Cyprus, or at least of its military bases, was emphasised later that year when it was used by French and British forces during the Suez Crisis.

## THE SUEZ CRISIS

British occupying forces had finally left the Canal Zone during 1956, although some civilian employees remained to look after the considerable quantity of stores and base installations left behind. Before leaving, the British Government had extracted certain concessions including landing rights at two of the former bases, Abu Sueir and Fanara, and a guarantee that the British-controlled Suez Canal Company would continue to run the Canal until 1968. Britain and the United States hoped to improve their standing in Egypt with its revolutionary leader Colonel Nasser – whose role was recognised as pivotal in the Cold War politics of the day – by offering loans to help build the Aswan High Dam, seen as crucial to meet the needs of a rapidly expanding population. However, when Nasser chose a policy of political non-alignment, and indeed appeared to favour closer ties with the Communist Bloc, the Americans withdrew their loan offer, closely followed by Britain. Nasser responded by nationalizing the Suez Canal, albeit with compensation, on 26 July 1956.

For the new British Prime Minister – still offended by the expropriation in 1951 of British oil assets in Iran and concerned at the loss of British influence and prestige in the Arab-speaking world – the nationalisation of the Suez Canal Company was a further blow, a slap in the face, and he determined to act using force if necessary to recover control of the Canal. He found an ally in the French who also had an interest in the Suez Canal Company, and were smarting at the support that Colonel Nasser had given to the independence movement in the French-governed North African colony of Algeria. During August, British and French forces began to assemble in Cyprus and Malta by air and sea; ships were taken up from trade to support the invasion force. RAF Transport Command was stretched to the limit, but was helped out in its task of flying reinforcements by BOAC; the latter had taken delivery of six of its new Britannias which had not yet entered commercial service because of an engine-icing problem leading to engine 'flame-outs'. Needs must, however, and their ample 100-seat capacity was put to good use by the government, the airline flying thirty-four sorties out to Cyprus. Charter airlines were also called up. Coordinated by Airwork they were involved in the build-up from mid-August: Hermes from Britavia, Airwork and Skyways operated sixty flights to Malta and Cyprus and Eagle flew an intensive series of twenty-one flights to Malta with its Vikings in a four-day period from 14 August to 17 August. Aquila flew out naval personnel to Malta in three Solents and then used the aircraft to fly a shuttle service between Malta and Fanara, a former seaplane base on the Great Bitter Lake, evacuating the civilian personnel and their families who then returned to England in the Hermes of Britavia.

Matters came to a head on 29 October when Israeli forces attacked Egyptian positions in the Sinai. Britain and France called on both sides to cease hostilities and withdraw from the area of the Canal Zone. When Egypt rejected the demand the British and French air forces began bombing Egyptian air bases and other targets, and landed troops at Port Said who quickly began advancing down the Canal. But world opinion (in particular anger on the part of the United States – which led to a serious loss of confidence in sterling) forced Britain and France to call a halt and then to abandon any further action, having achieved none of their goals. Colonel Nasser remained in charge and became a vocal and effective spokesman for the Arab cause; Eden himself resigned shortly afterwards. The Israelis had to withdraw from the Sinai. The Canal Company remained Egyptian-owned and run. The British lost all their military rights in the Canal Zone as well as the stores stockpiled there, worth £270 million. To save some face, United Nations forces took over from the British and French who were then evacuated. The Hermes and Vikings of the independents and BOAC's Britannias were once again put to good use. One casualty of the hasty evacuation was Britavia's Hermes G-ALDJ which crashed whilst trying to land at Blackbushe on 5 November on a flight back from Tripoli, Libya carrying service families. The accident report attributed at least part of the cause to lack of alertness by the crew who had endured a nineteen-hour duty day, prolonged by a six-and-a-half-hour delay at Malta with a magneto problem.

## THE HUNGARIAN UPRISING

Whilst France pondered the lessons it had learned from the Suez Crisis and went on to develop a more independent defence policy and to build up closer political ties with its European neighbours, the British quickly patched up their differences with the Americans as the two nations faced up to a new threat in Europe. Following rioting and demonstrations against the Communist regime in Hungary, the Soviet Union invaded that country in November whilst events in Suez and Egypt were providing other distractions and the uprising was put down with force, leading to a massive exodus of refugees who streamed over the border into Austria. From mid-November, for just over a month, the British Red Cross coordinated an airlift by British charter airlines and BOAC, carrying supplies into Linz in Austria and taking out around five hundred refugees a day. Over 7,500 refugees were flown out, many in BOAC's Britannias, performing a reprise of their role during the Suez Crisis, but the bulk, over 5,000 people, were carried in the Dakotas and Vikings of British independents, which performed 144 rescue flights.

# THREE

# IN THE DOLDRUMS
## 1957-1959

### NEW BLOOD

On 9 January 1957 Prime Minister Eden resigned; he had been in ill health and ill at ease after the Suez Crisis. His successor was Harold Macmillan, Chancellor of the Exchequer, who had been in Parliament since 1924 and a member of the Cabinet since 1951. The two had just finished collaborating over BOAC's future jet requirements, Macmillan agreeing to supply the dollars necessary to buy fifteen Boeing 707s: 'BOAC's Boeing purchase is a stop-gap though a necessary one', he wrote to Eden.[1]

Both corporations introduced new aircraft into service in 1957. Having won plaudits for the successful introduction of the Viscount in 1952, BEA now took delivery of the larger Viscount 802, seating up to sixty-five passengers, which allowed the corporation to retire its Ambassador fleet the following year. For its part BOAC introduced two new aircraft types early in the year: first, the long-range Douglas DC-7C 'Seven Seas' which permitted non-stop service to New York; and then the Britannia, the medium-range Series 102, which entered service on the South African route on 1 February. Despite their protracted development period the Britannias were still plagued with teething problems, causing serious delays to BOAC's services. With the DC-7Cs now in service, and having just ordered fifteen Boeing 707s, BOAC saw little point in taking delivery of the eighteen longer-range Britannia Series 312 it had on order, and tried to cancel them. No other major airline had ordered the Britannia. An American medium-range competitor, the Lockheed Electra, was about to enter service in 1958 having secured large orders from American carriers, always the biggest market. BEA had decided to order the Vanguard, optimised for its short-haul route structure and from the same stable as the successful Viscount, and so had no interest in the Britannia. Other airlines saw no need to introduce a complex new turboprop type which was due to be superseded in two years anyway by the faster and larger Boeing 707 and Douglas DC-8 jet transports – nor did BOAC, with a large inventory of aircraft in service and on order. Being a state-owned corporation has its obligations as well as its privileges, however, and the government was adamant that the order should stand. The standing charges of the Britannia fleet, together with all the heavy introductory costs of bringing the type into service for a very brief interim front-line operation, increased BOAC's overhead and financial burden and required massive debt write-offs later. Whatever advantages might have accrued to BOAC through the introduction of long-range turboprop aircraft had long ago been whittled away by the delay in bringing the Britannia into service, so that the long-range Series 312 was almost obsolete when it was finally introduced on the London-New York route by BOAC on 19 December 1957, some fourteen years after the Brabazon Committee had recommended manufacture of a transatlantic airliner. When it entered service, splendidly configured with just fifty-two deluxe first-class seats, it reduced flight times to and from New York by up to ninety minutes over Pan American's DC-7Cs and TWA's somewhat slower L-1649 Constellations. Nevertheless, BOAC remained very grumpy about its British-built aircraft:

> BOAC has been subject to the disadvantage of carrying an exceptional burden of expense and responsibility whenever they have been called upon to introduce a new British type of aircraft into service. It has fallen to the Corporation since the war to eliminate the teething troubles of successive types of long-distance British transport aircraft. There is no other country in the world which expects its airlines to bear the additional expense entailed by this work of developing a new aircraft to make it fit for competitive service and for export.[2]

Such protestations did not prevent the corporation from ordering thirty-five Vickers VC10s off the drawing board early in 1958, a few months before the first of its new Comet 4s entered service. BOAC had a requirement for a second-generation jet to use on some of its more demanding routes, in particular the hot-and-high airfields at Kano, Nairobi and Johannesburg. Vickers proposed a sophisticated design, the VC10, which had four Rolls-Royce Conways mounted at the rear, ensuring a clean wing and good airfield performance. It was somewhat smaller than the Boeing 707, but that seemed more suitable for the thinner, former Empire routes.

Between them, Watkinson and d'Erlanger sanctioned the acquisition of fifty new jets to add to the corporation's newly acquired fleets of nineteen Comets, ten DC-7Cs and over thirty Britannias. At the end of 1956, BOAC's somewhat sparse front-line fleet consisted of just over fifty piston-engine airliners: Stratocruisers, Constellations and Argonauts. As The Aeroplane pointed out,[3] for this huge increase in capacity to work it would require a quadrupling of output over the next ten years, a heroic assumption and one, of course, which was to lead in large part to BOAC's problems in the coming years.

Just under a year later the first British charter airline introduced the Britannia into service. On 1 October 1958 Air Charter began flying a series of charter flights for the Ministry of Defence between Stansted and Christmas Island transporting personnel to the H-bomb tests in the South Pacific, using Britannia 307 G-ANCE. Transair had been the first independent to introduce turboprop aircraft on trooping flights when its new Viscounts took over the West Med trooping flights to Gibraltar, Malta and Libya in October 1957. This was something of an irritation to the losing bidder, Eagle, whose chairman, Harold Bamberg, wrote to Flight:

> The facts are that Eagle have satisfactorily operated the predecessor of this particular contract (as well as others) for nearly two years, using Viking aircraft. Some months before the issue

of the invitation to tender for the renewal of this contract, we offered to convert the existing contract for operation with Viscounts, but the Government rejected this on financial grounds. Subsequently, in response to the invitation to tender, we, as holders of the existing contract, again offered Viscount aircraft, which we had ordered primarily for this type of work. [4]

The Treasury's gain was someone else's loss, but it showed how vulnerable carriers were with short-term contracts. Indeed, the Air League observed:

> We were informed that 80 to 85 per cent of the independents' traffic, carried under licence in the case of passenger traffic, and under government contract in the case of trooping, is on a basis of three years or less, with a substantial majority of one year or less. This is clearly an impossible basis for any commercial operation. [5]

The Air League recommended that both trooping and service freight carriage should be extended and noted approvingly that the comparative cost of RAF Transport Command and civil air transport was in the ratio of three or four to one, although it warned that 'so meagre is the return… that the committee finds it difficult to believe that the majority of these companies can continue to operate indefinitely on their present basis of earnings'. Ominously, though, there was talk of an expanding role for RAF Transport Command, with new Comets and Britannias coming on line, at the same time as the continuing withdrawal from the Canal Zone was decreasing movements by 50,000 passengers a year.

The West Med contract was important for Transair, which now operated twenty-five to thirty-five flights a month to bases in the Mediterranean: around half for Malta, five to Gibraltar and ten to Tripoli and Benghazi in Libya, giving about 2,000 hours of utilisation for its two Viscounts. This was the kind of bread-and-butter work that the independents needed if they were to re-equip; inclusive-tour flying, largely limited to a four-month summer season, could at best give 1,000 hours flying, so year-round flying had to be the key to buying modern but expensive new aircraft. Only trooping and the Colonial Coach Class services guaranteed that level of utilisation, or so it seemed at the time. Inclusive-tour flying, still hamstrung by associate agreements and an IATA fare structure, eventually overcame these obstacles and that of a short holiday season; but that was yet to come.

## FLIGHT TIME LIMITATIONS

The government had been quick enough after the war to implement legislation covering the economic regulation of airlines: it took somewhat longer to legislate on the operational aspects of airline regulation. To a certain extent the industry was already self-regulating when it came to operations and safety in the air. The Air Registration Board (ARB), first established in 1937, and with Lord Brabazon as its long serving chairman, comprised representatives from government, the airlines and the manufacturers. Its function was not dissimilar to that of Lloyd's Register of Shipping and it enjoyed similar independence. As well as setting standards for aircraft manufacturers the ARB also covered maintenance and inspection requirements, made recommendations to the Minister for the granting of

Air Charter's Bristol Britannia G-ANCE in flight. Freddie Laker stole a march on his competitors by being the first independent to fly this large, long-range turboprop airliner. (Richard T. Riding)

certificates of airworthiness, gave approval to airline flight manuals and licensed aircraft maintenance engineers.

The Civil Aviation Act enabled the Minister to introduce Orders and Regulations to cover air-safety standards and requirements which had been agreed under the auspices of a United Nations organisation, the International Civil Aviation Organisation (ICAO). There was further legislation in 1954 when the Air Navigation Order set out the responsibilities of the pilots, the so-called Rules of the Air. One outcome of the Act was a committee under the chairmanship of Sir Frederick Bowhill to investigate the question of air crew duty hours.

Duty hours, or the maximum length of time that pilots and cockpit crew could remain on duty, had always been at the discretion of the airlines and were set out in the relevant operations manual; an airline had to have its operation manual approved by the Ministry in accordance with the Air Navigation Order and so an important secondary check was already in place, but no detailed requirements were laid down. After much debate arising from the work of the Bowhill Committee, and with little advance notice, the government published new rules covering flight time limitations in May 1957; they only applied to flight-deck crew at this time.

The revised Air Navigation Order specified outline requirements. Pilots and flight engineers were limited to a maximum of 125 hours flying in any period of thirty consecutive days. If there was only one pilot on the aircraft, he could not fly more than twelve hours after beginning duty, or for fourteen hours if it was split with seven hours required on the ground; if there were two pilots they could fly up to sixteen hours and if there were three or more pilots, including two qualified captains and provision for sleeping facilities on board, then the crew could remain on duty for twenty-four hours. Furthermore, the pilot in command could still exceed these limitations in exceptional circumstances at his discretion. There were also specified minimum rest periods, although with no jets yet in service, the issue of 'jet-lag' had not yet arisen so there were no provisions to cover local time differences. Cabin crew were not covered by any of these requirements.

Charter airlines tended to fly with heavy crews and night stops, as there was little possibility of pre-positioning slip crews for flights that would often be fixed at short notice. If, however, a reasonable frequency along a specific route could be maintained, as happened with certain trooping flights to the Far East, then slip crews could take over at intermediate points; this was normal practice with scheduled airlines.

## CIVIL AVIATION POLICY – 'CONGRATULATIONS ON MAKING THE BEST USE OF THE CRUMBS'

'You have long listened to the bleats and moans of this Association,' said the chairman of BIATA at the Association's annual dinner on 9 December 1957, addressing himself to the Minister, Harold Watkinson, 'and you have spent many a long hour trying to see what is best for British air transport.'[6] After five years of Conservative Government and now with a new Prime Minister, the independents were fretting that so little was being achieved in their field of endeavour; despite having created many opportunities for themselves and exploited many and varied niche markets, they had reached the limit of the commercial opportunities available to them. In his foreword to the 1956-57 BIATA Annual Report, the chairman, Gerald Freeman of Transair, noted:

> Dealing first with the year's operations, the very general picture which emerges is that progress and expansion was achieved in some directions whilst in others there was some reduction and traffic declined. In both scheduled and non-scheduled operations, however, the total capacity produced showed a decrease on the previous year….In broad terms, the total effort of the independent airlines has not kept pace with the general world-wide upward trend, although some individual categories of operation enjoyed varying degrees of expansion.
>
> This, therefore, is the broad background of the year which is now under review and it clearly emphasises, once again, the urgent need for considerable re-thinking on the question of the future of the independents and of British air transport. More than anything, perhaps, it indicates that the limits of current Government policy have been reached in all but a few cases as far as the independent airlines are concerned.

The government, however, was disinclined to stretch those limits any further. The Minister was more inclined to make jokey references to the long-running 'crumbs from the table' metaphor than to allow the independents a larger slice of the cake. Although the independents had carried well over a million passengers in 1956, BEA had carried twice as many and was heard and listened to in Whitehall, as was its sister corporation BOAC. The government was more influenced by Treasury concerns than competition policy. Now that both corporations had come into profit, the government was not minded to take any action that would prejudice this state of affairs and it received plenty of advice from other ministries and the corporations that competition from British airlines would be detrimental to their financial well-being. BEA did not need competitive disruption in its own backyard, having stitched up numerous revenue-sharing and other pooling arrangements all round Europe. By 1 April 1959 the corporation had pooling agreements with thirteen of its fourteen European rivals; the only exception was TAP in Portugal, and it was soon to succumb. Mike Ramsden, writing in *Flight*, questioned the value of so many pooling agreements:

> While some pools are undoubtedly necessary, a 'pool-everything' policy must inevitably diminish the effort to be competitive and efficient; it must mean the destruction of the precious little freedom which politics allows an airline; and it must undeniably lead to questions about cartels.[7]

The corporation already objected to applications for inclusive-tour flights from British independents, pointing out in its 1956-57 annual report:

> The volume of these services to the main Continental holiday centres has, however, now grown beyond the scale which could be regarded as economically helpful in dealing with peak traffic demands... In our view these operations have caused material diversion of traffic from BEA's services.

Fortunately this was not a view shared by the Air Transport Advisory Council.

## THE COMMITTEE ON CIVIL AVIATION POLICY

Boyd-Carpenter's well-meaning attempts to quicken the pace of change had foundered, enmeshed in a bureaucracy more concerned with procedure than the content of his proposals. His successor, Watkinson, abandoned Boyd-Carpenter's step-by-step approach and evolved an altogether more ambitious scheme, one that would have surely led to the formation of a British airline monolith akin to Russia's Aeroflot,[8] and just as unwieldy. His proposals were summed up by the Treasury thus:

> In brief the Minister proposes to combine public and private interests in the existing Air Corporations, BOAC and BEA, by:
> (a)   converting the Corporations to 'holding' companies which would purchase and own aircraft, recruit and train crews and handle passengers and traffic.
> (b)   forming 'operating' companies by joint investments from the Corporations and private interests to do the actual route and charter flying. The companies would hire aircraft, crews and other staff from the Corporations. They would be represented on the Boards of the Corporations and would each be allocated particular routes.
> (c)   as a second stage, permitting the progressive reduction of the present Government holdings in the Corporations to that of a minority interest only.[9]

The Treasury viewed these ideas with a disapproving eye, arguing that this scheme could not be achieved without a change in legislation; it pointed out that even partial de-nationalisation was counter to the intent of the existing Civil Aviation Act, which had been specifically brought in to nationalise the remaining post-war companies, and to use the same Act to undo these changes was stretching credibility too far. The Treasury was also concerned that it would lose control of the purse strings – 'conferring the benefits of

Government credit on private interests,' as a senior Treasury official put it[10] – and would lose all hope of ever being repaid the extensive deficiency grants to the corporations, totaling over £51 million since the end of the war.

Nevertheless the Cabinet established a Committee on Civil Aviation Policy to examine Watkinson's various proposals, which met periodically in 1956 and early 1957. After the Treasury had successfully killed off the joint-venture proposal, Watkinson drew up a second scheme which was to amalgamate the four larger charter companies, Airwork, Hunting-Clan, Skyways and Britavia – those with shipping interests – into one large 'chosen instrument' which would have a monopoly of all trooping and military freight services and any new scheduled services that might arise. For this to work the Minister wanted the Service Ministries to award trooping contracts of up to seven years' duration, also regarded as the minimum period required to lease the three Ministry of Supply Britannias, which were still in play. This time not just the Treasury objected. The Service Ministries, supported by the Treasury, were not prepared to lose the benefits of competitive tendering by entrusting all civil trooping flights to just one company and certainly not under seven year contracts. They rightly pointed out that Britain's overseas garrison requirements were constantly changing, and resisted the imposition of anything but short-term contracts. Other ministers objected too. John Maclay, now at the Scottish Office, thought it wrong that other charter airlines should be excluded; he had in mind Scottish Airlines but also noted that Air Charter and Eagle stood to lose under these proposals, as did the corporations. The latter point invoked a warm endorsement from the Treasury, which appreciated the benefits of competitive tendering amongst charter airlines, but remained resolutely set against them competing with the corporations on scheduled routes.

By this stage Watkinson was in something of a dilemma. He felt obligated to the shipping companies, which with government encouragement had invested in the charter airlines and wanted to offer them some improvement; but at the same time could not give them anything which appeared to take something away from the corporations. The following extract from the Minutes of the Committee of 25 February 1957 shows how the government was boxed in:

The Minister of Transport said that various proposals had been put forward over the previous fourteen months, for widening the opportunities for the independent civil aviation companies... A report by officials had shown that the scope for expanding these opportunities was limited in extent, and had drawn special attention to the importance of air-trooping contracts to these companies. In 1954/55 these contracts had accounted for approximately two-thirds of the total passenger miles flown by the independent companies and these proportions were not materially different now. On further consideration, he had decided that it would not be practicable to proceed with the proposal to combine the independent companies and the Air Corporations into mixed corporations on the lines he had originally envisaged. Nor was a merger between the four major independent companies likely to materialise; the more probable development was the absorption of the smaller independent companies by the larger.

If, therefore, anything was to be done towards fulfilling the Government's stated policy, action must be taken to resolve two main outstanding issues. These were the future of the colonial coach services built up by the independent companies, and the provision of long-term assurances concerning air-trooping contracts.[11]

So it was that the Service Ministries were reluctantly coerced into agreeing longer trooping contracts of no less than three years duration, in an attempt to secure better terms for the independents' re-equipment programme. And after all the huffing and puffing the only improvement that the government was able to offer the independents and their shipping backers came down to this: Hunting-Clan and Airwork would be allowed to introduce more modern aircraft on the Colonial Coach Class routes in exchange for giving BOAC a share of this low-fare traffic. In future independents would be allowed to carry around 30 per cent of the low-fare tourist traffic, leaving BOAC with the remaining seventy per cent which it would offer at a new fare below the existing tourist rate. BOAC was introducing Britannias on its African services and was doubtless anxious to fill the greater capacity now available, but even so it was a curiously one-sided arrangement which forced the independents to give up a significant proportion of the market that they had developed to the state corporation. 'We are dealing with the traffic which was unwanted by BOAC and was developed at the risk of the shareholders monies by private enterprise… the Corporations are to be given 70 per cent of somebody else's business' was one view expressed in a debate in the House of Commons on 22 July 1957. The independents were glad enough to have been allowed to retain some share of the cake, however, and to be able to introduce more modern equipment. Hunting-Clan took back its three Viscounts which had been on lease to Middle East Airlines and inaugurated turboprop 'Safari' service to Nairobi on 17 October, followed the next day by service to Salisbury, Rhodesia. Two flights a week to East Africa and one flight a week to Central Africa were scheduled, with one night stop in each direction. Early in 1958 Airwork procured two Viscounts from the Norwegian airline Fred Olsen to fulfil its share of the flying.

## 'I ALSO WANT TO HELP THE INDEPENDENTS TO KEEP GOING'

Britavia, however, was not one of the airlines that benefited from the very minor concessions made, although it was not for want of trying. Its all-freight service to Australia, first applied for in 1954, was no nearer gaining approval from the Australians and in April 1956, Britavia persuaded the Earl of Home,[12] Secretary of State for the Commonwealth Relations Office, to write to the Australian Prime Minister, Robert Menzies, in support of its application. Clearly untutored in the Treasury view, Home made the heretical connection between the benefits of competition and its effect on the corporations:

> Experience of the past few years has convinced us that the initiative and enterprise shown by these private companies not only expands the field of air transport development but also stimulates the Corporations to greater efforts…. It is not without interest that, since we introduced this policy of providing opportunities for the private companies, both the State Corporations have transformed their annual losses into profits.[13]

Menzies was unimpressed. Any new services would wipe out Qantas's profits, he said, and besides, all-freight services did not work; look at what happened to Airwork's North American service. No, he continued, all reasonable public needs were being met. And that for the time being was that. But another opportunity arose a year later when Qantas was looking beyond London traffic rights to the United States. Britavia asked the government to try again. This time Watkinson was pressed into service, who hatched a scheme to get Mcmillan to write to Menzies on a personal basis, citing his embarrassment at not being able to offer the independents more opportunities when his government was on the verge of securing new concessions for the corporations.

> The inability to reach agreement with your Government about it has therefore already, as you can imagine, caused my colleagues and me some not unimportant political embarrassment and this would become more serious if it were publicly announced that major agreement had been reached between us to the benefit of two publicly-owned corporations with no regard for the commercially comparatively trivial interests of the only independent concerned...I am sorry to have to raise with you personally this relatively small question. My reason, which I know you will understand, is that I am in great difficulty about finding useful opportunities for independent air operators on which there are very strong feelings among my supporters.[14]

Macmillan approved the draft letter, and added a hand-written note: 'I also want to help the independents to keep going because they really are, like the merchant navy in the old days, our second line of defence so far as air transport is concerned.' For some reason this was omitted from the message that was sent to the Australians, possibly because it is almost illegible; a novel insight into the mysteries of government policy-making. Although Watkinson's approach was cynical, for he only wanted to delay the final Australian response to some time beyond the party's next political conference and would have been happy with a non-committal, face-saving reply in order to placate some of his more vociferous colleagues in the Tory party, the Australians responded courteously and even gave some ground, offering perhaps one service a week to Perth, but heavily circumscribed with restrictions. Britavia finally gave up the struggle. With the loss of its long-haul trooping contracts early in 1959, the Hermes were returned to Silver City for further use on IT services and short-haul trooping contracts to Germany.

## CONSOLIDATION

As for the next stage, Lord Mancroft explained the government's plans, or lack of them, in the House of Lords on 11 December 1957, just two days after the 'bleats and moans' BIATA Dinner:

> BOAC and BEA have over a number of years built up a strong position on their international routes. Their reputation and general goodwill are valuable assets to British civil aviation, and the Government have no intention of undermining the position that they have established. There is therefore no question of taking away from the Corporations their existing routes and handing them over to the independent companies.

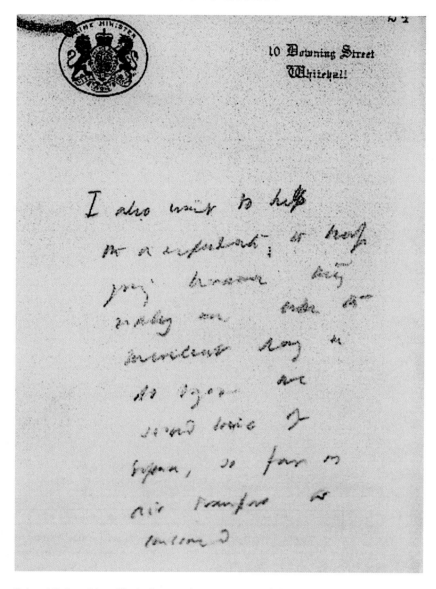

Prime Minister Macmillan's view on the importance of charter airlines, its essence somewhat lost in transmission.

No formal approval or licence is needed to set up a company. It is therefore for the companies themselves to decide on amalgamation or other rationalisation. I must, however, make this clear: that the Government would welcome some reduction in the number of companies if this is likely to result in the formation of larger and more firmly based companies. Such companies would be better able to afford the high cost of re-equipping their fleets with modern aircraft; and with a better fleet the companies would be able to bid more effectively in the international field for charter work, as well as to operate more efficiently the scheduled services allocated to them.[15]

The government set great store by rationalisation and amalgamation, economic concepts that went back to before the war. In January of the following year, Airwork duly complied and bought a controlling interest in the Air Charter group of companies – bringing Laker into the fold – and Aviation Traders. Just as far-reaching was the takeover of the Union-Castle Mail Steamship Company by the Cayzer family, who merged it with Clan Line to form British and Commonwealth Shipping. British and Commonwealth was to set the pace in the next decade when the independents began to do the Minister's bidding and started to consolidate.

But the more dramatic changes were those about to take place in the aircraft manufacturing industry, which had come under increasing pressure from the government since 1957 to rationalise itself. The government no longer favoured a multiplicity of relatively small manufacturers, ready in times of crisis to provide the production capacity to execute major rearmament programmes speedily, as had happened so magnificently during the war. Larger companies seemed to be financially stronger and were easier to deal with administratively. If there was any cake on offer, it was much easier to divide it up amongst fewer mouths; this was especially true of the aircraft manufacturers. Now government attention began to focus on the aircraft and engine manufacturers, as they struggled to develop successors to their earlier range of aircraft.

## SOME NEW OPPORTUNITIES

Whilst the major independents pondered the outcome of the government's latest review, the growth of inclusive tour (IT) business was attracting new entrants. In an otherwise stagnating market, inclusive tours had doubled in 1957 over the previous year, and there were plenty of newcomers eager to help out. In 1956 Independent Air Transport, under Captain Kozubski, was flying ad hoc and IT charters from Blackbushe and Bournemouth with Vikings and later Skymasters. Orion started flying its attractive two-tone green and white Viking, also from Blackbushe, in August 1957. Then in 1958 another new operator, Tradair, was formed to carry inclusive-tour passengers from its base at Southend, with two Vikings acquired from Airwork. By the end of 1959 there were further new entrants: Overseas Aviation, Air Safaris, Falcon, Continental, Trans European, and North-South, the last primarily a scheduled-service airline. On the other side of the coin, inclusive-tour operators were becoming more adventurous; during the summer of 1958 pioneering Horizon Holidays chartered Aeroflot's Russian-built Tupolev Tu-104 jets to fly holidaymakers to Moscow.

Other airlines sought new opportunities elsewhere. When boxed in by the lack of opportunity in the UK, we have already seen how the major independents tried to diversify abroad, setting up subsidiaries overseas to exploit markets that were not regulated by the British Government: Airwork had its African and New Zealand subsidiaries, Hunting-Clan had associated companies worldwide with interests in surveying, as well as aircraft manufacturing and maintenance concerns closer to home.

Bamberg had turned his interest to the north-west in 1957 when Eagle Aviation started flying scheduled services out of Manchester to Hamburg and Copenhagen, to complement the London routes he had started to La Baule, Saragossa, Luxembourg, Innsbruck and Perpignan. Although he was confident enough to order three of the

Eagle's Bermuda-registered Vickers Viscount VR-BAX *Enterprise*, with which the airline inaugurated Bermuda to New York services on 1 May 1957. (MAP)

bigger, longer-range Viscount 810 series, it was frustrating to be relegated to such secondary routes, yet release from the straightjacket, in the United Kingdom at least, was unlikely. Charter work, trooping and inclusive tours bulked out the business but it was still a hand-to-mouth existence; scheduled services gave the promise of year-round higher revenue earnings, and more importantly, were longer term. But something more lucrative than second level routes to Europe was needed. Now it was the turn of Eagle to look overseas. It established a subsidiary company in Bermuda – to this day still a British colony – and successfully applied for a licence to operate from Bermuda to New York and Montreal in direct competition with BOAC. Early in 1958 Bamberg was in Bermuda to launch the service and was helped in a practical way by a former comrade-in-arms, Air Commodore Powell, who had recently left Silver City on health grounds and resettled in Bermuda, his old home. On 1 May Eagle launched a daily service to New York, using its Bermuda-registered Viscount VR-BAX named *Enterprise*, seating forty-two tourist and twelve first-class passengers. By the end of the year Eagle (Bermuda) had also received approval from the Bermudan Board of Civil Aviation to fly to London using Douglas DC-6s or Britannias, opening up the prospect of transatlantic competition from a British independent for the first time. It was to be almost three years however before the British Government condescended to uphold the Bermuda Government's designation and allow Eagle to operate into London. During those years Eagle established itself as a significant competitor on routes between Bermuda and the United States; dual designation by BOAC and Eagle increased British participation on the New York route from around 20 per cent to 30 per cent over the next three years. Moreover the Eagle contribution was limited to Viscount and the occasional Britannia operations, which were competing against Pan American and Eastern Air Lines jets, underlining the quality of its service and underscoring the success of the Bermuda carrier in attracting new, mainly United States-originating traffic.

Airwork was allowed to introduce Vickers Viscounts, like G-APND, on its Safari services to Africa in 1958. (MAP)

## FORMER COLONIAL COACH CLASS

After Airwork and Hunting-Clan had been allowed to introduce Viscounts on the Safari services to East and Central Africa, it was the turn of the West Africa services to be upgraded. The faster Viscount allowed a speedier journey with only one night-stop: the new routing was Lisbon, Las Palmas (night stop), Bathurst, Freetown and Accra, which was inaugurated on 6 January 1958. The crew and the aircraft then took a night stop at Accra before setting forth northwards again. The pattern of operation allowed the airlines to avoid the need for slip-crews down the line; the same crew flew the round-trip. Now that Ghana had been granted independence, colonial coach principles no longer applied, so airfares charged had to be the same as those of BOAC. The corporation had been flying Argonauts, but under the spur of competition replaced these with Stratocruisers which made the journey to Accra overnight. The BOAC service was quicker but did not serve the intermediate points; the independents stressed the more leisurely comforts of the Viscount in their advertising, given that they were not able to charge less than BOAC:

> Nightstop at LAS PALMAS included in the fare! You fly only by day on VISCOUNT SAFARI. By night you sleep sound in the night-stop hotel. For this new service cuts the total journey time while still retaining a night stop. Yet this pleasure and nightstop leisure flying costs you no more than the price of your through ticket… all accommodation and meals are included in the fare.

Passengers had around fifteen hours in Las Palmas, enough time for an evening meal and a reasonable night's sleep, with an 0800 departure the next morning. The frequency was just one flight a week shared between the two airlines, Airwork and Hunting-Clan. However with the three other African Safari frequencies – twice weekly to Nairobi and once a week to Salisbury (each round trip took four days, with two departures on Mondays, to Nairobi and Accra, one on Thursday to Nairobi and the Salisbury flight leaving on Fridays) – the airlines were able to achieve around 2,000 hours utilisation on each of their combined fleet of five Viscounts. Moreover the Safari services left the Viscounts available for weekend charter work, especially useful for inclusive tours.

## THE PLAYERS

By 1958, the charter airline industry numbered some twenty-nine airlines and helicopter operators, with a further small number of air-taxi operators. Here is a reminder of who they were, what they flew, and where the business came from:

Southend-based Air Charter and its associated engineering company, Aviation Traders, had been acquired by Airwork in January 1958, but continued to operate as a separate unit. With three Skymasters, six Avro 'Super Traders' and six Bristol Freighter car-ferries, services ranged from the 'Channel Air Bridge', trooping flights to Cyprus, Ministry flights to Australia and a dwindling number of passenger and freight services between Berlin and Hanover.

Air Kruise was absorbed into Silver City in 1958.

Airwork, still the doyen of the independents, with three Hermes, two Viscounts and five Vikings, retained the trooping contract to Singapore in conjunction with Skyways, operated the Safari Colonial Coach Class services with Hunting–Clan and carried on with its leave service flights, now for the Sudan Government, the Cameroons Development Corporation and the Ghana Chamber of Mines.

Aquila Airways, entering what was to be its last year of service, operated its three Solents out of Southampton to Lisbon, Madeira, Genoa and Santa Margherita.

Autair operated six Bell 47 helicopters on contract charter work overseas, having started in 1953.

BKS Air Transport continued to develop IT charter flights from Newcastle and Southend; new scheduled routes from Newcastle in 1958 were those to Belfast, Basle, Bergen and London. The last quickly became the airline's prime trunk route and was followed in 1960 by a new route between London and Leeds-Bradford. The first of three fifty-five-seat Ambassadors bought from BEA entered service early in 1958 joining the three Dakotas; a Bristol Freighter was added later in 1958, used in large part to ship new Vauxhall cars from Luton to Northern Ireland. The airline had a subsidiary, BKS Air Survey, which undertook aerial survey work with a Dakota, a Consul and an Anson.

Bristow Helicopters operated its helicopters for various oil companies throughout the world in connection with seismic, geological and gravity survey work as well as in support of oil exploration and production. In January 1960 the company sold out to Airwork and later transferred its base to Redhill. At the time of the takeover the fleet comprised ten Whirlwinds, six Widgeons and seven Bell 47Gs, as well as various light aircraft.

Britavia, the long-range operating division of British Aviation Services, used its five Hermes on trooping flights to Aden and East Africa, European IT flights and even on passenger charters across the Atlantic.

Cambrian Airways flew its Herons and Dakotas to the Channel Islands from Cardiff,[16] Bristol, Swansea, Staverton, Liverpool and Manchester; and internationally to Paris from

Channel Airways DH104 Dove G-AOZW about to take off from Shoreham's grass airfield. (MAP)

Cardiff via Bristol and Southampton. On 7 February 1958, BEA acquired a 33 per cent interest in Cambrian, strengthening its role as a feeder airline, but the airline faced a crisis late in 1958 following very disappointing summer traffic results on its Channel Islands and Paris routes. Services were suspended for the coming winter and the Herons sold, although Jersey Airlines continued to operate the Manchester-Cardiff-Bristol-Jersey service. Services were successfully relaunched in March 1959 to the Channel Islands and Paris using Dakotas, at first leased and then bought, from BEA. Derby Aviation took over the service from Staverton.

Channel Airways flew its two Bristol Freighters and five Doves on scheduled services from Southend to Ostend, Rotterdam, Le Touquet and the Channel Islands. There were seasonal summer services to the Channel Islands from Portsmouth and Shoreham. The airline also operated many freight charters into and out of Rotterdam.

Continental Air Services shared its chairman, Ronald Myhill, with Overseas Aviation. Myhill and his partner Bernard Dromgoole had helped establish LTU as a charter airline in Germany and earlier Myhill had been associated with Autair. Continental at this time had two Vikings which were based at Rotterdam and flew on behalf of a Dutch shipping concern.

Dan-Air Services now had five Yorks, two Bristol Freighters and two Dakotas at its Blackbushe base, mainly carrying freight but with some IT business. The company held an Air Ministry freight contract between Lyneham and Singapore and in 1959 the airline won a two year contract to fly BEA's domestic freight services between London, Glasgow and Manchester. Some well-known Dan-Air personalities had recently joined, including Captain Larkman and Alan Snudden, formerly a RAF movements officer at Lyneham.

Derby Aviation ran a mixture of scheduled services and IT charters mainly from Derby's Burnaston Airport and Birmingham, using three Dakotas and its three unique Marathons. After Derby-based Rolls-Royce opened its maintenance and overhaul base outside Glasgow, Derby Aviation began running year-round scheduled services between Derby and Glasgow, starting in 1957; the service was underwritten by Rolls-Royce in the early years. The following year the decision was taken to change the name of the airline to Derby Airways. All-year-round services to the Channel Islands began in 1959, the airline's 21st anniversary, followed by a new year-round service between Derby, Luton and Dublin.

Don Everall Aviation flew its Dakota on IT flights from Birmingham and Coventry to Basle, Perpignan for the Costa Brava and Zagreb for the Dalmatian coast, and on scheduled services to the Channel Islands.

Eagle Aviation operated seventeen Vikings and two Viscounts, mainly on IT and trooping contracts (to West Africa, and around the Mediterranean). Its associate company, Eagle Airways, a member of IATA, was developing international services from London, Birmingham and Manchester; more than the other British independents Eagle concentrated on international services, serving Basle, Dinard, Innsbruck, La Baule, Luxembourg, Ostend, Pisa and Rimini. A new colour scheme had just been introduced, featuring a maroon roof and tail and grey cheat-line along the fuselage. In late 1958 two DC-6As were delivered, able to carry either ninety-eight passengers or twelve tonnes of freight. The Douglas DC-6 proved to be a versatile and reliable addition and in all six would pass through the fleet.

One of the DC-6s set a new record for British airlines by flying 3,804 hours in one year. The record had been held previously by a BOAC Argonaut which flew 3,597 hours in 1955. The Eagle DC-6 travelled far and wide on its journeys: Air Ministry trooping on contract services from the UK to Aden, Nairobi and Nicosia; Air Ministry ad hoc charters carrying passengers and freight from the UK to Christmas Island, Gan (a newly built RAF staging post in the Maldives), Negombo (Ceylon), Hong Kong, Adelaide (Australia), Bombay, Aden, Bahrain, Nairobi, Nicosia, Teheran, New York, Kingston and Malta; commercial charters from the UK to Basle, Zurich, Kuwait, Paris, New York, Buffalo, Bradley Field; Amsterdam to Teheran and Tel Aviv to New York; scheduled passenger services from the UK to Rimini, Pisa, La Baule and Dinard.[17]

Fison-Airwork, by now a substantial helicopter operator with nineteen small Hillers and five Westland Whirlwinds, was involved in crop-spraying, power-line inspection and oil and gas support work, mainly in Pakistan and Nigeria.

Hunting-Clan Air Transport, now one of the senior British independent companies, had extensive interests in Africa, and two Dakotas based there for Hunting-Clan African Airways. As well as the Viscount Safari services the airline flew the Africargo all-cargo service for which two Douglas DC-6As had been ordered to replace the existing fleet of Yorks, and which entered service at the end of 1958. Vikings and Viscounts were used for contract charter work and the airline had developed crew-training programmes for other Viscount operators. Less certain was the future of the Britannias on order.

Independent Air Travel, based at Bournemouth (Hurn), was chaired by Captain Kozubski who had ambitious plans for its fleet of six Vikings and two Skymasters operating IT services. Captain Kozubski however registered a new company, Falcon Airways, at the end of 1958.

Jersey Airlines, 25 per cent owned by BEA, was by now well-entrenched running services from the Channel Islands to the British mainland and France in addition to inter-island services. There were now seven Herons in the fleet, helped out by a Bristol Freighter and three Dakotas were added in 1959; a Rapide operated the inter-island routes. Traffic to the Channel Islands reflected the increasing proportion going by air, around two thirds by 1959, during which year Jersey Airlines carried just under 200,000 passengers, not far short of the numbers carried by Silver City on its cross-Channel services. Jersey even began operating a short-lived car-ferry service between Jersey and Dinard:

> The service was quick, efficient and marvellously convenient. It was possible to be on the road in France within an hour of leaving home in Jersey, yet the service was unprofitable, despite rather high charges. When required seats could take the place of cars, for extra passengers, but even so, the operation ended in 1958.[18]

Manx Airlines' services were absorbed into Silver City's Northern Division during 1958.

Morton Air Services had taken over Olley Air Service in 1953 and flew six Doves and a Heron on its services out of Croydon Airport, scheduled summer services to Jersey and Le Touquet and a year-round service to Rotterdam. Charter work continued: race-meetings, executive charters, newspapers, freight and air ambulance work. 1958 was to see the end of Morton's independence; faced with the impending closure of Croydon, Captain Morton sold out to Airwork at the end of the year.

Orion Airways, based at Blackbushe, flew its Vikings on IT charters.

Overseas Aviation (CI), another company run by Messrs. Myhill and Dromgoole, started operations with Vikings in 1958. Using Dromgoole's extensive contacts in Germany, where he had previously been European manager for BKS, the airline picked up contracts to fly German holidaymakers to European destinations, and was active in the Berlin charter market. Aside from its initial involvement with the German airline LTU, Overseas assisted with the formation of a number of European carriers, including Aviameer in Belgium, Martin's Air Charter (later Martinair) in Holland and Flying Enterprise in Denmark. From November 1958 the airline began operating Argonauts acquired from BOAC.

Scottish Airlines, a shadow of its former self, still flew two Yorks on charter services and operated a Dakota service to the Isle of Man.

Silver City Airways had by now taken over all the short- and medium-range operations of British Air Services' many subsidiary companies – Air Kruise, Manx Airlines, Lancashire Aircraft Corporation and Dragon Airways – as well as continuing to operate its own vehicle-ferry services. IT services were flown from Ferryfield and the Northern Division flew scheduled services from Newcastle, Blackpool and the Isle of Man. The group's fleet consisted of fourteen long-nosed Bristol Freighters and six of the earlier version, nine Dakotas, two Herons and various smaller aircraft. The airline cut fares across the Channel yet again and was rewarded by another major increase in cars and passengers.

Skyways, another illustrious name, had evolved into a curious hybrid of an airline. Dedicated to cooperating with the corporations, it flew Hermes freighters on behalf of BOAC from London Airport to Singapore and provided five Yorks for BOAC and Pan American for use on their engine transport service; there was the Crusader Colonial Coach Class service to Cyprus, another to Malta which operated via Tunis, and it still shared the main Far East trooping contract out of Stansted with Airwork, all of them operated by Hermes. In complete contrast, the airline also flew the ultra short-haul Coach-Air service between Lympne and Beauvais with four Dakotas, carrying over 85,000 passengers a year; this was now extended to other points in France, albeit at much

Tradair's Vickers Viking G-AIXR, bought from Airwork, shows off the dark blue 'pinstripe' livery outside its Southend base. (MAP)

lower frequencies. Late in 1958, Rylands bought an 80 per cent interest in Bahamas Airways from BOAC, another example of the continuing close relationship between the two airlines.

Starways, the Liverpool-based airline, flew an increasing number of IT charter services from Liverpool and Glasgow to Spain, France and Switzerland. The airline had also started scheduled services between Liverpool and London Airport, and from Glasgow to Jersey. Starways' fleet comprised three Dakotas and two Skymasters.

Tradair, based at Southend, flew its two Vikings on IT services and at the end of 1958 added three Vikings bought from the Royal Flight, contributing to the airline's upmarket image.

Transair, by now owned by Airwork, had three Viscounts and eleven Dakotas. It still flew scheduled mail and newspaper flights from its Croydon base to Paris, the Channel Islands, Belgium, Dublin, Dusseldorf and Hannover, but had become an important IT airline and had also taken over the West Med trooping contract with its newly delivered Viscounts. It flew from London Airport, but in June 1958 switched all its services and maintenance facilities to Gatwick Airport, which had been recently reopened by Her Majesty The Queen. During the summer of 1958 Transair operated daily Viscount services for Air France between London, Paris and Nice.

Transair was not the only airline to have to consider moving to Gatwick. Croydon was due to close on 30 September 1959 and at the same time the Ministry announced that Blackbushe would be closed for air transport movements from the end of May 1960, affecting a number of independents. Of the airlines based at Blackbushe, Eagle chose to move to London Airport, and Airwork switched to Gatwick, as did Dan-Air.

## THE AIR MARKET OF THE BALTIC EXCHANGE

The Baltic Exchange was an important element in the marketing of the charter airlines' services, especially as few of them had extensive selling organisations and therefore relied on brokers to secure loads for them, freight in particular. There was now less of a need for perishable foodstuffs to go by air as surface links had been largely re-established in Europe, but some livestock still travelled by air, which was also better-suited to the carriage of fresh-cut flowers. Otherwise the business was much as it had been: chemical products, heavy machinery – such as spare parts for ships – and newspapers.

The main brokers were:

Instone Air Transport, representing the British Aviation Services' group;

Furness Withy, which had a stake in Airwork;

Lep Air Services, looking after BKS and Channel Airways;

Lambert Brothers, representing Cambrian, Eagle and Olley (but see Lanes below);

EA Gibson, with two well-established airlines, Hunting-Clan and Skyways;

Lanes (Aircharters), which represented Starways and Mortons;

Davies and Newman of course looked after Dan-Air.

On the passenger side, there was a growing business in inclusive tours; brokers increasingly assisted smaller tour operators in finding airline capacity for their programmes.

## SILVER CITY: TEN YEARS ON

On 14 July 1958 Silver City celebrated ten years of cross-Channel vehicle-ferry operations. The main corridor between Ferryfield and Le Touquet still provided the backbone of the company's operations and was a model of efficiency. There were over two hundred flights a day; aircraft were turned round in just ten minutes and every few minutes another Freighter would leave with its load of three cars and up to twenty-three passengers for the twenty-minute flight to France, starting at 0715 in the morning and continuing to 2015 in the evening. In addition to freight and new car deliveries the company had introduced the Silver Arrow service, catering for passengers without cars and offering good connections between London and Paris; all the older short-nosed Freighters and two of the longer aircraft were converted to carry passengers only. Over the ten-year period, 575,000 passengers and around 185,500 cars, together with 70,000 motorcycles, had been carried on the short air crossings. For 1958 the fares were cut again, and the routes reduced to Le Touquet, Calais and Ostend from Ferryfield and Cherbourg from Southampton, but both car and passenger numbers increased over the previous year; for the first time over 50,000 cars were carried. Fares were cut yet further for 1959 and in anticipation of burgeoning vehicle traffic, Silver City decided in June to transfer its 'Silver Arrow' service to another airfield in Kent – Manston, on the Isle of Thanet. Using sixty-eight-seat Hermes, now surplus following the loss of its major trooping contracts and repainted in Silver City livery, the service still followed the same rail-air formula, with passengers travelling by rail to Margate, then being transferred by coach to Manston for the flight to Le Touquet.

Silver City was also developing its Northern Division, bringing together the various subsidiaries – Manx, Lancashire, Dragon – under one name although the networks remained disparate, based in the Isle of Man, Blackpool and Newcastle. By this time Air Commodore Powell had stood down as Silver City's managing director. He remarks in his autobiography that with the benefit of hindsight, the company was near the zenith of its meteoric growth at the time of its tenth anniversary. There were still some good years ahead but the airline was already at the peak of efficiency; any growth would have to come from new and larger equipment, and P&O, the airline's owners, were not willing to make the investment. Nor was it obvious where the airline should go to buy the larger aircraft. The company needed an aircraft that could carry six to eight cars together with accompanying passengers, but no such aircraft existed. It was left to Laker to try and resolve that problem but in the meantime, British Railways, without the financial restraints of a modestly capitalised private company, was able to continue investing in ever larger and more efficient ferries and its share of cross-Channel traffic subsequently increased.

## CHANNEL AIR BRIDGE

Although Air Commodore Powell comments in his autobiography that the traffic taken from Silver City by the Channel Air Bridge was insignificant, nevertheless Air Charter's Channel Air Bridge had built up a steady business at Southend. By 1958 it was flying nine Bristol Super Freighters, some modified and extended by Aviation Traders themselves, on three routes, with over 400 flights per week to Calais, 172 per week to Ostend, and fifty-nine per week to Rotterdam. Even the shortest flights, those to Calais which took twenty-eight minutes, were almost 50 per cent longer than the average Silver City sector out of Ferryfield, and not surprisingly, Channel Air Bridge achieved much better utilisation from its Bristol Freighters than did Silver City, with consequently less punishment to the airframe, engines and systems. Competition from British Railways' ferries was also less acute as the alternative route from north of the Thames was the Harwich-Hook of Holland service which sailed overnight. By mid-summer the company was carrying over 3,500 cars a month. When the Home Office allowed no-passport day trips by air, Air Charter introduced DC-4s on the Southend-Calais route in response to the enormous demand for staff outings which the new service encouraged; the day return fare was just under £4. Channel Air Bridge also faced the problem of how to replace the Freighter. The airline did not want a complicated car-carrier with two decks and internal hoists, ramps and so on; it preferred a long tube, the longer the better. When he was unable to find such an aircraft, Laker, as ever resourceful, decided to build the aircraft himself, drawing on Air Charter's and Aviation Traders' experience of operating DC-4s, which were now plentiful on the second-hand market for under £70,000; a Bristol Super Freighter new cost about £120,000. The Aviation Traders ATL.98 Carvair,

Channel Air Bridge Carvair G-ANYB *Golden Gate Bridge* demonstrates the scissor lift needed to load this Humber Super Snipe car at Southend. (Flight)

details of which were released in June 1959, was a modified DC-4 with an entirely new nose section which put the flight deck above the main cabin and had two large nose doors, not unlike the Freighter. The Carvair could carry four or five cars and twenty-five passengers and had more range than a Freighter; it was hoped to use the type on longer-haul routes to the Continent. The aircraft stood higher off the ground than the Freighter; instead of a simple ramp which allowed cars to be driven directly into and out of the aircraft, the Carvair needed a scissors lift to load cars, which extended turn-round times. The total cost of the converted aircraft was estimated to be around £130,000, not much more than a Bristol Super Freighter, for an aircraft that should be rather more productive.

## AQUILA AIRWAYS

Silver City was not the only airline in the Britavia Group that was facing difficulties re-equipping. For the last nine years Aquila had been flying from Southampton to Madeira via Lisbon, first with Sunderlands, then with the larger Solents. The service had not been without its problems: the flying boats were expensive to operate and maintain, and the company had to provide its own landing and handling facilities at Southampton and down route. For the same reasons it was not easy to use the aircraft on charter work. Passenger numbers were moving up slowly, around 16,000 passengers a year were carried latterly, but then the airline began to experience operating difficulties on its main route to Madeira, where due to abnormal sea conditions, the swell off Funchal made it impossible to land outside the harbour. The aircraft had to land off the north coast of the island, where there were no suitable facilities, so that the turn round then became very protracted. Over time the airline had suffered a number of non–fatal aircraft losses, the flying boats being vulnerable to gale damage when at their moorings, but on the night of 15 November 1957 an Aquila Solent struck the cliff face of a chalk pit at Chessel Down on the Isle of Wight shortly after taking off from Southampton, killing all forty-six passengers and crew. Finally, like Silver City's future fleet replacement of its vehicle ferries, it was not at all obvious how the elderly Solents could be replaced. The accumulation of bad luck and uncertainty over the future prospects caused the Britavia Group to decide to withdraw from the route and close down Aquila. On the evening of 30 September 1958 Solent G-ANYI, flying a 59ft paying-off pennant, made the airline's last landing at Southampton Water. Madeira would have to wait for the building of a runway at Funchal before it was to see regular air services again.

## ACCIDENTS AND REPUTATIONS

The loss of the Solent was only one of a number of fatal accidents that affected both corporations and independents during 1957 and 1958. BEA was to lose three Viscounts during the course of this period, but the most notorious accident involved one of its Ambassadors which crashed on take off at Munich on 6 February 1958, killing a number of the Manchester United football team. BEA also lost an Air Ambulance Heron on Islay in Scotland in September 1957, killing its two crew members and the nurse Sister Jean Kennedy. The independents suffered too. A Viking of Eagle's crashed at Blackbushe and a Silver City Bristol Freighter was lost when it struck Winter Hill on a flight from Douglas, Isle of Man to Manchester. At the end of 1958 a Hunting-Clan Viscount crashed shortly after take-off on a test flight, killing all five crew members.

Prior to that, a further accident, involving a Viking of Independent – which crashed on 2 September – had serious repercussions both for the airline, its chairman and managing director Captain Kozubski, and for the reputation of charter airlines generally. The Viking was carrying two Proteus engines on a charter for El Al, the Israeli airline, when one of its own engines failed; the captain elected to return to its base at Blackbushe. After flying off track, and unable to gain altitude, the aircraft crashed into a house in Southall. At the subsequent inquiry it transpired that the aircraft had been above its permitted all-up take-off weight, the crew had exceeded their flight-time limitations and that neither of the two people who had worked on the aircraft's engines were licensed engineers. This led to Independent becoming headline news in March 1959 and the airline subsequently had to undergo drastic reorganisation. Captain Kozubski sold out and turned his attention to Falcon Airways, which he had already formed. Independent changed the name on its aircraft to Blue-Air and lasted another season, before closing down for good at the end of 1959. All charter operators were tarred by this accident, which led to calls for tighter regulation of the independent airlines.[19]

## HOLIDAY FLIGHTS

The Suez Crisis had led to another economic 'blip' as Britain used up more dollars to buy oil to replace losses in the Middle East; petrol rationing was introduced for a time and the government raised the bank rate steadily to 7 per cent, its highest level for thirty-seven years. By the end of 1958, bank rate was down to 4 per cent again and the economic situation was more favourable, with growth in bank advances, extension of hire-purchase credit, an increase in the travel allowance and a relaxation of restrictions on imports from dollar areas. In April 1959 taxes were cut and after the General Election in October the Conservatives under Macmillan increased their majority in the Commons to one hundred.

There had been some slowing down of air transport which affected all carriers, but by 1958 this had begun to pick up again. Some of the biggest percentage increases were evident in the leisure market, as rising expectations and a higher standard of living encouraged more people to travel further afield for their holidays. The bulk of the traffic carried by the independents was now in response to leisure demand, to holiday destinations in the Channel Islands and the Isle of Man, by taking the family car to the Continent or crossing the Channel to take continental tours by coach, or flying in search of the sun on inclusive tours.

*Total Number of Passengers Carried (to Nearest 1,000) by Independent Operators on Scheduled Services, Inclusive Tours and Contract Charters*

|  | 1954/5 | 1955/6 | 1956/7 | 1957/8 | 1958/9 |
|---|---|---|---|---|---|
| Channel Islands | 69,000 | 98,000 | 153,000 | 209,000 | 187,000 |
| Isle of Man | 54,000 | 67,000 | 81,000 | 102,000 | 80,000 |
| Other Internal | 25,000 | 54,000 | 64,000 | 38,000 | 32,000 |
| International | 65,000 | 92,000 | 178,000 | 239,000 | 229,000 |
| Vehicle Ferries | 112,000 | 182,000 | 156,000 | 173,000 | 225,000 |
| Colonial Coach | 10,000 | 13,000 | 15,000 | 17,000 | 17,000 |
| Inclusive Tours | 23,000 | 46,000 | 96,000 | 137,000 | 180,000 |
| Subtotal | 358,000 | 552,000 | 743,000 | 915,000 | 950,000 |
| | | | | | |
| Contract charter | 66,000 | 258,700 | 322,500 | 307,700 | 331,700 |
| Air trooping | 214,600 | 204,700 | 157,000 | 137,800 | 142,000 |
| | | | | | |
| Total | 638,600 | 1,015,400 | 1,222,500 | 1,360,500 | 1,423,700 |

(Source BIATA)

In fact the official figures understate IT and leisure traffic – and probably by a large margin – for the following reason: the ATAC had to take account of BEA's objections to IT flights, which were becoming increasingly vociferous as the corporation continued to claim that these flights were causing material diversion on many of its routes. Much of the skill shown by the ATAC was in its ability to give the independents at least part of what they wanted whilst sticking to its guns and pointing out to BEA that all carriers, including the corporations, were showing reasonable traffic growth over time. To its credit BEA did more than just make protesting noises; the corporation introduced IT equivalent fares in 1959 and certainly captured significant market share.

Nevertheless that still meant the ATAC rejected a fair proportion of IT applications, particularly those out of London airports; but of course the demand did not go away. One solution was to repackage the application and hope for better luck the next time, which sometimes worked; many things in life are just a lottery. But an easier way was to operate the services outside the scope of the Act, and two categories developed to take advantage of the loopholes. First, 'aerial tours' or circular tours, in which a group would fly from city to city travelling in the same aircraft – the airline equivalent of a cruise – had always been exempted from the restrictions of the Act and so could be operated without any associate agreements; but tour operators found they could legally reduce the itinerary to a mere two stops thus allowing two-centre holidays to be developed. For example, a two-centre holiday could be sold covering a fortnight's holiday, one week to be spent in Barcelona for the Costa Brava, the second week to be spent in Majorca. The aircraft operated a triangular pattern and picked up the passengers at Barcelona after the first week, taking them on to Majorca for the second week. Secondly, a less expensive and ultimately much more popular solution was to bypass the regulations altogether: either by operating the flights in a non-systematic way, which in practice meant not more than three flights to any one destination, or by offering the holiday package to closed groups, which had always been exempted from regulatory restrictions. Many bona fide organisations existed, of course, such as the Overseas Visitors Club, the Royal Automobile Club and the British Civil Service's Whitehall Travel; but inevitably the boundaries got pushed out and tour operators were not above creating clubs and organisations specifically to charter flights for inclusive tours. If the ATAC turned down an application after bookings had been taken, it was often simpler to recast the flight as a closed group charter than to reapply for another licence. IT licences were of very limited duration and seldom granted for more than one year, unlike scheduled-service agreements which could be granted for up to ten years; it meant that there was always a huge backlog of applications being processed. Because of this pressure of work the Council often did not announce its decisions until shortly before the summer season had started, leaving participants little time to make alternative arrangements.

## PROVISION 1

There was another advantage in skirting around the licensing requirements. IATA rules on tariffs governed inclusive-tour holiday prices; as IT flights were still nominally operated under associate agreements it follows that their tariffs were also subject to regulation. In the case of holiday flights, the rule, which came to be known as Provision 1, stipulated that the cost of the inclusive tour must not be less than the lowest round-trip IATA air fare. As holidaymakers began to venture further afield, so this restriction began to bite, as charter-airline economics and scheduled-service mileage charges began to diverge. More efficient and larger aircraft meant that holiday flights to Majorca might not cost much more per passenger than short cross-Channel hops on older and smaller aircraft, but the

IATA fare structure was based on mileage, with only a slight taper over longer distances. Charter airlines and tour operators had to abide by this rule, which could be side-stepped if flights were unlicensed.

For the historian the disadvantage of this process was that such flights, with their passengers, went off the record. BIATA and the ATAC did publish statistics of passengers and freight carried but airlines that were not members of BIATA were not recorded in the association's returns. If the airline did not apply for associate agreements, it did not appear in the ATAC's returns either. As the ATAC was in time to recognise, its figures were understated; nobody knows how many passengers were actually being carried on British charter airlines during these years.

## PLUGGING LOOPHOLES

In 1958 the Minister decided to plug at least one of the loopholes, directing the ATAC to consider in future all circular tours in the same way that they already considered inclusive tours:

> In recent months … I have received a large number of applications for approval of Circular Tour services. Both in the choice of centres and in the type of holiday, the Circular Tours proposed have tended to become more and more like the Inclusive Tour holidays operated under Associate Agreements with the Corporations. In some cases, indeed, the application for the Circular Tour appears to have been made to take the place of an unsuccessful application for an inclusive tour. There was, therefore, a risk that, in approving Circular Tours, I might be undermining the work done by the Council in advising on appropriate capacity to be allowed for Inclusive Tour Service to the main European holiday centres. It is, in any case, clearly undesirable that airline companies should apply through two separate channels for permission to operate services which are intended to serve virtually the same kind of holiday traffic, or for similar applications to be dealt with under quite different procedures.[20]

As for the closed groups, the Ministry had found to its cost that it was powerless to do much about them. In April 1959 magistrates at Feltham threw out a prosecution brought by the Ministry in connection with a closed group. Hunting-Clan had applied to the ATAC for IT flights to Palma, Nice and Perpignan on behalf of Milbanke Tours, but they were refused; Milbanke Tours then told its prospective clients that if they all joined the International English Language Association (IELA), for which Milbanke was the official travel agent, they could still go on their holidays as the flights would be reclassified as charter flights. The Ministry prosecuted Milbanke but the magistrate dismissed the case, pointing out that the passengers were bona fide members of the IELA and so Hunting-Clan was entitled to carry them – anyway the airline was the carrier, not Milbanke. Incidents like this helped Watkinson to make up his mind that change was overdue.

## TIME FOR CHANGE?

The time for change was approaching. At the BIATA annual dinner on 12 November 1958 the Minister had hinted that the Ministry might at last be overcoming its hostility towards a licensing system, and would allow independents to fly scheduled and inclusive-tour-charter flights in their own right without having recourse to associate agreements:

> I think that it is worthwhile considering whether the excellent work done by the Air Transport Advisory Council combined with the idea… of an operator's licence, might not provide a clue to the right machinery for the future for solving these problems of conflicting or competing interests. I think there are attractions in the idea of a new ATAC with new powers, revised and wider terms of reference and wider discretion, to which might be entrusted the day-to-day and month-by-month handling of… conflicting requirements.[21]

Showing his usual grasp of the issues, *Flight's* Transport Editor, Mike Ramsden, went on to point out the new council needed to be up to the job:

> The Minister said that we ought not to consider anything as 'elaborate' or as 'long-winded' as the American CAB's[22] procedures. Long-winded? Only when airlines clamour to put up fares, and quite rightly so. Elaborate? If we think we can efficiently and fairly administer the expansion of all sections of British air transport without an elaborate executive council, we are probably deceiving ourselves. [23]

By February 1959 Watkinson was putting proposals to the Cabinet for an Air Transport Board. The government recognised that it could no longer continue to tweak the Civil Aviation Act in order to allow more flexibility to the independents, and that new legislation would be required. Apart from the formation of a Licensing Authority – and as a corollary – removing the monopoly of the corporations in scheduled services, he also was considering proposals for the various airports under his care. These ideas included establishing a London Airport Authority, which would remain in government ownership, but transferring some regional airports to their contiguous municipalities. He established an Air Transport Board Working Party to draw up proposals for the necessary new legislation and in the meantime continued to hold everybody at bay.

## EAGLE AND VERY LOW FARES

As 1958 drew to a close, Bamberg decided to launch his own bid for Colonial Coach Class services which he saw as offering a good vehicle for developing a Very Low Fare (VLF) market product, and one way out of the doldrums. There had been change already when at last the government had relented and allowed Airwork and Hunting-Clan to introduce more modern turboprop aircraft on the various African Safari routes. However, the Colonial Coach network had never developed beyond its original format; services were limited to Gibraltar, Malta, the colonies in Africa and Nicosia in Cyprus. Applications to extend the formula to the Far East and Aden had been turned down and frequency increases were determinedly resisted; demand was never fully met and the numbers carried on the services remained pitiably small. Between 1954 and 1958, total numbers had increased from 5,000 passengers a year to just 17,000 a year, a tiny proportion of the 1.3 million passengers carried by the independents. Even this segment was eyed covetously by BOAC, awash with new and unwanted aircraft, which persuaded the government to allow it to impose a traffic-sharing formula on the independents so that it could enter the market. Now Eagle wanted a share of this market too and put up wide-ranging proposals to operate VLF services with its Douglas DC-6s, not just to the existing destinations but also to Aden, Singapore, Nassau and Kingston in Jamaica, and Trinidad. Frequencies were low, mainly fortnightly; proposed fares were low too, lower than Colonial Coach Class, and considerably lower than the existing normal tourist rates.

Of course BOAC and BEA objected, and Airwork and Hunting-Clan put in similar applications, more in hope than with any great expectations. Support for VLF was strong in the colonies; a 10,000-name petition was handed in to the East African Air Transport Licensing Advisory Board, and some of the colonial administrations quickly gave Eagle's VLF applications their seal of approval: Aden, Bermuda, Bahamas, Hong Kong and Malta. Three colonies, Gibraltar, Singapore and Trinidad, left the decision to the British Government; Cyprus and Nigeria were about to achieve independence, so cabotage was no longer permitted. The British Government, meanwhile, delayed making any decision for over a year whilst it pondered what further steps needed to be taken to overhaul the entire regulatory structure in the United Kingdom.

A different proposal for VLF came from a new company, Trans-Africa Air Coach (TAAC), to exploit the market between the United Kingdom and South Africa. The South African Government now reserved low-fare services for its own carriers, but TAAC circumvented that restriction by flying to nearby Lourenço Marques in Portuguese Mozambique. The company used aircraft chartered from Overseas Aviation which had recently acquired some of the former BOAC Argonauts.

Flying his DC-6 through another loophole, Bamberg noticed that one of the aircraft was returning from Hong Kong to London with only a part load. Eagle advertised twenty cheap seats at £136 each in the local press and found thirteen takers. BOAC protested, but as Bamberg correctly pointed out:

> I knew I was within the law. I am quite entitled to make special flights at these rates provided I do not operate a regular schedule. I am not trying to prove anything. I am in business. I had an empty airliner coming through Hong Kong and I saw a chance to do business with it. [24]

What was significant in this case was that the airline was not operating a regular service so it did not have to apply for an associate agreement or operate the flight for a closed group. The airline went on to operate other 'non-systematic' VLF flights to Bermuda as well, to test the concept. Staying in the Caribbean, and following the success of its Bermuda airline, Eagle formed a further subsidiary in the Bahamas and duly received a permit from the American authorities to fly between the Bahamas and Miami; the Americans also gave Bahamas Airways a similar permit. Eagle used Viscounts; Bahamas used refurbished Hermes transferred from is owner, Silver City.

## CHANNEL AIRWAYS

By sheer dint of perseverance Squadron Leader Jones's airline hit its stride towards the end of the decade. Operating very small aircraft over short-haul routes and closing down for the winter, hardly made for rich pickings, but the airline and its tolerant pilots survived; it was not until 1954 that more than 10,000 passengers had been carried. In 1956 Channel inaugurated a year-round service from Southend to Rotterdam when the new airport opened, flying its ten-seat Doves once or twice a day during the year; even so, the rest of the operation closed down during the winter months. A big increase in capacity came in 1957 when the airline bought the first of two Bristol Freighters, and three more Doves, from West African Airways (WAAC). The Freighter, like the Doves, retained its basic WAAC livery, perpetuating a leitmotif throughout Channel's history: the airline seldom repainted the airliners it acquired second-hand. The forty-eight-seat Freighters could use the grass airfields at Rochester, Ipswich and Portsmouth, and flew the services to the Channel Islands as well as hauling freight to and from Rotterdam. By 1958 two thirty-six-seat Vikings had been added, flying out of Southend (Vikings were not suitable for operation from Channel's grass airfields) to the Channel Islands, Ostend, Rotterdam and Le Touquet, but they and the Freighters were still laid up that winter. In 1960 Channel introduced three Dakotas, better suited to Channel's airfield requirements than the Viking, and operated them out of Shoreham and Portsmouth – meanwhile the Doves maintained the feeder services into Southend from Ipswich and Rochester. Over 100,000 passengers were carried in 1960, testimony to the success of the Channel Airways formula, flying frequent, inexpensive short-haul hops across the Channel; unlike other charter airlines, Channel operated few inclusive-tour flights to Mediterranean destinations at this stage. The Channel Islands were a popular holiday destination in their own right, of course, but hardy British holiday makers would join coaches at Ostend and Rotterdam for the long trip along Germany's autobahns to resorts in Switzerland, Austria and Italy. Ostend, with its short flying time from Southend, became a major destination for the airline, and the Southend-Ostend route developed into one of the busiest international routes in the world.

## UNCERTAIN TIMES

By now the Conservative Government had been in power for over seven years and, as far as the independents were concerned, with little to show for it. It was unfortunate that pressure for change should have peaked just about the time that BOAC's finances were coming under extraordinary pressure. After the healthy profits of the Thomas era, BOAC had once again recorded a loss. The corporation blamed its losses of £2.8 million during 1958 on the high costs of introducing new aircraft and a fall in revenue; it was also losing money on its overseas associate airlines. All the government could do for the time being was to urge the independents to sort themselves into tidier and larger groupings and in the meantime the Minister would see what he could do. The way forward was not at all clear, the future uncertain. For the time being the charter industry was becalmed, still dependent on government favours whose value diminished every day, and unable to exploit fully the new opportunities which were arising.

British and Commonwealth's first Britannia, G-APNA, wears the shipping company's short-lived markings. (A.J. Jackson Collection)

Typical of the prevailing atmosphere of uncertainty was a bizarre episode towards the end of December 1958 when Peter Masefield, managing director of Bristol Aircraft, handed over the first of two unpainted Britannias to Sir Nicholas Cayzer, chairman of British and Commonwealth Shipping. Originally ordered by Hunting-Clan, the airline had hoped to use the aircraft on its services to Africa, and had also tendered for a whole range of trooping flights including the major contract to the Far East. BOAC's deal with Central African Airways had scotched any plans to fly the Britannia on African services, and decisions on the trooping contracts were nowhere near being reached; the Ministry of Supply still hoped that the successful tenderer would use its three Britannias, ordered for just that purpose, whereas both Air Charter and Hunting-Clan now planned to use their own aircraft. British and Commonwealth undertook the responsibility to finance the two aircraft, but there was no work for them; they could not be used on Colonial Coach Class services and were unsuitable for cargo work, which was in any case now being performed by Hunting-Clan's newly delivered DC-6s. The aircraft remained largely idle for some months, only operating occasional charters and crew-training flights; they were painted in the end, but not in Hunting-Clan colours, sporting instead British and Commonwealth titles and the shipping group's houseflag on the tail.

If Hunting-Clan seemed uncertain as to what to do about its new aircraft, Airwork's very future seemed uncertain. Early in 1959 it put up almost its entire fleet for disposal. With the end of its major Far East trooping contract approaching, Airwork offered for sale its remaining three Hermes and also invited bids for its four Vikings and two Dakotas. The Hermes were sold to Falcon Airways, two of the Vikings went to Tradair, and the other two eventually were bought by Air Safaris. Its pilots were made redundant and all that remained of this once-proud fleet at the end of the coming 1959 summer season were the Viscounts with which to maintain its share of the Safari services, and even those were soon transferred to Transair. Of course, Airwork owned other airlines, and had been adding more to its portfolio, but apart from the continuing Safari services and a new contract with Sudan Airways to operate its Blue Nile Viscount on scheduled services between Khartoum, London Gatwick and Cairo, Airwork's own cupboard looked very bare. Airwork, surely the pre-eminent independent airline of the 1950s, ended the decade a shadow of its former self.

## MEREDITH RENASCENT

In the charter airline business, certain names come around again and again. One thinks of Hugh Kennard, founder of Air Kruise, Air Ferry and Invicta, or Mike Keegan, the 'K' in BKS, who went on to form Trans Meridian and ran British Air Ferries as well. Another name that reappeared was that of Meredith, last heard of in the previous chapter when its Dakota was taken over by Dan-Air in 1953. Captain Meredith and his partners had then started another South African airline, Trek Airways, which operated between Johannesburg and Europe, using three ex-Airwork Vikings. Eventually DC-4 Skymasters were bought for the European service, and in 1958 two of the Vikings were transferred to Meredith Air Transport – still a British airline and now renamed African Air Safaris – with Alan Stocks as the general manager. Back on the British register the Vikings operated two seasons of inclusive-tour flying from Southend as well as South African charters, but in 1959 the aircraft-operating division was transferred to its associate Air Safaris, and moved to Gatwick.

## TROOPING: HUNTING-CLAN SCOOPS THE POOL

Finally the question of what British and Commonwealth should do with its two Britannias was resolved when Hunting-Clan was awarded the first of the longer term three-year trooping contracts, to operate around six flights a month to the Far East, from 15 May 1959. Configured with 114 seats and still in British and Commonwealth colours, the Britannias took about twenty-four hours for the journey to Singapore with no night stops, as compared to the three and a half days taken by the Hermes of Airwork and Skyways. The routing, with fuelling stops at Istanbul, Karachi and Bombay, highlighted one of the advantages of using civilian aircraft for trooping flights, which was the ability to land at Indian airports; RAF aircraft had to take a more circuitous route avoiding Indian airspace, otherwise prior permission was required from the Indian authorities. Even the Ceylon Government was anxious not to have too many RAF aircraft landing at Katunayake, so the British Government built a base at Gan, an atoll in the Maldives, which allowed military aircraft to avoid both Indian and Ceylonese airspace on their way to Singapore.

Hunting-Clan went on to gain further trooping contracts for both the Britannias and Douglas DC-6s. From 1 October of the same year the company was awarded the Cyprus,

Aden and East African contracts, a clean sweep and a blow to Eagle which had operated all those contracts during the previous year with DC-6s. Eagle was left with the Medair Viking flights within the Mediterranean, Transair held the West Med contract to Malta and Gibraltar, but Hunting-Clan had scooped all the other major contracts. There were other ad hoc flights and short-term contracts, like Air Charter's flights to Christmas Island. Skyways had a freight contract to Cyprus and Air Charter still held the Woomera contract with its Avro Tudor 'Super Traders', but following two accidents in 1959 the remaining aircraft of this type were withdrawn from service. As a result the contract passed to Dan-Air which used Bristol Freighters for the twelve-day journey to Australia. At the same time the RAF was itself taking delivery of its new Britannias and elected to undertake all freight flying with them as part of route-and-proficiency training, so Dan-Air's York contract to the Far East ended in 1959. For the next few years Hunting-Clan and its successor held all the major trooping contracts.

## NEW AIRCRAFT

This was a time of many new arrivals and some departures. As the Britannias entered service, so it was time for some of the old faithfuls to go. The last BOAC York had been bought by Skyways in 1957, and in 1958 the Constellations were withdrawn, the last four also sold to Skyways for operation of the BOAC freight contract to Singapore and Hong Kong. In May 1959 it was the turn of the Stratocruiser, which operated its last flight inbound from Accra to London; in April 1960 the last Argonaut flight, from Abadan, flew into London. For its part BEA withdrew its Ambassadors in July 1958.

On 4 October 1958, less than a year after the Britannia entered service on the North Atlantic, BOAC introduced the Comet 4 on the route to New York, with a refuelling stop westbound at Gander, Newfoundland. By the middle of November this type was operating a daily service, although some of the sheen of achievement was lost when Pan American introduced its new Boeing 707[25] on the New York-London route on 26 October 1958, just three weeks after the Comet 4. All this gave an opportunity for Watkinson to reflect on the development of British airliners:

> We always seem to have to pay the penalty for being first with a new project. We paid the penalty with the Comet because we were ahead of the world and did not quite understand enough about stresses and strains of flight at 40,000ft. We have had it with the Britannia, because this was the first big turbo-prop aircraft to fly through intense monsoon conditions… When the big Britannias start meeting the competition of the Boeing 707s nobody knows which will win.[26]

Really? There were already 199 Boeing 707s and 133 Douglas DC-8s on order, and the order books were filling up. BOAC had ordered thirty-three Britannias, other airlines an additional fifteen,[27] and there was a cancelled order for five.

Watkinson also wondered about his title, Minister of Transport and Civil Aviation: 'Aviation, in my opinion, is not civil and, again in my opinion, aviation is transport.' He had other issues to ponder. By now second-generation jets were beginning to appear.

The French were building the Caravelle, a short-haul twin-engine jetliner, which entered service with Air France in 1959. BEA would have preferred to stay with ever larger turboprops, indeed the Vickers Vanguard had yet to enter service, but by 1956 the corporation realised that the advent of short-haul jets would require some competitive response, and issued a specification for a 600 mph turbojet tailor-made for its network.

The government favoured the proposal by a consortium of Bristol Aircraft and Hawker Siddeley, whereas BEA preferred de Havilland's project. BEA was under some pressure from the government to go along with its wishes; the Prime Minister's office file was even given the heading, 'New jet airliner required by BEA. Government to encourage BEA to place order with Bristol Aeroplane Co. rather than with de Havilland'.[28] The Bristol/Hawker proposal, the Bristol 200, may have seemed attractive as it brought together two aircraft manufacturers at a time when the government was trying to encourage consolidation; also the consortium was talking extremely optimistically of possible overseas sales, including to the US. The matter was taken up at Cabinet level, with Watkinson from the Civil Aviation Ministry and Aubrey Jones from the Ministry of Supply on different sides of the fence. Jones supported the Bristol/Hawker group; Watkinson did not want to compel BEA to accept the Bristol 200 against its better judgement. A memo from Burke Trend in the Cabinet Office, dated 3 February 1958, shows how manufacturing still coloured all expectations:

> Given the extent of Exchequer money involved, it is surely wrong that a contract of this magnitude should be placed solely by reference to BEA's own preference and without any regard to its possible contribution to the reorganisation of the British aircraft industry and its export capability.[29]

So de Havilland agreed to form a consortium, Airco, to build its DH121 tri-jet with Fairey Aviation and Hunting Aircraft. In the end it took a letter from Lord Douglas, exasperated by the shilly-shallying, to bring the matter to a close, pointing out that the Bristol 200 was bigger than BEA wanted:

> BEA does not want an aircraft larger than that specified in our original requirement... In any case, the whole position is most humiliating for BEA in that it is now being suggested that the corporation should leave the choice of its new aircraft to a foreign firm and one which is, in fact, a potential competitor... Indeed, it has even been suggested that Pan-American Airways are picking Bristol's brains and making themselves familiar with the BEA specification in order that they might pass this on to American manufacturers.[30]

Later named the Trident,[31] BEA ordered twenty-four early in 1958. However, as the aircraft was not due to enter service until 1964, five years after the Caravelle, an interim jet was required and so at the same time BEA ordered a specially modified short range version of the Comet, to enter service in 1960.

Nor were smaller aircraft forgotten. The Dutch company Fokker had pioneered the development of twin-engine short-haul turboprops with its commercially successful F27 Friendship, and reaped the benefit of its head start. Handley Page launched the Herald, originally powered by four Leonides piston engines, but then redesigned the aircraft to be powered by two Rolls-Royce Darts, like the Friendship. The aircraft, with around forty-four- to forty-eight seats was similar in size to the Friendship and also had a high wing. Meanwhile, Avro cautiously re-entered the civil market, ten years after the Tudor fiasco, by proposing a twin turboprop design, the 748, with a low wing and superior airfield performance.[32] The launch customer was Skyways, which saw the aircraft as an ideal replacement for its Dakotas on the Coach-Air service, and by June 1959 Eric Rylands had signed a letter of intent to buy three; BKS followed shortly afterwards with an order for two. The government, too, lent a hand, ordering three Heralds for use by BEA on its Scottish routes, and BOAC ordered 748s on behalf of some its overseas subsidiaries.

## LOOKING AHEAD

'Nobody in his senses imagines that the two corporations are all we require for full transport development; that these corporations are in any way omniscient; or that it is, overall, a good thing for them to be omnipotent.' That was the opinion of *The Aeroplane* expressed in November 1952. Seven years later that sentiment was still being echoed by Clive Hunting, one of the directors of Hunting-Clan and a family member, in the September 1959 issue of *Airlift*, an American magazine:

> Surely no one believes that however good (the) two great organisations are, they can be so invariably right and so alive to every opportunity that the country's air transport industry can hope to remain competitive if it is composed of them alone. There is a resurgent belief throughout the country in private enterprise, which is leading to the feeling that reliance upon two chosen and protected instruments cannot possibly produce the variety of endeavor and the clash of opinion which is the essence of progress, and which is essential in the face of world competition.
>
> Moreover this line of thought leads to the conclusion that the manufacturing industry also could be disastrously weakened if there are only two big customers to give a lead; once again, however carefully and honestly they state their requirements, is it natural to expect them to be right every time? As the chief executive of BEA has put it, 'BEA is in the very unenviable position of being able to make or break the British aviation industry.'[33]

He went on to explain the area in which independents could make the greatest contribution – low fares:

> The most fruitful field for the independents may well lie in slashing fares as far as economically possible. Many of us believe that economy and not speed (which is to some extent incidental) is what the independents, by virtue of their lean overhead structures, have to offer. If newer and faster vehicles are going to cost more both initially and operationally, which seems inevitable, then the only hope of broadening the market which is in everyone's interest is to cut fares and tariffs dramatically with the equipment at our disposal today.
>
> That this is possible some of us have already shown in a recent pattern of applications for scheduled services over cabotage routes where fares sought were about half the present

tourist level. Economic suicide? We cannot claim and do not want any subsidies (we are not even permitted to carry mail). If we were wrong we go out of business.[34]

He meant what he said. A few weeks later Hunting-Clan closed down its locally based African Airways venture, although this did not affect either its Africargo or its Safari Class services, which were British-based.

## NEVER HAD IT SO GOOD?

Finally, on 20 July 1959, Watkinson announced in the House of Commons that if the Conservatives won the next election they would introduce legislation to bring in a new licensing authority with enhanced powers. This would cover both operators and their operations, and might go some way to easing the tight reins on the independent airlines. After being re-elected in October, the government reorganised its ministries, splitting Civil Aviation off from the Ministry of Transport and combining it with the Ministry of Supply in a renamed Ministry of Aviation, responsible not just for civil airlines and aircraft manufacturers, but also procurement for the RAF. The long-standing rivalry and frequent dissent between the two ministries was finally to be laid to rest, as were Watkinson's semantic concerns noted above. Watkinson, after four years as minister responsible for aviation, was sent off to be the Minister of Defence. Duncan Sandys, who had been the Minister of Defence, became the new Minister of Aviation. Although he was interested in consolidating the charter airlines into larger units, his first task was to persuade the aircraft manufacturers that rationalisation was desirable and that it was necessary for them to be merged into bigger and, it was to be hoped, stronger units. As aircraft programmes became more complex, the government wanted to be sure that the manufacturers had the resources to carry them through: larger, stronger units would be the key to this. The manufacturers needed some persuading; moral pressure was all very well, but financial assistance in underwriting development costs was better. Best of all were firm orders. The aircraft manufacturers had been relatively flush with money during the 1950s, buoyed by the Korean War, the Cold War, large off-shore purchases through American aid and some successful civil programmes, notably the Viscount. Vickers had been confident enough to launch the Vanguard as a private venture, but then lost £10 million on the programme; faced with losing more on the next venture, BOAC had to be nudged into buying too many VC10s by the government in order to prevent Vickers from backing out of civil aircraft production entirely. BOAC had become resentful of its role as surrogate for government aid to the industry, maintaining that high introductory costs and the resolution of teething problems fell unfairly on its shoulders; the airline understandably had broader concerns than the support of the British aircraft industry. Now that the government had taken the first step, the time had come to implement its policy of rationalising the aircraft and the airline industry, as we shall discover in the next chapter.

# FOUR

# THE FUTURE LIES WITH THE STRONG:

## THE CIVIL AVIATION (LICENSING) ACT 1960

We are determined, when the opportunity comes again, to restore a wide measure of private enterprise in the air, to throw the lines open to private competition under proper regulation, and to have some system analogous to the Civil Aeronautics Board in the United States, which has given the benefit of coordination and the benefit of competition as well.

That was what Alan Lennox-Boyd had promised back in 1951. But nine years were to elapse before the Conservative Government started to redeem this pledge, and even then the promise was only fulfilled in part and in small measure. The new Minister of Aviation, Duncan Sandys, now made up for lost time; he managed to achieve more in four months than his predecessor, Watkinson, had in four years, forcing through his new Bill against the protests of the Treasury. 'The Ministry make things very difficult for us. Having suffered a rebuff in their attempt to steamroller through their policy and the Bill, they now seem to be having another shot at it,' complained Mr Goldman at the Treasury in February, a few days before the first reading.[1]

## THE BRITISH AIRCRAFT INDUSTRY

'The special task for which I have been appointed to this new post is to strengthen the structure of the British Aircraft Industry and to promote the expansion of the British air services.' Sandys tackled the manufacturing industry first, persuading most of the manufacturers to regroup into five larger groups, two producing fixed wing aircraft and missiles, two responsible for aero-engines and one producing helicopters. Hawker Siddeley Aviation, which already controlled Armstrong Whitworth, Folland, Gloster, Hawker and AV Roe (Avro), now took over Blackburn and de Havilland. A new creation, the British Aircraft Corporation, brought together the aircraft interests of English Electric, Vickers and Bristol Aircraft, to which was added Hunting Aircraft.

Left outside the two main groupings were Handley Page, Scottish Aviation, and Short Brothers and Harland in Belfast; the last was already majority owned by the State. The two aero-engine companies were Rolls-Royce and Bristol-Siddeley, the latter owned equally by the Hawker Siddeley Group and the Bristol Aeroplane Company, parent company of Bristol Aircraft. The helicopter manufacturer was Westland, which took over the helicopter interests of Bristol Aircraft and bought out Fairey Aviation and Saunders-Roe. The government intended to concentrate orders on the five major groups; to help persuade the aircraft manufacturers to accept the 'voluntary' restructuring, it promised to give increased support for promising civil aircraft projects and aero-engines, hopefully recouping its costs through participation in the sales proceeds. Apart from contributing to the launch costs of new types directly, the government in future would also contribute towards the cost of proving new aircraft and introducing them into airline service, long a gripe of BOAC, who claimed that it had had to assume that responsibility in the past. Launch aid, as established by Sandys, continues to this day; at the time it marked a watershed both for the industry and its future relationship with government; the latter, as Keith Hayward notes, would now provide the main financial support:

> The period between 1959 and 1964 was an important one in the relationship between Government and the civil aircraft industry. Under increasing pressure from firms struggling to finance civil projects, the Government was forced to concede the need for launch aid. Similarly, BOAC's financial problems led the Government to accept full responsibility for the nationalised airlines buying British. At the same time, the likely costs of developing a supersonic transport as well as the presence of wider political advantages stimulated interest in international collaboration. By 1964, the Government had again become directly involved with civil aerospace and was embarked upon a course of action which, by the end of the decade, left the state as the primary source of capital for the industry's civil activities.[2]

## THE 1960 CIVIL AVIATION (LICENSING) BILL

As for the airlines, Sandys published a new Civil Aviation (Licensing) Bill on 2 March 1960 which had four main features:

• It required all commercial operators to obtain an Air Operator's Certificate, issued by the Director of Aviation Safety, which took account of an operator's equipment, organisation and operational arrangements.

• It repealed Section 24 of the previous Act which had granted the monopoly of scheduled services to the state corporations, and would allow independents to apply for route licences without having to be 'associates'.

• It established an Air Transport Licensing Board (ATLB) which would grant licences to approved operators, approve domestic fares, and ensure airlines provided statistical and other financial information.

• It enlarged the circle of the licensing net. Colonial airlines, and certain classes of flight, such as sole-use flights,[3] would continue to be exempt from licensing requirements; any flight for which a passenger had paid a 'separate fare' now required a licence. Airlines would have to apply to the new Board for licences route by route, specifying frequencies, aircraft type, dates of operation, who the charterers were to be and so on. Abandoning its fruitless quest for the perfect definition of a scheduled service, the Ministry now brought into the net all flights for which a fare of any description had been paid. Occasional, non-systematic flights would now require a licence; so too would closed group flights, closing that loop-hole at last. The ATAC had been rather shrill about the inequities of spurious closed groups, a natural concomitant of being a regulatory authority. In its 1959/60 report the ATAC observed rather tartly:

> A feature peculiar to the year under review which merits special mention, however, is the sharp fall in (Inclusive Tour) traffic. It would be difficult to believe that, in a year when British air traffic generally showed a marked recovery from the 1958 pause in its expansion, fewer people should have taken inclusive holidays by air. The explanation of this paradox appears to lie largely in the fact that a growing amount of this type of holiday traffic is being carried by other means than Inclusive Tour Service approved under Associate Agreements. There is no doubt that the lower fares becoming increasingly available on Normal Scheduled Services are attracting more inclusive-tour passengers onto Normal Scheduled Services. What is less desirable is the great increase in the number of services purporting to cater for group travel and not for the general public... More and more services appear to cater for groups which have little or no purpose apart from the provision of cheap travel and whose membership is not limited so as effectively to prevent people joining merely to secure that particular benefit. The stage now appears to have been reached at which spurious 'closed group' operations are undermining the work of the Council and one of the objects of the Civil Aviation (Licensing) Act, 1960, is to bring services of this kind under proper control.

Even the ATAC had to refer to cheap travel as a 'benefit', and other commentators questioned if this criticism of charters was really justified. *The Economist* wondered why it should be felt that 'there is something improper and un-British in wanting to travel cheaply.'[4] J.E.D. Williams, an aviation economist and airline managing director, pointed out the absurdity: 'It is a peculiar feature of modern Britain that the provision of a service is most offensive when its benefits are available to the public.'[5]

The regulation of closed groups came into effect as soon as the Bill became law so that the interim licensing authority, the ATAC, had to devise new licences to cover them; all manner of organisations, respectable or otherwise, found themselves coming under scrutiny.

## AN OLD DOLL DRESSED UP IN A NEW GOWN

The government, of course, did not take anything away from the corporations; there was to be no free-for-all in route licensing. Instead the Board was given meagre terms of reference and no directions except for the platitudinous, 'to further the development of British civil aviation'. The Board would still have to consider 'the adequacy of' existing services and 'the extent to which any air transport service proposed would be likely to result in wasteful duplication of such services or in material diversion of traffic from any such service authorized by any Air Service Licence already granted.' So two old favourites, wasteful competition and material diversion, remained; the corporations, under their previous monopoly, would be automatically issued with Air Service Licences to cover their existing routes. They were also free to object to new applications. Furthermore, the Minister could still direct the Board to refuse a licence if it would involve international negotiations for traffic rights which he considered 'inexpedient for the time being to seek'. Hearings for new licences would be in public, unlike the procedure under the ATAC. Airlines had the right to appeal decisions and the final decision lay with the Minister.

One appointment received general approval, when Lord Terrington was asked to be the first chairman of the new ATLB. Seemingly severe as a regulator, he was pragmatic and earned the confidence of his ministers to the extent that they never questioned his decisions; he also reiterated time and again that he did not believe the operations of independent airlines had to any material extent affected the growth of the traffic of the two corporations. BIATA was unusually demonstrative in its delight at his appointment:

> Although we have continuously criticised the circumstances under which the ATAC has worked, this has never implied any criticism of the ATAC itself and (we) must once again, on behalf of the Association, record our sincere appreciation and gratitude for the patience, courtesy and careful consideration which has been given unstintingly by the members of the ATAC and its staff. The work which the ATAC has done will have many lasting effects to the benefit of British air transport. [6]

Otherwise the response to the Bill was lukewarm. Traditionally low key, BIATA considered '… that the new legislation provides a reasonable basis for the future conduct of the affairs of the industry.' [7] Others talked of disappointment and voiced fears that the Board would be a puppet of the Minister. The older established carriers, though, welcomed the steps taken to improve overall safety and financial standards through the award of the Air Operator's Certificate; competition from new entrants was beginning to bite. George Woods Humphery, general manager of Imperial Airways before the war, was able to see through the smoke and espy the dangers:

> The Civil Aviation Licensing Act purports to give the Licensing Board wide powers, and it has even been suggested that, with this Act in force, the monopolies of the two government-owned corporations will be at an end. A study of the 'small print' conditions, however, indicates that this is but the old doll dressed up in a new gown. Even the Board itself is to be subject to the instructions of the Minister – which means, of course, the Ministry – which can instruct the Board to do anything that it orders, *inter alia,* to hold hearings in camera not only for diplomatic, but 'for other' reasons. That leaves the door wide open for the suppression of any views that might be unpalatable to the Ministry, and for more Star Chambers. Surely all hearings should normally be held in public, but with discretion left to the Board to have private hearings if it considers it to be in the public or national interest. One would hope that the Board will be composed of men who would be just as good judges of what is or is not in the national or public interest as the Ministry.

The whole basic idea that the government knows best is devoid of imaginative or healthy thinking.

The C A B systems and procedures are far from ideal, and have suffered from the progressive application of Parkinson's Law, but they are still a whole lot better than this new piece of legislation.[8]

John Brancker, who worked for many years with BOAC and then IATA, had his doubts too:

The new legislation setting up the ATLB has gone at least far enough to make the processes legal, but it is still not clear whether the whole affair is an honest attempt to give the independents a viable and permanent share of British air transport, or whether it is closer to being a political gesture designed to pay lip service to a declared policy, but not intended to make much difference in fact. So long as those words 'material diversion' are to govern the outcome one cannot help feeling that the real intention is to avoid rocking the boat.[9]

Brancker seems to question the bona fides of the Act, but there is no reason to doubt that both Ministers, Watkinson and Sandys, were sincere in their wish to create more opportunities for the independents, and as Conservatives they may well have wished for these exponents of free enterprise to prosper. Watkinson was minister for four years and so better placed than most of his predecessors to enact changes, but instead frittered away the opportunity by chasing after grandiose and impractical schemes, leaving it to his successor to push the new legislation through Parliament. Sandys achieved major structural changes in the manufacturing industry, but was unable to achieve a similar rebalancing of the airline industry. Ten years later, the industry was still dominated by the corporations and the independents were still unhappy with their crumbs; the Act, even though it 'removed' the corporations' monopoly and purported to give the independents more opportunities, did little to further the development of British civil aviation.

## IT'S NOT A BAD REPORT, AND PRETTY WELL KNOCKS THE MINISTER'S PROPOSAL AS REGARDS THE INDEPENDENTS WELL AND TRULY ON THE HEAD.[10]

Why did the Act fail? Perhaps the answer lies in a mismatch between the aims of the Minister and the underlying intentions of his subordinates in the Ministry. The ministers concerned may well have wished to open some doors for the independents: but not their civil servants. They had a completely different agenda. Far from doing the Minister's bidding, his officials knowingly subverted the plans in furtherance of their own ends, which were a great deal more prosaic. All that the men from the Ministry wanted to do was to clear up the legal anomaly of the old Civil Aviation Act being used to permit competition with the corporations; then to close the door on unlicensed charters.

This is how they did it: only days after Watkinson had announced in July 1959 that he was going to introduce a licensing scheme for the independents, a Working Party from his Ministry in its turn issued a final confidential report on his proposals to abolish the corporations' monopoly and establish an Air Transport Board; its terms of reference had been:

> To consider the possible scope and functions of an Air Transport Board possessed of powers to licence civil air services: and in particular to consider the scope for extending the activities of the independent airlines, having regard to consequent effects on the viability of the Airways Corporations and the need to control non-scheduled operations.

Note how the Minister's prime concern appeared to be to extend the scope of the independent airlines – for the Working Party very quickly concluded that as, in its view, the prime purpose of government policy was to protect the corporations, there was really no scope for extending the activities of the independents at all:

> Changes that would significantly affect the earning capacity of the Corporations would be highly controversial; it would be argued that the commercial morale of the Corporations would be sapped and the public's investment prejudiced.
>
> The abolition of the statutory monopoly of the Corporations and their associates, and the establishment of an Air Transport Board would not in themselves improve the independents' prospects.
>
> Any significant departure from the existing relationship between the Corporations and the independents would require fundamental changes in government policy. What is more important is that at almost every turn questions of international and Commonwealth relations are involved, and as all such matters must be entirely within the control of the government this at once poses the problem of the degree of autonomy that the Air Transport Board should enjoy. In our view all the principal means of increasing the independents' opportunities would fall outside the locus of the board because of either the international relations difficulties or the need to maintain the viability of the Corporations.[11]

The Working Party went on to dismiss the various options which might have given the independents greater scope:

• Territorial demarcation, which was practised by the French, would have reserved for the independents the UK share of some readily defined and large market, like Africa. This was rejected because it would have restricted the future earning power of the corporations.

• Surrender of selected routes had been proposed by BIATA, which suggested that independents could take over routes that were operated by the corporations at a loss. Although the Working Party observed that this idea had 'superficial attractions', it too was rejected because the group thought that 'the public might be less well served than it had been by the Corporations'.

• Allocation of categories of service; in this case the Working Party conceded that as the corporations had no interest in vehicle-ferry services, perhaps these could be reserved to the independents, and maybe non-scheduled helicopter services?

• Double designation, that is allowing two British airlines to compete on international services, as already happened in the USA, would give rise to 'formidable difficulties and dangers. On domestic and cabotage routes parallel operations would result in an immediate loss of revenue to the Corporations.'

Ten years later the Edwards Report recommended the surrender of routes, double designation on some intercontinental routes and territorial demarcation. That all lay in the future; for now, the trite and superficial analysis of the various options open to the independents was made by officials in the department, which in time would advise the Minister on licensing decisions and appeals under the 1960 Act.

Before examining the proposed Board's possible terms of reference, the group concluded:

> It now seems unlikely that the annual growth of traffic in the fields in which the independents are established will suffice to maintain their share of traffic in the face of mounting competition from the Corporations. The inclusive-tour market is already threatened by BEA; BOAC is prepared to introduce low-fare services that will undermine Colonial Coach operators; the declining strength of British garrisons abroad, coupled with the ending of National Service and the re-equipment of Transport Command, have caused a marked fall in trooping work. It is only in the specialised fields, e.g. vehicle-ferry services, that the independents' prospects are bright. Nonetheless we decided that the establishment of an Air Transport Board could be justified if on no other grounds than the need to introduce an orderly and coherent machine in place of the makeshift ATAC the vires of the existing arrangements being disputable. The Council has worked well but it is now constantly encountering difficulties that it has neither the authority nor the ability to overcome; it is, moreover, becoming less easy to maintain the fiction that the Council is a wholly independent body. An ATB with statutory authority and executive powers would relieve the Minister of much embarrassment and would make administration of air-service policy much easier.[12]

What would Lord Terrington have thought had he known that he was not viewed as 'independent'? Nor did the Air Transport Board relieve the Minister of 'much embarrassment'; the Minister soon found himself ensnared in antagonistic decisions that he had little control over. The group's forecasting was no more on target than its regulatory analysis; charter airlines still provide low-fare and Inclusive Tour Service to this day, and the trooping contracts were to run for another ten years, whereas vehicle-ferry services were about to peak and start their decline into oblivion.

When it came to suggesting terms of reference for the Air Transport Board, the Working Party was at pains to ensure the paramountcy of 'material diversion':

> This rather elaborate formula contains several safeguards designed to make it particularly acceptable to the Corporations. It is cast in a largely negative form so that the chief burden of demonstrating the merits is thrown on the applicant (who in most cases is likely to be an independent); much stress is laid on consideration of responsible objections (most of which are likely to come from the Corporations); and the criteria that established services must satisfy in order to be considered worthy of protection are those that the Corporations are especially well qualified to match because of their elaborate organisations.[13]

The Working Party then devoted eight lengthy paragraphs to discussing the problems of unlicensed flights, and concluded that a new definition, based on 'separate fare' rather than 'scheduled service', would bring into the regulatory net all the outstanding and troublesome categories that had so far evaded the long arm of the Ministry, such as occasional, non-systematic charters and closed groups. In this the Working Party was undoubtedly successful; most of its recommendations found their way into the new Act.

The Treasury was cock-a-hoop at the tone and content of the report. 'It's not a bad report,' wrote Mr Goldman, 'and pretty well knocks the Minister's proposal as regards the independents well and truly on the head.' His colleague Mr Painter was more circumspect: 'In very broad terms the draft report was comforting from the Treasury's point of view – it squashed the idea of significantly more scope for independent operators at the expense of the Corporations.' But the Minister, Sandys, could still be tiresome:

> There is a case on its own for improved licensing arrangements, but the Minister of Aviation also envisages these arrangements as enabling the Government to allow more scope to independent operators. We doubt whether this can be done without damaging the Air Corporations and thus increasing their financial burden on the Exchequer, and we would like to see this whole question of 'independents-versus-Corporations' thrashed out before the treasury are committed to the new licensing arrangements.[14]

The Treasury was won over when they were finally persuaded that, 'the Ministry's scheme does not threaten a major change in the relations between Corporations and independents and a threat to the Corporations' financial integrity.' Even the corporations approved the new Bill, rightly perceiving that their status would remain unchallenged, although they did try unsuccessfully to strengthen the 'material diversion' provisions. In a last desperate attempt to salvage something for the independents, Sandys proposed that the new Board would make recommendations as to what licences should be granted to existing operators, rather than nodding through transitional licences for approval, which would have given him a final opportunity to transfer routes, if he so wished. The Treasury was indignant:

> I would suggest that the Chancellor should resist this proposal. It would mean that the new Licensing Board would have to start by an exhaustive investigation of all existing services, invite objections from potential competitors – all of which would take a long time and involve existing operators in a great deal of uncertainty. It is difficult to see what lies behind the Minister's suggestion. Certainly his officials are at a complete loss about it.[15]

That proposal was quickly dropped too; it would undoubtedly have caused some consternation among officials.

Sandys was to prove adept at cajoling and coercing the Treasury to do his bidding, but in this case he was in too much of a hurry to set the wheels of his new legislation in motion, and therefore seems to have accepted his Ministry's proposals more or less at face value, give or take the occasional wobble. He was happy to accept the status quo in this matter, though not in others:

I can tell the House what the Bill will not do, and is not intended to do. It is not intended to undermine the position of BOAC and BEA. Large sums of public money have been invested in them and they have to face fierce competition from foreign rivals.[16]

Almost in the same breath, he went on to describe the 'fierce competition'; 'Another thing that the Bill will not do is to break up the partnership agreements the corporations have concluded with Commonwealth and foreign airlines. These pooling arrangements have proved valuable in eliminating wasteful duplication.' At least he had the good grace to substitute 'duplication' for 'competition'.

The Bill passed through the committee stages largely unscathed and on 2 June 1960 the Civil Aviation (Licensing) Act became law. Regulations were then published covering licensing procedures and the different classes of licence which amongst other matters reined in the closed groups, now classified as 'affinity groups'. Passengers on affinity group flights must have been members of the group for at least six months before they were eligible to travel, and the organisation or society must have been established for some purpose other than travel, a pointless but malicious stipulation; also, the organisation could not have more than 15,000 members and could only advertise its services to its members. One important innovation was that all hearings for contested licences would be in public and the Board would have to publish its reasons for refusing a licence. There was the right of appeal, too, although no guidelines were set as to admissible evidence; appeals would be heard by a commissioner appointed by the Minister, who would then make his recommendation to the Minister, who had the final say, of course.

## THE CORPORATIONS

The passing of the Bill found the two corporations experiencing different fortunes. BEA had enjoyed yet another profitable year, its sixth in succession and had just carried three million passengers in one year for the first time. The 1950s, the corporation's decade of the Viscount, were good years for BEA which had the right equipment in place, enjoyed growing demand in an increasingly prosperous market, and thrived in a heavily regulated environment which masked out most competition, and promoted the corporation's monopoly strengths. Even the competition, which came from the independents offering IT charter flights to European destinations, was effectively blunted by continual objections to the ATAC on the one hand, and by responding competitively with IT fares on the other. BEA ended the decade by bringing into service two new aircraft types, the Comet 4B and the Vickers Vanguard, which introduced a smart new livery: black fuselage cheat-line, red wings and the letters *BEA* in a red square on the tail. The corporation was to make another profit in 1960/61.

BOAC, meanwhile, was going through a difficult patch. The corporation had started making losses again, its subsidiary companies overseas[17] continued to lose money, and following the introduction of its Comet and Britannia fleets, the airline had to write off their 'abnormal development costs' as it called them. Smallpeice claimed the corporation had to shoulder more than its fair share of the introductory costs of new British-built aircraft, something that it did not have to do when it bought American aircraft. He also thought the airline paid too much money to the government for the privilege of bankrolling it. Since 1956 BOAC had had to go to the Treasury for exchequer advances in order to raise capital; previously capital requirements were met by issuing British Overseas Airways stock. BOAC's requirements therefore now fell under the country's annual budget and could be subject to Treasury cuts, and the corporation had to go on paying a fixed rate of interest on its capital, in good times and bad. The chairman said in the 1957/58 Annual Report:

> The Corporation bears a charge for interest on the whole of its capital whether or not a profit is earned. By contrast many of our overseas competitors normally have a material proportion of their capital in equity form which does not attract a dividend unless profits are available.

The rate of return was not especially high, at 4 per cent, but the more BOAC lost, the more money it had to extract from the Treasury and the debt, on which more interest then had to be paid back to the Treasury, became greater; it was a downward spiral. The problem for BEA was less acute as it was profitable and so could 'afford' to pay interest. But BOAC thought it had to pay the equivalent of hefty dividends even when it was making a loss, although the corporation was doing no more than any other business which needs to borrow money to invest, with the added benefit of having access to low interest funds provided by the State:

> It is true that the corporation has to pay interest in lean years as well as in fat ones. But this is the price of relatively cheap State capital; it is a relief to see that BOAC are no longer describing these payments as 'guaranteed dividends.' Certainly any airline with loan capital has to pay for its borrowings just as it has to pay for fuel, maintenance or anything else.[18]

To depress morale further, four of BOAC's new Comet 4s were badly damaged in a series of landing accidents within the space of nine months between June 1959 and March 1960. The corporation also began to suffer from periodic and prolonged strikes by its workers. There was a further change at the top. Sir Gerard d'Erlanger ended his career in aviation by stepping down from the chairmanship of BOAC at the end of July 1960, having been bullied by the Ministry of Aviation into committing the corporation to buy ten more VC10s on top of the thirty-five already ordered. His successor, Rear Admiral Sir Matthew Slattery, lately of Short Brothers and Harland and also the Bristol Aeroplane Company, faced the challenge of managing the corporation's financial deficit as world traffic growth was declining.

However, on a cheerier note, the first Boeing 707 entered service on 27 May 1960 on the service to New York, just as production of the Bristol Britannia was drawing to a close with eighty-five built; and the corporation reintroduced services to Brazil, Uruguay, Argentina and Chile, operated by Comet 4s.

## THE INDEPENDENTS

The charter airlines meanwhile reacted to the new Act cautiously, but not unfavourably. Harold Bamberg, in an interview with Frank Beswick for *Flight*, was candid:

I'm a bit of an optimist, and if you believe in air transport you naturally believe in your own future.

Some say there is now a great future for independents, and others that there is no future at all; some think the corporations will be badly damaged and others that they won't be touched. We see our future largely in terms of international scheduled flying, both passengers and freight. Trooping, charter and inclusive-tour work don't lend themselves to planning ahead.

Like others, I accept that the corporations' basic interests must be protected; they are a vital part of British aviation. But there is still scope for parallel services and the new board has the job of deciding where they will be.

The first important question is whether the existing operator is getting an adequate share of the traffic for Britain. Then an applicant may be capable of new specialized operations in the future but wants a conventional basis. The last thing we must do is to protect an existing operator who has built-in unnecessary high costs.[19]

Others looked to increasing the share of British aviation too. Group Captain Wilcock – chairman of Derby Aviation and Labour Member of Parliament for Derby North – observed that even if the ATLB's decisions were detrimental to the corporations' interests they would not necessarily be detrimental to the overall British air transport effort. He espoused the cause of more flexible fares but looked for greater security as well: 'If we can offer a cheaper ride on an older, slower but equally safe machine, then why should not the passengers be free to travel with us if they choose?'[20] Eon Mekie, the chairman of British Aviation Services, which had been active in taking over some of the smaller airlines, wondered about the benefits of rationalisation, something that Sandys and his predecessors had been urging on the independents:

There is no gain in being gargantuan; the task is to ensure that we get true economies from the maximum utilisation of equipment and staff. Certainly it seems to me that there are too many small concerns led by dedicated and honest people, but without the facilities that are required. Within the foreseeable future I should estimate that the number of independent operators or groups will be reduced to three or four.[21]

## BRITISH UNITED AIRWAYS

Indeed, Airwork had been acquiring airlines for some years of course, in pursuit of its own plans for rationalisation, and just as the Minister was introducing the Bill for its second reading in the House of Commons on 2 March 1960, the airline issued a brief statement on cue:

Mr M.D.N. Wyatt, chairman of Airwork Limited, Mr P.L. Hunting, chairman of Hunting-Clan Air Transport Limited, and Sir Nicholas Cayzer, chairman of the British and Commonwealth Shipping Group, announce that it has been decided to merge their air transport interests.

In view of the close cooperation between the two airlines, their similarity of equipment and market development, the merger came as no great surprise; it was another example of establishment airlines doing what was expected of them. The largest shareholder was British and Commonwealth; Whitehall Securities retained a substantial shareholding, as did Loel Guinness, and the other shareholders were Blue Star, Furness Withy, and Hunting.

The airline was not called British and Commonwealth. Whitehall Securities, whose aviation interests stretched back to before the Second World War, started United Airways in 1935, and had then amalgamated it with Spartan Air Lines and Hillman's later that year, to form the first British Airways. Whitehall now agreed to allow the United Airways name to be resurrected for the new airline, with the addition of 'British', and as a first step on 19 May, Airwork changed its name to British United Airways (BUA). Then on 1 July all the other operating companies were brought into British United. Some of the old familiar names died: Airwork, Hunting-Clan, Air Charter and Transair. Channel Air Bridge, Aviation Traders, Bristow Helicopters and Morton continued for a while as semi-independent fiefdoms and retained their names. The Group had over 3,000 employees and the combined fixed-wing fleet amounted to fifty-two aircraft, including four Britannias, two DC-6s, eleven Viscounts, four Skymasters and thirteen Bristol Freighters, all due to be repainted in the very conservative BUA scheme of dark blue cheatline, white tail and red lettering: the colourful and distinctive Hunting-Clan 'dayglo' orange tail disappeared. The helicopter division now had fifty-four helicopters, including fifteen Westland Whirlwinds, based at Redhill. The Cayzers, ready to diversify out of shipping into other areas, emerged as the main shareholder and intent on playing a more pro-active role. The merger was good for Laker, too. He became the airline's managing director, winning that contest over the older Gerald Freeman who had successfully been at the helm of Transair for many years. Maurice Curtis, managing director of Hunting-Clan, left, as did Alan Muntz, Airwork's original founder, who had remained the airline's vice chairman over the years.

Laker, ever an enthusiastic proponent of the British aircraft industry, went on to launch the newly formed British Aircraft Corporation's BAC One-Eleven with an order for ten. An attractive short-haul twin-jet, the sixty-nine seater was seen as a direct replacement for the eleven Viscounts in the fleet, with the range to serve Malta non-stop and capable of operating the Safari services as well. Smaller than the Trident, it was better suited to British United's route structure. British United followed this with an order for three VC10s, passenger aircraft but equipped with large freight doors; in a very short space of time British United had invested heavily in the products of the British aircraft industry with little fuss and no talk of subsidies.


## CUNARD AND BRITISH EAGLE


During March 1960 the holding company for the Eagle group of companies, Harold Bamberg Holdings, changed its name to British Eagle International Airways, and the airline acquired its first Britannia, a Series 318 on lease from the Cuban airline Cubana. The livery was changed too, introducing the familiar red, white and black colours, with a very large 'E' emblazoned on the tail. But the most significant change was the announcement made at this time that the great Cunard Steam Ship Company, owners of the famous *Queen Mary* and *Queen Elizabeth* transatlantic liners, was going to buy a majority share-holding in British Eagle.

Airwork's Vickers Viscount G-APND was absorbed into the fleet of British United Airways. It is seen here at Manchester Airport, assisted by Manchester Airport Agencies, with a RAF Blackburn Beverley in the background. (MAP)

Cunard had long interested itself in aviation, seeing air and sea travel as complementary, and even before the Second World War its then chairman, the redoubtable Sir Percy Bates, had held talks with Imperial Airways and tried unsuccessfully to become involved in its first transatlantic airline ventures. During the war it became clear to him that fast air services carrying passengers, mail and freight could compete seriously in the future with his large liners. Once again Bates tried to persuade the government to allow Cunard to operate air services, but after much tedious and frustrating negotiation, the government decided that BOAC would be its 'chosen instrument', although it did suggest that Cunard, together with the other Atlantic lines, Canadian Pacific and Anchor, could participate by securing a limited interest in BOAC's Atlantic services. Cunard would have been offered between 5 to 7.5 per cent and would have agreed to act as the corporation's booking agent. It was a cause of much bitterness to Sir Percy when the Labour Government subsequently decided that all scheduled air services were to be under government ownership and control:

> I think that the decision is open to criticism, but I do not wish to press the point… after being invited to participate, shipping companies are now no longer wanted. Well, speaking for our group, I accept the decision, yet I still believe that the two methods of transportation are complementary rather than competitive.[22]

Now, with the imminent passing of the new Civil Aviation (Licensing) Act, Cunard's interest in aviation was reawakened. Cunard was drawn to Eagle, the only large airline without any shipping interests, because it already operated scheduled services within

Europe and was active in Bermuda, the Bahamas and North America. Eagle held a Bermuda-London licence, which after two and a half years still awaited final approval from the British authorities, and also a Nassau-London licence. Cunard had ambitions to offer air service in parallel with its flagship routes between England and the United States; London to New York would do very well for starters. At the same time as it acquired Eagle, which it renamed Cunard Eagle Airways, Cunard was also talking to BOAC about air-sea cooperation, which allowed passengers to travel one way by air and return by sea and still qualify for the return discount. BOAC too was attracted by the strength and power of the Cunard name, especially in North America, although it was not immediately obvious how the government-owned airline could ally itself more closely with the private-enterprise shipping company at this time. Cunard was negotiating with the government over the construction of a new Cunarder, the Q3 project, to replace the ageing *Queens*. In April 1961 the government offered to provide around three-fifths of the estimated £30 million needed to build the ship, part low-interest loan and part direct contribution to the building cost, but Cunard was facing further decline in its transatlantic traffic and was therefore hesitant about committing itself to another specialised transatlantic liner.

## THE PASSING OF COLONIAL COACH CLASS AND THE INTRODUCTION OF SKYCOACH - VERY LOW FARES (VLF)

Eagle withdrew all its applications for VLF services once the shape of the new legislation became apparent, and Hunting-Clan followed suit. The Minister then announced his approval for lower coach air fares, to be called 'Skycoach', on certain cabotage routes, and told the independents that they would be allowed to share traffic on these routes with the corporations along the lines of the previously formulated thirty:seventy ratio. BEA would share the Gibraltar route with British United and the Malta route with Skyways. BOAC would share 'third class' (formerly Colonial Coach Class) African services with British United, Central African Airways and East African Airways. Cunard Eagle would be allowed to participate on routes to Bermuda and the Bahamas. The old Colonial Coach Class was to be revamped; the name was no longer altogether appropriate as more and more colonies sought – and were granted – independence. The lowest fares would only be available to residents of the United Kingdom or the respective colonies, and were set at around 25 per cent below the normal tourist fare. There were stipulations regarding service – cold meals only, which had to be paid for, no bar service, 33lb baggage allowance and 32in seat pitch.

Skycoach was launched on 4 October 1960 with the first in a fortnightly service to East Africa, followed by a fortnightly service to Central Africa. Although Central African Airways and East African Airways were participants in Skycoach, their flights were operated by British United's sixty-two-seat Viscounts so that BUA in fact operated forty-six of the ninety-five Skycoach services; BUA also continued to operate its Safari services, now at IATA economy fares, to East Africa, Central Africa and to Accra. In October 1961 BUA withdrew its Viscounts from the African services, which were taken over by eighty-seven-seat Britannias; the Viscounts were redeployed and two additional Britannias were leased from BOAC.[23]

Caribbean flights were next, operated just once a month; so too were BOAC's Skycoach flights to the Far East. However Cunard Eagle was allowed at long last to start its full-fare scheduled services from Bermuda and Nassau to London, on a weekly basis;[24] these offered both first and normal economy fares, and when the frequency was increased in 1961 to four times a week, Skycoach fares became available too. The flights were operated by Cunard Eagle (Bermuda) using Britannias chartered from its parent company. In a complicated cross-leasing arrangement, Cunard Eagle was now able to offer through plane service from London to Miami; it was already operating a four times a day Viscount service between Nassau and Miami – these flights were operated by Cunard Eagle (Bahamas) using Viscounts chartered from Cunard Eagle (Bermuda) – and could route its Britannias from Bermuda via Nassau to Miami. Cunard Eagle's western operations, now under the direction of Messrs. Guinane and Snelling, benefited considerably from the marketing prestige of the Cunard name as well as from more tangible assistance in the shape of sales outlets and reservations units.

Skycoach services were never a success; the combination of minimal service and very limited frequencies, together with the more competitive fares available on regular scheduled flights, militated against the concept which was not marketed with any great degree of enthusiasm by BOAC. The corporation was not best suited to providing low-cost services and even in those days was unhappy about the effect of such flights on its image.

## BIATA AIRLINES – THE FIRST ELEVEN?

The creation of British United Airways and Cunard Eagle, both of which remained in BIATA, still left a sizeable team of independent airlines, many now developing scheduled

Dan-Air's Airspeed Ambassador G-AMAH, the last of twenty-three built, was purchased from Australian airline Butler Air Transport. (MAP)

services, expanding IT flying and otherwise batting away on what was often a sticky wicket. Dan-Air launched a new scheduled network out of Bristol and Cardiff, using eight-seat Doves, and had acquired three Ambassadors for passenger work; these were used for charters, proving popular for visits to *grand prix* racing circuits and increasingly for inclusive tours, with the occasional scheduled flight, especially on the busy summer-only weekend service between Gatwick and Jersey. Its four Yorks were committed to flying freight services for BEA and occasional long-haul flights to the Far East and Australia for the government, achieving a creditable 2,000 hours annual utilisation. Two Dakotas and three Freighters made up the rest of the fleet which were maintained at the airline's engineering base at Lasham in Hampshire; flight operations had switched from Blackbushe to Gatwick. Early in 1961 Dan-Air bought what remained of Scottish Airlines from Scottish Aviation, taking over its Dakota and the Prestwick-Isle of Man route.

Another member airline, Derby Airways, was beginning to break out of its Midlands fastness and deploying its aircraft further afield. Joining Dan-Air at Bristol and Cardiff, the airline inaugurated services in 1960 to Ostend, Palma, Luxembourg and Perpignan (for the Costa Brava), and by now was well-established as an operator to the Channel Islands, which it served from Derby, Northampton, Cambridge, Luton and Staverton. Its links with Rolls-Royce extended beyond support for the Glasgow service as its Dakotas were frequently used to transport Avon engines down to Toulouse, where Sud Aviation installed them on the Caravelle; all told, 254 engines were airlifted.[25] Derby flew inclusive tours out of various Midlands' airports for Midland Air Tour Operators, as was to be expected, but also flew an extensive programme for Wenger Air Tours out of Gatwick to many points in Spain and to Zagreb, Calvi and Dinard. In July 1961 it carried its millionth passenger.

Starways, based in Liverpool, also began looking further afield. The airline introduced a new service from Liverpool to the West Country in 1959, and quickly followed up with new services to Cornwall and Exeter from other points in England and Scotland. The acquisition of Viscounts released the Skymasters for inclusive tours and other contract work; Starways was a major contractor to Sabena during 1961 when the Belgian airline was responsible for airlifting United Nations troops around war-torn Congo, and even had one of its Skymasters destroyed on the ground there.

Silver City, meanwhile, was having some success with its coach/air services which it had transferred from Ferryfield to Manston. Now operated by sixty-eight-seat Hermes, these aircraft saw further use from October 1960 when Silver City was awarded a new trooping contract to Germany, underscoring just how far the Service Ministries had gone in accepting air transport in preference to trooping by sea. Around fifty flights a month were operated to Dusseldorf and RAF Wildenrath. Silver City also joined the small band of airline operators, like Hunting, BKS and Derby, which were active in the arena of commercial non-airline flying, principally air surveying; it was awarded a five-year contract by the Ministry of Aviation to calibrate ground radio-aids at Commonwealth airfields in Africa and the Middle East using a specially modified Dakota. At a more terrestrial level, in 1961 French Railways agreed to build a spur to the airport at Le Touquet and a station on the airport itself, which would speed transfers for the users of the Silver Arrow service.

Jersey Airlines decided to boost its fleet by placing a launch order for six of the twin-turboprop Handley Page Dart Heralds. The first aircraft, a series 100 leased from the

Handley Page's demonstrator Herald G-APWA was leased to Jersey Airlines during the summer of 1961, here performing a low-level pass at Jersey Airport. (Flight)

manufacturer, entered service on 19 May 1961. With the coming of larger and faster aircraft, the airline began to chafe at some of the restrictions placed on its services; a proportion of its Manchester-Jersey flights had to stop at Bournemouth, for example, and half of its Gatwick-Jersey sectors had to make a second landing elsewhere in the Channel Islands. In trying to remove these restrictions, Jersey ran into objections from its minority shareholder BEA, which led the corporation to reassess its relationship with Jersey; eventually it decided to dispose of its 25 per cent shareholding.

Rylands and his partner David Brown sold Bahamas Airways back to BOAC in December 1960, following considerable losses which were manfully born by BOAC when it regained control of the airline, another example of the favourable treatment BOAC extended to Skyways in general; the corporation installed Air Commodore Powell, of Silver City fame, as chairman and managing director, but the losses continued and were to cause a further dent in BOAC's already battered finances. Skyways went through a restructuring at the end of 1961. Rylands bought out the Bibby Line shareholding and so regained control of the company. He then split the airline up into two, Skyways and Skyways Coach Air, the former being the charter operation; for good measure he renamed his Samlesbury Engineering company, Skyways Engineering.

Another airline with a fine engineering heritage, BKS, continued to expand apace into the new decade. Further Bristol Freighters were acquired and a vehicle-ferry service launched between Liverpool and Dublin which operated throughout the summer of 1960 and 1961. Two Viscounts were leased from Maitland Drewery in 1961, flying schedules during the week and IT programmes at the weekend, backed up by the small fleet of Ambassadors. But just as Cambrian had suffered a set-back at the end of 1958, which had led to its temporary closure and from which the carrier had happily emerged, so now it was the turn of BKS to face an uncertain future. In the wake of the difficult trading conditions arising from the collapse of a number of charter airlines (which made it hard to obtain credit, especially from fuel suppliers), BKS was forced to appoint receivers at the end of 1961. The Viscounts were returned to Maitland Drewery and the car-ferry services abandoned; some other services were suspended. The airline had three Avro 748s on order, earmarked for Leeds services, and delivery of these was deferred, but the receivers were optimistic that there would be no further changes in the flying programme.

## NON BIATA AIRLINES

The late 1950s and early 1960s saw the birth and rapid growth of a large number of inclusive-tour-charter airlines, usually followed by their premature demise. They developed largely in response to demand for low-fare holiday flights; as living standards improved during the Macmillan era, people wanted cars, better-equipped homes and now they also wanted foreign holidays. With low overheads and well-worn equipment these airlines initially were able to meet the peak summer demand for holiday flights, but problems arose during the long-drawn-out trough of the fallow winter months which invariably absorbed any summer profits that had been made. Those airlines that had trooping contracts, or flew the Colonial Coach Class routes, or operated freight services, managed to survive through the lean winters, but holiday airlines faced an almost complete shut-down. There were some winter sports holiday flights but these too tended to be the preserve of the longer established BIATA airlines. Inadequate backing, cash-flow problems, weakening demand – especially during the summer of 1960 – and the more stringent financial and operational requirements introduced with the 1960 Act, were to lead to their early dismissal in 1960 and 1961; the financial failure of Overseas Aviation in particular had a domino effect.

In alphabetical order, the Second Eleven, with a record of its innings, was:

|  |  | Fleet at October 1960 |
|---|---|---|
| Air Condor | (1960 only) | One Bristol Freighter |
| Air Safaris | (1958–61) | One Hermes, two Viking |
| Continental | (1958–60) | Two DC-4, four Viking |
| Don Everall | (1951–60) | One Dakota, one Viking |
| Falcon | (1959–61) | Two Hermes, one Viking |
| Maitland Drewery | (1960–61) | Two Viscount 700, two Viking |
| North-South | (1959–61) | One Bristol Freighter, two Heron |
| Orion | (1957–60) | Three Viking |
| Overseas Aviation | (1958–61) | Six Argonaut, six Viking |
| Pegasus (Claydon) | (1958–61) | Three Viking |
| Tradair | (1958–62) | Two Viscount, seven Viking |

During 1960/61 two of the airlines joined BIATA, Air Safaris and Tradair, but that did not help them in the long run. Air Safaris – previously known as African Air Safaris and Meredith – expanded rapidly, first acquiring Don Everall's airline operations and later the two Hermes of Falcon Airways. From Don Everall Air Safaris inherited a considerable number of scheduled licences, mainly from the Midlands to the Channel Islands and Isle of Wight, some of which were operated by Air Safaris in 1961; but most of the airline's business came from IT flying out of Gatwick and the regional airports. The airline entered the history books in a small way when its IT licences were the first applications to be approved by the new Air Transport Licensing Board. Following the collapse of Overseas in 1961, trading conditions became difficult for all the independents; we have already seen how BKS had to call in the receivers and on 2 November Air Safaris suspended operations due to a lack of working capital. Two of its directors, Alan Stocks and Captain de Bounevialle, subsequently joined a small Dakota operator, Air Links, bringing with them three of the Hermes (of which only one ever entered service); the Vikings were sold the following year to Eros, founded by the owner of Cyprus Travel. That was another short-lived charter airline, lasting just two years.

Tradair, meanwhile, continued as an upmarket charter airline flying for Lord Brothers, Hickie Borman and Wings, with Viscounts bought from Aer Lingus. In 1961 it applied for a number of scheduled-service routes, but with a difference in that the services would only be available for block bookings by tour operators. Rather than take the risk of chartering a whole aircraft, tour operators would be able to block somewhat smaller allocations of seats on services to popular destinations; they would be restricted in their days of operation and so would not have complete flexibility, but it was an attractive proposal, trading on the airline's image. The idea was never put into practice, however, as in November 1961 Barclays Bank appointed a receiver. The receiver was given the mandate to achieve profitability within a year and his first action was to ground the Viscounts for the winter, although he secured a contract for one of them to fly for BEA on its internal German services the following summer.

Maitland Drewery stands out for its ambitious purchase of Viscounts, but was unable to find enough work for them and so leased two of them to BKS for the summer of 1961 and then sold them on to Silver City when Maitland Drewery closed down. Leeds-based North-South operated its Herons on domestic scheduled services and the Freighter on inclusive-tour flights; Air Condor used its Freighter on ad hoc charters. Continental was taken over by Keegan in 1959 but after the 1960 summer season, when the airline had carried 40,000 passengers, he closed the airline down and absorbed the aircraft into his other businesses. Pegasus was started by an enterprising Luton builder, Cyril Claydon, and flew its cheerfully painted Vikings around Europe for four years; it even started a scheduled-service link between Gatwick and Blackpool before closing down in October 1961. Two of the airlines achieved greater fame, indeed notoriety: Overseas and Falcon.

By 1960 Overseas had a sizeable fleet of twelve aircraft, and three more of its Argonauts were used by the Danish airline Flying Enterprise. Overseas was trying to move its base to Gatwick, but faced delay getting approval to build a hangar there, meeting with the official obstructionism which was to plague it throughout its short life. Myhill and Dromgoole were still contracting German tour operators out of Berlin, Hamburg and Dusseldorf, and inclusive-tour flying from British regional airports was being developed, helped

A night-time shot of Vickers Viking G-AHPL of Pegasus Airlines, about to depart Newcastle. (MAP)

by the range of the airline's sixty-five-seat Argonauts. Long haul ad hoc charter flying continued and the airline flew regular services to Lourenço Marques from Southend for the Overseas Visitors Club, and from Luxembourg for Trans-Africa Air Coach: attempts to develop other such services to Australia, which Overseas planned to serve through Noumea, fell foul of the Australian authorities.

When finally Overseas was able to open its new hangar at Gatwick in 1960, Dromgoole took the opportunity in a speech to criticise the attitude of BIATA:

> I have not suggested that BIATA have refused membership to Overseas Aviation, but that we
> have been made to feel that we would not be welcome. My view is that there cannot be two
> standards in this business, one set by the Ministry and another by BIATA. This allows BIATA
> to subject companies not favoured by them to non-objective criticism.[26]

BIATA represented some of the older, more established airlines, and there may well have been a feeling prevalent that new airlines should earn their spurs before being allowed to join; historic, grandfather rights always seem to matter in aviation. It meant that the membership was not fully inclusive; it was therefore not only unrepresentative but its members were unable to cooperate with the newer airlines. Competition issues apart, one wonders why an airline with the energy and marketing skills of Overseas should have been shunned by its fellows: 'There is no doubt that non-BIATA independent activities are growing, there now being eleven such operators, some of them, particularly Overseas Aviation, with high reputations, well-run operations and highly competitive prices.'[27]

Overseas began casting its net wider in 1961, applying for a number of domestic scheduled services and evaluating different aircraft types; it was also at last, allowed to become a member of BIATA. The airline purchased fifteen Canadair North Stars from

Trans-Canada Air Lines, similar to the Argonauts. With a fleet of over twenty four-engine aircraft Overseas was turning into a very big player. But Overseas was having trouble paying its bills, although with a last show of bravado the airline inaugurated a 'walk-on' service from Gatwick to Prestwick via Manchester on 31 July. On 15 August the airline's parent company, registered in the Channel Islands, went into voluntary liquidation, owing over £500,000 after BP, its fuel supplier, and Rolls-Royce had applied for the airline to be compulsorily wound up. The liquidators found there were very few assets, however. Overseas Aviation (CI) had no aircraft of its own; these had recently been transferred to, and were now chartered in from, Overseas Aviation Limited, a separate company owned by Mr and Mrs Myhill, which was not affected by the winding-up order. The airline stopped operating, leaving around 5,000 passengers stranded at various European destinations. In the longer term Derby Airways stepped into the breach and acquired five of the former BOAC Argonauts, but the need to re-protect their passengers saw many tour operators scrabbling around for aircraft capacity wherever they could find it; Starways, Air Safaris and Pegasus were the main beneficiaries. The rescue operation worked, nevertheless, and around 18,000 passengers were still able to go on holiday although the tour operators had to carry a loss on the recontracted aircraft, which inevitably were more expensive than the original Overseas' flights.

Falcon, Captain Kozubski's latest airline,[28] moved its fleet of Hermes from Blackbushe to Gatwick during the summer of 1960 where it continued to fly entirely 'off the record'. It managed this by flying for tour operators in a 'non-systematic' way, that is, not to a regular schedule or routing although the tour operators were still able to offer all the usual destinations: Italy, Spain, Corsica, even Morocco. Such tour operators usually offered deep discounts and hefty commissions. Falcon also flew for closed groups, many of which arranged inclusive tours for their members through a travel agent. The writing was on the wall for these operations, however; the new legislation required all charter flights that were resold to individuals to be licensed, regardless of whether they were for closed groups or operated in a non-systematic way. For 1961 the airline had bought four Constellations, all of which needed considerable modifications before they could be operated on the British register; one was duly modified to ARB requirements and when that was completed, a second was sent to Field Aircraft Services for similar work; the third aircraft was placed on the Austrian register with Aero Transport as the operator. Falcon had signed contracts with Captain Langton's Sky Tours to start flying in May, but was already in trouble by March when Kozubski flew the first Constellation, with a plane-load of West Indian immigrants, from Gander to Gatwick with unserviceable radio and navigation equipment and insufficient dinghies on board, for which he was later successfully prosecuted. He did start his summer flying in May but the first aircraft was then withdrawn for further engineering work at the end of June and remained out of service throughout July. Eventually the second Constellation was brought into service in July but was then promptly sold to Trans European, a new and very short-lived airline. Kozubski hoped to fulfil his contracts by flying the Austrian aircraft, but the Ministry, having already imposed extra conditions on the airline's AOC – the airline was limited in its operations to Europe and the Mediterranean – refused to allow the Austrian aircraft, which had not been modified to meet British requirements, to operate Falcon's flights. Falcon was effectively grounded and Air Safaris picked up the Sky Tours contracts which

After the collapse of Overseas, one of its Canadair C-4 Argonauts is seen here in appropriately derelict surroundings at Gatwick. The aircraft carries a Canadian registration and had just been bought from Trans-Canada Air Lines. (MAP)

it flew with its Hermes. The first Constellation returned to service in August and, with the help of the Trans European aircraft, operated a number of flights; in September, after the collapse of Overseas, the Ministry relented and allowed Falcon to use the Austrian aircraft flown by Captain Kozubski and a British crew. Later, in September, the Ministry launched its prosecution (mentioned above) in respect of the Gander-Gatwick flight in March, to which Kozubski pleaded guilty. He and the airline were fined a total of £300 at Bournemouth magistrates' court. On 21 September, with no publicity, the Ministry withdrew Falcon's AOC. It was to be the end of Falcon, which early in 1962 was placed in the hands of a receiver. It was not, however, the end of Kozubski, who continued flying for Aero Transport out of Vienna until October 1964 and then re-emerged briefly in 1965, trading as Britair East African Airways and flying charters between Kenya and Europe. He even managed to re-acquire one of the former Falcon Constellations which he put on the Kenya register, but this venture was short-lived and by the end of the year operations had been suspended.

The combined fleet of this 'second eleven', as at October 1960, came to fifteen four-engine aircraft, and thirty-one twin-engine aircraft, together with some smaller aircraft; equivalent to about one quarter the size of the total BIATA fleet. What is striking is just how few of these airlines had associate agreements approved by the ATAC. Some simply bypassed official channels altogether; Falcon does not appear on any ATAC listings at all. When all airlines had to apply for IT licences from 1961, which now had to include closed groups, *Flight* magazine was somewhat stunned to discover that 75 per cent of the applications came from non-BIATA airlines.[29] Unfortunately it does not follow that these airlines carried 75 per cent of the IT business; many applications were speculative and many more were refused, with dire consequences for the airlines concerned, which

BOAC had bought Lockheed Constellation G-AMUP in 1953, and then sold it on to Capital Airlines. It returned to the British register in 1961 to join Falcon Airways, Capital's eagle symbol doing further duty as a falcon! (MAP)

now could no longer circumvent the regulations. Nor did the number of applications themselves reflect the extent of the flying; applications could cover single flights or whole series, short series, long series and even amendments to previous licences, such as a change of operator or aircraft type:

*Total Number of Passengers Carried (to nearest 1,000) by Independent Operators on Scheduled Services, Inclusive Tours and Contract Charters.*

|  | 1959/60 | 1960/61 | 1961/62 |
|---|---|---|---|
| Channel Islands | 217,000 | 299,000 | 420,000 |
| Isle of Man | 95,000 | 121,000 | 155,000 |
| Other Internal | 54,000 | 125,000 | 241,000 |
| International | 275,000 | 405,000 | 479,000 |
| Vehicle Ferries | 291,000 | 358,000 | 366,000 |
| Colonial Coach | 19,000 | 12,000 | |
| Inclusive Tours | 167,000 | 199,000 | 273,000 |
| Subtotal | 1,118,000 | 1,519,000 | 1,934,000 |
| | | | |
| Contract charter | 173,900 | 396,000 | 301,100 |
| Air trooping | 119,500 | 171,100 | 314,700 |
| | | | |
| Total | 1,411,400 | 2,086,100 | 2,549,800 |

(Source BIATA)

This table is taken from BIATA sources, and covers the critical three years of this chapter. Of note is the increase in contract charter flying, mainly for closed groups, in 1960/61; the table does not include any estimates for closed group flights by non–BIATA airlines, although the figures for scheduled and Inclusive Tour Service are comprehensive, as they are derived from ATAC sources.

# FIVE

# CHANGES
## 1961-1962

## WIND OF CHANGE

Britain's Prime Minister, Harold Macmillan, having led the Conservative Party to victory after its most recent 'Imperial' adventure at Suez, then set about dismantling the British Empire with gusto, famously observing in a speech in 1960 at Cape Town:

> In the twentieth century… we have seen the awakening of national consciousness in peoples who for centuries lived in dependence upon some other power… Today the same thing is happening in Africa, and the most striking of all the impressions I have formed since I left London a month ago is of the strength of this African national consciousness. The wind of change is blowing through this continent, and whether we like it or not, this growth of national consciousness is a political fact.

By the end of the next decade every colony in Africa, apart from Rhodesia, had been granted independence. When the British realised that they did not actually need to retain the whole of Cyprus for their strategic-defence purposes the island was granted independence in 1960, thus side-stepping union with Greece; Britain retained just two so-called Sovereign Base Areas for its own purposes. Malta became independent in 1964; the Federation of Malaya had already achieved independence in 1957 and became Malaysia in 1963 when Singapore, Sabah and Sarawak joined, although Singapore seceded in 1965. Most of these nations retained their links with Britain and with each other through membership of the Commonwealth; Britain in turn maintained its military-treaty obligations with the former colonies as it did with the Gulf States. The end was not yet in sight for Britain's overseas garrisons and bases and there was still another decade of trooping flights to contemplate.

Whilst Harold Macmillan respected the ties with the Commonwealth, he inevitably looked in new directions. Relations with the United States were sometimes strained. After Dean Acheson – formerly the American Secretary of State – had claimed in a speech given at West Point in 1962 that, 'Great Britain has lost an empire and has not yet found a role', Macmillan caustically responded: 'In so far as he appeared to denigrate the resolution and will of Britain and the British people, Mr Acheson has fallen into an error which has been made by quite a lot of people in the course of the last 400 years.' Although he enjoyed good relations with the new American President, John F. Kennedy, Macmillan looked now to Europe and its developing Common Market, led by France and Germany. Macmillan's ties with the French President, General de Gaulle, however, went back to the Second World War, a difficult time for the General as he struggled to maintain the dignity of his defeated country in a largely Anglo-Saxon alliance. The change of focus away from the Commonwealth and former Empire was perhaps too abrupt; moreover the Common Market was structured around an agricultural policy that was a lesser priority for Britain's trading economy. Declaring at a press conference in Paris on 14 January 1963, 'England is insular, maritime, linked by trade, markets and food supply to very different and often very distant lands. She is essentially an industrial and commercial nation, and her agriculture is relatively unimportant', General de Gaulle vetoed Britain's application to join the Common Market.

## THE AIR TRANSPORT LICENSING BOARD (ATLB)

The ATLB set up its stand on 1 December 1960 preparatory to issuing licences from 1 April 1961. Applications for new licences began to roll in. Cunard Eagle's controversial London-New York application, A.1000, was the Board's first. Both British United and Cunard Eagle were quick to put in numerous applications for scheduled services within Europe, within the United Kingdom and further afield, to Africa and the Far East in the case of British United; Cunard Eagle specified London Heathrow or Gatwick, British United wanted Gatwick alone. Frequencies were low, anything between twice daily and twice weekly. In view of later developments it should be remembered that the corporations had no frequency restrictions; they were free to operate as many or as few services as they wished.

The ATLB got off to a bad start when its first chairman, Lord Terrington, died on 7 January 1961. If ever an organisation needed a safe pair of hands to help it through its first paces, it was surely the ATLB which was venturing into new and sometimes hostile lands. Lord Terrington would undoubtedly have been more conservative in his decisions than his successors, and he might well have rejected some of the more glamorous applications; but he would have had the skills and authority to ensure that the Board's decisions were respected.[1] In his place the government appointed Professor Jack, an economist. Although there were no fireworks at the first ever public hearing of the ATLB on 14 March 1961, *Flight's* Air Transport Editor, Mike Ramsden, found the procedures lax, noting that accusations against airlines could be made in public without supporting evidence, which he thought was disquieting: 'No doubt the allegations could have been so supported, but in principle it seemed quite wrong for a man to be pilloried in public without a shred of evidence except that supplied by the accuser.'[2] In short that summed up the structural weakness of the ATLB, which was to remain an amateurish organisation; although it acquired greater knowledge in its chosen field over the following ten years, it never acquired authority, and increasingly lacked conviction.

By mid-summer the Board had a busy programme of hearings planned. Even the corporations were applying for routes and not just objecting to all and sundry. BEA had an interest in new services to Genoa, Malaga and Madeira, but loftily dismissed any suggestions of a deal with British United over European routes. BOAC applied for more African routes, and of course was the major objector to Cunard Eagle's New York bid. British United and Cunard Eagle were slugging it out for European and domestic routes, whilst Starways had applications in for provincial services. Silver City was also applying for passenger routes to Genoa and Madeira, whilst Tradair had its innovative application for scheduled services which would only have been available to travel agents making block bookings for inclusive tours. British United and Cunard Eagle cut a deal before the major European hearing whereby British United withdrew its domestic applications, leaving the field open to Cunard Eagle, and Cunard Eagle in turn withdrew many of its European applications, conceding those routes to British United. Independent airlines, unlike BEA, did not disdain pragmatic and cooperative solutions to licensing issues.

## CUNARD EAGLE AND THE NORTH ATLANTIC

The first 'heavyweight' application to be heard by the Board, starting on 16 May 1961, was from Cunard Eagle, to fly between London Heathrow and New York, although in the manner of all applications, a string of optional points was also inserted (Manchester and Prestwick on the UK side, 'other United States terminals designated in the US-UK agreement' and Montreal and Toronto in North America). Cunard Eagle had already ordered two Rolls-Royce powered Boeing 707s; the announcement of the order was low key as malignant commentators might have wondered aloud how it was that Cunard was perfectly able to finance new jet aircraft when it was at the same time in rather tortuous negotiations with the government over the financing and building of the new Q3 Cunarder.

This was the first hearing in public in which applicant and objectors were represented before the Board by counsel. Cunard Eagle used Norman Ashton Hill, a director of the company and a solicitor; BOAC fielded Henry Fisher QC, son of the then Archbishop of Canterbury. The format followed trial cases. The applicant had already submitted written evidence including traffic forecasts. Ashton Hill opened by stating his company's case and then had to spend most of his time trying to show that if granted, the licence would not cause 'material diversion' from BOAC. Bamberg was called as a witness, as was Sir John Brocklebank, chairman of Cunard, both of them being quizzed on the financing of the proposed Q3 liner and subjected to professed astonishment that Cunard could find £6 million to buy the new Boeings but was unable to afford £12 million for a new liner. Much time was spent going into traffic forecasts. BOAC claimed that it had sufficient aircraft in its fleet to meet all 'reasonable' demand and maintained any incursion by Cunard Eagle would divert traffic away from them. Cunard Eagle put up an impressive witness, its Washington lawyer Robert Beckman, who was thoroughly familiar with CAB procedures and made short shrift of traffic rights issues. Several days later it was the turn of the objector BOAC to state its case, so the procedure was run through again, with Fisher making an introductory statement and then calling his own witnesses, including Smallpeice, all of them cross-examined in turn by Ashton Hill. BOAC's main argument was that it had taken all the time and trouble to develop the market, and now some upstart airline wanted to come along and grab a slice of it, without having first suffered in the way that BOAC had suffered; an argument that was to become all too familiar over the ensuing years and which curiously ignored the restrictions placed on the independents up until the passing of the 1960 Act. Smallpeice did, however, at least try to put a quantifiable figure on 'material diversion'; he thought the loss of 1,000 passengers, representing revenue of £150,000, would be material. The two lawyers concluded the hearing, spread out over five days, by summing up their cases.

Three weeks later the Board announced that it had approved Cunard Eagle for a once-daily service on the London-New York route, which could also serve Manchester, Prestwick, Philadelphia, Boston, Baltimore and Washington DC but not Canadian points. In practice the New York sector was the preferred route. The Board accepted there might be diversion, but thought it wrong that British capacity should be frozen at BOAC's present and future fleet size. BOAC was 'surprised and deeply disappointed' and immediately announced it would appeal against the decision, hinting darkly that it might have to cancel some of the VC10s on order,[3] a threat rightly calculated to throw the Ministry of Aviation into a fit.

## EUROPEAN AND DOMESTIC APPLICATIONS

The tone of the European and domestic hearings which took place in June and July was somewhat more cordial than the Cunard Eagle North Atlantic case, but the hearings were more complex with a large number of competing applications and cross objections. Cunard Eagle was already operating a European network, however small, but apart from some Italian routes preferred to concentrate its applications on domestic routes which would serve as feeders for its long-haul traffic, not just to Bermuda and the Caribbean but now to New York. British United was not, at this stage, a significant scheduled-service operator; aside from the African services, Morton's third-level routes, and the Channel Air Bridge, it was primarily a charter airline and principal contractor for trooping flights, indeed it had just been awarded the German trooping contract to add to all the other contracts it held. Regional and domestic scheduled routes were flown by non-BUA companies such as Silver City, BKS and Jersey Airlines. However British United intended to invest in scheduled services and had recently announced plans to build a terminal at Victoria railway station which would serve the fast, electric train services to Gatwick Airport station. Laker was one of the main witnesses; he pointed out that a major company like British United needed a share of scheduled services to provide a reasonable degree of security and as compensation for the future loss of business; trooping contracts were marginal, and he thought inclusive-tour-charter flights could be finished within ten years as a result of the incursions made by BEA and its ITX fares (special IT fares available on scheduled services). Understanding this point helps explain why British United laboriously realigned itself over the next few years away from charter operations and into scheduled services. Scheduled services were always perceived as more prestigious, and had, in any case, effectively been denied to the independents since the war, but Laker's analysis was at variance with a number of other airline operators, many of whom successfully operated IT charters for the next three or four decades. Cunard Eagle worked to a different commercial blueprint which envisaged its business as being supported by three 'pillars', namely scheduled services, inclusive tours and government contract work; should one of these fail there would always be two other pillars to support the airline.

When it came to making its case BEA called many distinguished witnesses, including Sir George Cribbett to help on international issues. Traffic rights and bilateral agreements figured largely in the various examinations; there was genuine uncertainty as to how other European countries would react to the designation of a second British airline. BEA also called Stephen Wheatcroft, a consultant and economic adviser to the corporation and author of one of the first studies of airline economics, *The Economics of European Air Transport*. Though undoubtedly an expert witness he must have wished at times that not quite so many people had read his book, as passages from it were used against him by the other applicants who gleefully quoted his then expressed views on pooling, competition and cross-subsidisation, all of which seemed at variance now with his views as economic adviser to BEA, the arch-advocate of pooling arrangements in Europe. He riposted that some time had passed since the book was written and conditions had changed.[4] There was further embarrassment when the Board came to consider some of the specific applications, in particular the route to Genoa. BEA had objected to British United's application on the grounds that there was no potential need or demand for the service. One month later the corporation had then put in its own application for the Genoa route, claiming that traffic would exceed that to Milan or Nice. Anthony Milward, chief executive, had the good grace to admit that the two statements did not appear to 'clew up' but went on to claim that if there was to be any 'wasteful duplication', he would prefer BEA to do its own duplicating. His socialist chief Lord Douglas fulminated in the witness stand, one moment claiming that the independent airlines were attempting in effect a takeover of part of a nationally owned undertaking without payment of compensation,[5] then issuing threats about the future of his Trident orders:

> We had previously foreseen a requirement for additional aircraft, and we had hoped to be able to meet this requirement by ordering a developed version with larger seating capacity... But it is obvious that decisions of this kind cannot be made at the present time: far from knowing that we have a requirement for more developed Tridents we cannot currently feel sure that the aircraft we already have on order will actually be required in the years ahead.[6]

## CUNARD EAGLE, THE NORTH ATLANTIC AND THE APPEAL

'It is my intention,' said Duncan Sandys when Minister of Aviation 'that the Board shall be independent.' Under the new regulations the Minister appointed a commissioner to hear the appeal, but he was not bound by the Commissioner's recommendation. *Flight* summed up the situation neatly:

> It is by no means a foregone conclusion that Cunard Eagle will get their licence, particularly as the Minister must be as concerned as BOAC about the corporation's really serious surplus of capacity on the North Atlantic. But if he vetoes the Board's first major decision he will confirm what has always been suspected – that the Board is only as independent as the Minister, guardian of the corporations, wants it to be. The Minister will have to balance his responsibilities to BOAC with those that he bears towards the British aircraft industry.

He will also have to take into account possible trade union reaction towards independent competition on one of BOAC's plum routes.[7]

The Minister duly appointed a retired High Court judge, Sir Fred Pritchard, to hear the appeal. The Commissioner had first to consider whether the Board had interpreted the law correctly. Unfortunately he was also allowed to consider any new evidence that either party, the original applicant or the appellant, might lodge; this meant that the Commissioner was in effect re-hearing the whole case. It was a sloppy process, and fatal to the working of the 1960 Act and to the credibility of the Board. Considering and, if necessary, correcting the Board's interpretation of the law was a proper function of the Commissioner: re-hearing the case was not. The North Atlantic appeal was not the first appeal to be heard; that dubious distinction went to Falcon Airways which had appealed a decision not to allow it to fly a short inclusive-tour series to Tangiers and Malaga. In that case the Commissioner had given a Solomonic judgement (he had been rather shocked by the lack of veracity shown by both the Falcon and the BEA witnesses) but the Minister decided to dismiss the appeal.

When the North Atlantic appeal came to be heard in September the two parties disagreed over the issue of new evidence. Not surprisingly BOAC, which was suffering a decline in its North Atlantic traffic, exacerbated by two strikes in June, argued that this affected the traffic forecasts; Cunard Eagle dissented, but the Commissioner agreed to hear the new evidence and accepted the argument that BOAC had sufficient capacity for its needs on the routes in question. In its evidence BOAC also declared cynically that it had a duty to support the British aircraft industry:

> BOAC has as a matter of policy assisted the development of new British aircraft by giving firm orders… If some of the traffic is taken away from BOAC and there is an ever present threat that, as soon as they have developed a route and made it profitable, a second operator will be allowed in on it, BOAC will not be able to give these firm orders in the future.[8]

Unremarked at the time, in May BOAC had just ordered three more Boeing 707s; indeed, apart from Concorde, BOAC never ordered another British built aircraft. It cancelled a few, though. Aside from this bluff BOAC did however have some real problems in 1961; it had a surplus of aircraft, and was dilatory in adjusting its route structure to accommodate weakening demand, which led to a ten-point drop in its load factor. The corporation therefore made a substantial operating loss in the year, which meant it could not cover its fixed interest dividend, so had to borrow more, which merely increased the deficit still further. The worsening crisis was known, if not always understood, at the Ministry. As it steeled itself for more bad news from the corporation, the Ministry had to reconcile these unpalatable facts with its stated intention of allowing the ATLB its 'independence'.

## DECISIONS, DECISIONS

The Commissioner sent in his recommendation on the North Atlantic appeal to the Minister on 10 October 1961, but it was not divulged until 21 November. There was then a positive rush of mostly bad news: in very short order the new Minister of Aviation, Peter

Thorneycroft, first accepted the Commissioner's stunning decision to revoke Cunard Eagle's North Atlantic licence; he then announced in a debate in the House of Commons two days later that BOAC was going to lose £10 million that year, the corporation's largest ever loss; the following Tuesday, 28 November, the ATLB announced all its decisions in the European/domestic/Channel Islands route applications.

'The Minister's decision is unfortunate not because an independent is not to be allowed to compete with a corporation, but because it is a decision that undermines the authority of the Board,' so opined Ramsden in *Flight*.[9] Thorneycroft's decision undermined the fledgling Board's authority from the very start of its existence, but of course his decision did not merely encompass the rights and wrongs of the case. The Commissioner was influenced by the very short-term downturn in traffic which all North Atlantic carriers were experiencing as they swamped the routes with newly bought Boeing 707s and Douglas DC-8s, but his main disagreement with the Board was over the matter of 'wasteful duplication'. He accepted the contention that BOAC had sufficient aircraft on hand and on order to cater for all traffic that might reasonably be expected over the next five or six years, and that was good enough for him. But Thorneycroft also perceived ambivalence on the part of Cunard which seemed forever to be re-evaluating its future policies and interests, including its aviation investment. More seriously, Cunard had decided in October not to go ahead with the building of the Q3 express transatlantic liner despite generous government assistance, which the Cabinet regarded as a blow to the ship-building industry and an affront to the government. Finally, the Commissioner had ruled in favour of BOAC, however dubious the legal process; doubtless the men from the Ministry were not too sorry to see the new Board emasculated so early on.

Reaction was mostly unhappy. British United immediately withdrew its pending long-haul applications, saying that such a decision made a farce of the Act and of hearings by the Board. Ramsden, writing in *Flight* magazine and having recently complimented Cunard Eagle on its professional level of service, was dismayed:

I can well appreciate the bitter disillusionment of Cunard Eagle and of its parent – disillusionment that must amount almost to a feeling of betrayal. My own reaction is one of regret that the name Cunard, a national asset which in America has the prestige of the name Rolls-Royce, is not to be allowed to serve Britain in the air as it has for so long (until air transport intervened) on the sea. This seems not only unfortunate, but unjust.'[10]

*The Aeroplane* thought the right decision had been made but for the wrong reasons:

The justification for the decision rests with the present situation for the air transport business in which – because of the competitive over-purchase by the World's airlines of long-haul turbojets – far too much capacity is already being offered and … it will be two or three years before the North Atlantic traffic has caught up with this capacity.[11]

The magazine did not accept that the decision should have been influenced by BOAC's aircraft purchases and regarded the whole process as a costly fiasco. Cunard's interest in its airline evaporated overnight; what happened subsequently is told later but for the time being the airline industry lost the value of the prestigious Cunard name as well as the undoubted marketing assistance that this powerful organisation could have given its airline, especially in the western hemisphere. The airline decided to suspend all its scheduled-service operations out of Manchester and began to hunt for a buyer for the now surplus Boeing 707s it had ordered.

J.E.D. Williams summed up the Cunard Eagle debacle succinctly in his 1967 Barnwell Memorial Lecture to the Royal Aeronautical Society:

> The test of whether the government of the day really would permit competition came with the Cunard Eagle application in 1961 to operate the North Atlantic in competition with Pan American, TWA and BOAC. The portents could not have been more favourable. Eagle was a successful independent which had been taken over by Cunard, the leading passenger carrier on the sea route. Cunard provided the capital and the marketing skills and resources in the US. Boeing 707 aircraft had been ordered for the job. Virtually since the end of the war there had been two American carriers and one British carrier. The British carrier had always carried the kitten's share of the traffic. Indeed, BOAC only operated thirty-nine out of the 113 services offered weekly on the London-New York route in the summer of 1963. The application was heard, the licence was granted on 10 July 1961 for fifteen years. BOAC appealed, the Minister, a Conservative, revoked the licence. The Civil Aviation Licensing Act would never be the same again and few indeed are the international routes on which independents have been allowed to compete with the corporations, although independents do have a growing share of scheduled international services by the development of traffic from other UK centres or to destinations not served by the corporations.[12]

Perhaps the final word on the decision can appropriately be left to the victor who thought the whole process had just been a nuisance and a waste of time; Smallpeice's comment points up the corporation's disdain for the new order: 'The outcome was very gratifying. Though the time we had to spend in warding off this threat was wholly negative, it did serve to establish future guidelines for the Licensing Board.'[13]

After the setback of Cunard Eagle's New York licence, the Board's decisions on the European and domestic applications came as an anti-climax, now that the licensing process was revealed as merely the first step in obtaining the route rights. The Board explained its guidelines on competition and how it should affect BEA. First of all, there was to be no competition until the end of the 1962/63 year; then competition would be regulated so that only some of BEA's estimated traffic growth during the ensuing three years would go to the independents and, after three years, BEA's traffic could resume its growth. It must have looked convincing in graph form, but in practice frequency restrictions hobbled any worthwhile competitive challenge; the independents were only to be allowed to carry the 'growth', in other words the demand curve would flatten out for BEA, but the independents could aspire to the putative area of demand that was left – had the curve continued rising. Traffic rights issues were also sidestepped, although the Board was aware that the same Ministry that had effectively cut the ground away from under its feet was also going to be responsible for negotiating traffic rights for a second British airline, though with rather less enthusiasm.

One small point in the independent's favour, however, was BEA's profitability. Owing to the fact that BEA was not in crisis, it did not need quite so much pampering as BOAC.

Furthermore the Ministry knew that there would be a good chance that many of the European governments would refuse to accept a second British carrier, or insist that its share came from the British half of the pool; whereas there was every reason to believe that the Americans would have accepted a second British carrier on the New York route. Even so, the Board still managed to refuse more than it granted when its decisions became known. British United appeared to do best, in what was only the first step in a lengthy and uncertain process, gaining the new route to Genoa as well as Paris, Amsterdam, Zurich, and Milan, together with the predominantly IT routes to Basle, Athens, Tarbes, Barcelona, Palma, Malaga, Lisbon and Madeira; but it was refused anything to Germany, Brussels, Rome, Naples and Dublin. Frequencies were either once a day or fewer, except for Paris, which was twice daily. Cunard Eagle gained some domestic routes from London Heathrow to Edinburgh, Glasgow and Belfast – each route with seven frequencies a week, but the Edinburgh route was cut back to only five flights a week during winter – and also was awarded some European points at low frequencies, Geneva, Copenhagen, Stockholm, and Dublin. Starways gained Chester-Isle of Man but all the applications by Channel, Tradair and Silver City were refused. BEA was awarded Marseilles and Malaga. The airlines all reacted differently. Predictably BEA appealed all the decisions whilst British United quietly accepted its grants and refusals. Cunard Eagle appealed both the refusals and the frequency limitations and so did Starways. Silver City threw in the towel and accepted all of its adverse decisions, as did Channel and Tradair.

## YOUNG HOPEFULS IN 1961

Despite the setbacks, new airlines were anxious to get started. One such was Lloyd International which bought a Skymaster and began freight and ad hoc passenger charter flying from Cambridge; its chairman, Jaime Ortiz-Patino, was Bolivian but the two managing directors, Brian Lloyd and Alasdair Macleod, gave the airline its name and 'Dunvegan Castle' crest respectively. Air Links, a new Dakota operator based at Gatwick which went on to assume the mantle of Air Safaris, found there was still business to be had if one went out and looked for it; some of their deals were reminiscent of the early post-war days of charter flying, flying for oil companies out of Las Palmas, carrying live lobsters to France, operating freight services for scheduled airlines within Europe. Autair, the helicopter operator, bought Dakotas and launched an IT flying programme in 1961. But the year which saw nine charter airlines close down also saw the birth of two new airlines, both of which helped change the course of British aviation: Caledonian and Euravia, later known as Britannia.

Caledonian started flying on 28 November 1961, its DC-7C leased from the Belgian airline Sabena. Originally formed with the backing of Max Wilson's Overseas Visitors Club, which had previously used Overseas, the new airline planned to participate in the long-haul affinity group market. Indeed, its second flight was to Lourenço Marques, the unofficial charter gateway to South Africa. Some well-known names joined the company early; John de la Haye as managing director and Captain Adam Thomson as deputy managing director, Frank Hope as the commercial director and David Parlane as the operations manager.

Autair's Dakota G-AMGD spent most of its time leased to a short-lived British carrier, Continental Air Services. Previously Autair had flown helicopters. (MAP)

Euravia was formed by aviation economist turned consultant J.E.D. Williams and his partner John Harrington, a former operations director at BOAC who had joined Imperial Airways in1931; they were backed by Captain Langton and his company, Universal Sky Tours. It was a carefully crafted airline; much thought was given to the relationship between the tour operator and the airline, the size and range of the aircraft relative to the flying that would be required, and the utilisation that was feasible. The airline needed three aircraft with around eighty seats each; the aircraft needed to be inexpensive because annual utilisation would be low initially; the plan was to convert to more modern aircraft, most likely Britannias, in three years' time. So the carrier bought three eighty-two-seat Constellations from El Al, from whom they also acquired Derek Davison, its first Chief Pilot. The Constellations had a lower initial cost than the comparable DC-6, important as the aircraft were to be amortised over the short four-month summer season; the airline aimed to achieve around 3,500 hours for the three aircraft during the summer, with another 1,500 hours in the remaining eight months. Universal Sky Tours, scarred by its experience over the past three summer seasons, was the first tour operator to participate in a dedicated charter airline. During 1959 it had contracted with Independent and suffered from the bad publicity following the airline's Viking crash. The following year the tour operator bought its own Skymaster which was operated for it by Continental, but that airline closed down at the end of 1960. The next year, Universal Sky Tours thought it had picked another winner in Falcon, and then saw most of its summer operation subchartered out; the flying was eventually taken over by Air Safaris and its Hermes, hardly an alluring prospect given the Hermes's limited range. Air Safaris also failed. After such a bad experience, the tour operator thought there must be a better way and approached Williams. The new airline was based at Luton and was called Euravia, in

Caledonian's Douglas DC-7C G-ARYE *Flagship Bonnie Scotland* was leased from the Belgian airline Sabena in 1962. (MAP)

An aircraft with a history, Euravia's Lockheed Constellation G-AHEL had flown previously for Captain Kozubski's airline Falcon Airways, and subsequently returned to him and his airline Britair East Africa in 1964. (MAP)

tune with Britain's Common Market aspirations at the time; as these were subsequently rebuffed by General de Gaulle, its later name, Britannia Airways, is also appropriate!

## KEEPING THEM FLYING

An airline like Euravia quickly established its own maintenance organisation; Caledonian preferred to entrust its engineering to the airline from which it was leasing the DC-7C, Sabena, at least for the time being. In 1952 Eagle had bought out Britavia's engineering company at Blackbushe, Aviation Servicing, thus securing its own maintenance facilities. Dan-Air established its engineering organisation at Lasham in Hampshire. Each airline adopted a course of action appropriate to its requirements. Another solution was to contract with an independent maintenance organisation and by the late 1950s many of the smaller start-up airlines used such contractors, one of the reasons why so many were able to begin operations; strategically located at Gatwick, Air Couriers was much in demand. The same principle applied to aircraft ground- and passenger-handling; Dan-Air was an early concessionaire at Gatwick, providing handling services for some of the smaller airlines, and like Derby Airways, was quick to offer handling at regional airports too.

Airlines that started operations immediately after the Second World War had perforce to devote a great deal of time, money and energy to keeping their aircraft in the air. A legacy of wartime requirements, some engines barely managed fifty hours between overhauls. Airline operators had to assemble large engineering organisations to stay in business. Skyways had employed over 1,000 people at its base at Dunsfold in Surrey and others – like Airwork and Scottish Aviation – also had large engineering establishments which had been at work flat out during the war and now turned to commercial work: overhaul, maintenance, rebuilding and modification to civil requirements. Even if an airline did not have its own engineering function, it could still turn to another commercial organisation. Bond Air Services were kept flying during the Berlin Airlift through the efforts of Laker's Aviation Traders, and many small airlines depended on the other centre of engineering excellence at Southend, BKS Engineering. At this stage pre-war methods of inspection were still implemented; maintenance entailed a pre-flight inspection and the issue of a daily Certificate of Safety, followed by periodic inspections. The Certificate of Airworthiness for each aircraft was renewed at yearly intervals, and before renewal it was usual to undertake a complete overhaul of the aircraft involving dismantling and opening up which could cause an aircraft to remain out of service for periods up to two months. From 1948 the Air Registration Board, in cooperation with the various operators, began to draw up maintenance schedules for each type of aircraft, defining inspection periods and checks, routine maintenance and the times at which various components were to be overhauled. The concept of major overhaul before the renewal of the Certificate of Airworthiness was abandoned, and the intention was to maintain a good continuous standard of airworthiness, rather than allow a gradual fall-off until the major annual overhaul.

As the annual utilisation of aircraft in the immediate post-war years was moderate, seldom exceeding 1,000 to 1,500 hours, the cycles of routine inspections seem restrictive by modern standards. A large airliner typically had a check cycle of: Check A, daily; Check 1, after 50 hours flying; Check 2, after 150 hours; Check 3, after 300 hours and

Hunting Dakota receives attention during a periodic maintenance check at sister company Field
Aircraft Services. (Flight)

Check 4, after 1,200 hours. Hunting's Vikings needed a Check 1 each time the aircraft
returned from a Colonial Coach service to Nairobi. But this system did obviate the need
for an annual two-month overhaul and in 1949 the requirement for the issue of a daily
Certificate of Safety was also withdrawn. Further changes to maintenance requirements
came about as a result of the Berlin Airlift after it was realised that increasing check cycles
and overhaul periods as an emergency measure had had no real adverse effect. By the
beginning of the 1960s annual utilisation in some cases had increased to 3,500 hours, but
experience had shown that there was no reduction in safety standards from an extension
of the various maintenance and overhaul periods; a Check 3 might now take place after
6,000 hours, and a Check 4 after 12,000 hours.[14]

As more modern and more reliable aircraft entered service, heavy-engineering
workloads eased, although the lack of flying opportunities in winter had at least allowed
aircraft to be overhauled prior to the next season's summer flying. However, Airwork was
justifiably pleased when it first managed to obtain approval to extend the time between
overhauls on its Hercules engines to 1,000 hours; many airlines were grateful for the
reliability of these legendary engines which powered the ubiquitous Viking, Hermes and
Bristol Freighter variants. When the first Viscounts entered service in the late 1950s they
brought with them even greater reliability but at a financial cost. Their Rolls-Royce Darts
may have had an overhaul life of 3,000 hours – sometimes even as high as 5,000 hours –
but the Viscount's expensive purchase price required year-round business opportunities.

## BRITISH UNITED GETS BIGGER

The backers of British United Airways had formed Air Holdings on 3 November 1961, which now held the issued share capital of the airline and was to be the vehicle for acquiring further companies. On 23 January 1962, Air Holdings announced it was taking over British Aviation Services – Britavia – the parent company of Silver City and Manx, thus bringing together the two largest independent airline groupings. P&O retained a minority shareholding, now with the other shipping lines, British and Commonwealth, Furness Withy and Blue Star Line. Silver City and Manx were significant scheduled-service operators, but as we have seen, Britavia had had almost no success developing long-haul flying; it was almost the reverse of the British United experience. British United was profitable, having turned in surpluses both in 1960 and 1961, but Silver City had accumulated a deficit of around £1.5 million over the previous three years. One of the Group's first actions was to transfer Silver City's passenger operation out of Manston to Gatwick, bringing the Silver Arrow service with it; the car-ferry services at Ferryfield were not affected. Then the car-ferry operations were combined with Channel Air Bridge under the British United Air Ferries name; the services were largely unchanged but now came under the control of Douglas Whybrow, Laker's commercial manager. Silver City and Channel Air Bridge had complementary rather than overlapping car-ferry networks; Southend-based Channel Air Bridge had by now successfully introduced the Carvair on to its longer-haul flights from Southend to Basle, Geneva and Strasbourg, and Silver City ran its high-frequency shuttle between Ferryfield and Le Touquet.

In May it was the turn of Jersey Airlines to be acquired by Air Holdings, bringing its dynamic managing director Maldwyn Thomas into the group, as well as a sizeable and well-run organisation. In October the two 'island' networks, Jersey Airlines and Silver City's Northern Division, were amalgamated under Thomas to form British United (CI) Airways, based in Jersey, and the respected name of Jersey Airlines disappeared. The combined fleet was soon repainted in British United colours and comprised four Heralds, with two more on order, thirteen Dakotas and two Herons for the Alderney services (which had a short 950ft grass runway). The four Heralds boosted capacity during the busy summer period, carrying over 124,000 passengers in their first year of service, flying from Jersey to Glasgow, Manchester, Exeter and Paris, and via Guernsey to Gatwick and Bournemouth. During the winter months they were also used to operate leisurely inclusive tours direct from Jersey to Tenerife and Marrakesh, and from Gatwick to Athens and Rhodes, chartered by Stephen and Christopher Lord, the Lord Brothers. Their entry into service was remarkably trouble-free, in contrast to BOAC's unhappy experiences with the Britannia. Silver City's radio-calibration contract passed to Morton Air Services, Air Holdings' jack-of-all-trades subsidiary which had also taken over many of the newspaper contracts previously held by Transair; its Herons and Doves flew mainly third-level services, but the fleet of four Dakotas transferred to it had allowed a rapid expansion of charter work.

In a reprise of Airwork's role in the early post-war years in the Sudan, British United took over the management of Sierra Leone Airways in 1961, following Nigerian independence and the break up of the West African Airways Corporation. A Heron and Twin Pioneer were based at Freetown for local services, and British United operated a weekly Britannia flight to London Gatwick on behalf of Sierra Leone.

Morton was a long term user of the DH104 Dove. G-ANAN spent time chartered to the oil company Burmah Oil. (MAP)

The new airline made other news. For two months during the summer of 1962 British United operated the world's first passenger hovercraft service, using a Vickers VA-3 twenty-four-seat craft to ply across the Dee Estuary between Moreton and Rhyl. Although the experimental service proved popular, the hovercraft was plagued by technical problems and bad weather, which led to around 40 per cent of the services being cancelled. More successful was Myles Wyatt's address to the Institute of Transport on 11 February 1963 when he delivered the twentieth Brancker Memorial Lecture 'British Independent Aviation – Past and Future', the first time that anyone connected with the independent airlines had been so honoured. Wyatt had been at the helm of Airwork and its successor for over sixteen years, and his lecture marked the passing of those years as he looked back over the development of civil aviation, wondered why the shipping companies had become involved in air transport and worried about the future. The lecture is reproduced in full at Appendix Six.

In a parallel development the French independent airlines were also regrouping into larger units at this time; on 1 October 1963 the two largest privately owned airlines, TAI and UAT, agreed to merge to form Union de Transports Aeriens (UTA). UTA was much like British United, a company that enjoyed substantial backing from shipping companies. The combined fleet ran to six Douglas DC-8s, two DC-7Cs, fifteen DC-6s and six DC-4 Skymasters; what is noticeable is the quality of the French equipment: modern turbojets as well as relatively new piston-engine aircraft. Furthermore, under a more enlightened government policy the French independents were able to operate long-haul scheduled services to Africa, the Far East and French possessions in the Pacific; Air France withdrew from some African markets to allow UTA sole French rights in most of Africa, from which evolved a 'spheres of influence' policy. Eventually UTA would emerge as the French flag carrier in Africa, to the West Coast of the United States and in the Pacific. This left Air France routes in Europe, North and South America, the Middle and Far East. Domestic services were in the hands of Air Inter, part-owned by Air France and the other French carriers, and French Railways also had an interest. The French approach was pragmatic and met the aspirations of many sectors of the French transport industry; it compared favourably with the strife which was such a feature of the British air transport industry.

## INCLUSIVE TOURS

The Air Transport Licensing Board issued the first large batch of IT licences at the beginning of 1962. The most popular destination was Palma, Majorca, followed by Perpignan in France – the entry point for the Spanish Costa Brava. Basle was also important as a centre for coach tours. British United picked up extra business from Air Safaris and Tradair, and was by far the largest and most successful applicant, followed by Silver City and Derby. BKS, still in receivership, at first had its applications refused – reflecting a tougher attitude on the part of the Board towards financial fitness – but the Board eventually relented. There were some new names: Euravia, Caledonian, Lloyd International and Air Links.

The Board refused more applications than it granted, continuing its predecessor's tradition of managing the process like a lottery. This procedure, designed to protect European scheduled carriers and BEA, had by now evolved into one of those classic British scenarios wherein the British happily cut off their nose to spite their face. British charter airlines needed traffic rights to fly to the countries of destination, mainly France, Spain and Italy. As tourist development boomed in these countries, they too began to form their own charter airlines in order to participate in the traffic. Of course French, Italian and Spanish charter airlines had in turn to apply to the British authorities for traffic rights in order to pick up holiday-makers in the United Kingdom, but the British had no legitimate excuse to refuse these applications, and possibly understood that any refusals would have been met by reciprocal action on the part of foreign governments; if the British denied an application by a Spanish airline, the Spanish authorities would start refusing applications for traffic rights from British airlines.

The tour operators understood this but nevertheless needed to secure their holiday programmes. In the past they might have restructured their flying operations or signed up their clients to join a closed group, but these options were no longer available. Now, if an application was refused by the Board, the tour operator merely contracted the flying to a foreign airline, secure in the knowledge that this second application could not be denied; by 1961 around a quarter of the business was in the hands of foreign airlines. Through its actions the Board was effectively giving business to foreign airlines which it had denied to British carriers, contrary to its policy objective 'to further the development of British Civil Aviation'. By 1962 the foreign airlines' share of the inclusive-tour business had gone up to a third,[15] although some of this business would have been garnered legitimately following the collapse of so many British independent airlines in 1960 and 1961.

The government further tightened the screws on charter airlines when it decided that from 1 May 1963 charter flights 'operated on a frequent basis' would be banned from London Heathrow (previously known as London Airport) and would have to use London Gatwick instead, starting a tiresome sequence of actions that would ultimately reserve Heathrow to the corporations and foreign airlines, and deny it to British independents. Cunard Eagle with its base already firmly established at Heathrow was not affected, but it meant that British United was consigned to Gatwick.

Newcomer Euravia found itself being objected to by a slew of airlines, BEA, British United and Cunard Eagle, when it sought licences formerly applied for by Tradair and Air Safaris. Even the Board was disgruntled, claiming that the tour operator should not have advertised the service until the licences had been approved. Nevertheless the Board did approve the bulk of the applications, and Euravia took to the skies on 5 May 1962 – flying from Manchester to Palma. At this time package holidays usually lasted one or two weeks. Universal Sky Tours wanted to pioneer the eleven- and twelve-day holiday, believing there was a market for holidays of that duration which would compare favourably in price with those already offered by coach operators, but allow much more time at the holiday destination. The Board was suspicious at first and rejected most of these applications for 1963; Williams was outspoken in his criticism of the Board's actions:

> What the Board is really doing is deciding which tour operators will be allowed to fly (under their own trade-mark) by British airlines to which resorts. Even if such a decision were desirable, the Board is incompetent for this task; its terms of reference do not provide adequate criteria for decision. The only possible effects of this major facet of ATLB activity is to prevent people in the lower-income groups from having air holidays abroad, to divert British passengers to foreign charter airlines of varying standards of safety and to harass British airlines and travel organisations and render them economically less efficient.[16]

But by 1964 the Board relented sufficiently to allow Universal Sky Tours to sell these tours of longer duration, and Euravia and Universal went on to exploit the strong economic framework of their joint enterprise. IT flying of that era was concentrated at weekends, but this caused scheduling problems; Euravia's fleet of aircraft might fly fourteen flights on a Saturday or Sunday but never more than four flights a day in mid-week. By flying the aircraft both mid-week and at weekends Euravia evened out the peak somewhat, and increased the utilisation of its fleet, spreading the capital costs and overheads over more flying hours. By concentrating on just a few destinations the tour operator was able to boost volume at those resorts and, by offering them more business, negotiate better deals for hotel rooms; by applying these system-design principles, the airline and tour operator were able to fill the aircraft seats and the hotel beds so that there was no wasted accommodation. The two companies were also quick to understand the importance of regional marketing in the inclusive-tour business; Universal and Euravia brought the business to the local airports, establishing departure airports at Newcastle, Glasgow and Manchester. They were not the first – indeed many other tour operators had appreciated the strength of demand in the north of England and Scotland and had operated accordingly – but it is typical of the professional way that Universal and Euravia chose to do business that they were able to draw together all the components of a package tour and deliver an attractive product.

A familiar name reappeared on the licensing scene in mid-summer when Wing Commander Hugh Kennard applied for IT licences for a new Manston-based airline, Air Ferry, which he proposed to form in association with his long-standing tour operator partner, Leroy Tours, following the example of Euravia. Leroy had built up an extensive programme of flying with Silver City but following its exit, needed a new carrier. Manston's now empty concrete runways tipped the scales in preference to Rochester as a base, the latter a more attractive location but handicapped by its grass runway. Equipped with two Vikings and two Skymasters, Air Ferry was duly launched on 30 March 1963 flying mainly inclusive-tour flights for Leroy Tours.

Harold Bamberg brought together two well-known names in British tour operating when he combined Sir Henry Lunn and Poly Travel late in 1962, forming Lunn Poly Travel. Both were very old names; Sir Henry Lunn had been knighted for his services in making travel arrangements for the German Kaiser and Poly Travel was a pioneer of inclusive tours by air that had used Airwork in the immediate post-war years.

## OTHER LICENCES

BEA was not alone in objecting to charter licences. BOAC took an aggressive stance against newcomer Caledonian when the latter applied for a licence to fly to New Zealand on behalf of Max Wilson's Overseas Visitors Club (OVC); curiously the corporation had not objected to similar applications from British United on behalf of the OVC to fly to Rhodesia. BOAC claimed that the OVC was advertising in breach of charter regulations and the Board accepted the claim, denying Caledonian the licence. This was followed by further bad news when the South African authorities denied Wilson's operating company in South Africa a licence, forcing him to continue to use Lourenço Marques as his entry point. Trek Airways was by now the designated South African carrier on the low-fare route to Luxembourg, having entered into a symbiotic relationship with South African Airways, and put up a vigorous objection to Wilson's airline, which would have used Caledonian's aircraft. Caledonian itself suffered a major setback on 4 March 1962 when its DC-7C crashed at Douala, in the Cameroun Republic, killing all 101 passengers and ten crew whilst operating for Trans-Africa Air Coach, another of Wilson's companies. But the airline quickly secured a replacement DC-7C from Sabena and was operating again from 5 April. Wilson sold out and control of the airline passed to Airways Interests (Thomson), a Scottish company formed by the directors of Caledonian.

Caledonian then had to face the next challenge from BOAC, which applied to restrict its fifth-freedom operations, in an attempt to prevent it from carrying its long-haul affinity passengers into and out of Europe; this would have had a severe impact on its Luxembourg-Lourenço Marques flights for OVC. Caledonian chose to use its American lawyer Leonard Bebchick to represent it before the Board; not the first time that an American lawyer had appeared before the ATLB, as Robert Beckman had already appeared as a witness for Cunard Eagle, but it was the first time an American lawyer had led. American aviation lawyers were already familiar with tribunal processes through the CAB, and brought a degree of expertise and professionalism to British hearings. He pointed out that restricting the licence would merely take business away from a British

Air Ferry's Skymaster G-APYK came to the airline in 1963 from another independent, Starways of Liverpool. (MAP)

airline; Caledonian had taken over the contract from the Finnish airline Kar-Air and doubtless if Caledonian were not allowed to operate, the contract would revert to another European airline. Nevertheless the Board was cowed by BOAC and although it refused to grant the BOAC application in this instance, it warned that in future it might 'impose a general condition restricting fifth freedom charter flights to those not of the character of a scheduled service.'[17] Of course, the decision begged the question as to what was, or was not, a scheduled service, a definition that had eluded Britain's regulators for the past fifteen years.

By this time Caledonian was turning away from South African flying and beginning to look for new markets. Both the Luxembourg and Portuguese authorities had begun to restrict fifth freedom operations. Instead, Caledonian decided to enter the European inclusive-tour market, and in a further move, to develop low-fare charter flights to the United States, planning fifty such flights for the summer of 1963. After no more than the usual bureaucratic delays, and against objections from Pan American and TWA, President Kennedy signed the order granting Caledonian its permit for three years on 17 June 1963, the first charter permit granted by the Americans to a British airline.[18] Successfully trading on its Scottish name, the airline began to operate affinity group flights to and from Prestwick in Scotland as well as serving the English market.

## TROOPING

By now there were only two main trooping contractors, British United and Cunard Eagle.[19] Cunard Eagle retained the Medair contract around the Mediterranean bases and now held the West Med contract to Gibraltar, Malta and North Africa. British United flew to Germany and was the prime long-haul contractor to Singapore, Hong Kong, Aden, Cyprus and Nairobi. After a dip in numbers the totals had begun rising again, following the award of the German contracts. In 1961 the number of troops carried by air surpassed the number carried by sea for the first time. Even though carriage by air was steadily rising, the government had put into service – as recently as 1956 – two new troopships, the *Nevasa* and *Oxfordshire*, which were mainly used on the Singapore run. Following recommendations from the Estimates Committee, the Minister of Defence, still Harold Watkinson, bowed to the inevitable and accepted that all future trooping contracts would be by air, announcing in May that the contracts for the *Oxfordshire* and the *Nevasa* would not be renewed when the existing charter expired in 1964 and terminating early the charter of the smaller *Devonshire*.

There were other changes in 1962. British United, operating around nineteen flights a month from Stansted to the Far East, another twenty a month to East Africa and Cyprus and with a further thirty flights a week to Germany, remained secure in its trooping contracts, but Cunard Eagle was about to lose its DC-6 West Med contract in September of that year. September also saw the end of Cunard Eagle's Medair contract which had relied for many years on Vikings based in Malta and Cyprus. As a consequence the last Viking left Eagle's fleet in October after nigh on ten years service with the airline. However, Cunard Eagle was awarded a modified contract which gave it two flights a week by Viscount, operating from London to Malta and then round the bases in the Mediterranean before returning to Malta and London.

Although the major contracts, now lasting up to three years, were awarded to only the select few, there were still plenty of short-term and ad hoc Ministry contracts available, especially during the summer months. The Ministry of Defence evolved a formula of inviting tenders on a month-by-month basis to cover these extra requirements which could cover a multiplicity of tasks: cargo flights to the Middle and Far East, extra trooping flights to Singapore and large-scale summer movements of Territorial Army and School Combined Cadet Force units, mainly to Germany and Cyprus. On the back of the regular military contracts there were also a number of private-enterprise flights for service families, so-called welfare flights, which were usually contracted and administered by a military entity – for example a Sergeants' Mess – which allowed forces' families access to cheaper fares in the same way that an affinity group catered to special groups. There were welfare flights to wherever there were British military installations, providing valuable and legitimate business to charter airlines, especially true in the case of the longer hauls to Singapore and Hong Kong.


## TROUBLE AHEAD - THE TREASURY INTERVENES

Trooping had become the mainstay of Britain's long-haul independent airlines, and the award of major contracts to British United had done much to consolidate that company in its early years. The government was inclined to reward those companies that did its bidding and acted on its advice, and British United's behaviour was exemplary. As a result the company was given some latitude. When it became obvious that Hunting-Clan's original trooping bid had been hopelessly optimistic, the Air Ministry quietly renegotiated the contract.[20] At the same time the Air Ministry tightened up the terms for contractors. Frightened by the aftermath of Caledonian's crash at Douala,[21] the Ministry decided that in future only companies with at least one year's operating experience would be eligible. There were other changes just visible on the horizon, changes that spelled the beginning of the end, for the government, especially the Treasury, was increasingly minded to redirect trooping to the RAF now that Transport Command was acquiring long-haul jets.

By the middle of 1960 the RAF had taken delivery of its fleet of twenty Britannias, plus the three originally intended for civil charter, which found a new home with the RAF. Remember the decision made back in Chapter Two: 'The only firm decision is that they are not to be taken over by Transport Command.' Eleven VC10s had been ordered for the RAF, and during the first half of 1962 the Service took delivery of five new Comet 4Cs for operation by No. 216 Squadron. The Treasury, however, was becoming restive; why pay good money to the independents to perform trooping flights when the RAF appeared to be accumulating a sizeable fleet of long-range transports? The difficulty lay in two areas.

First, due to fiscal restraints, the RAF was limited in the amount of flying that it could undertake with its transport aircraft and most of that flying was already earmarked: training, route flying, special purposes and VIP flights, joint exercises with other services and, most importantly, as the strategic reserve. To increase the flying would mean an increase in establishment, maintenance costs and the service vote, that is the money voted to the Service Ministries by Parliament, and the service chiefs knew well that any extra money for transport flying would have to come out of some other area of their budgets. It was cheaper to use commercial charters than their own resources for trooping flights and if there was an emergency, the RAF's own transport aircraft were not tied up on routine scheduled flying and were thus available for strategic support. There had been such an emergency in Kuwait in 1961 which had entailed the flying in of reinforcements under Britain's treaty obligations.

Secondly, the government had time and again reiterated its policy on trooping flights:

Apart from a small number of ad hoc movements which have been undertaken either by Transport Command or by the Corporations, and apart from the carriage of individual passengers on scheduled civil air lines, the policy of the Government has been to invite the independent companies to carry out the air movement task.

Under this arrangement, Transport Command is free to concentrate on its operational role of being ready to provide air movement support for the Services. The Corporations are able to concentrate on the highly competitive task of operating world-wide scheduled services. And, last but by no means least, the trooping work is of great value to the independent companies, whose civil opportunities are necessarily limited.

Thus Harold Watkinson, in the debate on air estimates on 9 May 1957, although the matter went beyond that as the Services also appreciated the value of having a sizeable strategic reserve.

## THE TREASURY'S TROOPING REVIEW

However, the Treasury was not about to be deterred by these wider issues. After some judicious prodding, the matter was raised at the Estimates Committee of the House of Commons, questions were asked in the House and the Treasury was given the task of trying to ascertain by what means more troop flying could be performed by the RAF and less money paid to the independents. So, on 12 February 1962, Mr Peck of the Treasury sent out a circular letter asking for suggestions as to how expenditure on charter trooping could be reduced respectively by £500,000, £1 million and £2 million per annum by 1966/7.[22] The Air Ministry was spending around £6 million a year on civil trooping, the main beneficiary being British United, which held all the major long-haul contracts and had recently taken over the German contract as well.

As happens, events intervened which were to force the pace and prejudge the outcome. Having received its new Comet 4Cs, the RAF then decided that it still wanted to hold on to its early model Comet 2s, and could extend their lives for a few more years by flying at lower altitudes and with reduced cabin pressure. The extra cost of retaining the fleet was set at around £1.1 million a year, but perhaps this could be offset by allowing the RAF to take over the West Med contract, to Malta, Gibraltar and Libya, from Cunard Eagle. The Cunard Eagle contract was due to expire at the end of September 1962, albeit with the option of renewal.

The economics of this particular case are puzzling. The Comet 2s would be used for the West Med trooping contract, and for conversion and continuation training, but for nothing else. The conversion and continuation training was needed to ensure enough crews could operate the air-trooping movements; but no other operations were envisaged as the aircraft were limited in the hours they could fly and the tasks they could perform (they could no longer fly out to the Far East, for example). In order to save £450,000 a year in charter costs, the RAF and the Treasury were willing to sanction the expenditure of over £1 million instead. Even by Treasury standards the arithmetic is flawed. The logic points to a determined effort by the RAF and the Treasury to bring more troop flying in-house and thus overset government policy by careful oiling of the wheels. Both parties had an interest in doing so; the Treasury, because it now wanted to divert funds away from the independents to the RAF and the RAF because it wanted more flying. The Air Ministry was neutral but under pressure from the other Services, which did not have to pay for trooping when the flying was performed by the RAF. There were some operational advantages; the Comet 2 was a much smaller aircraft than the DC-6 – seating only forty-two passengers – so frequencies would have to be substantially increased which suited the garrison in Gibraltar but came at a much higher cost in real terms.

Only the Ministry of Aviation was unhappy at this breach of government policy, but as had happened before, the Treasury and the Service Ministries rode roughshod over the civilians. The Ministry was a bit-player, with little idea as to the costs involved and so unable to make any worthwhile contribution to the debate; its officials were inclined to haul up the white flag.

The proposal has obvious financial attraction for the Government and is free from some of the general objections applying to the use of Transport Command for trooping. It has some attractions for the Services, because the use of Comet 2s instead of the larger DC 6s at present on this contract would mean more frequent flights and a greater degree of flexibility. The independents' need of trooping contracts to keep them alive has lost some of its force.

This case can be treated as a special one, without prejudice to the general question of trooping policy.[23]

This somewhat naïve view was rightly treated with suspicion by the departmental chief:

I'm not very keen on this. It seems a straight departure from policy; should one accept that simply because 'its only a little one'? I'd have thought not, especially when a major review of trooping policy is under way.

Can we have a word, please?

In reality Michael Custance, the Deputy Secretary, was no more able to stop the wheels turning than his hapless underling. Doubtless he had his word, but a few days later agreed to the proposal 'with some misgiving, and on the understanding that this is entirely without prejudice.' Of course, it was the thin end of the wedge.

Once the Air Ministry had disposed of the Ministry of Aviation's objections, confirmed the new arrangements with RAF Transport Command and allowed Cunard Eagle's existing contract to lapse, it was time to return to the main issue: the Treasury's quest to reduce trooping by the charter airlines. Any additional flying would need to come from the Britannia fleet, but the Services were loath to impair the viability of the existing contract with British United, which undertook to fly at least 1,250 hours a month with five dedicated Britannias. (By comparison the RAF's fleet of twenty-three aircraft was permitted only 2,000 hours a month flying.) The Far East trooping flights were to a large extent sacrosanct; these long flights carrying wives and families were better suited to operation by civil aircraft which routed more directly by overflying Pakistan and India, and could use existing civilian facilities en route. The question was how to redirect the other trooping tenders; the Cyprus contract was the favourite. It was just not possible to increase the RAF's Britannia flying without also increasing the number of flying hours, which the Treasury would have to sanction. The Treasury meanwhile wanted it both ways: more flying at no additional cost, another example of the Treasury's quirky economics. The arguments between the service ministries and the Treasury raged for over a year, with the hapless Ministry of Aviation lost somewhere in the middle. The service ministries did not want any flying hours diverted from its other commitments, the Treasury endlessly tinkered with the figures. It was not until late 1964 that the Treasury finally conceded and granted the RAF an additional 400 flying hours a month, which allowed the RAF to take over the Cyprus contract at the end of September.

## TROOPING AND THE CORPORATIONS

Had they but known it, the independents were being assailed on other fronts too. As we have seen, by 1963 there were ominous signs that the government and the corporations were having second thoughts about the existing air-trooping policy. The arguments for allowing the corporations to tender exhibited the muddled thinking that somehow always worked to the disadvantage of the independents; if the independents were allowed to apply for the right to operate scheduled services, then surely the corporations should be allowed to compete on what was traditionally the independents' turf. The corporations, through the monopoly powers granted them over fourteen years, had built up sizeable scheduled fortress networks which were to remain largely impregnable after 1960, given their accumulated mass and the government's own regulatory barriers; it was, however, entirely in the government's gift to take away business from the independents and give it to the corporations. Laker explained the realities in his usual robust way:

> If we were to take a substantial part of the corporations' scheduled traffic, then it wouldn't be wrong for them to have an equal opportunity to tender for trooping. But this isn't the case. No independent has ever taken a passenger mile from BOAC – on the contrary, their North Atlantic position has been strengthened – and it is on BOAC's network that the bulk of the trooping is performed by the independents. And where has BUA taken any traffic from BEA? If you are going to say that BEA have sole rights to all European traffic, then you can say that every passenger we carry is a BEA passenger. But the boot is on the other foot – how about the inclusive-tour business which we developed and created? How about the hundreds of thousands of ITX passengers carried on scheduled services by BEA? But this debate about diversion is sterile – I'm much more interested in getting new business into British aircraft, because while I'm worrying about somebody taking part of our business they are taking the rest of it.[24]

The Treasury, the RAF, and now the corporations were steadily chipping away at the solid base of the trooping contracts, remorselessly, unstoppable.

1. Avro Yorks of Skyways at Heathrow in 1959, seeing out their later years as freighters. (Peter M. Corbell via Air-Britain/C505130)

2. Another veteran of the Second World War, the Dakota continued in airline service well into the 1960s. Silver City used G-AMWV on its north of England scheduled services. (MAP)

3. Famous for playing its part in the Berlin Airlift, Douglas DC-4 Skymasters entered service with Britain's independent airlines in many roles. Lloyd used G-ARWI to carry ship's crews and freight to Hong Kong. Note the MacLeod Dunvegan Castle crest on the nose. (MAP)

4. Lockheed Constellations entered service with BOAC in 1946. Formerly named *Baltimore* with BOAC, G-AHEN returned to Britain to see further service with Euravia. (MAP)

5. Vikings were the mainstay of BEA in its early days, and of many charter airlines in the 1950s. G-AGRS looks wonderful in Orion's two-tone green livery. (MAP)

6. One of the Brabazon Committee's most successful projects, the de Havilland Dove was successful as business aircraft and feederliner. Morton's G-AJDP sports a period livery. (MAP)

7. The other successful Brabazon type was the Vickers Viscount. Here an early model version, G-ALWF, carries Cambrian's Welsh colours. (MAP)

8. The Airspeed Ambassador was another Brabazon design, to the same specification as the Vickers Viscount. G-AMAE stayed in service with Dan-Air until 1971. (MAP)

9.   Channel Airways used the Bristol Freighter for passenger flights. Here G-AIFO shows the minimal changes made to its former owner's livery, West African Airways. (Peter M. Corbell via Air-Britain/C505133)

10.   A larger four-engine development of the Dove, the de Havilland Heron continued the manufacturer's tradition of building practical small airliners. G-AORH is one of seven Herons used by Jersey Airlines. (MAP)

11. BOAC relied on its Argonauts, a Canadian-built development of the Douglas DC-4, for many years. G-ALHP was used for long-distance charters to South Africa by Overseas in 1960. (MAP)

12. Airwork's Handley Page Hermes G-ALDA at Blackbushe, in full civil colours. (James J. Halley via Air-Britain/C551138)

13.  Eagle introduced a sophisticated livery in 1957, sported here by Vickers Viscount G-APDK. (MAP)

14.  Hunting-Clan had an exotic name as well as an attractive livery, with its distinctive 'day-glo' orange tail, shown off here by Douglas DC-6 G-APNO. (James J. Halley via Air-Britain/C513009)

15. Cunard Eagle introduced the stylised E on the tail, and it was retained by British Eagle. Bristol Britannia G-ARKA waits in the sun at London Airport. (Eric W. Sawyer via Air-Britain/C520139)

16. A tribute to a fine aircraft and its owner. Dakota G-AMSX looks immaculate nearly twenty years after it was built, a credit to Derby Airways and its engineers. (MAP)

# SIX

# PICKING UP THE PIECES
## 1962-1964

## CUNARD EAGLE

Cunard Eagle picked up the pieces of its shattered commercial plans and still met with difficulties. Bamberg offered the Boeings to the Air Ministry for trooping flights, but was turned down on the grounds that they were too expensive. Then his proposed programme of charter flying to the States was blocked by the United States Civil Aeronautics Board; Cunard Eagle was allowed a small percentage of 'off-route' charter flying as a result of its scheduled services from Bermuda and Nassau, which the airline wanted to utilise on flights to and from London, but the CAB obdurately refused to allow it to increase them above this restricted level. Despite support from the British Government, which even threatened retaliatory action against American charter airlines, Cunard Eagle was forced to abandon its charter programme.

The company took delivery of its first Boeing 707 which entered service on the Bermuda-New York route; Cunard Eagle was the first British independent to operate jets. In May the Boeing took over the London flights to Bermuda and Nassau, and on to Miami and Jamaica; it was the first jet connection by a British carrier between London and Miami, the world's third-busiest airport, and was marketed as 'the Londoner' in the west and as 'the Cunarder' out of London. Better news for the airline was the award by the government of the Woomera support contract to Adelaide in Australia from June 1962, providing excellent utilisation for its DC-6 fleet. There was talk of forming a subsidiary in Jamaica; there was even talk of re-applying for the London-New York licence. All these developments did not go unnoticed at BOAC, which relied on Britannias for many of its competing Caribbean services, and already endured a certain level of disaffection on the part of the colonial governments, who always seemed very ready to support the enterprise of Cunard Eagle.

## PICKING UP THE PIECES

Other airlines had to pick up other pieces. The collapse of nine airlines in the previous two years had led to a substantial loss of charter capacity; over time the vacuum was to

Cunard Eagle's Boeing 707 VR-BBW carried a Bermuda registration initially but was soon to join the BOAC fleet as G-ARWD. (MAP)

be filled by existing airlines – which expanded and re-equipped – by new airlines like Euravia, and by foreign airlines.

Derby Airways took over some of the Argonauts from the former Overseas fleet, bringing three of them into service for inclusive-tour work in 1962 to supplement the Dakotas, which were increasingly needed for its developing scheduled services from Derby, Birmingham, Cardiff and Bristol. The Argonauts, by now decidedly long in the tooth, stayed in service until 1967 but according to Captain Cramp, the airline's commercial manager, the choice was not a happy one:

> Although not appreciated at the time, the decision was a disastrous one insofar as the aircraft were concerned, cheap as they were, they were very expensive to operate and did not have either the range, capacity or cargo doors of the DC6B.[1]

Despite that, the aircraft were extensively rebuilt and an extra row of seats added, bringing seating capacity up to seventy-five seats. In another development Derby took over Executive Air Transport of Birmingham, which included amongst its assets a ground-handling company at Birmingham Airport, Midland Airport Services. Derby was now able to offer third-party handling at a major airport and consolidated its own handling under the Midland Airport Services name. Anticipating the forthcoming transfer from Derby's old airfield at Burnaston to the newly built airport at Castle Donington, now named East Midlands Airport, Derby Airways changed its own name to British Midland Airways on 1 October 1964 and announced an order for two Handley Page Heralds for use on the scheduled services out of the new airport to Birmingham, Newcastle, Leeds, Glasgow, Belfast and the Channel Islands.

Starways introduced Viscounts on its Liverpool routes, including the all-important route to London which it now served direct as well as via Chester (Hawarden). Another

DC-4 operator, Lloyd International, was looking to trade up and acquired a DC-6 from Alaska Airlines in 1964. The airline, based at Gatwick but with strong Hong Kong connections, specialised in ship's crew movements but also undertook ad hoc charters worldwide. Lloyd had established a relationship with Mercury Holidays, a Glasgow tour operator; normally one DC-4 was sufficient to operate the summer programme but during the 'Wakes' weeks, when Glasgow and Edinburgh close down for the summer holidays, additional aircraft were operated out of Glasgow, including the new DC-6.

Mercury Airlines – no connection with Mercury Holidays – whose Herons had done much of the flying for the now defunct North-South Airlines, emerged as a new name operating out of Manchester; its previous identity, Overseas Air Transport, was a little too close to the other 'Overseas' for comfort, even though there had been no connection between them. Another Heron operator – Biggin Hill-based Metropolitan Air Movements – had found its niche flying domestic charters, especially for the Pressed Steel Company, but by 1962 was exploring new horizons, operating oil-support flights in Libya.

A new Dakota operator, Tyne Tees – formed with the help of Keegan and based at Newcastle – immediately ran into difficulties with the Board, which refused to grant it a general charter licence on the grounds of financial fitness. Business opportunities were therefore extremely limited. The airline was forced to lease out two of its aircraft, and after it lost its appeal late in 1963, ceased operations in 1964.

A different new entrant was Aviation Charter Enterprises, otherwise known as ACE Freighters, which was formed at Gatwick on 1 March 1964 by Captain Chegwidden to fly cargo charters, and used a freight-door-equipped Constellation supplemented by two DC-4s; the airline soon picked up Ministry contracts to carry freight to the Middle and Far East, as did another cargo airline, Trans Meridian. Hardly a newcomer, but a new entrant nevertheless, Trans Meridian was just the latest, but by no means the last, manifestation of Keegan's aviation enterprises. Trans Meridian used two DC-4 Skymasters leased in from another Keegan company, Trans World Leasing.

## OUTPOSTS: THE WEST COUNTRY

In the West Country two new entrants showed early promise. Squadron Leader Cleife's Mayflower had operated frequent charter flights between Plymouth and St Mary's in the Scilly Isles during 1961, and in 1962 had been granted a scheduled-service licence for the route. Flying a single Rapide and helped by his wife, who took the bookings, Cleife earned an enviable reputation for reliability; it was not unknown for him to continue operating into St Mary's when BEA's own Rapide services were grounded by bad weather at its base at Land's End. In 1963 a second Rapide was acquired but on 20 July Cleife was severely burned after his Rapide crashed and caught fire whilst attempting to take-off from St Mary's. Although his wife and the second pilot gallantly tried to keep the airline going, at the end of the season Cleife sold out to Scillonian Air Services, a newcomer operating Aero Commanders between Gatwick and St Mary's.

Further east, at Exeter, Westpoint Aviation had started operations with two Dakotas, but they spent much of 1961 and 1962 flying IT charters out of Gatwick. In 1963 the airline tried unsuccessfully to buy Mayflower, but persisted and the second time around was able

Wartime DH Rapides remained in use in the west country of England well into the 1960s. BEA sold Rapide G-AHKU to British Westpoint for further use on the routes to the Scilly Isles. (MAP)

to buy the airline from Scillonian in 1964, for by now Scillonian was in trouble and indeed shortly afterwards had its Gatwick–St Mary's licence revoked. Competition of a new order emerged on the St Mary's route, however, when BEA introduced a radically new type, the Sikorsky S-61 helicopter. BEA had abandoned scheduled helicopter services early in 1957 but maintained a charter unit; this was now reformed as BEA Helicopters. Operating initially from Land's End, BEA Helicopters transferred the service to a new heliport at Penzance on 1 September 1964; the service has operated successfully ever since. BEA disposed of its Rapides to Westpoint, now named British Westpoint Airlines, which used them on the former Mayflower routes to the Scillies from Exeter, Plymouth, Newquay, Bristol and Cardiff; the Dakotas were now also used on a scheduled service between Newquay and London Heathrow. In September 1965 Metropolitan Air Movements took British Westpoint over, but neither airline survived beyond 1966.

The other main operator to the West Country was Starways, which in 1959 had pioneered flights to Newquay in Cornwall from Liverpool and other points in the north, before adding a route from London.

## CHANNEL AIRWAYS AND TRADAIR

Tradair was still in receivership but managed to keep its Vikings flying during the winter months with ad hoc work and aerial cruises, and by developing air-freight business to Sweden. One of the Viscounts went back into service that summer, flying for BEA in Germany; the other was sold to Starways. Come November 1962 one year had elapsed since the receiver had been appointed and the situation was no better for the airline.

By way of complete contrast, BEA inaugurated helicopter service between the Scilly Isles and Cornwall in 1964. Newly delivered Sikorsky S-61G-ASNM is here at Land's End Airport in Cornwall. (MAP)

Southend Council accepted an offer from the airline to write off most of the outstanding debt, and the receiver then sold the airline to Channel Airways in December. Channel thus acquired seven Vikings and its first turboprop, the remaining Viscount, which was retained for the longer summer runs to the Channel Islands. At the end of 1963 Channel bought seven Viscount 701s from BEA, some of which were leased short-term to Eagle, the remainder entered service early the next year, flying mainly to the Channel Islands, Ostend, Paris and Rotterdam. Rotterdam and Paris were important destinations during spring; Rotterdam attracted day-trippers visiting the Dutch tulip fields and Paris was the centre for short three- and four-day breaks. During the summer of 1964 Channel began using the Viscounts on inclusive-tour-charter work, sending the aircraft further afield – from Southend and Manchester, to Spain, Italy and France. 1964 also marked the end of Viking operations for Channel; four Dakotas remained in the fleet and a Douglas DC-4 Skymaster, seating eighty-eight passengers, had been acquired for the lucrative Southend-Ostend route.

## CAMBRIAN AND BEA

Under its managing director, Wing Commander Elwin, Cambrian had managed to bounce back from its earlier troubles, and with its fleet of eight Dakotas had rebuilt its network out of Cardiff and Bristol to Manchester, Liverpool, the Channel Islands, Bournemouth, Paris, Cork and Glasgow. In September 1962 BEA announced it was going to transfer its Irish Sea routes to Cambrian – the services from the Isle of Man together

Channel Airways put 88 seats into this Skymaster, G-ARYY, and it spent most of its life shuttling back and forth between Southend and Ostend in Belgium. (A.J. Jackson Collection)

with the Liverpool-Belfast route – from April the following year. In return Cambrian would buy five Viscount 701s from the corporation and take over its ground-handling unit at Liverpool. BEA already held a 33 per cent interest in Cambrian, but it was another turnabout of policy for the corporation which had formerly been loath to concede any part of its route structure to the independents. However, losses of £500,000 a year on these routes could no longer be tolerated in the climate of the time, and by nominating Cambrian, BEA hoped to retain a measure of control. BEA and Cambrian had to apply to the Board for the transfer of the licences, and faced opposing applications from British United (CI) Airways and Starways, both of which airlines had strong connections with the Isle of Man and Liverpool respectively. BEA's Secretary, Henry Marking, was asked why Cambrian expected to make a profit when it was proposing to use the same aircraft that BEA had used. His answer summed up many of the cost advantages that the independents had achieved over the state corporations; Cambrian paid its pilots less, expected them to fly more and managed to get by with fewer people on the ground. Elwin went further, saying BEA staffing levels were 'far too luxurious.'[2]

British United (CI) had a good case, the Herald's operating costs were lower than those of a Viscount (the fifty-six-seat Herald carried almost as many passengers as the early model Viscounts with two fewer engines) and it was better suited to the route structure; but the Board duly awarded all the licences to Cambrian, which took delivery of the first of the Viscounts on 24 January 1963 and inaugurated the Irish Sea services on 1 April. The impact of the new routes on Cambrian was striking, catapulting the airline into a different league. In 1962 the airline had carried around 115,000 passengers; the following year, this figure had more than doubled to over 256,000 passengers.

American built light aircraft, like this Piper Aztec G-ATBV, found a growing market with British air-taxi companies. Norfolk Airways operated this aircraft on behalf of locally based insurance company, Norwich Union. (MAP)

## AIR-TAXI OPERATIONS

With the advent of light American twin-engine aircraft like the Piper Aztec there was a renewal of interest in air-taxi operations in the early 1960s. Norfolk Airways and Anglian Air Charter, veterans of the 1950s, still made a living from pleasure flying at the holiday resorts in Essex and Norfolk, but Norfolk Airways had moved on, buying an Aztec to fly on behalf of locally based Norwich Union. Other newcomers looked to business and executive travel for the bulk of their business. Based at Denham, Gregory Air Taxis had seven twins in operation by 1965, supported by its own engineering facility. In Scotland a civil-engineering contractor, Duncan Logan, began an on-demand air-taxi service between Dundee and Edinburgh with a Piper Aztec in 1964. He called the airline Loganair, and in time it became the spiritual successor to the pre-war Scottish Airways,[3] eventually re-opening services within the Orkney Islands which had been abandoned by BEA after the Second World War. Another civil-engineering contractor, Sir Robert McAlpine, established an Aviation Division at Luton in October 1963, offering air-taxi and engineering services.

## 'A KNOCK-OUT BLOW AT THE MOST ENTERPRISING OF BRITAIN'S PRIVATE AIRLINES'

As Eagle and Bamberg were such pioneers, constantly pushing out the boundaries of commercial endeavour, any occurrence affecting them had an immediate impact out of proportion to its ultimate significance. Eagle's history through the years is punctuated by seismic shocks, and Cunard Eagle was about to deliver another jolt: on 6 June 1962 BOAC and Cunard announced the joint formation of BOAC-Cunard to take over the Western Hemisphere operations of both BOAC and Cunard Eagle.

After the revocation of Cunard Eagle's New York licence, Smallpeice realised that he might only have won a short reprieve in his tussle with Cunard Eagle. Cunard had invested heavily in its new airline and was also familiar with the ways of government; a Conservative Government might yet grant it another licence. He decided to act quickly and suggested further talks with Cunard over a joint venture:

> It might just appeal to Cunard (as distinct from Eagle) in that it would bring their name into transatlantic aviation and give them a lasting interest in it. My idea was that we should set up a subsidiary company to hold some of our transatlantic Boeing 707s and Cunard would get their minority interest in this joint company in exchange for their two aircraft.
>
> I then asked R. F. (Dick) Taylor of Cunard and Harold Bamberg of Eagle to talk about the situation resulting from the loss of their licence, now that the dust had settled a bit. They came to my office at BOAC headquarters at London Airport on 27 April 1962. I outlined my tentative ideas. Harold Bamberg remained quiet throughout. But I had been right: and it became evident that Dick Taylor thought Cunard could well be interested in the possibility of promoting a company jointly with BOAC. We would have further talks after he had referred back to his chairman, Sir John Brocklebank.
>
> It seemed that John Brocklebank and his board approved because matters went ahead fairly rapidly.[4]

The government accepted the proposal after the Chancellor had expressed some concern over the size of Cunard's shareholding; he wanted Cunard to put up 50 per cent of the capital, whereas BOAC wanted them to have less than 25 per cent. Cunard contributed its two Boeing 707s, its Bermuda and Bahamas operations and thirty of Bamberg's pilots to the joint operation in which it was agreed that it would hold a 30 per cent stake. Cunard achieved the link with aviation that it had been seeking, but remained the junior partner in the deal which in truth did little for either company. Although in retrospect it is not relevant – because the partnership did not endure – the venture did represent a partial de-nationalisation of a state corporation. If anything, the benefits for BOAC were greater; the corporation did not need much marketing or selling assistance from Cunard, but with one blow BOAC effectively disposed of all present and future competition on the North Atlantic, not just to New York, but from Bermuda, the Bahamas, Jamaica and all the other destinations that Bamberg and his colleagues had in their sights.

For Cunard Eagle the about-turn in its fortunes was little short of astonishing. Only one month previously Bamberg and one of his fellow directors from Cunard Steam Ship had been happily photographed together during the inaugural jet 'Cunarder' and 'Londoner' flights to and from Bermuda; there had been talk then of more services and a robust response. We now know that BOAC and Cunard had already started their fateful negotiations. Instead the airline was to be dropped from the Cunard portfolio, leaving Bamberg to pick up the pieces. 'The new arrangement does have disconcerting implications,' was the indignant response in a *Flight* editorial, which continued:

Now in full BOAC livery Boeing 707 G-ARWD shows off its Rolls-Royce engines at Heathrow. (MAP)

A bright independent light could – for all the Minister of Aviation, Cunard Steam-Ship and BOAC appear to care – have been snuffed out. *Flight* feels no particular passion about the relative merits of private and State enterprise; what we do believe is that independent operators enrich the country's airline industry by providing a second measure of airline worth and an alternative fount of ideas and employment.

All this must be obvious to a Minister of Aviation who stands for private enterprise; yet it is the second time in six months that he has sanctioned, when an alternative formula might have been found, the delivery of a knock-out blow at the most enterprising of Britain's private airlines.

The effect on the whole of the independent industry, representing one quarter of the world's second-biggest air-transport effort, must have been depressing. Hardly a single employee can have gone to work on the morning of June 7 without wondering how his or her future might be affected by the stroke of a BOAC or BEA pen. Such an unsettling situation is good for nobody.[5]

One immediate effect of the sell-out was that Cunard Eagle dropped its application to the American CAB for charter rights, sparing the British Government the embarrassment of a confrontation with the Americans over the issue. Change came about quickly. The Boeings were repainted in BOAC colours, the New York-Bermuda Viscount service suspended, the London-Jamaica service re-routed over New York, and the Nassau-Miami Viscount flights transferred to Bahamas Airways. Both Bamberg and Ashton Hill joined the board of BOAC-Cunard, although Smallpeice made it quite clear that as far as he was concerned, there was no difference between BOAC and BOAC-Cunard except for the

Three generations of airliners: Skyways Avro York, BOAC Bristol Britannia and Pan American Boeing 707 share a wet ramp at Heathrow. BOAC and Pan American used the Yorks to dispatch replacement engines for aircraft-on-ground (AOG). The coming of much more reliable jet aircraft meant the service was about to end, as was Skyways. (Flight)

name on the side of the aircraft. The colonial governments of Bermuda, the Bahamas and Jamaica were dismayed at the outcome; they were not consulted beforehand by BOAC, and Bermuda in particular was nervous over the future of its flag carrier, and with good reason. BOAC's services had previously been erratic; Cunard Eagle had brought some stability to services to the United States, not to mention cheap fares and better links with London.

## SKYWAYS AND EURAVIA

Colonial governments were not the only casualties of BOAC's pervasive influence. At the end of March Skyways's Far East freight contract with BOAC expired, and was not renewed; nor, with the advent of more reliable jet aircraft, did BOAC and Pan American need to keep Skyways's York freighters any longer on stand-by to carry jet engines for Aircraft on Ground (AOG) and other emergencies. Overnight a large part of Skyways's revenues evaporated and the long-haul freight operations of this once-mighty charter airline ended. Skyways still flew its low-fare passenger services to Malta, Cyprus and Tunis, but the airline had never made an impact on the inclusive-tour market; instead it made a virtue of its close association with the corporations, a fatal attraction when BOAC withdrew its support. Other airlines might just have gone into liquidation; not, however, an airline owned by Eric Rylands.

He sold the aircraft and the company's liabilities to Euravia, which needed the additional Constellations for its growing IT business; later in the year Euravia also acquired the two by now notorious Constellations, G-AHEL and G-AMUP, previously with Captain Kozubski. For a year or so Euravia continued to operate one of the Constellations in Skyways colours for the Crusader services before finally abandoning those routes. Euravia even retained the four Yorks, again in Skyways colours, for ad hoc freight- and engine-carriage work. The last Skyways York flight, and the last York flight by a British airline, was on 8 October 1964 when G-AGNV positioned from London Airport to Staverton.

Nor was that the end for Rylands. He still retained his engineering interests, the freehold of Lympne Airfield and Skyways Coach-Air, which by now had introduced the Avro 748 on its Lympne-Beauvais service. The first entered service on 17 April 1962, originally in a forty-seat configuration which was soon increased to forty-eight. Skyways also flew to other destinations in France – Lyons, Vichy and Montpellier, but on a limited basis, and it retained some of the Dakotas for charter work and for its developing air-cargo business on the Lympne-Beauvais route. Neither Skyways nor BKS were over-endowed with funds, and both companies originally leased the aircraft from the manufacturer. The early 748s shuttled back and forth between the two companies, working for Skyways during the summer and being used by BKS for its Leeds-London service during the winter.

The receivership at BKS was terminated in 1963, but the airline continued to look at alternative ways of acquiring aircraft. In 1964 BKS began using a ninety-two-seat Britannia 102 bought for the company under an innovative financing deal by the Newcastle tour operator, Airway Holidays; the aircraft was used on IT services to Rimini, Barcelona and Palma at weekends but flew the Newcastle-London route three times daily during the week, a measure of how successful this flagship route had become. The Britannia represented a formidable advance for Airway Holidays whose charter programmes had been flown previously by Ambassadors; the economics were further improved when the aircraft's capacity was increased to 117-seats. The arrangement also demonstrated a happy marriage of two sources of demand, a template copied by many other independent airlines; the aircraft flew on business routes during the working week, and were then free to fly holiday charters at weekends. Finally BKS found a solution to its financial problems in June 1964 when it sold a 30 per cent stake to BEA. The corporation now held significant stakes in two independents, Cambrian and BKS.

Avro 748 G-ARMX was used by Skyways on its coach-air service to Beauvais in France during the summer and by BKS for its London to Leeds service in the winter. (MAP)

## THE AIR TRANSPORT LICENSING BOARD

The Board received some sort of endorsement from the new Minister of Aviation, Macmillan's son-in-law Julian Amery, when he and the Commissioner upheld most of the decisions it had made at the long European routes hearing in 1961, only revoking two of the licences, those to Geneva and Zurich. A year had since gone by, and many of the awards subsequently proved meaningless as the British Government proved unable or unwilling to negotiate traffic rights overseas. British United was confirmed as the new operator to Genoa and as the second operator to Amsterdam; the airline was also confirmed on two holiday routes, Barcelona and Palma. Cunard Eagle was confirmed as second airline on the domestic trunks to Glasgow and Edinburgh but the frequency restrictions remained. The Commissioner, Sir Arthur Hutchinson, approved the Board's guidelines for allowing competing services and remarked austerely of Cunard Eagle's appeal: 'The grant of unrestricted frequency would be quite inconsistent with "regulated" competition and would enable an operator to drive a coach and horses through the Board's carefully balanced scheme.'

British United, good establishment airline that it was, made appropriately grateful noises for its 'minimal route network'. BEA, fresh from announcing its first annual loss in seven years, talked ominously of too many empty seats being the 'natural road to ruin'. Cunard Eagle could barely contain its anger:

> We are very disappointed. It is pathetic that we have had to wait two years since the alteration of the Civil Aviation Act and now find that the Minister's decisions give us enough work for between two and three aeroplanes at the most. The frequency he has granted us on the

London-Glasgow route, for instance, one of the densest routes in Europe and currently operated as a monopoly by BEA, is seven flights per week only, whereas BEA are at present operating no less than fifty nine services per week. Furthermore, BEA are free to put on as many more services as they wish. BEA's talk about competition from us on domestic routes such as this is a complete farce because we are given frequencies which are pathetically restricted: they can drive us off the route by putting on even more than the fifty-nine services they currently operate on this particular route. The word competition hardly fits the case.[6]

When the dust had settled, Cunard Eagle reapplied for revised capacity on the routes, this time specifying seats per week rather than frequencies, in accordance with the Board's European formula, and applying to restrict BEA's capacity, so that together the two airlines would offer no more capacity than the estimated forecast for the next three years. It was likely to be a complicated formula and it was the first time an airline had sought to restrict BEA's licences. In the meantime Cunard Eagle made plans to inaugurate its domestic services regardless, using Britannias.

The Board still found itself on the wrong end of appeals. The latest put-down involved Autair, which had applied to the Board for a licence to fly between Luton and Blackpool; Silver City then applied for a similar licence from Gatwick. Although there was little to choose between the airlines, and indeed, Luton showed some operational advantages, the Board decided to award the route to Silver City on the grounds that it commanded greater resources and was the more experienced carrier. Autair appealed the decision, and in another arbitrary reversal the Minister decided to revoke Silver City's licence and award it instead to Autair, on the strength of the Commissioner's somewhat diffident recommendation:

> Though the material before me is not sufficient to enable me to make a precise assessment of all the factors, I find that on balance the advantages of the proposed service via Luton are sufficient to outweigh the admitted advantage enjoyed by the respondent (Silver City) in respect of resources and experience.[7]

Silver City had done nothing wrong, indeed, it had already started flying the route; it now had to suspend the operation and hand over the service to Autair. The decision further undermined the authority of the ATLB, but Autair was 'extremely pleased' about it; smaller airlines took comfort from the fact that sometimes bigger was not necessarily better. Autair used Vikings initially, but had just bought three Ambassadors which it used on the route as well as on IT flights. Autair took over the service on 1 October, flying six services a week from Luton with a dedicated coach link from the tarmac to the north London terminal. At the same time the airline changed its name to Autair International Airways and introduced an attractive two-tone blue livery.


## BRITISH UNITED AND THE GENOA ROUTE

Very few of the international licences granted were ever implemented. However, the Ministry enjoyed one success. When the government tried to persuade the Italian authorities to allow British United on to the Genoa route at first it met with a blank refusal; the Italians claimed they were not prepared to countenance an additional British carrier into Italy, especially when they had already accepted both BEA and BOAC. The British, prodded into action by Laker, retaliated by limiting the frequencies on the route of Alitalia, the Italian State airline; BEA sportingly joined the fray by applying to have British United's licence revoked and reapplied for the route itself. Exasperated by this malevolence Laker commented: 'Law-abiding citizens, however much they may disagree when they have exhausted the processes of law as laid down by Parliament, accept the verdict, but not BEA.'[8] When he learned BEA had been lobbying its pool partners to create difficulties for British United, knowing full well that most European airlines were merely an extension of their respective governments, he continued: 'The thing that disturbs me the most is the hate by the corporations for the independents, which is almost fiendish. It would appear that the foreigners can do anything they like with the two corporations, but any form of cooperation is impossible if you happen to be British.'[9] The corporations were always most anxious to protect their overseas pool partners.

This time BEA's tactics failed. The Italians, surprised by the strength of the reaction, and doubtless baffled by the waywardness of British aviation policy, backed down and allowed British United to start operating the route in May 1963. It was a rare win for British negotiators, but even so it came at a cost. BOAC found that it was now required to pay a royalty to Alitalia for stop-over rights at Rome.

## BOAC'S DAY OF RECKONING

Paying royalties was the least of the corporation's worries. BOAC may have trounced Cunard Eagle and the ATLB in the battle over the North Atlantic routes, but that could not defer for ever its next impending crisis; BOAC now began hinting that all was not well, suggesting that losses for the year would be the highest ever. Having increased its capacity by a third the corporation had uplifted only 10 per cent more traffic. All airlines were facing difficulties following re-equipment with jet aircraft; problems of too much capacity were compounded by fleets of obsolete aircraft still on the books and which were insufficiently written down. With its array of nearly new and already obsolete aircraft, BOAC faced more drastic capital losses than most but nevertheless, its decision to write off £33 million in its 1961-62 accounts – to which was added an operating loss of £14 million – outraged everybody, especially the government. The corporation now had an accumulated deficit of over £64 million, and this figure ignores previous write-offs and treasury grants of £34 million; neither corporation had the comfort of Treasury deficiency grants to fall back on, for that privilege had been rescinded in the mid-1950s. Commentators wondered why the losses should have been so understated in previous years, and were unsympathetic to the usual BOAC moans about paying interest on its loan capital, pointing out that the corporation had access to cheap state finance and everybody had to pay interest on borrowed money. The chairman, Sir Matthew Slattery, did not improve matters at the press conference announcing the losses when he returned to the subject of BOAC's 'obligations', and opined that the way the government handled BOAC's finances was 'bloody crazy'. Relations with the government subsequently became somewhat frosty. 'Isn't Slattery rather an ass?' asked Prime Minister Macmillan. 'He has made some very foolish statements about money. Sholto Douglas is clever – but shallow. Where is the Beeching?'[10] continued Macmillan referring to Dr Beeching who had recently knocked some economic sense into Britain's sclerotic railways. Macmillan was a man of his age, he had fought in the First World War, witnessed the terrible effects of unemployment in the 1920s and 1930s and was anxious to promote the expansion of employment in British industry. He was a keen supporter of British-built aircraft, so Smallpeice also came in for some criticism when the latter appeared to be writing, 'rather freely in the BOAC news-sheet about what he will and won't do about Vickers and Boeings. No more Boeings, I hope.'[11] Yet the government maintained that it had never obliged or forced BOAC to do anything against its wishes or commercial judgment; indeed Britannias and Comets had been anticipated eagerly at the time and d'Erlanger had agreed to order up to forty-five VC10s. But Smallpeice notes that the government had ways of making its wishes known without ever leaving any traces for the record:

> The Treasury could impose capital cuts which would reduce our profitability for budget reasons quite unconnected with BOAC, or indeed with civil aviation.
>
> We had such a cut in 1957. It was only a few hundred thousand pounds... Pops d'Erlanger and I argued strongly with the Minister against the cut. The matter was settled only by the Minister telling a London Airport board meeting that we had damn well got to accept it.
>
> Parliament had properly conferred on Ministers the power to give BOAC instructions, wisely adding that he should exercise that power only in the form of a written directive which should be published in our annual report. So we asked him for the necessary directive. He just laughed and said: 'Not bloody likely! What do you take me for?' In the fourteen years I worked in BOAC, there were several occasions when the chairman's or the board's arms were well and truly twisted by Ministers. But they all baulked at issuing a written directive.[12]

Of course, the BOAC board did have some recourse, such as resignation, but Smallpeice rightly points up the flaws of government behind closed doors. Embarrassed by the suddenly massive deficit and unamused by Slattery's remarks, Amery duly launched an inquiry, appointing an accountant, John Corbett, to investigate BOAC's losses and to recommend what changes were needed to put the corporation on a sound financial basis.

## HAROLD BAMBERG AND BRITISH EAGLE

Early in 1963 Bamberg and his fellow director and solicitor Ashton Hill resigned from the board of BOAC-Cunard; Bamberg also resigned as a director of Cunard Steam Ship. Then on 14 February there came about another of those seismic shocks when it was announced that Bamberg had bought back a 60 per cent share in Cunard Eagle, with an option to buy the remaining 40 per cent. The airline still flew two Britannias, three DC-6s and two Viscounts, had some valuable Ministry contracts, operated European IT and scheduled services, and had been granted some challenging domestic routes. With the airline again under his control Bamberg set about re-equipping it, first by expanding the airline's Britannia fleet. He turned to BOAC and started buying the corporation's long-range Britannias which had begun leaving the BOAC fleet just six years after first entering service. In the end he bought fourteen of BOAC's Britannia 312s, converting three of them into freighters, and endowing them all with splendid names like *Endeavour, Perseverance, Resolution, Team Spirit, Justice*, and *Good Fortune*. Two of the DC-6s went to Saudi Arabian Airlines in exchange for three of their DC-4 Skymasters which he used for inclusive-tour work. Eagle then applied to the United States Civil Aeronautics Board for a transatlantic charter permit similar to the one just granted to Caledonian. As Eagle no longer operated services in the Western Hemisphere it was now free to apply for a charter permit. On 9 August the airline changed its name, reverting to British Eagle but retaining the stylish Cunard Eagle 'E' on the tail.

Before launching its domestic trunk services British Eagle ran into another obstacle when the Board refused its application to increase frequencies, and to limit BEA's frequencies; it also refused the London-Manchester application. Rather dispiritingly the Board in its decision observed:

> We are satisfied that the capacity provided by BEA is reasonably adequate to meet the needs of the public. While it will probably remain the case that at peak times not every intending passenger will be able to obtain a seat this is a common feature of public transport everywhere.

With regard to 'swamping' and 'sandwiching' by BEA, the Board concluded naively: 'There was little or no evidence in support of the view that BEA would engage in these practices'. Meanwhile BEA was busily adjusting its schedules so that its flights would parallel those of British Eagle; it also increased capacity by some 50 per cent. British Eagle, of course, appealed the decision.

The Glasgow service was launched on Sunday 3 November 1963, the Edinburgh and Belfast routes the next day; frequencies were less than daily at five or six services a week, but allowed passengers a full day in London. Passenger amenities included trickle loading on flights to London, seat selection and full meal service; there were sixteen first-class seats on the Britannia and eighty-seven seats in tourist class. BEA followed suit, introducing full meal service, trickle loading and seat selection. When called on to comment, BEA said rather huffily:'BEA have been expanding their routes and services for seventeen years to cater for the growing demand for air transport and we do not really need to borrow any ideas from Bamberg as to when and how to operate air services for the benefit of the travelling public.'[13] At the end of the year British Eagle took over Liverpool-based Starways which became British Eagle (Liverpool), adding another trunk route to London, and providing competition for Cambrian which had recently become ensconced in Liverpool. To cope with the expansion British Eagle leased in more Viscounts from Channel Airways and operated some of the Liverpool-London flights with Britannias. The DC-4s it had acquired from Saudi Arabia were brought in to fly the former Starways inclusive-tour programmes. Before signing off on the year 1963, Bamberg, who had been the year's Chairman of BIATA, made the following plea to the corporations on behalf of the Association, echoing Laker's views:

Another scene in Cornwall, as British Eagle Viscount G-ATDU prepares for its passengers at Newquay.
(MAP)

I think it may be important to express on behalf of my colleagues in BIATA our general philosophy regarding the State Corporations: we are not always in a position to appreciate the way in which they react to our participation in this Industry but for our part we believe that there is a place for both private and nationalised sectors: in this context we wish our nationalised corporations well. We would like them to subscribe to our philosophy of 'live and let live' so that we may, as the total British effort, obtain the maximum possible British share of the international market.[14]

## THE CORBETT REPORT

Amery never published the report submitted to him by Corbett; no member of BOAC's top management ever saw the report.[15] Although subsequent events were overshadowed by the assassination on 22 November 1963 of President Kennedy, the denouement of the crisis at BOAC was dramatic and engrossing. First the chairman, Sir Matthew Slattery, and his managing director, Sir Basil Smallpeice, were sacked, and in their place Sir Giles Guthrie – a merchant banker and existing BEA Board member – was appointed chairman and chief executive. The Minister then announced these comings and goings in Parliament on 20 November, at the same time publishing a rather thin White Paper which laid the blame firmly on the two outgoing directors. Accusing them of 'very serious weaknesses in management', Amery cited four main areas that needed stronger management: unsatisfactory handling of associate companies; unduly optimistic traffic forecasting (leading to over-ordering of new aircraft); ineffective financial control and excessive maintenance costs.

Corbett delivered his report to Amery on 24 May 1963; it took Amery six months to steel himself to announce his conclusions and remedies, and he was only saved further embarrassment by the news of the assassination of President Kennedy which obliterated any other news in the ensuing days. Almost the last comment that Prime Minister Macmillan made on aviation matters before he himself resigned on 18 October, says it all:

> From what I have seen of it, Mr. Corbett's report on BOAC is a damaging document. I am not surprised that the Minister of Aviation does not want to publish it. Although he has told the House that they would only get a White Paper I am not sure that that would not do us as much damage without the advantage that frankness in publishing the report might bring.[16]

'My task is to advise as to whether the organisation is efficient rather than to advise the executives as to the detailed steps which they should take to correct any shortcomings,' wrote Corbett to the minister, by way of introduction.[17] Corbett writes in an understated manner, making very few direct criticisms, but leaving it to his reader to draw the appropriate conclusion, to understand the subtext. For example, 'I make no specific recommendation about the Managing Director' led to the sacking of Sir Basil Smallpeice. Smallpeice emerges as the main culprit, but the others, Watkinson the minister, d'Erlanger the chairman, Cribbett, former civil servant turned deputy chairman, are also found wanting. Slattery got a good report card, but was still sacked. Corbett himself concentrated on a number of specific issues, and then called for additional reports on aspects of the corporation's activities. He asked Urwick, Orr and Partners to report on BOAC's marketing effectiveness in the UK and Europe. Peat, Marwick and Mitchell were asked to investigate the Financial Comptroller's Division, Smallpeice's erstwhile fiefdom; he also asked AIC Associated Industrial Consultants for a comprehensive report on the Engineering and Maintenance Division. The areas of Corbett's special interest were: capital losses on aircraft; the associated companies; the Vickers VC10, and current and future operations.

Corbett's style is to start at the beginning and proceed step by step, as best he can. D'Erlanger had already died, Cribbett was critically ill – so Corbett was unable to interview him – and as he acknowledges, it was 'particularly distasteful to criticise either directly or by implication' when they had no opportunity of putting their side of the case. Nevertheless he is still forced to impute motives to d'Erlanger and speculate as to his reasoning. Corbett tackles the major issue of the capital losses first. By 1961/62 the accumulated deficit of BOAC stood at £67,293,838, and it included provision for losses on the Britannia aircraft of £22.4 million, on the DC-7Cs £4.6 million and on the Comet 4s £4.7 million; the associated companies accounted for a further £13.8 million, and interest £27.9 million.

He could not understand why the amortisation of the various aircraft had been kept at their existing levels, namely seven years straight-line depreciation to 25 per cent of the residual value, when that did not reflect their planned service life, four years in the case of the DC-7C and six years for the Britannia. 'Was it right to apply this to a turbo-prop aircraft (Britannia) which came into service 2½ years late?' He continues: 'In the two years 1959/60 and 1960/61 the Corporation continued to charge the same rate of obsolescence on its aircraft and in each year a profit of over £4 million was shown on the Operating Account.' He criticises the Board: 'I can find no evidence that an increase in the obsolescence charge was considered – there is certainly no evidence that it was ever considered with the Ministry.' Corbett has to suspend belief repeatedly: 'I find it hard to believe that Sir Gerard (d'Erlanger) was contending that a seven-year life with 25 per cent residual value was realistic.' He brushes off excuses that the Minister objected to the obsolescence charge being increased and was entitled so to direct them. 'I find it hard to believe that Sir George Cribbett, who had been deputy secretary in the Ministry, could have been under the impression that the Act gave the Minister such power.' Corbett says of the Minister, Watkinson:

> I am at a loss to understand why (so far as the written record is concerned) no one in any quarter pressed for an increase in the obsolescence charge… I think that by 1959, if not earlier, it should have been obvious that the rate of obsolescence which was being charged in the BOAC accounts was entirely inadequate.

Criticism does not come much stronger than 'I am at a loss to understand.'

As for the associated companies, around £12 million of the deficit had accumulated over the past six years, roughly the time of Cribbett's tenure. Corbett found a lack of any clear policy and a complete lack of financial and management control:

> Occasional references are found that the loss of a particular company must not exceed a certain figure, but there were few signs of speedy action having been taken when such a figure was in fact exceeded… Although the value of feeder traffic was often claimed as one of the advantages that was derived from the associated companies, it is clear to me that up to July 1962 the Board had no recorded estimates as to the extent of this traffic.

His conclusions are echoed elsewhere in the report: 'I think the Board felt that it was acting in the national interest in making these investments.'

Corbett allows BOAC its share of gripes, and lays great stress on the perceived threat posed by the newly enfranchised independents:

> BOAC maintains, and I think justly, that the new licensing procedure introduced by the 1960 Act encourages attempts by independent operators to run services competing to a greater or lesser extent with the Corporation's network… The present position whereby BOAC faces increased competition on its routes either from or by reason of the independent operators and yet can get no share in the trooping contracts is very hurtful to it.'

Whether BOAC actually believed that is open to doubt, certainly the government and its civil servants did not, but it shows BOAC's skill in drawing fire away from its deficiencies, and pulling the wool over the eyes of an intelligent man. As the Edwards Report was to remind us in later years, the only services ever licensed to compete with BOAC, 'were not really for new routes but were reaffirmation of 'grandfather' rights which had been granted in the period before the 1960 Licensing Act was introduced.'[18]

Turning to organisation and management, Corbett learned from Watkinson that d'Erlanger had not wanted the job of chairman after Thomas quit, and had had to be pressed to accept, which he did on condition that he had an additional full-time executive to help him. Watkinson chose Cribbett, which was another mistake because of the clash of personalities which ensued:

> … and some means had to be found to enable Sir George Cribbett and Sir Basil Smallpeice to work together under the Chairman. I believe that for the four years prior to Sir Matthew Slattery's appointment the administration of BOAC was weak. I think the position was aggravated by the fact that the Chairman and Board were conscious of their obligation to act in the national interest and this, I think, they construed as being synonymous with the Minister's wishes, and they paid all too little regard to the cost in which BOAC was involved.

Corbett struggles briefly with temptation, then succumbs:

> It is very tempting to attribute to the Managing Director a large share of the blame for the shortcomings of the d'Erlanger administration. It should, however, be remembered that many of the matters criticized in the report were handled personally by the Chairman, and it was the Chairman who set the tone with emphasis on expansion and prestige. I think, however, that the Managing Director should have taken a much stronger line.

It did not help that the corporation was rather inward looking: 'During this period there has been very little intake of senior executives from outside, almost all the vacancies created as a result of retirements and expansion having been filled from within the organisation. I am not sure that this has proved a good thing.'

On engineering, Corbett was critical of the relatively higher costs of BOAC, blaming bad organisation procedures and management, and poor labour relations: 'For example, faced with a substantial figure of redundancy of employees in 1957, management has nevertheless authorised the recruitment of some 2,000 employees over the past five years.' As for sales and marketing, he discovered that not everyone thought British was best:

> It is significant that most of the small minority of people who are critical of BOAC are frequent business travellers who have flown by a number of different airlines. The main criticisms are of poor and unfriendly cabin and ground service, lack of variety of food and inadequate use of foreign languages.

Thus suggesting that the British are prepared to put up with second best, and foreigners do not like British food. In other organisational issues, he goes on to pin much of the blame squarely on Smallpeice: 'As regards the organisation generally, I would say that far too much is centred on the Managing Director's office. This may well be the cause of a second criticism of lack of delegation in a number of divisions of the organisation.' Corbett believed in making the best use of the material at hand, and pays moving tribute to the senior executives, 'who could be given the chance to run the airline within a clearly defined commercial policy, inspired by a firm lead from the top… would not be found wanting. The loyalty, amounting almost to devotion, of the senior executives in the Corporation is quite outstanding.'

There, then, is the VC10 Story. I have included the full text of this chapter, paragraphs 208-364, as Appendix Seven, in view of the continuing controversy surrounding the VC10. He starts during the spring of 1957, following BOAC's decision in autumn 1956 to order Boeing 707s. In order to launch the VC10 project, Vickers needed firm orders for thirty-five aircraft at £1.7 million each; BOAC wanted twenty aircraft at £1.6 million each. There was also a difference in estimated operating costs; Vickers put the figure at 13.7 pence per ctm, whilst BOAC wanted costs of 12 pence per ctm. Despite this, the BOAC Board was prepared to order twenty-five aircraft, with options on another ten, and on 30 April 1957 d'Erlanger wrote to the Minister seeking approval for thirty-five VC10s at an estimated price of £1,770,000 each. As Corbett observes, within seven days of the previous meeting, BOAC had decided it could, after all, take thirty-five against twenty or twenty-five aircraft, pay the higher price and accept the higher operating cost, even though the yardstick, the Boeing 707, had operating costs of 12 pence per ctm. The government approved the order on 22 May 1957. By the end of 1957, the cost of each aircraft had escalated to £2,107,000, yet on 31 December 1957 the BOAC Board formally approved thirty long-range VC10s for southern and eastern routes, although it proposed reducing the order as at the same time it concluded that the VC10 would not be competitive with the Boeing 707 on the North Atlantic. Just eight days later Smallpeice submitted a paper based on findings of the Royal Aircraft Establishment (RAE) which claimed to show that in fact the VC10, because of its superior take-off characteristics, would turn out to have a cost per ctm on the North Atlantic of 12.5 pence per ctm, as opposed to the Boeing costs of 12.7 pence per ctm, so the Board ordered thirty-five aircraft after all. Corbett did his own research on the findings, and comments that the RAE was not dealing with operating costs, so the figures that Smallpeice used were BOAC's calculations.[19] By this time the Minister was having doubts, and there followed an exchange of letters that Corbett calls extraordinary, in which the Minister asks BOAC to confirm that it really is satisfied with the performance and likely operating costs of the VC10. As Corbett says, 'the extraordinary features about this correspondence are, first, that BOAC as the buyer should be prepared to rate the VC10 aircraft higher than Vickers as the seller were prepared to guarantee, and, second, that the chairman of BOAC, who is later on record as saying that he never wanted to buy the VC10 but always wanted a Boeing, should have confused himself into assuring the Minister that BOAC felt the VC10 would be as good as the Boeing... If d'Erlanger did not want the VC10, here was a golden opportunity to lay before the Minister the very heavy annual burden that would be placed on flying it rather than the Boeing.' The order for thirty-five VC10s was signed on 14 January 1958 and there follows a comparative lull until January 1960, when Vickers said that they had seriously underestimated the costs of making the thirty-five VC10s, and the position was so serious that they needed an order for an additional ten aircraft at £2.7 million each immediately for them to be able to continue production. Although the evidence is circumstantial and weak, BOAC felt it was under pressure to order more aircraft, but they were interested in a larger aircraft, a stretched VC10. So a few days later d'Erlanger went to see Sandys, and BOAC ordered ten more VC10s. Sandys's letter to the Board, which went on the public record, noted that although he had made it clear that he was not asking them to adopt this course, the decision was 'most helpful' to the aircraft industry. Corbett's comment is, 'contrary to what it says, I believe it supports the Board's case of ministerial pressure.'

'I pass now to May 1960 and to the first record I can find of any dissatisfaction being expressed by BOAC to the Ministry about the economic viability of the VC10 fleet': on 12 May 1960 d'Erlanger wrote to the Minister to tell him in a rather roundabout way that the fleet of VC10s was going to cost £7.5 million more per annum to operate than their competitor's comparable fleet. Corbett says he is satisfied that the Ministry knew that BOAC's total costs were going to be 20 per cent higher than rivals, and that there would be between £5 million and £10 million in introductory costs for the VC10.

Just before he resigned, d'Erlanger wrote to the Minister on 12 July 1960 to say that if BOAC had had the choice, it would have ordered Boeings, but the government had made it clear that it would not sanction any more 707 orders. Between September 1960 and January 1961, the VC10 order was revamped and there were further changes to the size and specifications of the two versions of the aircraft. Instead of thirty-five standard and ten stretched VC10s, fifteen standard and thirty Super VC10s were to be ordered, the thirty Super VC10s being slightly smaller than the original stretched version. These came at higher cost, but the government said that the overall cost of the purchase could not be increased, so the order for the standard VC10s was then reduced to twelve, making forty-two VC10s of both types in all, and Vickers were paid £600,000 compensation for the cancelled order.

After Sir Matthew Slattery took over as chairman, he wrote to the new minister, Peter Thorneycroft, setting out the 'grave' disadvantage of operating VC10s instead of Boeings; the annual penalty of between £7 million and £11 million would need an increase of six percentage points of load factor to eliminate the penalty. Vickers disputed the figures, so BOAC asked Stephen Wheatcroft, the aviation economist, to review the matter. He arrived at a figure of £10.7 million in 1966/7, going down to £7.5 million after the early years.

Corbett goes on to deny the oft-repeated claim that somehow the VC10s higher operating costs should be offset against its greater passenger appeal and subsequent better load factors: 'I do not agree.' He says that any sound commercial board 'would have required considerably improved "consumer appeal" as an offset to the heavy costs of developing and installing a new type of aircraft and the recurrent additional annual costs of running two fleets instead of one.' The passenger appeal should have been factored into the higher purchase and introductory costs of the aircraft, and, he continues, the operating costs of the aircraft should be on a par, at the very least, with the previously delivered 707s.

> In my view, if, when the VC10 fleet is fully operational, the annual costs of operating it are higher than the costs of operating an appropriate fleet of Boeings, excluding in each case pre-operational or development costs, the difference is the true measure of the burden on BOAC which arises from the decision to buy British aircraft.
>
> The whole trend of the VC10 negotiations is very bewildering. There is no question that in the autumn of 1956 the Government insisted that BOAC should buy British... The negotiations about the VC10 were handled personally by Sir Gerard d'Erlanger and I think he genuinely felt that he was acting in the national interest if he met the Minister's wishes.

He concludes by saying that he thinks BOAC only needs twenty-nine VC10s, not forty-two.

Now it was time for Corbett to address other issues; after some criticisms of the BOAC-Cunard venture, and observing the management at BOAC encouraged its planners to use forecasts that were too optimistic. He points out that the revenue figures for 1962/63 were actually less than those for 1961/62: 'The revised budget contemplated a surplus of nearly £1 million, whereas in fact a deficiency of nearly £5½ million appears to have been suffered.'

## RECOMMENDATION AND IMPLEMENTATION

Corbett sums up as follows: as of 1961/62, BOAC had accumulated deficiencies of £67 million, and by March 1963 there was a further deficiency of £14 million, an aggregate deficiency of £81 million for an organisation which is 'extravagantly staffed.' BOAC has on order thirteen more aircraft than it needs, which are:

> … likely to have direct operating costs substantially higher than those of the Boeing which its competitors are flying… I conclude that it should have been obvious by 1959, if not earlier, that the rate of obsolescence which was being charged in the BOAC accounts was entirely inadequate.

He does not blame d'Erlanger for the mixed fleet that had been introduced, that was down to earlier management, but 'I think that the budget (for 1962/63) was prepared on a far too optimistic plane.'

> I think the wise thing to do would be to write the Comets and Britannias down to their estimated residual value at 31 March, 1963, which would cost £12 million and would increase the loss for the year to £26 million. The total accumulated losses would rise to £93 million. I must advise you that there is no prospect of this enormous loss ever being recovered and it is quite unrealistic to imagine that BOAC will ever be able to earn sufficient to pay interest on this lost capital… I am sure the sensible course is to allow it to be written off by the cancellation of an equivalent amount of indebtedness to the Government.
>
> I question whether the dual role of having to operate commercially and yet to have regard to 'interests of a national and non-commercial kind' is in practice really satisfactory. I am convinced that during the period I have reviewed the dual obligation on the Board of BOAC has led it into some very confused thinking, particularly in connection with the VC10 negotiations and the administration of associated companies.

He thinks that if there was ever a conflict between commercial interest and national interest, then the Minister should issue a directive. There is some small acknowledgment of the independents:

> I have referred in paragraphs 99-106 to the way in which independent airlines have been permitted to encroach upon BOAC's previous preserves. I have suggested that you may feel

it would be fair both to the two international airlines and also to the independents that you allow the matter to be reviewed so as to determine the part which the independents should be permitted and expected to play in the provision of air services.

As to the VC10, he is disappointed that the only recommendations he can make are either to pass the thirteen surplus VC10s to the RAF, or to take the aircraft over and lease them to BOAC at a rate comparable to the Boeing 707. And for the future: 'Fundamentally BOAC needs two things – strong and efficient management and aircraft that are competitive.'

Had anything changed since 1940? Now the government had to act. The new Prime Minister, Sir Alec Douglas-Home, received plenty of advice from his staff:

> BOAC is in a financial mess and new management is needed; the financial mess has been made worse as a result of the Government's pressure on them to buy the VC10; the report by Mr Corbett has revealed all: is the Government now to tell all?[20]

These were the spirited comments from Timothy Bligh, the Principal Private Secretary he had inherited from Macmillan. The short answer was no, the government was not about to tell all, and indeed had spent the best part of six months figuring out how it could avoid doing so, sometimes to the dismay of the Cabinet Secretary, Sir Burke Trend:

> The White Paper is not an expurgated version of the Corbett report; it is the Government's own analysis of the reasons for BOAC's parlous position, prepared by a group of ministers on the basis of Corbett's findings. If so, it is essential that the status of the White Paper should be made clear and that public opinion should have no grounds for supposing that it is a bowdlerized version of the Corbett report itself…The main points at which the White Paper is most vulnerable (i.e. the main points where it diverges from the Corbett report) are these…'[21]

Trend went on to point out where the Government proposed a few economies with the truth. In the event, not even this White Paper made it into the public domain, as an even shorter version was published, causing Trend to mutter: 'The fact that the revised version owes so little to Corbett could be argued to imply that Corbett's criticisms had been deliberately omitted or toned down, particularly those which attributed some blame or default to the Government themselves.'[22]

Corbett's report, without the numerous appendices and accompanying reports, ran to 139 pages. The White Paper *The Financial Problems of the British Overseas Airways Corporation* ran to thirteen and a half pages, and as *Flight* remarked disgustedly, 'nine of those merely retrace the familiar historical background or restate facts already well known.'[23] The remaining four and a half pages threw very little light indeed on the problem areas that required stronger management: unsatisfactory handling of associate companies; unduly optimistic forecasting; ineffective financial control and the excessive maintenance costs. Readers may well wonder where are the references to the VC10. So did *Flight*: 'The big VC10 issues are ignored, and there is no reference to BOAC's estimates… of the £8 million–£14 million excess annual operating cost of the new fleet.' But the government got away with it, behind closed doors.

BEA shows off its de Havilland jets, Trident 1C and Comet 4B. (Royal Aeronautical Society Library)

Sir Giles Guthrie was given a year to get BOAC back on its feet, the implication being that if matters did improve the Government would consider writing off the £80 million deficit. The Government intended all along to forgive the corporation its debt, but heads had to roll before the government could steer the restructuring through Parliament. All the more galling, therefore, that BEA was able to announce its 'most golden summer', anticipating a substantial profit for the financial year; to make matters worse, Air Holdings, British United's holding company, announced a profit of over £1 million for the same period. In the meantime BOAC's borrowing powers were extended yet again.

Smallpeice left to become chairman of Cunard. Also leaving the arena, albeit for different reasons, was BEA's chairman Lord Douglas, retiring in 1964 after fifteen years at the helm. BEA was able to announce profits for the year of over £3 million, a measure of now much BEA had changed over the years; another measure was that the corporation now carried just under 5 million passengers a year, making it the largest carrier outside the US and Russia. BEA seemed more at ease with the nation's aircraft builders, during this period buying British-built aircraft exclusively and with relatively little fuss; indeed the Trident had just entered service with BEA during March 1964. Lord Douglas was succeeded as chairman by Anthony Milward, and Henry Marking became chief executive. Lord Douglas himself performed something of a 180-degree turn and became chairman of Vladimir Raitz's tour-operating company Horizon Holidays. Forgetting past battles over IT licences, Lord Douglas said: 'I regard inclusive tours as the particular province of the independent air companies who should concentrate on this work rather than compete against nationalised airlines on scheduled services.'[24]

## BRITISH EAGLE SET TO SOAR

Early in 1964 British Eagle's perseverance seemed at last to pay off when the Commissioner overturned some of the Board's decisions on its domestic routes. The Commissioner, Sir Arthur Hutchinson, by now something of an old hand at hearing appeals, still refused to grant a London-Manchester licence but did increase British Eagle's frequencies, up from seven to ten on Edinburgh, and from seven to twelve on Glasgow. So many of his conclusions were at variance with the Board's that a significant regulatory layer was now perceived as having been added. The Board now became merely the first step in a lengthy and expensive process; the final decision rested with the Appeals Commissioner (often Hutchinson who was developing some expertise), and then the Minister. British Eagle introduced the higher frequencies on 1 April 1964, and substituted Viscounts for the Britannia on the Belfast service which was still restricted to once daily. On 1 June the airline inaugurated scheduled services from London to Stuttgart, a new international route.

British Eagle enjoyed further good fortune when it was awarded the Far East trooping contract from 10 May 1964, worth some £3 million and 11,000 flying hours a year, to operate five Britannia flights a week to Singapore and Hong Kong. In July the airline started flying the government contract to Adelaide with a Britannia freighter, which it had converted itself with a large freight door at its extensive Heathrow engineering facility. Further Australian flying followed in October, after British Eagle was awarded a contract by Qantas to carry around 6,000 new immigrants to Australia as part of the Assisted Passage Scheme, taking over flights that had previously been operated by BOAC. President Johnson signed the airline's '402' charter permit in March, so British Eagle became the second airline after Caledonian to receive charter rights to the US. There was, however, still some rain to fall on Bamberg's parade.

When he bought back Eagle from Cunard, Bamberg agreed not to compete with BOAC-Cunard on ATLB-licensed scheduled-service routes for three years from March 1963 or for as long as Cunard retained a shareholding. He was happy to be awarded his American charter permit, of course, but in no time he had registered a new airline in Bermuda, Eagle International Airlines (Bermuda). With a considerable store of goodwill in the colony, he doubtless wanted to emulate his previous and very successful ventures in Bermuda and the Bahamas. However, in an extraordinary act of mean-spiritedness and to the outrage of many colonial administrations, the British Government suddenly decreed that all aircraft registered in British colonies and protectorates would now be required to obtain a licence from the British Air Transport Licensing Board if they wanted to fly services into the United Kingdom. The new regulation meant any application by a Bermuda-registered airline to fly between London and Bermuda would require both approval from the Bermuda authorities and a licence from the British ATLB.[25] The British Government was able to push this change through by using a so-called Statutory Instrument which can be used to give the Minister emergency powers. There was no consultation with colonial governments beforehand, many of which pursued robust aviation policies and were consequently affronted by the high-handed behaviour of the British Government. Mike Ramsden, Air Transport Editor of *Flight*, understood the significance of this development completely:

The effect of this new regulation, passed without a murmur by Parliament, was to bring within UK jurisdiction any proposed operations by the Eagle Bermuda company to London....The new regulation was obviously aimed at Bermuda, and at Bamberg in particular. It seems extraordinary that what is in effect an Act of Parliament can be passed to defeat the specific purpose of a British company in this way.[26]

It certainly stayed Bamberg's plans in Bermuda, and gave him added impetus to try and buy out the rest of Cunard's shareholding. Just to make doubly sure that Bamberg would not try again, the Board then revoked the airline's 'B' licence which would have allowed the airline to operate IT charter flights for Sir Henry Lunn to Bermuda and the Bahamas; the licence had been actively supported by the Government of Bermuda. British Eagle was no luckier when it tried to operate IT charters to another colony, Gibraltar. The Board found that there was sufficient capacity offered by the two scheduled airlines, BEA and British United, setting a precedent in favour of scheduled services to the Rock that was to last many, many years.

## BRITISH UNITED AND THE VC10

The VC10 entered service with BOAC on 29 April 1964 on its West African services. The controversy over the VC10 orders, and BOAC's subsequent highly publicised difficulties, cast a shadow over this fine aircraft. In marked contrast British United, and especially its managing director Freddie Laker, were unabashed enthusiasts for the type, eagerly looking forward to its entry into service. At Farnborough that year the British Aircraft Corporation demonstrated a One-Eleven and VC10 in British United's colours, the Super VC10 appearing only in house colours, a telling comment on where the aircraft manufacturer thought its future prospects lay. The VC10 was in any case well suited to British United's requirements, smaller than the Boeing 707 and with the performance it needed for the African routes; it was able to fly Nairobi-London non-stop. The aircraft were specified to a higher standard than the corporation's aircraft, with a large freight door and extended wing tips for better performance.

Intended primarily for use on the airline's African services, British United was also successful in tendering for renewal of the trooping contract with the jet to Aden, East Africa and Bahrain from 1 October; British United planned to install 129 rearward-facing seats for this contract but otherwise could configure the aircraft for up to sixteen first-class and ninety-three tourist-class passengers, depending on the amount of freight to be carried. The airline was not awarded the Cyprus contract; we saw how this was given to the RAF after the Treasury's intervention. The award of these trooping contracts compensated British United in some measure for the loss of the Far East air movement task which had been given to British Eagle. Laker had been very unhappy at the loss of this contract which British United had held for five years. He complained that British Eagle had been able to undercut his airline's tender only because BOAC agreed to lease Britannias to the airline at a rate of around £55,000 a month, whereas British United had to pay BOAC £122,000 a month for its leased Britannias. The airline was also saddled with four Britannias that its predecessor companies had bought new and was painstakingly depreciating over a ten-year period. He complained bitterly to the Air Ministry, even accusing it of being 'most unethical' in its handling of the tendering,[27] but the Ministry was unimpressed. The Air Ministry wanted to maintain two long-haul charter contractors, and so was not inclined to place all the major contracts with British United; furthermore, as the Ministry reminded Laker, it had been very accommodating in renegotiating the Far East contract after British United had terminated the original Hunting-Clan agreement. Indeed British United had held the contract for five years in total, two years longer than usual. Laker had little choice but to accept, leading to the run-down of Stansted as the major trooping centre in the United Kingdom, with a consequent loss of jobs. British Eagle's flights were operated from its base at Heathrow, and the new Aden, Bahrein and East African services were to be flown by the VC10s out of Gatwick. Stansted would remain in the doldrums until the development of North Atlantic affinity group flying at the end of the decade.

## NORTH ATLANTIC DEVELOPMENTS

The developments at Cunard Eagle may well have stayed its activities in that market but interest in low-fare traffic to and from the United States remained live. Caledonian followed up its award of an United States charter permit by applying for an inclusive-tour licence and, more controversially, for a low-fare scheduled licence flown with propeller aircraft. The Icelandic airline Loftleiđir had pioneered the concept, offering a 10 per cent price advantage over normal IATA fares on its service between New York and Luxembourg, which transited Reykjavik and was operated by Douglas DC-6s. Caledonian wanted to develop its own low-fare discount service, using DC-7Cs and trading on its Scottish heritage. BOAC objected although it had just sold a DC-7C to Caledonian. The Board rejected the scheduled-service bid although it allowed the IT licence; the demand, however, was not for relatively expensive inclusive tours, but for price-competitive seat-only charters, and this was now met by affinity group travel. The closed group, or affinity group, may have been effectively stifled on routes within Europe but the concept was enjoying a new lease of life on the Atlantic; almost one quarter of a million passengers had travelled on affinity charters in 1963 between the USA and Europe. Most of these passengers were carried on IATA airlines, such as BOAC, Air France, KLM, Lufthansa and Sabena, but that did not prevent nasty spats erupting amongst the Association's member airlines. The luckless members of the Midland Dahlia Society found themselves stranded at Heathrow one day in September 1964 after an Alitalia staff member had allegedly procured a ticket on the Society's BOAC charter by answering an advertisement in *The Times*. He then reported the breach of charter rules, and in order to avoid an IATA-imposed fine BOAC felt obliged to cancel the flight.

## SIR GILES GUTHRIE RETRENCHES

As well as negotiating with the government over the cancellation of the £80 million deficit, Sir Giles Guthrie began some pruning of his own. He was in a relatively strong position after the expulsion of his predecessors, having received a directive from Amery that 'the interchange of views between the Government and the Corporation should not blur the fundamental responsibility of the Corporation to act in accordance with their commercial judgment.'[28] He now decided to exercise his commercial judgment and returned to the subject of the VC10; he wanted to cancel all the thirty Super VC10s on order. The government was appalled. It was estimated 4,500 people would be thrown out of work, it would be the end of the VC10 programme, and it would have repercussions throughout the aircraft industry:

> The VC10 contract was one of the foundations upon which the Government persuaded Vickers and other firms to join in setting up the British Aircraft Corporation. To allow this contract to be cancelled would shake the confidence of the aircraft industry in the Government's aviation policy.[29]

To make matters worse, Guthrie wanted to replace the cancelled VC10s with six Boeing 707-320Cs. 'This is a fearful decision,' was Douglas-Home's comment. So the Ministry of Aviation proposed that the Boeing 707s should be sold, and all the VC10s kept instead. These were the days before pendulum arbitration, so the Treasury was called in to broker a deal and arrived at the least costly solution; to cancel the ten VC10s which had not actually been built. It was estimated that would save around £27 million by comparison to either of the other two proposals. So the total order was reduced to twenty-nine aircraft, the figure suggested by Corbett; in order to mitigate the blow to the British Aircraft Corporation, the ten aircraft were not exactly 'cancelled' but 'held in abeyance', and the government agreed to transfer three of the putative BOAC order to the RAF, which now found that it was to have fourteen VC10s rather than the eleven originally ordered.

In the next exercise of its commercial judgment, BOAC decided in February 1964 it could no longer maintain the South American services to Brazil, Argentina and Chile and asked the government for a subsidy. The South American services had had a chequered development, first at the hands of BSAA, after which they were taken over by BOAC and as quickly dropped by them following the Comet disasters. Eventually reinstated in 1960, the service was operated twice weekly by Comets at an annual loss of £1.25 million. The Foreign Office, concerned with British prestige, wanted to offer a subsidy, but Boyd-Carpenter at the Treasury was unimpressed, pointing out that the government was trying to get BOAC to run on commercial lines and the Government had already refused the shipping lines when they had asked for such a subsidy. Guthrie piled on the pressure, insisting that he would withdraw service at the end of September. The Government finally floated the idea that maybe another British airline should take the routes over. The only serious contender at this stage and at such short notice was British United, which had just accepted two VC10s, and energetically took up the challenge; minutes before the bell, on 24 September 1964, BUA announced it was taking over the east-coast route to South America. To an outgoing Conservative Government, one by now somewhat irritated by the short-comings of at least one of the state corporations in its charge, the opportune circumstance of an independent airline having the resources, will and ability to assume part of the state's commercial responsibility might have seemed a vindication of the party's supposed espousal of private enterprise. Had the Conservatives remained in power, greater encouragement and more opportunities might have been offered to the independents; there would have been less incentive to protect the state corporations at all costs if a viable private enterprise airline could offer a safety net instead. Up until now Tory policy had merely produced two different sorts of monopoly: one for the corporations and a second for government trooping contracts. Sir Myles Wyatt had talked of the independents 'basking in the pale sunshine of the Conservative Government.'[30] Had the Conservatives' aviation policy evolved further at this juncture, the independents might have acquired more of a glowing suntan.

It was not to be, however. The Macmillan era was over; the new Prime Minister called an election for 15 October 1964, when it was widely predicted that the Labour Party, after thirteen years of Tory rule, would win a commanding majority. It was the end of another era, too. Pioneer aviator and motorist, sportsman and politician, Lord Brabazon had died in May; fascinated by civil aviation up to the very end, he was still campaigning for greater safety in the air, a restless subject in a changing world.

# AIRCRAFT TYPES

At the end of the war, there were twenty-seven firms designing and manufacturing aircraft, and a further eight building aircraft engines. They had to make the switch from wartime production to the demanding requirements of the post-war era, and were guided in this by the War Cabinet, which had asked Lord Brabazon to advise what civil aircraft the manufacturers should design and build; between 1943 and 1945 his committee proposed what became known as the Brabazon types, listed in the introduction. Manufacturers also produced so-called 'interim' types, usually bombers converted to transports at various levels of complexity. The Avro Lancastrian, for example, was a more or less standard Lancaster bomber converted to carry up to thirteen passengers; whereas the Avro York used the wings, tail and engines of the Lancaster, but substituted a larger fuselage. As well as the interim types, and the later Brabazon types, manufacturers also launched their own designs. These had to be approved by the Ministry of Aircraft Production, which controlled the supply of materials and resources; this became the Ministry of Supply after the war and had different responsibilities from those of the Ministry of Civil Aviation, which was the regulator for civil air transport. That just added to the general confusion.

## AIRSPEED (LATER DE HAVILLAND) AMBASSADOR.

The Ambassador was built to the Brabazon Committee's Type 2 recommendation for a short-haul aircraft, originally intended as a DC-3 replacement. BEA ordered twenty of the piston-engine aircraft, but after it had taken over Airspeed, de Havilland, already heavily committed to the Comet, decided not to build any more. BEA withdrew the type in 1958 but Ambassadors continued to give good service with the independents, flying for BKS, Autair and Dan-Air. The aircraft could carry up to fifty-five passengers over a distance of 1,000 miles and so needed a refuelling stop to reach destinations in Spain.

## ARGONAUT

See Douglas DC-4 Skymaster/ Canadair C4 (DC-4M).

BEA was the only airline to buy new Airspeed Ambassadors, and G-ALZW, now with BKS, shows signs of its previous owner's livery. (MAP)

## AVIATION TRADER ATL.98 CARVAIR

Conceived as a replacement for the Bristol Freighters used on vehicle-ferry services, the Carvair was based on the DC-4 with a new bulbous nose and larger tail, and could carry five cars and twenty-five passengers. Aviation Traders built twenty-one of them, which saw service in Europe and Australia as well as on their intended cross-Channel routes. Although DC-4s were plentiful and cheap to buy, the conversion was expensive, and the old DC-4s were not as reliable as the Freighters. Cars had to be hoisted on a loader up to the door, which slowed down turn-round times, and left the Carvair better suited to the deeper-penetration routes in to Europe, in themselves a move away from the short, high-frequency services that sustained the operations of Silver City and Channel Air Bridge during the 1950s. Nevertheless it was a technically ingenious solution to a unique challenge.

## AVRO YORK

Based on the Lancaster bomber, but with a new large-capacity square-section fuselage, 258 Yorks were built between 1942 and 1948. The backbone of the RAF's transport capability immediately after the war, new Yorks also entered service with BOAC, BSAA and Skyways. Carrying thirty passengers, or up to nine tons of freight over 1,000 miles, Yorks were used extensively by British charter airlines in the 1950s. Skyways, Eagle, Air Charter, Scottish Aviation, Hunting and Dan-Air operated sizeable fleets. Skyways and Dan-Air withdrew their last Yorks in 1964.

## AVRO TUDOR

Rejected by BOAC, and contributing to BSAA's downfall, the Tudor nevertheless proved to be a good load carrier, especially during the Berlin Airlift. The versions that are relevant to this story are as follows:

Channel Air Bridge's Carvair G-ANYB showing off its hump. It could carry up to five cars. (MAP)

Four Rolls-Royce Merlins power up Avro York G-AMGM as it starts another freight flight for Hunting-Clan. (MAP)

## Tudor 1:

The original short fuselage version, seating between twelve and twenty-four passengers. It was not accepted by BOAC and most were subsequently rebuilt as Mk 4s for BSAA.

## Tudor 2:

The longer fuselage version, seating up to sixty passengers, of which only four were built; they were the only Tudors allowed to carry passengers after the passenger certificates for the Mk 4s were withdrawn in 1949.

Avro Tudor 2 G-AGRY at Southend, with Laker's Rolls-Royce Silver Dawn parked in front of its Rolls-Royce Merlin engines. (MAP)

## Tudor 4:

With a fuselage 5ft longer than the Tudor 1, this was the version used by BSAA and Air Charter. It had a range of 4,000 miles, and could carry up to thirty-two passengers, but Laker's plans to use them for passenger work were thwarted when the military refused to allow them to be used for trooping flights; he converted them into freighters instead.

## Tudor 5:

With the same fuselage length as the Tudor 2, the six aircraft built were used on the Berlin Airlift as fuel carriers by BSAA and AVM Bennett's Fairflight.

## AVRO 748 (LATER HAWKER SIDDELEY 748)

When Duncan Sandys declared in 1957 that there would be no future requirement for manned-military aircraft, Avro, manufacturers of the Vulcan bomber, decided that a return to the civilian market would be timely, following its difficulties with the Tudor. The company chose to re-enter the market with another essay at a DC-3 replacement, a twin turboprop low-wing aircraft, tough, durable, easy to maintain, cheap to operate and with superior airfield performance. At the same time the Indian Government was keen to build a replacement for the many DC-3s still in service in India, both with the Indian Air Force and Indian Airlines, and agreed to build the 748 under licence at Kanpur. Skyways was the launch customer for the initial Series 1 version, which first flew on 24 June 1960 and the first Indian built aircraft flew on 1 November 1961. The aircraft achieved worldwide sales on every continent, and was continuously developed throughout its life.

# BELL 47

The two-seat Bell 47 helicopter first flew in December 1945, and many thousands were built before production ceased in 1973. BEA and Autair used early versions. In 1964 Westland acquired a licence to build over 200 for the British army and subsequently sold sixteen to Bristow for helicopter training.

BKS liked its passengers to know that they were flying in an Avro Prop-Jet 748. G-ARMX was shared with Skyways during the early years. (MAP)

Bell 47G G-ASYW of Bristow Helicopters, used for training. (MAP)

# BOEING STRATOCRUISER

A development of the C97 military transport, the Stratocruiser had a capacious 'double-bubble' two-deck fuselage, with seating in BOAC service for fifty-two passengers together with a number of sleeping berths on the upper deck, and a lounge-bar and freight holds below. BOAC pioneered its luxurious 'Monarch' service with Stratocruisers in the early 1950s.

BOAC's Stratocruiser G-ANTX *Cleopatra* shows off its impressive bulk. There was a cocktail lounge on the lower deck. (MAP)

Boeing 707 G-ARWE in blue and gold BOAC-Cunard markings. This aircraft was ordered by Cunard Eagle but delivered to BOAC after the take-over. (MAP)

## BOEING 707

A development of the 367-80 prototype and its KC-135 military derivative, the Boeing 707-120 entered service with Pan American on the New York-London route on 26 October 1958. Like the Comet 4, the 707-120 was not intended for long-haul over-water stages and was only used on those routes until the larger, longer-range versions of the same design, the 707-320 and 707-420, became available one year later. The 707-420 was powered by Rolls-Royce Conway by-pass engines, and was ordered by a number of airlines apart from BOAC.

## BRISTOL TYPE 170 FREIGHTER/WAYFARER

Owing much to the pre-war design of the Bombay, the Type 170 was to have been used to carry vehicles and supplies to jungle airstrips during the Burma campaign but the war ended before this could be realised. Bristol adapted the design to have a stronger floor and large opening nose doors, calling it the Freighter, and a passenger-carrying version without the nose doors, the Wayfarer. Tough and very reliable, the aircraft was sold to air forces and airlines throughout the world but is perhaps best remembered for its role in the 1950s as a vehicle ferry with Silver City, Channel Air Bridge and British United Air Ferries. The Freighter could carry two cars and up to fifteen passengers; the later and larger Super Freighters could carry three cars and up to twenty-three passengers. As a freighter, the aircraft could carry up to five tons over 380 miles, slowly.

After Silver City took over Air Kruise, they transferred to it some of the Bristol Freighters which had been converted to all-passenger Wayfarers. G-AHJI is shown at Blackbushe in 1956. (MAP)

Bristol Super Freighter G-AMWD, formerly with Silver City. After the take-over British United Air Ferries generously endowed the type with a more uplifting name, 'Superbristol'. (MAP)

## BRISTOL TYPE 175 BRITANNIA

Although the Brabazon Committee's Type 3 recommendations failed to mature, BOAC's requirements for a Medium Range Empire (MRE) transport were not dissimilar. Bristol at first proposed a licence-built Constellation 749 powered by its Centaurus engine but the Treasury turned down this proposal on foreign-exchange grounds, and Bristol instead produced its own design, the Type 175, originally a forty-four-seater and still powered by the Centaurus. Successful bench-running of the Proteus turbine engine allowed the design to be scaled up, ninety passengers could be carried and the design further improved to give transatlantic-range capability. The Centaurus version was dropped, and the aircraft was given the name Britannia. It first flew on 16 August 1952, but its development was troublesome, the Proteus engines being prone to flaming out in certain conditions and a cure was not easy to find. Although the first of the shorter-range Britannias were delivered to BOAC in December 1955, it was not until February 1957 that they entered service with the corporation, initially on Australian and Far East routes. The longer range 312 series entered service on United States routes on 19 December 1957, only one year before the Comet and Boeing 707. BOAC began to dispose of the 102 series as early as 1960, and the final BOAC Britannia service was flown on 26 April 1965. New Britannias were bought by Air Charter and Hunting-Clan but the type went on to have a successful second career in the 1960s and early 1970s with a number of British independent airlines, many of which acquired large fleets.

## DAKOTA, DC-3, DC-4, DC-6 AND DC-7

See under Douglas.

## DE HAVILLAND

See under DH

British Eagle's Bristol Britannia G-AOVG about to leave on another trooping flight from Singapore's Paya Lebar Airport. (MAP)

Olley Air Service de Havilland Rapide G-AGSI still shows its wartime nationality markings on the tail, when it operated with the Associated Airways Joint Committee. (MAP)

## DH 89 RAPIDE

Rapides were the mainstay of British airlines before, during and immediately after the war. An elegant biplane, carrying six-to-eight passengers on two Gipsy Queen engines of 200hp each, the Rapide flew at 115 mph and had a range of 400 miles. Some were still in service in the early 1960s.

## DH 104 DOVE

First flown in 1945, the Dove resulted from Brabazon Committee recommendation Type 5B to replace the Rapide and proved very successful for de Havilland, with over 500 built. Most

Dan-Air's eight-seat de Havilland Dove G-AIWF was used on services out of Bristol. (MAP)

were sold as executive aircraft or to the military, but a small number were used by British charter airlines, both for charter and scheduled services, seating up to eleven passengers. However, its high purchase price and 50 per cent greater operating costs than the Rapide ruled it out for most charter airlines.

## DH 106 COMET

Designed to meet the Brabazon Committee's Type 4 specification for a jet-propelled mail carrier, the first prototype Comet flew on 27 July 1949 and went on to break world records, flying at over 450 mph and cutting journey times in half. Orders began to come in from overseas airlines. BOAC inaugurated the world's first jetliner service, to Johannesburg on 2 May 1952. Lord Swinton, a former Minister of Civil Aviation, said in the House of Lords: 'I feel that we have such a lead in civil jet aircraft, and these machines have established such a reputation for themselves, that we may not only get orders from all over the world but possibly corner the market for a generation.'[2] Then the accidents started. On 6 October 1952 a Comet failed to become airborne at Rome and was damaged beyond repair, although only one of the passengers was injured. On 3 March 1953 there was an identical accident at Karachi involving a Canadian Pacific Comet on delivery to the airline, with the loss of eleven lives. On 2 May 1953 a BOAC Comet broke up in a storm after taking off from Calcutta. All this was bad enough, but on 10 January 1954 the first production Comet G-ALYP disappeared off Elba with the loss of all forty-three on board. The fleet was grounded and after minute examination by BOAC of its remaining fleet had revealed nothing untoward, BOAC resumed operations on 23 March. Just two weeks later, on 8 April, Comet G-ALYY, on charter to South African Airways, disappeared off Stromboli with the loss of twenty-one lives. Next day the British Certificate of Airworthiness was withdrawn and production of all aircraft halted. With the help of the Royal Navy about three quarters of the wreckage of G-ALYP was salvaged

Air France Comet 1A F-BGNX touches down, but further export sales evaporated after the crashes. (MAP)

BOAC Comet 4 G-APDE, longer than the Comet 1A, it has oval windows and tip tanks. (MAP)

and taken to the Royal Aircraft Establishment, where it was eventually pieced together. After extensive pressure tests at Farnborough, the cause of the failure was eventually pinpointed to a tiny rivet near a cabin window which had begun to crack, as had the corner of the cut out for the Automatic Direction Finder aerial. The official Court of Inquiry report published in 1955 stated that 'the accident to Comet G-ALYP was caused by structural failure of the pressure cabin brought about by metal fatigue, and the accident to G-ALYY might have been due to the same.'[3] It was the end of many hopes, and although the Comet 4 did make a comeback and indeed inaugurated transatlantic jet service for BOAC on 4 October 1958, the pioneering lead was lost never to be recovered. BEA used a shorter-range version, the Comet 4B. The

Dragon's de Havilland Heron outside HM Customs shed at Newcastle; G-ANYJ is the later Series 2 version with retractable undercarriage. (MAP)

RAF bought the ultimate Comet type, the 4C, which combined the slightly longer fuselage of the 4B with the greater range of the original Comet 4.

## DH 114 HERON

An enlarged, four-engine development of the Dove, the Heron first flew in 1950. There were two main versions, the Series 1 with a fixed undercarriage and the Series 2 with a retractable undercarriage, which was some 20 mph faster. The Heron carried fourteen passengers over 1,000 miles, at a speed of 165 mph (Series 1). The design grew out of a requirement proposal from BEA for a DH89 Rapide replacement, and indeed three were used by BEA for air-ambulance work and services to Barra in the Western Isles. The largest British users were Jersey Airlines and Morton Air Services, but Cambrian, Dragon Airways, Dan-Air and Channel Airways also operated the type, as did HM The Queen, who undertook some epic journeys around Africa in the Herons of the Queen's Flight.

## DH 121 TRIDENT

Tailored to BEA's requirements, the three-engine Trident as originally proposed would have carried up to 111 passengers, powered by three RB141 Medway engines of 12,000lb thrust, over short and medium ranges, at a speed of 600mph. However, early in 1959 and before signing the contract, BEA forecast that there was going to be a sharp drop in demand and decided that the proposed aircraft was too big. De Havilland was persuaded to crop the design and Rolls-Royce instead developed the RB163, the Spey, of 9,800lb thrust. The new design which BEA

BEA's Trident 1 G-ARPP, in the new livery of black cheat line and red BEA square, at Heathrow. (MAP)

eventually ordered could seat up to ninety-nine passengers, but in BEA service usually carried eighty-seven passengers, only a few more than the twin-engine BAC One-Eleven. In his book *Government and British Civil Aerospace*, Keith Hayward explains what happened next:

> In 1959 Boeing launched the 727, a similar tri-jet aircraft. Significantly, Boeing was influenced by the De Havilland design, but from the outset built the 727 with a larger capacity (up to 131 passengers) capacity. Boeing also optimised the 727's airfield performance, whereas the Trident was designed to reflect BEA's insistence on a higher cruising speed than the Caravelle. The 727 also had plenty of 'stretch' and it entered service before the Trident. The American aircraft ran away with the market, selling over 2000 copies to the Trident's 115. Its capacity, performance, delivery were all better than the Trident's, but above all the 727 was of a size more suited to most airline requirements. BEA's pessimistic forecasts about the market proved false, and the airline continually sought larger versions of the Trident. Eventually, BEA even wanted to buy the 189-seat 727-200.[4]

## DOUGLAS DC-3 DAKOTA

Most Dakotas operated by British airlines came from RAF stocks after the war, and so are conversions of the C-47, the military designation of this fabulous twin-engine workhorse airliner. It could carry up to thirty-two passengers or three and a half tons of freight over 1,500 miles at a speed of around 170mph. In BEA service it outlasted the Vickers Viking which had been introduced to replace the Dakota after the war. Most early post-war charter airlines operated the Dakota which had excellent airfield performance and was supremely versatile.

Skyways's Dakota G-AMWX shows the Lympne-Beauvais Coach-Air emblem on its nose. Just one of the over 300 Dakotas that were registered in Britain after the war. (MAP)

## DOUGLAS DC-4 SKYMASTER/ CANADAIR C4 (DC-4M)

The DC-4 entered service with Skyways in 1947 but they were sold off in 1950. Laker re-introduced the type in 1955 and other charter companies began to follow suit in 1958. Able to carry up to eighty-eight passengers, or around eight tons of freight, the DC-4 had a range of some 2,500 miles. It was the basis for the Aviation Traders Carvair, a conversion designed to carry up to five cars and their passengers across the English Channel. The Canadians built a version of the DC-4, powered by Rolls-Royce Merlins and known by BOAC as the Argonaut, which was pressurised and somewhat noisy. Unlike British-built interim types, the Argonaut had a long innings with BOAC, remaining in service for eleven years until 1960. They saw further service in the 1960s with British independents, notably Derby Airways and Overseas.

## DOUGLAS DC-6/DC-7

A straightforward development of the DC-4, but with a pressurised cabin, increased accommodation and payload and higher performance, the DC-6 evolved into the most efficient piston-engine commercial transport with the lowest operating costs recorded until the advent of more efficient jet airliners. In a high-density layout, the DC-6B, 5ft longer than the original DC-6, could carry up to 102 passengers, and its freighter equivalent, the DC-6A, could carry twelve and a half tons over 3,000 miles. Hunting-Clan introduced the type into Britain, using them as freighters on its Africargo service from December 1958; other operators included Eagle, Lloyd International and Air Ferry. The DC-7 was the ultimate development of the DC-4 design, further lengthened, and re-engined with four

Douglas DC-4s were the mainstay of the Starways fleet. G-APEZ is operating a scheduled flight from London Airport, but was also used for charter flights out of its Liverpool base. (MAP)

The Canadair C-4 was a development of the Douglas DC-4, pressurised, and powered by Rolls-Royce Merlin engines. Derby Airways had just become British Midland as this volume concludes. (MAP)

Eagle was an enthusiastic user of the Douglas DC-6, achieving high utilisation with a wide range of services. G-APON displays the new red and black livery. (MAP)

Former Airwork Handley Page Hermes G-ALDA nearing the end of its service life with charter airline Air Links. (MAP)

Wright R-3350 Turbo-Compound engines. The final version, the DC-7C Seven Seas, was the first truly long-range airliner, capable of flying the Atlantic non-stop in either direction; it entered service with Pan American in 1956. BOAC bought ten as timely insurance against delays in the delivery of its Britannias, and Caledonian was launched with a fleet of DC-7Cs taken over from Sabena, the Belgian airline.

## HANDLEY PAGE HERMES

Powered by four Bristol Hercules engines, with a pressurised fuselage and a new tail with single fin and rudder, the Hermes shared the engines and wing design of the wartime Halifax bomber, and was produced in a military variant, the Hastings, still with a tail wheel, whilst the handsome passenger carrying Hermes 4 boasted a tricycle undercarriage and was some 13ft longer. The Hastings went on to give many years of service to the RAF, participating in the Berlin Airlift and only finally being withdrawn in 1977. The Hermes 4 was selected by the Ministry of Supply and BOAC for the Empire routes, replacing Yorks and the flying boats on African services, but had a very brief career with the Corporation, between 1950 and 1953, before being replaced in turn by the Comet[5] and the Argonaut. The fleet of low-time, modern, pressurised aircraft was, however, put to good use by the independents, especially on the growing number of trooping contracts. There was a further secondary use of the type by charter airlines on IT work, with the last flight being in 1964. The fairest description of the Hermes is as an enhanced interim design, because it still used the basic Halifax wing – eleven years old by this time – and this penalised the aircraft's range, as did its propensity to fly tail-down. With a full payload of up to sixty-eight passengers, its range was not much more than 1,400 miles.

Derby Airways was the only airline to operate the four-engine Handley Page Marathon in Britain. G-AMGW is pictured at Liverpool's Speke Airport in 1958. (MAP)

## HANDLEY PAGE/MILES MARATHON

The original Brabazon Type 5 specified a small feederliner intended to replace the DH Rapide. Miles Aircraft persuaded the Committee to recommend a larger, four-engine feederliner as a replacement for the four-engine DH86, and proposed the M60 Marathon, powered by four Gipsy Queen engines, an all-metal high-wing aeroplane which would carry fourteen passengers. By the time Miles was looking for a production order the company was in serious financial trouble and receivers were appointed in 1948, but the Ministry of Supply was not anxious to lose the design team and so persuaded Handley Page to take over the project. Handley Page increased the capacity to eighteen passengers and secured an order from the Ministry of Civil Aviation for fifty aircraft, thirty for BEA and twenty for BOAC. However, BEA refused to take delivery, preferring to stay with Rapides for the Scottish services, and BOAC had very limited success in persuading its associated companies to take the type. The RAF received twenty-eight for use as navigational trainers, and Handley Page closed down production after forty aircraft. Derby Aviation bought a small number for its services out of Derby in the mid-1950s.

## HANDLEY PAGE DART HERALD

Conceived as a DC-3 replacement, and looking somewhat like a bigger version of the Marathon, the Herald was originally powered by four Alvis Leonides piston engines, and first flew in 1955. However, by that time the Rolls-Royce Dart engined Fokker Friendship – of similar size and configuration but better performance – was gaining sales and pointed the way to the future. Accordingly Handley Page re-engineered the Herald to be powered by two

Darts, and the type entered service with Jersey Airlines in mid-1961, some three years after the Friendship entered service. Slightly larger than its Fokker and Avro competitors, it could carry up to fifty-six passengers or six and a half tons of freight. It never caught up with the Friendship in terms of sales, and was shunned by the RAF when Handley Page refused to join one of the two aircraft manufacturing groupings ordained by the government in 1960.

Jersey Airlines was the first carrier to introduce the Handley Page Herald into service. G-APWE sported yellow and blue fuselage stripes. (MAP)

A beautiful aircraft, Lockheed Constellation G-ALAK looks unglamorous in bare metal as a stripped down freighter for ACE Freighters. (MAP)

Scottish airline Loganair started commercial services with Piper Aztec G-ASER. (MAP)

## HERALD

See under Handley Page Dart Herald.

## HERMES

See under Handley Page Hermes.

## HERON

See under DH 114 Heron.

## LOCKHEED CONSTELLATION

The Constellation started life in 1943 as the American C-69 military transport, although the majority of those built were completed after the war as civil aircraft. BOAC was allowed to buy the earliest model, the L049, immediately after the war ended, in order to start transatlantic services. The corporation subsequently also bought the developed, longer-range L749 version, which could carry up to sixty-four passengers. A few were converted into freighters and passed on to Skyways. Charter airlines, especially Euravia, used Constellations on inclusive tour services during the 1960s.

Short Solent 4 flying boat G-AOBL retained its former name Aotearoa II after it was sold by New Zealand's TEAL to Aquila Airways. RMA stands for Royal Mail Aircraft. (MAP)

Vickers Viking G-AHOW saw service with no fewer than nine British airlines, as well as Trek Airways in South Africa, in its twenty-three-year existence. It was looking good with Air Safaris at the end of the 1950s. (MAP)

## MILES MARATHON

See under Handley Page/Miles Marathon.

## PIPER PA-27 AZTEC

All-metal six-seat development of the four-seat Piper PA-23 Apache, the Aztec was introduced in 1959. Powered by 235hp Lycomings, over 100 have been in use either privately or for charter operations in the United Kingdom.

## SHORT SUNDERLAND/BOAC HYTHE CLASS

The mighty Sunderland was one of the truly exceptional aircraft of the Second World War, and over 800 were built. After the war BOAC modified the aircraft by fairing in the gun turrets at the nose and tail, and upgrading the passenger accommodation. Named the Hythe Class, and carrying up to twenty-two passengers, they were used to re-open routes to the Far East and Australia. Withdrawn from service in 1949, twelve were eventually sold on to Aquila Airways, which operated them successfully on its services to Lisbon and Madeira.

## SHORT SOLENT

The Solent can be distinguished from the other Sunderland-derived boats by the curved dorsal fin. Fitted with more powerful engines, the aircraft could carry thirty passengers over 2,200 miles and were used by BOAC to reopen the flying-boat service to South Africa in 1948, taking over from the York. The Solent was in turn displaced by the Hermes in 1950, ending BOAC's flying-boat services. Aquila Airways acquired three Solents and used them to inaugurate service in 1954 to Capri and to Las Palmas in the Canaries in 1956.

## TRIDENT

See under DH 121 Trident.

## VICKERS VIKING

The most successful of the post-war 'interim' airliners, the Viking was a development of the wartime Wellington bomber with a new fuselage that could seat up to thirty-six passengers. It sold relatively well, and many saw service with British charter airlines, flying well into the 1960s. The Viking was significantly faster than the Dakota although it had slightly higher operating costs and needed longer runways. When the German charter airlines began taking to the sky in the mid-1950s, over twenty Vikings were used, their higher speed proving a real benefit on the longer sectors to Spain and the Balearics.

## VICKERS VISCOUNT

Development of the Viscount, the world's first turboprop airliner, was helped by the experience that Vickers gained in the commercial market through building the Viking. One of the Brabazon-recommended designs, the project languished for a while and the piston-engined Ambassador, built in parallel, might have assumed the mantle of Britain's contribution as a medium-range passenger airliner. But Vickers persisted and with the help both of BEA and Trans-Canada Air Lines, produced a truly world-class airliner bought by many significant airlines. The Viscount was the first foreign-built airliner to be sold in any quantity in North

An airline with an exotic, if not incomprehensible name, Maitland Drewery operated Vickers Viscount G-ARBY for a short time. It is seen here at Gatwick in 1960. (MAP)

BEA's Vickers Vanguard G-APET in front of the passenger terminal at Luqa, Malta GC. (MAP)

America, but it also dominated European skies for a decade until the advent of the jet Caravelle. The original 700 series, seating up to sixty-three passengers, was superseded by the 800 series which could seat up to seventy-one passengers. 445 Viscounts were sold between 1953 and 1964, the last aircraft being delivered to the People's Republic of China. Transair and Hunting-Clan bought new Viscounts, but many independent airlines subsequently built up large fleets bought second-hand, including Channel, Cambrian and British Midland.

## VICKERS VANGUARD

Both BEA and Trans-Canada Air Lines were satisfied Vickers customers, and as early as 1953 each approached the manufacturer regarding a replacement for their large fleets of Viscounts. BEA was especially enamoured of the concept of a large turboprop transport, believing its economics would be unbeatable, and not for the first time a British manufacturer developed an aircraft too closely tailored to the Corporation's requirements; only BEA and TCA bought

BOAC Vickers VC10 G-ARVJ on the ground at Heathrow, as a BOAC Boeing 707 lifts off in the background. (MAP)

the aircraft, between them accounting for forty-three Vanguards. Vanguards could carry up to 139 passengers and were undoubtedly economical to operate, but suffered from having to compete with jets; they remained in BEA passenger service until 31 March 1974, proving especially useful on low-revenue holiday routes to Malta and Gibraltar. BEA converted nine for cargo work, with a large door and useful twenty-ton payload.

## VICKERS VC10

Smaller than the Boeing 707, and entering service in 1964, some five and a half years after the introduction of its rival's intercontinental version, the VC10 and larger Super VC10 offered superior airfield performance, being particularly well suited to operation from hot and high airfields for which they were designed. The rear-mounted engines imposed a weight penalty, however, and the type's operating costs were commensurately higher. British United, with its African operations, was an obvious customer for the VC10, a decision which stood the airline in good stead when BOAC pulled off its South American routes, allowing BUA to operate them with modern jet equipment. But after Caledonian took over British United, the VC10s were disposed of and the combined fleet consolidated on the Boeing 707. The VC10 could carry up to 151 passengers, or twenty tons as a freighter; the larger Super VC10 managed up to 174 passengers or twenty-six tons of freight. By way of contrast, the 707-320C carried typically up to 189 passengers in a one-class configuration, and around forty tons as a pure freighter.

## WESTLAND

In 1947, Westland signed an agreement with United Aircraft to build Sikorsky helicopters under licence. The agreement allowed Westland to incorporate British components, to

Westland Whirlwind G-AOHE of Bristow Helicopters, hovering near a Dakota of Derby Airways. (MAP)

develop the helicopters, and to sell them world-wide except in North America. The company employed Alan Bristow as a test pilot between 1947 and 1949, a link that was to stand the company in good stead in later years.

## WESTLAND S-51 DRAGONFLY

Used by BEA for its experimental cross-country scheduled and mail services between 1948 and 1951, examples of this four-seat helicopter were also owned by Silver City, Autair, Bristow and the *Evening Standard*. Westland subsequently developed the type into the more powerful, five-seat Widgeon, and Bristow used five in the Persian Gulf for oil rig communications flying.

## WHIRLWIND

Westland continued its association with Sikorsky when it began building the larger S-55 under licence in 1952 for the British military. The early Series 1 model had a US-built piston engine, the Series 2 had a British-built Alvis Leonides piston engine and the Series 3 was powered by a Bristol Siddeley/Rolls-Royce Gnome turboshaft engine. Carrying up to seven passengers, the largest civil operator of this type was Bristow Helicopters, which at one time or another operated twenty-five between 1961 and 1969, and modified a number of Series 1 to Series 3 standards. Christian Salvesen bought a fleet of six for whaling operations in the 1950s, and BEA inaugurated its short-lived scheduled services from the South Bank in London with a float equipped version.

# APPENDIX TWO
# LIST OF ABBREVIATIONS

| | |
|---|---|
| AAJC | Associated Airways Joint Committee |
| ARB | Air Registration Board |
| ATA | Air Transport Auxiliary |
| ATAC | Air Transport Advisory Council |
| ATLB | Air Transport Licensing Board |
| AVM | Air Vice-Marshal |
| | |
| BEA | British European Airways (Corporation) |
| BIATA | British Independent Air Transport Association |
| BOAC | British Overseas Airways Corporation |
| BSAA | British South American Airways (Corporation) |
| BUA | British United Airways |
| | |
| CAA | Central African Airways |
| CAB | Civil Aeronautics Board |
| CI | Channel Islands |
| ctm | capacity ton mile (the product of aircraft payload and the miles flown) |
| hp | horse power |
| | |
| IATA | International Air Transport Association |
| ICAO | International Civil Aviation Organisation |
| IT | Inclusive Tour |
| | |
| KLM | Royal Dutch Airlines |
| | |
| LAC | Lancashire Aircraft Corporation |
| lb | pound (weight) |
| London Airport | Now known as Heathrow |
| MAP | Ministry of Aircraft Production |

| | |
|---|---|
| MCA | Ministry of Civil Aviation |
| MEDAIR | Trooping Contract for inter-Mediterranean flights |
| MoS | Ministry of Supply |
| | (formerly Ministry of Aircraft Production) |
| MP | Member of Parliament (British) |
| mph | miles per hour |
| MTCA | Ministry of Transport and Civil Aviation |
| | |
| PS | Parliamentary Secretary |
| PPS | Principal Private Secretary |
| | |
| RAAF | Royal Australian Air Force |
| RAF | Royal Air Force |
| | |
| SBAC | Society of British Aircraft Constructors |
| STOL | Short Take-off and Landing |
| | |
| TCA | Trans-Canada Air Lines |
| | |
| VLF | Very Low Fare |
| | |
| WEST MED | Trooping contract for Gibraltar, Malta and North Africa |

# WHO'S WHO
# BIOGRAPHICAL DETAILS*

AIKMAN, Barry Thomson: director and general manager, Lancashire Aircraft Corporation, 1945-47; managing director, Aquila Airways, 1948-56; chairman, Barry Aikman Travel.

AMERY, Julian (later Lord Amery): MP (Conservative) Preston North, 1950-66, Brighton Pavilion, 1969-92; Secretary of State for Air, 1960-62; Minister of Aviation, 1962-64.

BAMBERG. Harold Rolf: chairman and managing director, Eagle Aviation, Cunard Eagle and British Eagle International Airlines, 1948-68; chairman, Sir Henry Lunn, Poly Travel, Everyman Travel and Rickards Coach.

BEBB, Charles William Henry 'Cecil': toured South Africa with Alan Cobham Aviation, 1933; with Olley Air Service, 1936-39; Chief Test Pilot, Cunliffe-Owen Aircraft, 1939-43; Chief Test Pilot, A.W. Hawkesley, 1943-44; Chief Test Pilot, Dunlop Aviation Research Dept, 1944-46; Chief Pilot, Olley Air Service, 1946-53; operations manager, Transair, 1953-60; operations manager, British United Airways, 1960.

BLIGH, Sir Timothy: Principal Private Secretary to the Prime Minister, 1959-64.

BOYD-CARPENTER, John (later Lord): MP (Conservative) Kingston-upon-Thames, 1945-72; Financial Secretary, Treasury, 1951-54; Minister of Transport and Civil Aviation, 1954-55; Minister of Pensions and National Insurance, 1955-62; Chief Secretary to the Treasury and Paymaster General, 1962-64; chairman, Civil Aviation Authority, 1972.

BRABAZON OF TARA, Lord (Lieutenant-Colonel John Theodore Cuthbert Moore-Brabazon): first English pilot to fly, holder of Aviation certificate No.1; Assessor, R101 Inquiry, 1930-31; Minister of Transport, 1940-41; Minister of Aircraft Production, 1941-42; president,

---

*Largely compiled from the annual editions of *Aeroplane Directory*, published by Temple Press.

Brabazon Committee, 1942-43; chairman, Air Registration Board, 1946-64; owner of number plate FLY 1.

BRANCKER, John William Sefton: son of Sir Sefton Brancker, Britain's Director of Civil Aviation who died in the R101 crash at Beauvais, John Brancker joined Imperial Airways in 1929 and transferred to BOAC on its formation. His last posting was as general manager, International Affairs, 1951-53, before he joined IATA as its Traffic Director, 1953-60. Thereafter he became an air transport consultant.

BRISTOW, Alan Edgar: Pilot, Fleet Air Arm, 1943-46; helicopter test pilot, Westland Aircraft, 1947-49; Chief Pilot, Antarctic Whaling Expeditions, 1950-53; managing director, then chairman, Bristow Helicopters, 1954-85; Director, British United Airways, 1960-70; managing director, British United Airways, 1967-70.

CAYZER, Hon. Anthony: chairman, British United Airways, 1968-70; deputy chairman, British and Commonwealth Shipping; chairman, British Island Airways.

CAYZER, Sir William Nicholas, Bt (later Lord): chairman of the following companies: Clan Line Steamers, 1938-87; Union-Castle Mail Steamship, 1956-87; British and Commonwealth Shipping, 1958-87; Caledonia Investments, 1958-94; Air Holdings, 1962-8; BUA (Holdings), 1968.

CHEGWIDDEN, Captain Laurence Charles: RNZAF 1939-46; Chief Pilot, Amphibious Airways, New Guinea, 1947-49; Qantas, 1949-53; Captain, Silver City Airways, 1953-58; Captain, Transair 1958-62; MoA Flight Safety Inspector, 1962-63; managing director, ACE Freighters, 1963-66.

CRIBBETT, Sir George: Deputy Secretary, Ministry of Civil Aviation, 1946-56 (Director of Civil Aviation); Deputy Chairman, BOAC, 1956-60; Director, BOAC Associated Companies, 1957-63.

CURTIS, Maurice Henry: joined Imperial Airways as trainee, 1930; station manager on overseas routes; commercial manager, European Region, BOAC, 1944-46; traffic manager, BEA, 1946-47; Director of Skyways (Far East) and Skyways (East Africa), 1947-49; managing director, Hunting-Clan Air Transport, 1949-60; Director, Curtis Greensted Associates.

DAVIES, S. Kenneth: formed Cambrian Air Services 1935, managing director until 1951; managing director, British Parachute Co.,1939-45; board member, BEA, 1951-67.

D'ERLANGER, Sir Gerard John Regis Leo: Member of London Stock Exchange, 1935-39, at that time associated first with Hillman Airways, then British Airways; Commanding Officer, ATA, 1939-45; Member of Board, BOAC, 1940-46; chairman, BEA, 1947-49; chairman, BOAC, 1956-60.

DORRINGTON, Peter: Skyways of London, 1954-60; commercial manager, Tradair, 1960-61; sales manager, Autair, 1961-70, sales director, Court Line, 1970.

DOUGLAS OF KIRTLESIDE, Marshal of the Royal Air Force Lord (William Sholto Douglas): AOC-in-C, Fighter Command, 1940-42; AOC-in-C, Middle East Command, 1943-44; AOC-in-C Coastal Command, 1944-45; Air C-in-C, British Air Forces of Occupation, Germany, 1945-46; C-in-C, British Forces in Germany, British Military Governor, 1946-47; Director, BOAC, 1948-49; chairman, BEA 1949-64; chairman, Horizon Travel, 1964.

ELWIN, Wing Commander LB 'Bill': a Canadian, he flew with the Royal Canadian Air Force during the Second World War, before joining BEA in 1947. In 1948 he was general manager of Westminster Airways at Blackbushe during the Berlin Airlift, and later with Silver City at Lympne. Joined Cambrian as general manager, 1950; managing director, 1959; resigned 1968. General manager, British United Island Airways, 1968-70.

GRANVILLE, Keith: sales director, BOAC, 1951-56; commercial director, BOAC, 1956-58; deputy managing director, BOAC, 1958; board member, BOAC, 1959 and deputy chairman, 1964.

GUINNESS, Group Captain Thomas Loel Evelyn Bulkeley: together with Lord Cowdray's Whitehall Securities, he was an early investor in Airwork. Member of Parliament for City of Bath, 1931-45; chairman, Airwork, 1943-51; then president, Airwork and from 1960, president, British United Airways.

GUTHRIE, Sir Giles Connop McEachern: winner, with CWA Scott, of the Portsmouth-Johannesburg Air Race, 1936; traffic officer, British Airways, 1938-39; served during the War with the Fleet Air Arm; Board Member, BEA, 1959-68; chairman and chief executive, BOAC, 1964-68.

HOPE, Sir Archibald Philip, Bt: joined Airwork, 1945; managing director, Airwork, 1952-56; chairman, BIATA, 1956; chief executive, Napier Aero Engines, 1962-63.

HOPE, Frank Albert: navigator, RAF, 1948-53; BEA Operations, 1956-57; planning manager, Cunard Eagle Airways, 1957-61; Caledonian Airways, 1961; deputy managing director.

HUNTING, Sir Percy Llewellyn: chairman, Hunting Group of Companies, which included Percival Aircraft, Field Aircraft Services, Hunting Aviation, Hunting Aerosurveys, 1927-60.

HUNTING, Wing Commander Gerald Lindsay: governing director, Hunting Group of Companies. Brother of Sir Percy, father of Lindsay Clive Hunting.

HUNTING, Lindsay Clive: joined Hunting Group, 1950; director, Hunting Group, 1952; vice-chairman, 1962; chairman, 1975-91; director, British United Airways, 1960; president, BIATA, 1960-62; president, SBAC, 1985-86.

JACK, Sir Daniel: Professor of Economics, Durham University; chairman, Air Transport Licensing Board from 1961.

JONES, Squadron Leader R.J. Jack: pleasure flying from Herne Bay Holiday Camp, summer 1946; registered East Anglian Flying Services (later Channel Airways), 16 August, 1946; first post-war operator out of Southend, 1947; managing director, and later chairman, Channel Airways, until 1972.

KEEGAN, Thomas Dennis 'Mike:' RAF 1943-46; ground engineer, Skyways, 1947; flight engineer, Pan African Airways, 1948; founded Crewsair, with Messrs Barnby, Stevens and Haley (the latter also had an interest in Pan African Air Charter and William Dempster), 1949; with Messrs Barnby and Stevens, founded Crewsair Engineering, 1951; became BKS Aero Charter (later BKS Air Transport), 1952; sold interests, 1959; acquired Continental Air Transport, 1959; founded Keegan Aviation (aircraft sales and service), 1960 and its associated companies, Airline Spares, Bembridge Air Hire, Kay Rings, Keystone (Southend) Finance, Trans World Leasing; founded Trans Meridian Flying Services, 1962.

KENNARD, Wing Commander Hugh Charles: served throughout Second World War in Fighter Command; formed Air Kruise (Kent) 1946, managing director and chairman, 1946-54; director, Skyfotos, 1948-59; director, Luxembourg Airlines 1947-51; joint-managing director, Silver City Airways 1957-60; director, Air Ferry, 1962-64; managing director, Invicta Airways, 1964.

KOZUBSKI, Marian Kozuba: Chief Pilot, William Dempster, 1950-53; chairman and managing director, Independent Air Transport, 1954-59; chairman, Falcon Airways, 1959-61; chairman, Britair East African Airways, Nairobi, 1965.

LAKER, Frederick Alfred: managing director, Aviation Traders, Aviation Traders (Engineering), and Air Charter, to 1960; managing director, British United Airways, British United Air Ferries and Aviation Traders (Engineering), 1960-65; director, Air Holdings, 1961-65; chairman and managing director, Laker Airways, 1966.

LEATHERS, Lord (Frederick James Leathers): associated with the Ministry of Shipping during the First World War; Minister of War Transport, 1941-45; Secretary of State for the Coordination of Transport, Fuel and Power, 1951-53.

LENNOX-BOYD, Alan (later Lord Boyd): MP (Conservative) Mid-Beds, 1931-60; PS, Ministry of Aircraft Production, 1943-45; Minister of State for Colonial Affairs, 1951-52; Minister of Transport and Civil Aviation, 1952-54; Secretary of State for the Colonies, 1954-59.

MACLAY, John (later Lord Muirshiel): MP (Conservative) for Renfrewshire West, 1950-64; Minister of Transport and Civil Aviation, 1951-52; Minister of State for Colonial Affairs, 1956-57; Secretary of State for Scotland, 1957-62.

MANCROFT, Lord (Stormont Mancroft Samuel Mancroft): Minister without Portfolio, June 1957-October 1958. Deputy chairman, Cunard Line, 1966-71.

MAITLAND, John Ramsey: RAF 1943-58; managing director, Maitland Air Charter, 1958-59; managing director, Maitland Drewery Aviation, 1959-64.

MASEFIELD, Sir Peter Gordon: joined editorial staff *The Aeroplane*, 1937; chairman, Editorial Committee, *Inter-Services Journal on Aircraft Recognition*, 1942-45; Personal Adviser Civil Aviation to Lord Privy Seal, and Secretary War Cabinet Committee on Air Transport, (Brabazon Committee), 1943-45; British Civil Air Attaché to USA, 1945-46; director general, Long-Term Planning and Projects, MCA 1946-48; chief executive, BEA, 1949-55; managing director, Bristol Aircraft, 1955-60; managing director, BEAGLE and Beagle Aircraft, 1960; chairman, British Airports Authority, 1965.

McINTYRE, Wing Commander David Fowler: Pilot to Houston Mount Everest Flight Expedition, 1933; Founder, with the Duke of Hamilton, Scottish Aviation, 1935; managing director, Scottish Aviation and Scottish Airlines, 1946; died 8 December 1957 in a Scottish Aviation Twin Pioneer which crashed during a demonstration flight in Libya.

MEKIE, Eoin C.: chairman, British Aviation Services and its subsidiaries, including Britavia, Silver City, 1949-62.

MELVILLE, Sir Ronald: entered Air Ministry, 1934; Assistant Under-Secretary, 1946; chairman, Committee on Air Trooping, 1950; Deputy Under-Secretary, War Office, 1960-63; Ministry of Defence, 1963-66; Secretary (Aviation), Ministry of Technology, 1966-71.

MILWARD, Sir Anthony Horace: Controller of Operations, BEA, 1946-55; chief executive, BEA, 1956; chairman, BEA, 1964.

MORTON, Theodore William 'Sammy': Civil Aviation 1931-40, with Hillman's, then with British Air Navigation (Banco) and latterly as Chief Pilot, Olley Air Service; Chief Test Pilot, London Aircraft Production, 1940-45; chairman and managing director, Morton Air Services, 1946-68; chairman and managing director, Olley Air Service, 1953; director, British United Airways, 1960-68.

MUNTZ, Alan: with British Petroleum, 1922-26, and Anglo-Iranian Oil, 1926-28; with Sir Nigel Norman founded Airwork and Heston Airport, 1928; with Banque Misr, Cairo, founded Misr Airwork, 1932; with R.E. Grant Govan, Delhi, helped found Indian National Airways, 1933; became vice-chairman of Airwork, after Whitehall Securities and TLEB Guinness (who became chairman) acquired an interest in Airwork; founded Alan Muntz and Co., 1937; with L.E. Baynes, founded Baynes Aircraft Interiors, 1954.

MYHILL, Ronald: founder/director, Autair, a helicopter operator, 1954; Proprietor, R.M. Overseas Motors, a Jaguar car agency in Germany; chairman, Continental Air Services, 1957-59; with Bernard Dromgoole, founded the following companies; LTU in Germany, 1955; (also with Alfred Meerbergen) Aviameer, Belgium, 1958; Overseas Aviation (Channel Islands), Jersey, 1958.

NEWMAN, Frederick Edward Fry: joined Davies and Newman, 1937; served Honourable Artillery Company and 9th Field Regiment, Royal Artillery, 1939-46; formed Dan-Air Services, 1953; chairman Dan-Air Services, 1953-89; chairman, Davies and Newman Holdings, 1971-90.

OLLEY, Gordon Percy: joined Handley Page Transport on first Continental air services, 1919; with Handley Page Air Transport, 1922-24; pilot with Imperial Airways, 1924-33; formed Olley Air Service, 1934-39; deputy manager and operations manager, Associated Airways Joint Committee, 1939-46; managing director, Olley Air Service, Air Commerce and Air Booking, 1946-58.

PAINE, Ronald R.: during the Second World War, Chief Engineer, Nos 16 and 28 Elementary Flying Training Schools; technical director, Air Schools, Wolverhampton Aviation, Derby Aviation, 1953; general manager, Elstree Flying Club, 1953; joint-managing director, Derby Aviation, Derby Airways, 1960; managing director, London School of Flying, 1960; managing director, British Midland Airways, 1962-69.

POWELL, Air Commodore Griffith James: Imperial Airways, 1929-39, as pilot Empire routes and Atlantic experimental flights, later operations manager in Bermuda; Senior Air Staff Officer, RAF Ferry Command, 1942-43; Senior Air Staff Officer, No.45 Group, RAF, 1944-45; managing director, Britavia, Silver City, British Aviation Services, 1946-57; director, British West Indian Airways, 1958-61; chairman and managing director, Bahamas Airways, and resident BOAC manager, 1961-65; European director, Invicta Airways, 1966.

RAMSDEN, J. Michael: joined *Flight* magazine, 1955; air transport editor, 1961; editor, 1964.

ROXBURGH, Wing Commander Henry Alan: joint-managing director (with R.R. Paine), British Midland Airways (and associated companies), 1962-63; chairman, 1962-65; president, BIATA, 1962-63.

RYLANDS, J Eric; chairman, Skyways; chairman and managing director, Eric Rylands; Samlesbury Engineering, later Skyways Engineering; director, Lancashire Aircraft; Skyways de France; Skyways Coach Air; Bahamas Airways; Middle East Airlines; Chairman BIATA, 1949-52 and president 1958-59.

SANDYS, Duncan (later Lord Duncan-Sandys): MP (Conservative) Streatham, 1950-74; Minister of Defence, 1957-59; Minister of Aviation, 1959-60 (ten months); Secretary of State for Commonwealth Relations, 1960-64.

SAUVAGE, John: Joined Eagle, 1951; managing director, British Eagle, 1965-66; managing director, Britannia Airways, 1967.

SLATTERY, Rear Admiral Sir Matthew: Director-General of Naval Aircraft Development and Production, MAP, 1941; and Chief Naval Representative, 1943; Supply Council, MoS, 1945-48; managing director, Short Bros. and Harland, 1948-52; chairman and managing director, 1952-60; chairman, Bristol Aircraft, 1957-60; director Bristol Aeroplane, 1957-60; chairman, BOAC, 1960-63.

SMALLPEICE, Sir Basil: director of Costs and Statistics, British Transport Commission, 1948-50; joined BOAC as Financial Comptroller, 1950; managing director, BOAC, 1956-63; chairman, Cunard Steam-Ship Co., 1965-71; a deputy chairman, Lonrho, 1972-73.

SNELLING, Henry Philip: joined Railway Air Services, 1934; superintendent, Great Western and Southern Air Lines, 1938; and manager, 1940; operations manager, Skyways, 1947; and general manager, 1951; operations manager, Lancashire Aircraft Corp., 1952; commercial manager, Skyways, 1953-55; general manager (commercial), 1955-61; general manager, Bermuda and Nassau, Cunard Eagle Airways (Bermuda), 1961-62; deputy general manager (Air), Cunard Steam Ship (USA), 1962; director, Bahamas Airways, 1962; director of Operations and Passenger Services, British Eagle International Airways, 1965-66; director marketing, 1966.

STRAIGHT, Air Commodore Whitney Willard: entered civil aviation 1934, having started in motorcar racing; formed Straight Corporation, which, before the Second World War controlled twenty-one associated companies operating airlines, flying clubs and aerodromes throughout Great Britain, and continued after the war, renamed Airways Union in 1949; served RAF 1939-45 as fighter pilot and later commanded Nos 216 and 46 Groups, Transport Command; Additional Air ADC to King George VI, 1944; deputy chairman, BEA, 1946-47; managing director and chief executive, BOAC, 1947-49; deputy chairman, BOAC, 1949-55; executive vice-chairman, Rolls-Royce, 1956; deputy chairman, Rolls-Royce, 1957-71; chairman, Rolls-Royce, 1971-76.

TERRINGTON, Lord (Horace Marton Woodhouse): chairman, Industrial Disputes Tribunal 1944-59; chairman, Air Transport Advisory Council, 1947-60; first chairman, Air Transport Licensing Board, 1960; Deputy Speaker, House of Lords, 1949-61.

THOMAS, Maldwyn Lewis: founded Jersey Airlines in 1948, although the registered name was Airlines (Jersey) Ltd, to avoid confusion with Jersey Airways, recently nationalised and now part of BEA. Managing director, 1948-62; director, British United Airways and managing director, British United (CI) Airways, 1962-65.

THOMAS, Sir Miles (later Lord): technical editor of *The Motor*, then editor of *The Light Car*, until 1924; with Lord Nuffield from 1924, finally vice-chairman and managing director, Morris Motors Group, 1940-47; deputy chairman, BOAC, 1948; chairman, BOAC, 1949-56; chairman, Monsanto Chemicals, 1956-63; chairman, Britannia Airways, 1967; director, Thomson Organisation, Thomson Travel.

THOMSON, Sir Adam: Fleet Air Arm Pilot; then various flying appointments involving BEA, West Africa Airways and Britavia; founder member of Caledonian Airways, 1961; chairman and managing director, 1965; chairman and managing director, British Caledonian Airways.

THORNEYCROFT, Peter (later Lord Thorneycroft): MP (Conservative) Monmouth, 1945-60; PS, Ministry of War Transport, 1945; President of the Board of Trade, 1951-57; Chancellor of the Exchequer, 1957-58; Minister of Aviation, 1960-62, Minister of Defence, 1962-64.

THRELFALL, Gerald Herbert Goodair: joined RAF in 1942, with the Air Ministry 1947-49; studied as architect, 1949-54; helicopter pilot training with World Wide Helicopters, 1954; subsequently manager of helicopter operations in New Guinea; operations manager, 1955-59; joined Autair International Airways, 1959; managing director, April 1960. director of Court Line; deputy chairman, Court Line.

TREND, Sir Burke (later Lord Trend): Second Secretary, HM Treasury, 1960-62; Secretary of the Cabinet, 1963-73.

WAKEFIELD, Sir Wavell (later Lord Wakefield): MP (Conservative) St Marylebone, 1945-63. Director, later chairman, Skyways Ltd

WATKINSON, Harold Arthur (later Lord Watkinson): MP (Conservative) Woking division of Surrey, 1950-64; PPS to the Minister of Transport and Civil Aviation, 1951-52; Minister of Transport and Civil Aviation, 1955-59; Minister of Defence, 1959-62; Cabinet Minister, 1957-62.

WHEATCROFT, Stephen: joined BEA as Commercial Research and Tariffs Manager, 1946; since 1954, acted as Air Transport Consultant and Economic Adviser to BEA; appointed Assessor to the Edwards Committee, 1967-68.

WILCOCK, Group Captain Clifford Arthur Bowman: MP (Labour) Derby since 1945, Derby North from 1950.; Deputy Director Manning, Air Ministry and Senior Personnel Staff Officer, Transport Command, 1939-45; chairman, Air Schools, Derby Aviation, Wolverhampton Aviation, Derby Airways.

WILLIAMS, John Ernest Derek 'Jed': RAF Navigator, 1941-46; navigator with Argentine Airlines and Swissair, 1946-52; with El Al, 1952-57 as planning manager and later technical adviser to the chairman; consultant with JC Harrington, 1957; managing director, Euravia (renamed Britannia Airways, 1964), 1961-66; chairman, 1966-67.

WOODS HUMPHERY, Major George Edward: general manager, Daimler Airway and Daimler Hire, 1922-24; managing director and/or general manager, Imperial Airways, 1924-38.

WRIGHT, Leslie Gordon: North West Frontier, India, with 28 Squadron, 1940; Burma, 1942-44; Bomber Command, 1944-45; managing director, Anglian Air Charter, 1952.

WYATT, Sir Myles Dermot Norris: assistant and later deputy secretary to the Commissioners for Port of Calcutta, 1925-33; joined Airwork as general manager, 1934; managing director, 1938; chairman and managing director, 1951-60; chairman and managing director, British United Airways, 1960; chairman, Air Holdings, 1961.

APPENDIX FOUR

# EVERYBODY'S AIRLINES*

## BY SQUADRON LEADER D. WEST

'Have a toffee luv' was the friendly greeting I got from a flying companion aboard a Manx Airlines Dakota bound from Newcastle-on-Tyne to the Isle of Man. Later, on that flight, I was asked by another passenger to have an 'Uncle Joe,' which turned out to be a large peppermint humbug. 'Uncle Joe' I discovered started making these sweets as a young man and, when he died recently, left a five-figure fortune. This matey atmosphere among the holiday fliers in the United Kingdom could very well be classed as a sort of 'theme song,' for I found it ever present during my travels on every flight I made during a tour of the UK in July. To start at the beginning, I decided early this year, when I saw that the Ministry of Civil Aviation was granting a number of licences for new routes within the British Isles, to fly with as many of the airlines as possible. The object being to see how these airlines were operated, what the airports were like, who flew on these routes, and how the airlines connected up the various towns.

Operators have been granted licences for new routes in the United Kingdom and to European countries. The licences are for periods of from three to 10 years, and licences for routes already in operation have been extended until 1955.

At the time of writing the number of licences issued exceeds 60. Included in these are licences for inclusive international tours and vehicle-ferry services. The licences are liberal and allow for a substantial number of flights. For example, between Bristol and the Channel Islands, Cambrian Air Services can operate up to 20 return journeys a week with more in accordance with demand. Between the Isle of Man and Glasgow, Manx Airlines can operate up to 22 plus return flights weekly and between the Isle of Man and Birmingham, Lancashire Aircraft Corporation can operate 20 or more weekly. Between Croydon and Le Touquet, Morton Air Services can fly up to 92 return flights a week, and from Croydon to Deauville, Olley Air Service has been granted up to 82 flights a week.

The first part of my journey was made with Hunting Air Transport Limited, who started a twice daily service with Dakotas between Bovingdon and Newcastle (Woolsington Airport) in May. The time of departure from the new Air Terminal at Waterloo, London, was 06 50 and

---

*Reprinted from *Aeronautics*, September 1953.

this meant that I was there at 06 15. As readers know, I always arrive well before departure time because much can be learnt about aviation that way.

On this occasion I was very surprised to see crowds of passengers milling around the departure gates at 06 20, many with their friends. They were going to Europe mostly. Many were starting their holidays, while others who were obviously visitors were returning from a stay in England. The situation in the café was the same, where people of all nations were buying our coffee with satisfaction, in spite of the fact that the world says we can't make it. The setting of the café is unique, because it occupies part of one of the Festival of Britain buildings. This café, which is open to the public, is worth a visit.

Near my departure time I looked for the sign which would tell me where I could buy my 5s coach-ticket for Bovingdon Airport, but there wasn't one. I then inquired, and was told to go to the window marked 'Cashier,' and here I bought my ticket, but even at this window there was no 'coach ticket' sign. The word 'cashier' usually suggests a place where you pay a bill after having received service, or settled for a purchase. I feel that an appropriate sign should be installed for passengers. At 07 00 I started my coach journey to Bovingdon, it took nearly an hour and this is an aspect of 'flying' that is always good for an argument. People say, 'I flew from Jersey to Northolt in 50 minutes, and then it took me the same time to get to Waterloo by coach.' Taking into consideration the time factor, it does seem crazy to hustle through the air at three miles a minute to finish up on the ground at a speed of one mile in three minutes.

The Hunting service between London and Newcastle has been started to cater mainly for business people, and allows them seven hours in either town in which to conduct their business. The air journey takes about 1 hour 45 minutes for the 400km (250 miles) journey. We took off at 08 40 which was a little late, the normal time being 08 15, and arrived at Newcastle at 10 25. Our course lay along the Amber 1 airway, on which we checked our position at Daventry and again at Lichfield. We then obtained a height to fly from the Northern Flight Information Region at Preston, and crossed Green 2 airway about 15 miles east of Oldham, with the final check point at Dishforth beacon near Ripon. We flew at 1 400 metres (4 500ft) and cruised at a ground speed of 250km/hr (155 ml/hr). I must say it was a comforting thought to know we could fly safely across G2 without fear of bashing into other aircraft operating along this airway.

During the flight passengers enjoyed light refreshments in the form of sandwiches, biscuits and coffee, which at that time in the morning was most acceptable, because most of us had had very early breakfasts. Later, to my surprise, the stewardess asked if I would like a drink. I thought she meant more coffee, but I found that whisky, gin, beer and other non-soft drinks could be had. Some brave souls said 'yes'. Mr Richardson, Hunting's station superintendent at Newcastle, told me that although the service was very new, there was good public response. On the previous Saturday, for example, there were 18 southbound and 12 northbound passengers and, of course, at the same time last year there were none. The fare, he said, of £3 10s single and £7 return was favourable. Huntings have a staff at Newcastle of nearly 30, plus nine hostesses, who share the Newcastle-London and Newcastle-Paris services. To become an air hostess is still a favourite and when Hunting secured these new services, over 200 applications were received for this fascinating job. Three-quarters of these were interviewed. The majority were already in jobs as stenographers. Altogether there are twenty hostesses on Hunting's staff.

Bookings for ex-Newcastle flights are handled on the airport, where inquiries from the town office and agents are dealt with. In addition there is a 'four o'clock' call each day to the London office for passenger checking purposes.

Squadron Leader West started his journey flying in a Dakota of Hunting Air Transport from Bovingdon to Newcastle. (MAP)

Although the airport buildings are small at Woolsington, they are adequate and comfortable. There is a very attractive restaurant here for passengers' use.

## Manx ahead

My next flight was with Manx Airlines Limited, who were operating a new service between Newcastle and Ronaldsway, Isle of Man, and I soon noted, when I saw the passengers, that here was an entirely new travelling public, at least, as compared with those I have encountered on my world flights. Nine out of 10 were holidaymakers, and I would say the same proportion had never flown before. We were late taking off, and all the passengers were waiting near the aircraft, eager to board. They were of all ages and circumstance. The elder couples, I noticed, were full of wonder at what was going on, and were content to follow the crowd when the signal to board was given. This signal, by the way, certainly showed me a new aspect of air traffic, because the passengers all moved forward in one rush, eager, it seemed to me, to be the first aboard. I have never seen this before, and I am certain that they had no fear of flying. It was aboard this Dakota, as previously mentioned, that I was offered toffee and 'Uncle Joes.' My near companions were like school kids, waving to their friends through the windows, joking with each other, making fun of the 'mal-de-l'air' bags, and spilling the holiday atmosphere everywhere. It was a new experience for me. Already that morning two Manx Rapides had taken 14 people to Ronaldsway, and here was another 32 bound for the same place.

I asked one passenger why he was going by air. He told me the journey only took 50 minutes. By train and steamer, the time was from 10 to 20 hours, according to the waiting times for boats, and this, he said, meant the loss of two days. Another passenger expressed the opinion – which I heard often repeated – that the holiday starts the moment he got on board the aircraft. There is, of course, a difference in fares. First-class return rail and boat fare between these towns is £5 13s 6d and third class is £3 19s 6d. The return air fare is £8. An added advantage in the air travel, of course, is the absence of baggage handling which is necessary

West continues his journey from Newcastle to the Isle of Man (Ronaldsway) in a Dakota of Manx Airlines. (MAP)

between train and boat. On this flight the stewardess checked the holiday addresses of all the passengers. This, she told me, was to enable the airline to get in touch with them should there be a delay or alteration in the return times.

## Ronaldsway

At Ronaldsway I met Mr Hankinson, a director of Manx Airlines, who told me the airline was operating four Rapides and two 32-seat Dakotas. The Dakota I had arrived in had recently been furnished and re-upholstered by BKS of Southend. The colour scheme was quite attractive – cream ceilings, plum walls, pale blue seats and red carpets. The wall colour, I thought, was sensible because it did not show stains or scratches. Mr Hankinson told me that the traffic for his airline – and the others operating into Ronaldsway – was ever on the increase, and that he and other operators were contemplating future business in terms of larger aircraft. This attitude I found everywhere I went. The sequence I gathered is for the Rapides to be gradually replaced with de Havilland Herons (14 seats) or by Devons (seven seats), the cruising speeds of which are 260 and 290 km/hr respectively. These speeds are more favourable than the 190km/hr which I experienced in one Rapide in which I flew. There is a lot to be said for retaining a seven-seat aircraft in service for, as Mr Hankinson said, they can always be put on to carry the few instead of having to put on larger aircraft which would in effect be flying nearly empty.

Many of these internal operators would like to see 60- or 80-seat aircraft in use. Manx Airlines is based at Ronaldsway, and has its maintenance hangars there. While I was inspecting them I was asked how much I thought a Dakota tyre would cost, but my guess was nowhere near the amount – £57.

This, I thought, was plenty, but by comparison it did not reach the amazing price I was told de Havilland charged for two seats for a Dove belonging to one of the airlines – £140! Think of it; when you fly in a Dove – your 'latter end' is comfortably housed in seventy quids worth of luxury. I am sure one could travel just as elegantly for far less if an enterprising firm set their minds to producing cheaper equipment. Mr Hankinson told me something of the popularity of flying in the north of England between the Isle of Man and Newcastle, Carlisle and Glasgow. Every year traffic rises by about 50 per cent, and on Saturdays in the season each of his aircraft has about nine hours utilisation. The timetable shows 16 movements out and the same number in to Ronaldsway. These are scheduled services but many additional flights are made to meet the demand. Passengers who have once used this method are anxious to book for the following year, and some even make provisional bookings before they leave Ronaldsway. General booking periods are in September and January, and by the following March/April the requirements for the coming season are clear. Manx operate between Ronaldsway and Glasgow and Carlisle all the year round. The Newcastle run, which is, of course, new this year, may also have a restricted winter service.

A busy man at the airport is the commandant, Mr Griffiths, who has been associated with the airport since before the war.

When he showed me the airport buildings I immediately recognised that they were outstanding and designed with considerable skill to meet the steadily growing traffic.

On one side of the large main hall are to be found all the airline booking offices, and immediately opposite – on the airport side – are the airline traffic counters where tickets are checked, luggage is weighed and passengers assemble immediately before departure. In the centre of the hall plenty of comfortable seating is provided.

There is a very convenient lounge with a snack bar at hand together with a first-class restaurant. Upstairs is a public viewing area, under cover, also with a snack bar available. Incidentally, this is one of the few large airports where no charge is made for the visitors' enclosure. The airport buildings cost £120,000. There is tremendous activity at Ronaldsway at the week-ends. On 4 July, for example, 2,229 passengers used the airport. There were 124 movements of aircraft. There is a steady upward movement week by week over the previous years of the number of passengers carried. Last year there were over 60,000 visitors who came by air. Five regular airlines use the airport – Manx, Lancashire Aircraft Corporation, Aer Lingus, B E A and Scottish Airlines. In addition, charter flights arrive every week. It has not always been like this, for Mr Griffiths told me that in 1948 there were no fewer than 80 private airlines operating into Ronaldsway. The majority were 'one-man, one-machine affairs,' and time has taken toll of them.

## Blackpool

I returned to Blackpool on the mainland in a Dakota belonging to Lancashire Aircraft Corporation. The crossing took 25 minutes for the 60-odd miles, which I thought was a leisurely journey.

LAC, I understand, is the only airline operating between Blackpool and Ronaldsway with daily scheduled services. In addition, a minimum of six supplementary services are put on Fridays, Saturdays and Sundays. On the other days there are five, but I was told on many occasions even more flights are put on. The motto being, 'if there is a customer, we'll take him.' To give some idea of the volume of passengers LAC handles, on 4 July I was told they carried more than 800 people between Ronaldsway and Blackpool. Mr R.V. Baker, LAC's manager at Blackpool, told me that his company had pioneered the idea of bringing Isle of Man holidaymakers to Blackpool by coach and then flying them over. This coach-air service has become 'the thing,' he said, and no fewer than 19 coach services are in the scheme, bringing people from all over England. Some through adult return fares I saw were: Burnley, £4 6s 6d; Derby £5; Edinburgh £5 13s 4d; London £5 12s 9d; and Newcastle £5 6s 9d. The London-Isle

Lancashire's Dakota G-ANAE carries the red Lancaster rose emblem on its tail. (MAP)

of Man coach-air service leaves at 09:00 and arrives at Isle of Man at 21:00 (twelve hours). In some districts the bookings have increased by 500 per cent. Most of the passengers are carried in Dakotas – last year only Rapides were used – and LAC are increasing their Dakota fleet.

I saw one in the service hangar, recently acquired from the RAF. It was undergoing a complete overhaul in order to be in service this summer, but, Mr Baker said, larger aircraft still were needed to cope with the ever-growing traffic. LAC are certainly enterprising in getting people to fly. One idea of theirs is to collect a number of villagers and bring them to Blackpool by coach, fly them over their village at a prearranged time, so that the remainder of the inhabitants can be ready to cheer, and then fix them up with seats at a show.

One such trip cost only 45s per head. As many as three air-loads of 35 people have been gathered from one village and inquiries from others are coming in all the time. Another popular 'do' is being arranged for September – a flight over the Blackpool illuminations for 12s 6d. Catering for the passengers at the airport restaurant is very well done. There is a restaurant, a bar, and a tea lounge. An unusual and attractive idea I saw at the bar was the use of maps as table covers under the glass table-tops. These showed the country for a large area around Blackpool. LAC have introduced a splendid system in their air hostess training. Most of them are able to do shorthand and typewriting, and are instructed in customs and manifest procedures. They are capable of making bookings and of handling traffic details and they stay with their passengers from the start to the end of their journey. At destination, they chaperone their charges to the coaches and see them safely on their way. After having done this they take care of the booking office at destination, relieving the hostess in charge, who is by this time ready to accompany her party aboard the same aircraft for their journey. This ensures a complete interchange of staff without loss of efficiency.

## Bristol and Cardiff

Now I come to the sad part of this story. Continuing my journey, I wanted to fly from Blackpool to Liverpool to join Cambrian Air Services Limited, but I found I could not do

West describes the de Havilland Dove of Cambrian Air Services in which he flew from Liverpool to Bristol as 'a grand little fellow'. (MAP)

this because there was no air service. Here are two important towns separated by a stretch of water and about 50km apart. It took me nearly one and three quarter hours to make this tedious journey in a bus, whereas the air hop, had there been one, would have been accomplished in about twelve minutes. I could not find an answer as to why there was no air service; to me it seems a 'natural' and well suited for a cheap day return service between each town. Anybody willing to have a go? It was not until I joined CAS that I was able to fly in a small aircraft. Up to then I had flown in Dakotas. Now it was to be in a Dove, and this was my first ride in one. I must say it is a grand little fellow, and with its cruising speed of 290km/hr a valuable aircraft for short and medium distances. Cambrian have three Doves and seven Rapides, and with them maintain a remarkable traffic network, connecting five towns in the United Kingdom, and Dinard and Paris.

I travelled with a few months' baby from Liverpool to Bristol. I learned from the parents that the mother and child had not flown before, but travelling this way meant hours saved on the journey – fifty minutes against several hours by train. The only time I heard the child was during the running up of the engines which frightened it, but as soon as we were airborne all was well. I found the Dove a very attractive aircraft with plenty of room for eight passengers. Incidentally, there is a variation in the charges for youngsters. LAC for example carry children under three years of age free, and between three and twelve at half price. Most of the others I flew with charge 10 per cent of the adult fares for children under two years, and the same for others up to twelve. Passengers are allowed 15kg (33lb) of luggage, but I found that very few have this amount. CAS told me that a survey of 7,000 passengers showed an average of 10 to 11kg each. The flight to Bristol was also on an advisory route, as are most of the other routes flown by CAS.

We flew in cloud most of the way, only coming into the clear by Clifton suspension bridge, a mile or so from Whitchurch Airport, our destination. For a town the size of Bristol I expected to see at least an attractive terminal, but I regret to say I was glad to get away from it. The small waiting room was neat enough but the place seemed dead. The only airport activity I could see was in the CAS office, and a Rapide receiving service on the apron. At the time I was there, a lot of polishing was going on, for a committee was expected who were to assess the suitability of Whitchurch and the airport at Lulsgate Bottom, a little further out, to enable them to decide which to adopt and develop as Bristol's airport. When that decision is made I have no doubt that Bristol will see to it that they have a first rate airport. When I visited CAS headquarters at Pengam Moors Airport, Cardiff, Mr Elwin, the managing director, told me how his airline was trying to encourage mid-week flying. Everybody, he said, wanted to fly on Saturdays and Sundays on the Jersey services because hotel accommodation is usually offered from Saturday to Saturday. On Fridays and Mondays he said the return fares were reduced by £1 and on Tuesdays, Wednesdays and Thursdays by £2. The last figure brings the return fare between Cardiff and Jersey at £8; below the first-class boat and rail cost. This reduction has had a favourable result, and people are beginning to travel mid-week. Of course, some of the hoteliers in Guernsey and Jersey have cooperated to make this possible. I was interested to see copies of the newspaper – *Cardiff Western Mail* – being loaded into the Dove. There were possibly 30 copies, and these, I was told, had a ready sale in Jersey and Guernsey where there are Welsh residents. I can understand the big dailies doing good trade but for a local newspaper to be exported like this is surely unique.

I understood Cardiff's new civil airport is to be at Rhoos, about 12 miles out, which is being modernised by the MCA. The one at Pengam Moors cannot be extended because of obstructions, houses and water on its boundaries.

I have been intrigued by the number of children flying today. On five out of the six aircraft in which I flew there were children. Flying has become such an accepted mode of travel that families do not take any notice of what must be to many an adventure. Back in 1948 in Canada when I flew with Trans-Canada Air Lines, a child aboard was a novelty, and much comment was heard, but now little notice is taken of them – unless they secrete chewing gum in awkward places!

## Jersey Airport

I continued my journey to Jersey with (Cambrian) in one of their comfortable Doves which are doing plenty of work. These and the Rapides, I understand, put in a total of about 1,000 hours per month, and as the longest journey is about two hours, the number of movements is very high. It was necessary to land at Guernsey to off-load passengers but the stop was only a few minutes. There is a hump across the airfield, and I noticed as we were waiting to take off that a BEA Pionair completely disappeared over the brow after landing. This showed how vital the 'permission to take off' signal is, because it was impossible to see if the aircraft had cleared the landing area. It took only 20 minutes to fly to Jersey, and here I think is to be found the most remarkable air traffic situation in Europe and perhaps the world. On Fridays and Saturdays it is literally bombarded with aircraft from all over England, which belong to BEA and the eleven private operators listed (below):

Scheduled Services by private operators from England to Jersey

| Company | Base |
|---|---|
| BKS Aerocharter, Ltd | Woolsington, West Hartlepool |
| Cambrian Air Services, Ltd | Cardiff, Manchester, Bristol, Liverpool |
| Derby Aviation, Ltd | Derby, Wolverhampton |

| | |
|---|---|
| East Anglian Flying Services, Ltd | Southend, Rochester, Shoreham |
| Jersey Airlines, Ltd | Exeter, Manchester, Coventry, Hurn, Gatwick, Eastleigh |
| Lancashire Aircraft Corporation | Blackpool |
| Morton Air Services, Ltd | Croydon |
| Olley Air Service, Ltd | Croydon |
| Starways, Ltd | Liverpool |
| Transair, Ltd | Croydon, Gatwick |

The peak period handling is at the rate of thirty an hour. On the Saturday before I arrived there were 281 movements (142 in and 139 out). This was an increase of sixty-five over the same day last year and a record. No fewer than 2,263 people were carried in those 145 aircraft, and 500 of those by the little aircraft, Rapides, Doves, Ansons, Consuls, Aerovans and Herons.

In view of the fact that air passengers are arriving at an ever increasing rate, 54,000 more in 1952 than 1951, I asked Mr Roche, the Airport Commandant, if he could see a saturation point ahead. I gathered that this was a remote possibility because there were some periods during the busiest days when more aircraft could be handled and that larger aircraft – Dakotas, Pionairs and Ambassadors – were beginning to come in carrying more people for less movements. I noticed, for example, that Jersey Airlines had a new 14-seat Heron which did the work of two Rapides.

The Heron, incidentally, is the only four-engined aircraft operating between Jersey and the UK. The senior Air Traffic Controller, Mr Dalton, MBE, was quite confident that his staff could handle any number of aircraft. If necessary, he said, he would use the 'flow control,' which in the case of Jersey would be under the eye of the A.T.C at Uxbridge. He did mention that it would be an advantage if beacons could be established at Alderney and Guernsey, to make a clockwise traffic pattern, instead of as present – aircraft coming in and out along the same lane. Mr Dalton showed me the Airfield Control Radar which enabled aircraft to be marshalled on the back beam. This cuts the normal SBA procedure time of 15 minutes to half. The ground handling of ever-increasing numbers of passengers will certainly need attention, said Mr Roche, and it is possible that a new departure area will be established. A good site I noticed was a hangar adjoining the airport buildings. Although the incoming and outgoing passengers do not clash, the traffic area is so small that congestion does occur.

While in Jersey I met Mr M.L. Thomas, managing director of Jersey Airlines, but only after waiting patiently on the pavement outside his office for a considerable time. I couldn't get a foot inside the premises. It was packed with customers. When I had a look at one of his timetables I was not surprised. On a Saturday, for example, his Herons and Rapides operate over six routes and are scheduled to take part in 48 movements, many of which are duplicated because of the demand.

(That) brings to mind a complaint I heard in the lower refreshment room at Jersey Airport. Here passengers, aircrew and airline officials use the snack bar. I heard a lady and her husband complain about the cost of a cheese roll at 6d, a ham roll at 9d and coffee at 6d. I was inclined to agree with them. The roll which surrounded the cheese could have been bought for 1d, the lady said, and the cheese could probably have been bought for 1½d, which if sold at 4d would give a good profit. The ham roll appeared to be a worst offender for, as the customer said, the roll was only small with little ham inside and a fair price for that, she declared, was not more

His final journey was made in a de Havilland Rapide of East Anglian Flying Services, better known by its later guise, Channel Airways. (MAP)

than 6*d*. The cup of coffee at 6*d* was certainly not worth the money, as compared with prices elsewhere. This snack bar, I understand, is run by BEA and I feel the prices should be revised. On the several occasions I visited this snack bar during my three days' stay it was packed, so there can be no excuse over lack of customers. Another situation at the airport which I feel wants looking into is the need of a comfortable waiting-room for people who arrive on the special cheap rate aircraft, usually about 02:15. By that time the waiting-room is closed for cleaning.

The Friday night before I left I was told there were 15 people who had to make do with resting on ordinary chairs in the entrance hall for from six to seven hours. They could not go to their hotels because their rooms were not ready until noon. There was nowhere for them to buy a cup of tea and, I should imagine, ' a miserable time was had by all.' I understand there is a staff canteen open all night, but not to the public.

I returned to Southend via Shoreham and Rochester with East Anglian Flying Services Limited in a Rapide. We had a full load and were one of several aircraft taking off at about the same time. This Jersey route has been operating for three years and is meeting with continued success. The return fare of £9 12*s* 6*d* from Southend compares favourably with the other airlines operating into Jersey.

Mr R.J. Jones, the managing director, told me that on his Southend, Rochester, Shoreham and Paris service about 75 per cent of the inquiries for Paris come from the Brighton area and 70 per cent of these are for single return bookings. Jersey bookings, he said, were usually in pairs and for both places they were practically all holiday people. Mr R.J. Jones told me that he plans to re-equip the Jersey and Paris routes with Dakotas, and use Herons for feeder purposes. Herons, by the way, cost £40,000 with a delivery in twelve months. He also hopes to rent and operate the Ipswich Airport and this should mean greatly extended business for East Anglian, because Ipswich will serve a big area which is now without a suitable airport.

I am full of enthusiasm about the service being offered to the British public on these internal lines, and the plans being laid by the operators for buying larger aircraft for the better handling and comfort of their passengers.

# REPORT ON CHARTER*
# FLIGHT AW/104/506,
## 30TH APRIL-3RD MAY 1957

## *Introduction*

1. Seventeen T.C.E.U. examiners travelled from the United Kingdom to Singapore on charter service AW/104/506 from 30 April to 3 May 1957. The service appeared to be operated jointly by Skyways of London and Airwork Ltd. The aircraft, a Hermes, carried Skyways markings and, on route, was flown by two Skyways crews and two Airwork crews. The service was scheduled as follows:

|            | E.T.A.  | E.T.D.       |
|------------|---------|--------------|
| London     | —       | 302000       |
| Brindisi   | 010215  | 010345       |
| Ankara     | 010805  | 010940       |
| Baghdad    | 011425  | 011555       |
| Bahrein    | 011905  | 012005       |
| Karachi    | 020100  | 030300       |
|            |         | (night stop) |
| Delhi      | 030620  | 030720       |
| Calcutta   | 031120  | 031250       |
| Bangkok    | 031730  | 031830       |
| Singapore  | 032305  | —            |

Assembly Centre, 209 Harrow Road, London W.1.

2. The assembly centre is operated by the Army, and on this particular service, arrangements for passengers and baggage reception were good. It would appear, however, that the stipulated reporting time of 15:00 GMT was rather early when related to the scheduled E.T.D. of 19:00 hours from Stansted. On the other hand, no reasonable complaint could be made about waiting in the assembly lounge, there being a snack-bar and adequate comfortable settees etc.

---

*TNA AIR 20/10924

Stansted Airfield

3. A poor quality meal (indifferently prepared potatoes, peas and meat pasty) was provided at Stansted prior to departure. Dining room conditions were satisfactory and reception generally well organised.

Stansted – Brindisi (Skyways crew)

4. Departure from Stansted was delayed until 21:45 GMT due to a 'mag' drop. The flight took place in smooth flying conditions and was notable for the extremely helpful and willing service given by the cabin crew, particularly to the mothers and small children. No member of the flight deck crew attempted to make conversation with passengers during the flight.

5. A daylight landing was made at Brindisi at 010350 hours GMT. The approach technique employed by the captain was markedly at variance with Transport Command procedure and would not be accepted by T.C.E.U. A low final 'turn-in' (during which full flap was lowered) was followed by a low 'drag-in' approach. The landing was satisfactory.

6. The meal at Brindisi was of very poor quality and served on filthy tables. Toilet arrangements at the airport were quite unacceptable. Wash basins were in an unclean state, only a very few taps operated, and lavatories were in a disgusting condition.

Brindisi-Baghdad (Airwork Crew)

7. Apart from fast taxying at Brindisi, no adverse comment can be made on aircraft handling on this 'leg'. The Captain, in contrast to his predecessor, spent much time with the passengers and was most helpful and informative. On the other hand the cabin crew did not go to any special effort to ease the lot of the mothers on board. It is considered they could have been more helpful.

8. The 'in-flight' lunch box was mediocre in quality but quantity was adequate. Tea, provided on arrival at Baghdad at 011245 hours GMT consisted mainly of fruit and was quite satisfactory, as were dining room and toilet conditions at the airport.

Baghdad-Karachi (Skyways crew)

9. Take-off time for this leg was 011410 hours GMT. Very indifferent and unnecessarily curt treatment was received from the cabin staff and no member of the flight deck crew spent any time with the passengers. This being the 'third' leg without rest for passengers, much greater consideration and help should have been afforded to mothers and children. The cabin staff appeared to do the absolute minimum of work.

10. Bearing in mind that the last meal (i.e. tea at Baghdad) was by nature rather frugal, food served on the Baghdad-Karachi leg (cheese sandwiches and biscuits) was inadequate.

11. On arrival at Karachi at about 012110 hours GMT tea and cake only was served, passengers having to wait until the next morning for a cooked meal. Subsequent meals served at Karachi, i.e. lunch, tea and dinner, were particularly good and were served in a pleasantly air-conditioned dining room. Hotel accommodation was adequate and reasonably clean.

## Karachi-Delhi (Skyways crew)

12. During the whole of this 'leg' the cabin temperature was kept at about 35° F above outside temperature (i.e. at about 87° F) and this despite numerous complaints from the passengers. This condition was particularly distressing for mothers and children. Cabin staff gave indifferent service.

13. Arriving at Delhi in the dark at about 021710 hours GMT the first approach resulted in an overshoot from about 10ft some 300 yards down the runway. On the second approach the aircraft was landed heavily, giving the impression of having been stalled on to the main wheels. The nosewheel came down heavily and developed a marked 'shimmy'. A large part of the hand baggage fell from the roof racks on to the passengers' heads and several sections of the roof light covers fell into the gangway. It was noted that the aircraft was then taxied in with differential engine power and brake as opposed to the normal method using the steerable nosewheel.

14. Reception arrangements at Delhi were good. Food was first class and served in congenial surroundings.

## Delhi-Calcutta (Skyways crew)

15. Take-off took place in darkness at about 022200 hours GMT. As the brakes were released and full power applied, the aircraft adopted a most marked nose-up attitude, suggesting that for some reason (possibly the nose-wheel shimmy experienced on the previous landing) the captain was attempting to lift the nosewheel clear of the ground at the earliest possible moment. The result was what appeared to be an excessively long take-off run accompanied by 'juddering' suggestive of a semi-stalled condition of flight. It is felt that if this nose-up technique was intentional, it suggested that the pilot suspected that the nose-wheel mechanism was faulty. If this was so the safer course would have been to delay the flight until a proper inspection could be made or as an extreme measure the take-off run might have been made with the nose-wheel on the runway to determine the possibility of further shimmy while still travelling at a relatively slow speed.

16. Once again the cabin temperature was 35 degrees above the outside air temperature for the duration of this leg. Cabin service was again rudimentary only.

17. After completing a holding pattern for some ten minutes a smooth, but markedly nose-up landing was made in the dark at Calcutta.

18. Reception arrangements and meals at Dum Dum Airfield were good.

Calcutta – Bangkok (Airwork crew)

19. Take-off was delayed from Calcutta for some 45 minutes due to a 'mag drop' and took place at 030050 hours GMT in daylight. In-flight snacks consisted of biscuits and tomato sandwiches, the latter (according to the stewardess) having been uplifted from Karachi. They had a peculiar taste and are suspected of having dire and painful results on many of the passengers after their arrival at Singapore. The flight was uneventful except for a very low approach (by Transport Command standards) at Bangkok. Cabin service was courteous and efficient during flight. Reception and food at Bangkok were good.

Bangkok – Singapore (Airwork crew)

20. This final 'leg' was carried out efficiently and uneventfully by the Airwork crew and the aircraft arrived at Paya Lebar Airfield Singapore at 031100 hours GMT. Reception arrangements were exceptionally good and no time was lost in conveying the team to Temple Hill Mess.

After effects of the flight.

21. Some 24 hours after landing the greater part of the team suffered chronic stomach pains accompanied by vomiting, diarrhoea and pains in arms and legs. This was attributed by the M.O. at Changi to food poisoning and is apparently a relatively common occurrence amongst passengers travelling by charter aircraft. Karachi is suspected by the medical officer as the source of the food poisoning. The germ or toxin causing this complaint has apparently not yet been identified and relief, as opposed to a cure, can only be administered to those stricken. The worst symptoms disappear after approximately 48 hours. The gravity of this complaint, if it was contracted by a young child, can only be imagined and it was noted that a fair number of young children travel by these charter services.

Conclusions

22. Generalisations cannot be made on the experiences gained from one flight. However, impressions gained from this flight were:-

(a) This type of charter schedule, involving only one night stop, is suitable for male and female adults unaccompanied by children. With the present facilities provided it is unsuitable for others accompanied by young children.

(b) Attention is required at some of the staging posts to the standards of cleanliness of toilets and washing facilities etc.

(c) In-flight meals and snacks were all of low quality.

(d) Meals at Stansted and Brindisi were sub-standard.

(e) Cabin service was of a widely divergent nature. In general it appears that stewardesses should be instructed to give more attention to mothers with young children.

(f) The piloting standard of Airwork captains was better than that of Skyways pilots. Both companies pilots, however, indulged in very low drag-in approaches of the type that precipitated the recent Hermes accident at Blackbushe. This tendency, together with the errors of airmanship and judgement of which the Skyways pilot is suspected of being guilty when landing at Delhi caused concern amongst the T.C.E.U. staff travelling on the service.
(End of Report)

## FOR OFFICIAL USE★

Director of Movements
War Office/Admiralty/Air Ministry

## AIR TROOPING – PASSENGER FLIGHT REPORT

Flight from: LONDON to SINGAPORE    Date and time of departure of: 2240 hrs.
Operating Company: SKYWAYS    Flight Number: AW 104/506

|      | ITEM | REMARKS |
|------|------|---------|
| 1.   | Passenger reception arrangements at emplanement airfield | Satisfactory |
| 2.   | Briefing before flight | – " – |
| 3.   | Seating and comfort in the aircraft | Satisfactory with exception noted below |
| 4.   | Cleanliness of the aircraft | Satisfactory |
| 5.   | Meals served in flight | – " – |
| 6.   | Meals at stopping places | – " – |
| 7.   | Suitability of childrens meals | – " – |
| 8.   | Accommodation at stopping places | – " – |
| 9.   | Care of family members | – " – |
| 10.  | Flight bulletins | – " – |
| 11.  | Maintenance of flight timings | – " – |
| 12.  | Passenger reception at final destination | – " – |
| 13.  | Suggestions | See below. |

| Signature | Rank: Major | Date: 3 May 57 |
|-----------|-------------|----------------|
| Name | Crosland E. | Unit: GHQ FARELF |

(BLOCK CAPITALS)

---

*Thus follows the comments on the Report by the Director of movements.

<u>Note to paragraph 3</u>

1. The cabin temperature at 9500', in the tropics, is too hot to be comfortable and caused distress, especially amongst the families. The air vents did NOT work satisfactorily and only by increasing height to over 11,000' could the temperature be reduced to an acceptable degree. It was understood from the Captain of the aircraft that it was not always possible to increase height until sufficient fuel had been used up. The aircraft was a Hermes Mark 4.

2. While it is appreciated that it is inevitable the ac may become hot while standing on the tarmac in the tropics, it is considered that full use should be made of the mobile air conditioner provided by BOAC at most scheduled halts to Singapore. This was not done. An observation to the air hostess brought the comment that it could only be used when NOT in use by BOAC civil ac. Enquiries at Bangkok brought the following comment from the maintenance staff that the service costs £10 a time which was NOT acceptable to the charter company.

Recommendation
3. The following recommendations are made:-
   (a) that until the air vents are modified to function correctly, ac should fly at 11,000' minimum between all scheduled halts in the tropics.

   (b) that clear instructions be given to the charter company and ground maintenance staff, that full use will be made of the mobile air conditioner at all scheduled stops EAST of and including Baghdad.

Comments on the Administrative Matters raised in a Report submitted by the Leader of a T.C.E.U. Team after Travelling in Charter Flight A.W.104/506, 30th April – 3rd May, 1957

Submitted under cover of letter from A.O.C.-in-C. Transport Command
Ref. TC/S.55525/ITAS dated 14th June, 1957

<u>Administration</u>

1. A particular fact to be borne in mind in connection with this flight is that it was the first to be undertaken straight through in one aircraft, when it became no longer necessary to operate the shuttle service. We were forced into the shuttle service when the Middle East air barrier caused us to over-fly Turkey; the contractor flew Mark IVs on the U.K./Karachi/U.K. leg and Mark IVA Hermes on the Karachi/Singapore/Karachi leg. To some extent the criticisms made in this report may well have arisen because of the inevitable teething troubles experienced on the change of flight schedule.

2. When the report is analysed and the administrative items are studied in isolation, the criticisms are by no means fundamental and reflect a reasonable administrative organisation; the latest report submitted by the Air Movements Liaison Officer consequent on an inspection flight undertaken by him in the latter part of May supports this contention. It is also of interest, to note that the official report submitted by the Officer i/c Passengers for this flight (Major

E. Crosland – G.H.Q. Far E.L.F.) indicates complete satisfaction with the arrangements made, with the exception of cabin temperatures experienced.

3. We have now been analysing flight reports on the Far East route for the past 12 months and, as a result, have become very much aware that no two reporting officers ever have the same ideas on such personal matters as food and drink, and flight schedules, and that the only way to achieve a uniform and constructive appreciation of air trooping is to study in detail reports submitted by the A.M.L.O.

4. Meals.
What is poison to certain individuals travelling on trooping aircraft appears to be very popular with others. An example is provided in this report under comment, in which it is stated that the meals provided at Delhi and Calcutta were 'first-class' and 'good', whereas it was mainly unsatisfactory meals and accommodation at these particular spots that decided the J.M.C.C. to restrict the use of these particular airfields to the barest minimum. Although we are by no means complacent on this aspect of airtrooping, we are fairly confident that as a result of experience, the institution of Officer i/c Passenger reports and publication of our Codification of Standards and Passenger Comfort, the average meal provided by the air-trooping contractors is reasonably satisfactory.

5. Ground Reception and Handling Arrangements.
We are aware that conditions at the International Airport at Brindisi are not very good, but at the same time they are equal to, if not better than, those prevailing at similarly controlled airfields. We are powerless to obtain any real improvement at these airports as they are under the control of governments other than our own, who strongly resent any suggestion that the British are interfering in their affairs. There is no alternative to the use of Brindisi on the Far East route under present conditions.

6. Arrangements in the Air.
The service etc., provided by aircrew and cabin crew is very much dependant on personalities as the reports shows. We have been advised by both Airwork and Skyways that they are having difficulty in crewing up their aircraft these days, especially during the summer season which accentuates the shortage of aircrew of all trades. The inadequacy of the Skyways crews described in this report will however be taken up with the contractor.

7. Ventilation in the Cabin.
We have experienced difficulty with high temperatures in the cabins of Hermes aircraft in the tropics ever since we started using them on trooping contracts. In fact, BOAC had the same experience before they sold them to Airwork and Skyways. Apparently, the pressurisation was designed originally for the cabin only, whereas after the aircraft was taken into use it was found necessary to extend the pressurisation to include the luggage hold underneath the cabin, whilst at the same time it was not found possible to boost up pressurisation machinery without incurring major modifications. Neither BOAC nor the independent operators were prepared to do this. Consequently, for the last two years, various makeshift efforts have been made to improve the situation without undue expense; during the past six months all

operators have installed more fans in the cabins. Such efforts will continue and at the present time Airwork are experimenting with the possibility of lowering the cabin pressure in flight in tropical areas to coincide with the pressure in the outer air; this, in theory, should reduce the cabin temperature. With present conditions, and bearing in mind that the Britannia should be available for use on the Far East route either towards the end of next year or early 1959, the J.M.C.C. consider that to incur major expense on the Hermes aircraft is not justified.

8. Medical.

The discomfort suffered by the Transport Command examining team on arrival at Singapore is not a new experience on this trooping route; the problem has been observed on already by the D.P.M.O. of Transport Command and the medical services in the Far East. Apparently, the cause of the pain, vomiting etc. is dehydration and a change that takes place in flight in the bowel flora of the body. According to medical Authorities, these symptoms are to be expected, although in fact the incidents of sickness of this nature amongst passengers on charter aircraft is reported to have fallen off considerably in the past few months. The opinion expressed by the Medical Officer at Changi that the symptoms were due to food poisoning appears somewhat irresponsible in the light of the foregoing.

9. To conclude, we have been made aware during the past few months that the performance of Skyways aircraft when employed on the Far East run compares unfavourably with that of the parent contractor, Airwork. It will be necessary therefore, if when the Far East contract is renewed, it is awarded on a 50/50 basis to Airwork and Skyways, that we make this fact known to the latter and ask him to ensure that his performance improves.

# BRITISH INDEPENDENT AVIATION – PAST AND FUTURE*

M. D. N. WYATT, C.B.E.

*The twentieth Brancker Memorial Lecture delivered in London on February 11th 1963. The Author is Chairman, Air Holdings Ltd*

I am honoured by being asked to present the twentieth Brancker Memorial Lecture. My choice of subject is one of which I like to think Sir Sefton Brancker would have approved. His whole approach to aviation was that of an enquiring and imaginative mind and he would, I am sure, have eagerly debated and would have contributed much that would have been of value to the problems affecting British independent aviation.

My lecture is designed both to cover the past and, if possible, to throw some light on the problems facing the independent companies in the future. The distant past, that is, up to the end of 1945, was fully and admirably outlined by Mr Peter Masefield in the 1951 Lecture and in a somewhat different context by Mr Keith Granville last year, so I will only touch upon it briefly and will concentrate on what has happened since 1945 and on what may emerge over the next few years.

*Between the Wars*
British civil air transport really began in 1919 when services were started by several companies.

As is only too often the fate of pioneers they lost most of their money. But they staked a claim and from that time to this private companies have always participated in British civil aviation, sometimes on a fairly large scale, sometimes in the face of almost insuperable political and financial difficulties.

Between 1919 and 1924 it can scarcely be claimed that these pioneer companies prospered, since their total losses were in the region of £500,000. Not a large sum by today's standards but since their total revenue was only about one third of their total expenditure, one cannot but admire the fortitude of their shareholders in continuing the operations for so long. Unfortunately, this early record of financial failure and loss is one which has dogged the industry from that day to this and it is sad that the air is the only form of transport which has never enjoyed even a short period of prosperity before settling down to the record of losses

---

* Reprinted with the kind permission of the Chartered Institute of Logistics and Transport.

or, at best, of meagre financial returns which seem to be the lot of all established forms of transport whether road, rail, sea or air.

In 1924, the four private companies which still existed were merged into the state-aided Imperial Airways. Imperial Airways lasted for sixteen years and nobody would deny that it flew the imperial flag with distinction and success. Indeed, Imperial Airways has become something of a legend. Unfortunately, all the efforts of its management and staff were unable to make it a financial success and it relied heavily on Government subsidies for the whole of its career.

In the late twenties and early thirties, although Imperial Airways' financial troubles were well-known, a number of new independent companies appeared on the scene, but the individual existence of most of them came to an end when they amalgamated to form British Airways in 1935. At this time the railways were also developing air services and individual developments were taking place in Scotland and the Channel Islands.

Between about 1930 and 1939, therefore, this country's air transport was developed by Imperial Airways and some sixteen independent companies. It was carried out basically on ordinary commercial principles, but with the Government playing an increasingly dominant role as more and more help became necessary in the form of subsidies and as strategic considerations became ever more important.

## The War Years

The war years themselves can be dealt with quite briefly. Imperial Airways and British Airways were amalgamated to form BOAC which, with the remaining private companies, carried out the wartime tasks allotted to them.

## Post-War Events

When civil flying started again after the war, air transport was one of a number of industries which was in a position without undue delay to embark upon a period of very substantial expansion. In the circumstances then prevailing, the establishment of three nationally owned Corporations was understandable enough. There was a Socialist Government in power which believed in the wide-scale nationalisation of industry; there were well-founded doubts whether air transport could be made to pay its way, at any rate until a series of post-war airliners had been designed and built; the large initial capital investment which would be needed to establish and develop worldwide services could only be found if it was backed by some form of Government guarantee.

The Civil Aviation Acts of 1946, however, by granting the three Corporations a complete monopoly of all scheduled services went far beyond the requirements necessary for an industry seeking financial support from the Government. Private enterprise was restricted to the right to carry out charter services, and it was clear from the speeches of Government spokesmen during the passage of the Bills that it was envisaged that this would mean no more than the provision of taxi services with small aircraft — a form of air transport which always had led and still does lead straight to ruin, unless it is massively supported by some form of long-term contract sufficient to provide basic turnover and continuity of work.

In other words, air transport was to be a fully nationalised industry from which private enterprise would be excluded. In retrospect the rigid monopoly thus established by the 1946 Acts appears all the more surprising when one remembers that they were drafted and came on the Statute Book at a time when no one could possibly tell how this new industry would be likely to develop.

Whilst there were and still are convincing arguments for the need for State participation at that time and possibly for all time, there has never been a convincing argument for the need to exclude private enterprise, either in its own right or in some form of partnership with the Corporations, and there is no doubt that the 1946 Acts were drafted so as to conform with Socialist political doctrine of widespread nationalisation which was so fashionable at the time. Politics thus became a major factor in British air transport and from 1946 onwards politics have largely dictated and bedevilled the shape and structure of the industry.

As we shall see, the need for a less doctrinaire attitude was soon established.

Despite the closely confined arena permitted to private enterprise, there was no shortage of individuals who thought that the possibilities of air transport were unlimited. Which of these bold individuals staked their capital in the confident belief that there was bound to be some loosening up of the rigid provisions of the 1946 Acts, and which of them allowed their enthusiasm for the air to outweigh commercial prudence will never be known, but the astonishing fact is that in the year 1946-47 there were no less than 69 private companies offering charter services. Statistics for that somewhat chaotic period are extremely sketchy, but, in this first post-war year, these companies carried about 119,000 passengers and 26,000 tons of freight.

These companies were almost without exception promoted by young ex-Servicemen who used what little money they had to purchase or lease war surplus equipment. Although only a comparatively small investment was required, most of the companies lacked sufficient financial resources and most of the managements had little or no commercial experience. They relied mainly on enthusiasm. The outcome was inevitable and companies went out of business almost as fast as they were formed. But a few were able to continue in existence, with sounder financial backing or because of greater ingenuity and commercial understanding.

The high failure rate did not deter others who hopefully started new companies and in 1948-49 the number of charter companies still stood at 39.

During this period, the Air Corporations were naturally very fully occupied in opening up scheduled routes throughout the world.

## The Berlin Airlift

In 1949, an unexpected event took place which proved to be one of the most important single factors affecting the development of British independent companies-namely the Berlin Airlift. The decision to make use of the independent companies for this task was based on strictly practical considerations. Very simply, no other aircraft were available to provide the British civil contribution unless the Corporations' fleets were used, and this would have entailed the most severe disruption of their services at a time when they were struggling to establish themselves on the main commercial routes of the world.

Twenty-three British independent companies participated in the airlift under the general direction of British European Airways. At its peak, 48 aircraft were involved – Dakotas, Tudors, Lancastrians, Haltons, Yorks, Bristol Freighters, Liberators and even Hythe flying boats. A strange collection, but they carried out the task and altogether, they uplifted 147,000 tons of freight.

The Berlin Airlift for the first time gave the independent companies a real job of work to do. It demonstrated not only the existence of these companies but also the extent of their technical and operational ability. But what was infinitely more important was that it demonstrated, for all to see, the benefits to be gained nationally by the existence of other operators in addition to the Government Corporations.

Admittedly, the circumstances of the Berlin Airlift were unusual and possibly unique, but a case for the Independents had definitely been made and the next question, inevitably, was how existing policy was to be amended in the light of the experience gained. To return to the pre-Airlift conditions under which independent companies could only participate in day-to-day charter business could only mean that, before long, they would disappear and that their experience, facilities and above all their flexibility would disappear with them. In the new atmosphere which existed, consideration had therefore to be given as to how these companies could achieve some element of longer-term security which would not only ensure that some, at least, of them would continue in business, but which would also attract the financial backing necessary to provide equipment and facilities of all kinds.

## The 'Associate' Device

The problem did not permit of any easy solution, since the 1946 Acts specifically excluded all except the Corporations from participation in scheduled services, and these alone offered the prospect of a continuing business, regular employment of equipment and personnel and the background necessary for forward planning and orderly investment. However, in the end a solution was found and looking back, one cannot but admire the ingenuity of it. Quite simply, it was decided that the independents could after all operate scheduled services provided they were nominated as 'Associates' of one or other of the Corporations. This device to get round the 1946 Acts, for that in fact is what it was, naturally enough was not welcomed enthusiastically by the Corporations, but they accepted it with a fair grace and it had to serve for eleven years from 1949 to 1960.

Thus, within three years, the architects of the 1946 Acts were finding ways round these same Acts in order to overcome the too rigid pattern they themselves had imposed and from 1949 the basic principle of a Government monopoly in British air transport ceased to exist in fact, although it was to continue as a legal concept for many more years. No wonder, therefore, that this statute monopoly rightly grew to be regarded as a mistake in concept and farcical in practice by nearly everybody in the industry and those concerned with its administration.

The immediate results of this change of attitude were not revolutionary. A ten-year licence was granted to Silver City Airways Ltd enabling it to develop vehicle-ferry services; other licences, mainly for one year, were granted for the operation of services to the Channel Islands and some short, cross-Channel routes.

## Trooping Contracts

At about the same time, the War Office and the Air Ministry were being urged by some of the independents to consider the advantages which would accrue from the carrying of troops by air. As a result, a one-year experimental contract was granted in 1950 to Airwork Ltd for the carriage of troops to various destinations in the Mediterranean and to West Africa. About 11,000 troops were carried in this operation. This first contract was carried out successfully and since that time civil air trooping has expanded very substantially. It still represents almost 40 per cent of the passenger mileage achieved by independent companies on all their operations.

These air-trooping contracts were and still are awarded by the Air Ministry on the basis of competitive tender. At first they were for short periods only, terminable by the Government at three months' notice, but more recently the practice has been to award contracts for longer periods sufficient to make it possible for the successful contractor to plan and carry out the operation on an orderly basis. So far the Corporations, bound by an undertaking not to maintain aircraft specifically for Charter or trooping work, have not tendered for long-term trooping contracts, although, of course, every year they carry out a very considerable amount of ad hoc trooping and general charter business. In 1962, British Overseas Airways Corporation was in fact the biggest charter operator in the United Kingdom.

## New Opportunities

By 1950-51, therefore, we find that Government policy had been dislodged from its initial ever-rigid position and that the independent companies had begun but only just begun to find themselves as an established part of the British air transport industry.

At this time, there were 26 companies in existence. Together they operated about 200 aircraft of very mixed sizes and vintages. The traffic carried by them consisted of about 55,000 passengers on scheduled services (10 million passenger miles) and 75,000 passengers (92 million passenger miles) on charter and contract operations. This certainly did not add up to a great deal by any yardstick and, at best, could only be regarded as the first faltering step towards creating conditions under which both State and private enterprise could make their fullest contribution.

The Conservative Government of 1951, finding itself preoccupied with a heavy legislative programme, decided to continue to use the methods and to a large extent the policies of the previous Government, using as its instrument the Air Transport Advisory Council and establishing it as an independent quasi-licensing authority. Existing legislation was to remain unaltered and the companies would continue to act as 'Associates' of the Air Corporations which would retain a monopoly of all normal scheduled services on routes operated by them at that time. But for the future, any independent Company, or either of the Corporations, wishing to operate a new route or under closely defined conditions, a new type of service along a route already operated by another carrier, would be required to make an application to the Air Transport Advisory Council.

This Council, which was originally formed chiefly to provide a medium for airline passengers to air grievances, was not an executive body and it was only empowered to make recommendations to the Minister. It is a most remarkable tribute to the work of the Air Transport Advisory Council and its outstanding Chairman, the then Lord Terrington, that on only one occasion out of the many hundreds of cases it handled did a Minister see fit not to accept a recommendation from the Council. It is, I think, worthy of comment that there was no appeal procedure in those days and the fact that operators had, in effect, to accept the decisions of an independent body does not appear to have done anyone any lasting harm.

During the next four years, the independent companies used the opportunities open to them to the full and expanded their activities at a high rate. Obviously, since they started from a very low datum point almost any expansion would show a high percentage gain. But the important thing about this expansion was that it proved the contentions of the independent companies that a measure of freedom would promote overall expansion and not result in disaster either to themselves or to the Corporations; and that, as a consequence, British civil aviation would gain.

Basking in the pale sunshine of the Conservative Government, the independent companies were able to embark upon the wholehearted promotion of Inclusive Tour Service based on the principle of a 'package deal' which included both the cost of air transport and holiday accommodation. The development of these Inclusive Tour Services gave new opportunities to the public both in convenience and price, and services of this type rapidly became and still remain a popular feature of European air transport.

'Colonial Coach' services were another development thought up by the independent companies about this time and they did their utmost to establish these services to all the then Colonial territories. Owing to the limitations of international regulations, 'Colonial Coach' services could only be operated on cabotage routes, and in order to avoid any risk of taking away existing traffic from the Corporations, it was required that these services should provide a lower class of comfort than that offered on normal scheduled services. Fares had therefore to be low enough to attract a new class of traffic.

Services on somewhat similar lines had been carried out on a charter basis for some time principally to East and West Africa by Airwork Ltd and Hunting-Clan Air Transport Ltd, and new services to Central Africa and Gibraltar were now introduced. Later attempts by Eagle Airways and others to introduce services to British territories in the Far East and the West Indies did not receive Government approval.

Vehicle-ferry services, another idea of the independents, were also started about this time. These services were initiated by Silver City Airways operating at first from Lympne and later from their own airport at Lydd. The Channel Air Bridge operating from Southend was started shortly afterwards. Both companies are now part of the Air Holdings Ltd group. The routes operated have gradually increased in number and distance, so that passengers today can fly their cars from Southend, Lydd or Hurn to Geneva, Basle, Strasbourg, Rotterdam, Ostend, Calais, Le Touquet, Cherbourg and the Channel Islands. The popularity of these services is shown by the fact that in 1962, no less than 141,700 vehicles and 419,200 passengers were carried.

## Investment by Shipping Companies

In the years 1953-54 several of the major shipping companies decided to become financially interested in air transport. Furness Withy, shortly to be followed by the Blue Star Line, made a substantial investment in Airwork Ltd; the P&O acquired a controlling interest in Silver City Airways, the Bibby Line made an investment in Skyways Ltd and the Clan Line went into partnership with the Hunting Group to form Hunting-Clan Air Transport Ltd; a good deal later, the Cunard Steam Ship Company acquired the whole of the share capital of Eagle Airways Ltd

There is no doubt that the shipping companies were encouraged by the Government of the day to make these investments, but just why they did so without a firm understanding of the Government's intentions with regard to the future will always remain something of a mystery. However, whatever their underlying reasons may have been, their financial strength and their worldwide connexions were very welcome additions to the industry. I think it would be generally agreed that their association with the air has, on the whole, been something of a disappointment to them in that experience has shown that there really is surprisingly little in common between the world of shipping with its basic concept of freedom of the seas and the closely circumscribed and restrictionist world of civil aviation.

The year 1956 saw what was certainly the largest and on the whole, one of the least successful ventures of any of the independent companies. Airwork Ltd, by means of the 'Associate' agreement device, obtained a licence to operate an all-cargo service between the United Kingdom and the Continent of North America. This licence was hedged about by restrictions. For example, the carriage of mail was entirely prohibited and after a short, but exciting experiment, lasting nine months, the service was withdrawn in November of that year. Several valuable lessons were learnt. Airwork Ltd discovered that playing in the First League was a very different affair to schoolboy football. It was clearly demonstrated that to run an all-cargo service hedged about with restrictions was entirely impracticable and that any cargo service, at any rate on the highly competitive North Atlantic, operated in isolation and unsupported by a massive network of passenger routes, was doomed to rapid failure.

## Wide-scale Mergers

After the failure of Airwork's North Atlantic venture and with the advent of a new generation of turbo-prop aircraft each costing as much as a whole fleet of older aircraft, it became more and more apparent that if they were to have any chance of success the number of independent companies would have to be drastically reduced and that wide-scale merging was inevitable. Indeed, on more than one occasion, the Independents were publicly urged to get together by the responsible Minister of the day. As a result, partly of these exhortations and partly due to the pressure of ordinary economics, a large number of mergers and takeovers took place between 1957 and 1962. Airwork Ltd took a leading put in this process and acquired control among others of Hunting-Clan Air Transport Ltd, Transair Ltd, Air Charter Ltd, the Channel Air Bridge Ltd, Morton Air Services Ltd, Silver City Airways Ltd, Bristow Helicopters Ltd and Jersey Airlines, together with a New Zealand Company, Straits Air Freight Express Ltd which it had formed in 1951 to carry freight across the Cook Straits under contract with the New Zealand State Railways. In the process, Airwork Ltd which was founded as long ago as 1928 lost its identity and became British United Airways Ltd. Later a purely holding company was formed under the name of Air Holdings Ltd with British United Airways as a wholly owned subsidiary. The Air Holdings' Group is by now far the largest of the independent companies. Accurate statistics for 1962 are not yet available, but during the year, it will have carried not less than 1,700,000 passengers, 141,700 vehicles, and 89,000 tons of freight.

## Growth of Independent Operation

In the last of its Annual reports (for the year ending March 31st 1961) the Air Transport Advisory Council produced the following table:

### THE GROWTH OF AIR TRANSPORT 1953-61

| YEAR | BOAC | | BEA | | INDEPENDENT COMPANIES | |
|---|---|---|---|---|---|---|
| | Passengers Carried | Load Short Ton Miles | Passengers Carried | Load Short Ton Miles | Passengers Carried | Load Short Ton Miles |
| 1953-4 | 286,582 | 133,362,000 | 1,656,779 | 53,119,000 | 252,550 | 8,100,000 |
| 1954-5 | 270,635 | 126,665,000 | 1,874,316 | 63,039,000 | 360,686 | 12,235,000 |
| 1955-56 | 362,507 | 149,606,000 | 2,224,747 | 77,903,000 | 552,326 | 23,453,000 |
| 1956-57 | 383,862 | 164,754,000 | 2,461,065 | 88,828,000 | 725,988 | 25,181,000 |
| 1957-58 | 447,835 | 181,582,000 | 2,865,591 | 101,246,000 | 903,427 | 32,548,000 |
| 1958-59 | 470,959 | 202,494,000 | 2,828,715 | 108,598,000 | 949,892 | 39,271,000 |
| 1959-60 | 597,561 | 252,612,000 | 3,289,606 | 127,304,000 | 1,118,235 | 44,761,000 |
| 1960-61 | 790,718 | 315,849,000 | 3,990,957 | 151,133,000 | 1,517,421 | 53,945,000 |

The report went on to comment on these results as follows:

It is encouraging to note that the steady expansion during earlier years for all operators has been followed in 1960-61 by even larger increases than in any past year. The table indicates the results of the policy of allowing independent companies to share in the development of scheduled air services as Associates of one or other of the Airways Corporations. A natural result of that policy has been that the independent companies' traffic on scheduled services has increased at a faster rate than that of the Corporations; between 1953-54 and 1960-61 the annual traffic (as measured in load ton miles) of independent companies increased about 6½ times and that of the Corporations 2½ times. Despite this faster rate of growth by the independent companies, the two Corporations were in 1960-61 still carrying 90 per cent of the total scheduled-service traffic of all United Kingdom operators, the independent companies' share of that traffic having risen from 4 per cent to 10 per cent over the period covered by the table. To express these developments in different terms, 86 per cent of the increase in scheduled-service traffic between 1953-54 and 1960-61 is attributable to the expansion of the Corporation's traffic and 14 per cent to that of the independent companies. The Council considers that these figures support its view that the increased participation of the independent companies in scheduled services has been achieved without materially restraining the growth of the Corporations' traffic.

So far as I am aware, no one other than the two Air Corporations has sought to contradict the conclusions drawn by the Air Transport Advisory Council.

## The 1960 Act

In the light of such a substantial change for the better, it may fairly be asked why the independent companies continued to press the need for the introduction of new legislation which would give them a wider measure of opportunity. There were several reasons. In the first place, there was an obvious need for more adequate control over technical and operating standards; it was also necessary to ensure that companies seeking to embark on public transport operations had adequate financial and material resources. A few 'bad eggs', by their low operational standards and financial failures, had gone a good way towards undermining public confidence in independent companies and had brought some discredit to British air transport as a whole. The situation could only be put right by amending existing legislation. It was also generally agreed that the statutory monopoly, linked as it was to the 'Associate Agreement' device bore no relation to current conditions and that a change was long overdue. This too could only be brought about by Act of Parliament.

If the statutory monopoly was to be repealed and if all operators were to be placed in an equal position in law, there must obviously be some provision for the general control of the industry. As a matter of administrative convenience it seemed that this could best be achieved through the medium of some form of licensing authority. During the passage of the Bill, the main argument centred round the issue of how independent such a Licensing Authority should in fact be and what were to be the extent of its powers.

In the end the Civil Aviation Act of 1960 came into being. The two most important features of it were the repeal of the Corporations' statutory monopoly and a provision for the setting up of an Air Transport Licensing Authority. Thus after a struggle lasting for fourteen years, the independent companies achieved their main objective and achieved in the eyes of the law an equal position with the Corporations.

The Air Transport Licensing Board, under the distinguished chairmanship of Professor Jack, consists of nine members and employs a permanent secretariat. Thus with greater resources than the old Air Transport Advisory Council, it has been able to delve more deeply into all aspects of air transport and, as a natural consequence, the hearing of cases has become more detailed and more complex. The hearings are in public; the Board's findings and supporting reasons are published. In addition, the 1960 Act provides for an appeal to a commissioner appointed by the Minister against any of the findings of the Board. The Commissioner in turn publishes his findings and the Minister, as the final arbiter, decides whether or not to uphold them. Thus, when one gets to the end of the long road, the Minister is still the sole arbiter in every disputed case.

All this procedure is exceedingly time-consuming and expensive. In the case of the applications to operate on certain European routes in parallel with British European Airways made in December 1960 by British United Airways and Cunard Eagle Airways, the final decisions of the Minister were not published until September 1962. In the course of the original hearing before the Board and of the subsequent hearing before the Appeal Commissioner, nearly 2,000,000 words were submitted in evidence, and the cost in Counsels' fees and in time spent in preparing and hearing the case must have run into many thousands of pounds. This particular case, of course, was of basic importance and the delay in arriving at a decision and the cost of obtaining it is fairly understandable, but it is to be devoutly hoped that future cases going to appeal before a commissioner will not entail what hitherto has in effect been a complete re-hearing.

I think I am right in saying that some simplification of procedure is possible without amending the Act and if this view is correct, let us all pray that the Minister may be moved to give the matter his effective attention at a very early date

In the main, with one dramatic exception, the Board's decisions have been accepted by applicants and in those cases where appeals have been lodged, the Board has been upheld by the Commissioner and the Minister. The chief exception was, of course the much publicised application made by Cunard Eagle Airways for a passenger service across the North Atlantic. A licence for this service was granted by the Board, but subsequently after appeal, the Board's decision was reversed by the Minister. The last stage of this affair was the forming of a joint company by the Cunard Steamship Company and British Overseas Airways Corporation to operate on the North Atlantic. This has only been in operation for a short time and no results are yet published, but whatever the outcome, it is a bold experimental partnership which will be watched with interest by everyone concerned.

A stranger to this strange industry might suppose that once a licence has been confirmed by the Minister, the coast would be clear for the licensee to start operations without further ado.

But this is very far from being the case. There remains the problem of obtaining the necessary traffic rights from the foreign Governments concerned. Between Great Britain and almost every other country there exist agreements, many of them of long standing, which regulate the amount of traffic which is permissible and the proportions in which it may be shared between the countries concerned. So before any new licence for an international route can be implemented, it is necessary to obtain, through the good offices of the British Government, the consent of the foreign Governments concerned. This at best is likely to take many months to obtain: at worst it may not be possible to obtain it at all.

We have now therefore reached in 1963 a stage where British air transport, largely regulated by the Air Transport Licensing Board, is composed of the two Government-owned air Corporations and about sixteen independent companies. These companies vary substantially in size from the relatively large British United Airways group backed by substantial shipping and other interests to the smallest companies, some of them owned and managed by one individual.

The air Corporations are still naturally by far the predominant element and still account for 90 per cent of this country's scheduled air services and about 70 per cent of its total effort. But taking it all in all, over the sixteen years which have elapsed since the 1946 Acts were passed, the independent companies have a record of achievement of which they may well be proud. Many of them have fallen by the wayside, but between them they have pioneered a number of entirely new forms of air transport including inclusive tours, colonial coach services, vehicle-ferry services, and the large scale carrying of troops by air.

Thus, after years of discussion and argument, sometimes acrimonious, but on the whole fairly good-humoured, the 1960 Civil Aviation Act would seem to point to a pattern of joint effort and regulated competition between the Corporations on the one hand and the independent companies on the other — a situation fraught with interest and carrying with it the most complex problems for the future.

## The Future

The three great problems for the future as far as the independents are concerned seem to be: firstly, whether they will be able to live alongside and in regulated competition with the Government Corporations; secondly, whether they will be able to survive the financial perils of an industry in which enormous capital investment is required, in which many, if indeed not the majority, of the largest units are conducted with at least as much attention to national prestige as to commercial considerations, and an industry moreover which is at the mercy of foreign and domestic politics to a quite exceptional degree; thirdly, assuming the two other problems are mastered, whether it will be possible to devise some satisfactory method of providing the very substantial finance which will inevitably be required by at least some of the independents if they are to take an expanding part in this still fast growing industry.

A satisfactory solution of the first of these problems I am sure can be arrived at but it will take time and it will certainly need the best efforts of all concerned. As far as I know, with the possible exception of road transport which is not really very closely allied to air transport, there is no other industry where a Government controlled and financed sector operates alongside and in competition with a privately owned sector. Still less, where the privately owned sector is absolutely at the mercy of the Government for its very life blood.

Theoretically, of course, it would be easy for any Government to make life impossible for an independent company, but that seems scarcely likely in view of all that has been said and done both inside and outside Parliament during the past eighteen years and in the light of the policy which has so slowly and so painfully emerged. Theoretically, also, it would be an easy matter for the Corporations to use their vast financial strength and their mass of unrestricted licences to kill any competition from the independents. In the rough world we live in that must clearly always be a risk which must be taken into account, but for my part, I am inclined to think that in normal circumstances, it is not a very serious risk. Apart from any other considerations (and there are several) there is enough public opinion in favour of private enterprise to render any such action on the part of a Government Corporation politically unattractive.

Nevertheless, in view of the apparent helplessness of successive Governments to exercise policy control over the nationally owned Corporations, the risk remains.

What seems to be a far more serious risk may well arise from the straightforward pressure of events, and this brings me to the second of the questions I have posed. What, for example, is to happen if the future shows that Great Britain's share of world traffic is not sufficient to support two Government Corporations in addition to one or more substantial privately owned airlines? Would the solution be some form of joint effort between Government and private enterprise, or is one or other of the two sectors to be entirely sacrificed? Let us hope that British efforts to obtain a sufficiently large share of world traffic will be so successful that this dilemma will never arise.

The third and last of these three problems is much more humdrum, but nonetheless of vital importance.

When Vickers produced the first Viking aircraft shortly after the war, it was sold at £37,500. Today a medium-range aircraft would cost not less than £500,000 and the next generation is likely to cost close on a million.

This increase in cost puts the replacement of existing fleets outside the unaided financial capacity of operating companies. Just as shipping companies have for many years had to rely upon the public and the financial institutions to finance part of the cost of building their new ships through mortgages and fixed interest debentures, so now the time has come when the air companies must look for part of their finance to private enterprise in the City. This is not going to be easy.

It is generally accepted that aircraft must be written off over a period of 7/10 years. It follows that any loans secured on those aircraft must be amortised over a similar or rather shorter period. Advances of this kind are regarded as too long for British banks and too short for insurance companies. Furthermore, the private investor who constantly reads of the vast losses made by many of the greatest of the world's airlines is by no means ready to subscribe to public issues of airline fixed-interest securities. The hire purchase companies who have in the past provided limited finance for the purchase of aircraft are hardly likely to have available funds on the scale contemplated, and the rates of interest normally charged would be far too high to permit of proper amortisation and economic operation. Thus most of the normal sources of finance are not available to aircraft operators. Fundamentally, the difficulty lies perhaps in the fact that in the City of London an aircraft, however efficient and costly and whatever its earning capacity, is still generally regarded as a hazardous form of property not worthy of the credit which is regularly accorded on the security of a tramp steamer. This attitude may in part be due to the unsatisfactory state of the law of England in relation to the registration of charges on aircraft to which reference is made later.

Thought in New York is much more advanced. There it has become the recognised practice of Banks to advance at moderate rates of interest up to 75 per cent of the cost of new aircraft upon the security of mortgages repayable over 5/7 years.

It has been possible in England for many years past to arrange finance for ship construction by means of mortgages regarding which special rules are laid down in the Merchant Shipping Act of 1894. But these rules do not apply to aircraft and as things stand, mortgages of aircraft are in exactly the same position as mortgages of any other ordinary chattel.

An international convention was signed in 1949 by the United Kingdom and a number of other States by which the contracting States agreed to establish registers in which mortgages of aircraft will be recorded and the contracting states have also mutually agreed to recognise rights duly recorded in the register of the aircraft's home state. But this convention so far has only been ratified by one or two of the signatories and only if it were ratified by a substantial number would the security of mortgages be materially improved. So far it has not been ratified by the United Kingdom.

At the present time, therefore, probably the best method of securing monies advanced to operating companies is by a floating charge. Floating charges, however, involve certain risks to the lender and in other ways are not entirely satisfactory. It might be, therefore, that the time has now come when the financing of aircraft fleets should receive the serious attention of the City with a view, for example, to forming an institution for the purpose which, on the strength of its own credit could purchase and own aircraft and charter them on a bare hull basis to operating companies who might or might not themselves be shareholders.

In conclusion, I should like to thank all those who have helped me in the preparation of this paper and in particular, Mr Blakemore, whose years of service as secretary of the British Independent Air Transport Association gave him a unique knowledge of the developments that have been taking place in civil aviation since the end of the last war.

# THE CORBETT REPORT
## (PAGES 82-98)

*Paragraph numbers are included.*

SECTION VIII – THE VC10 STORY

208. In the autumn of 1956, when the Government gave BOAC permission to buy 15 Boeing 707s, the Minister (Watkinson) made it clear that no further dollars would be available for the purchase of American aircraft and that, when the announcement for the Boeing purchase was made, it must be made clear 'that it was the firm intention that British aircraft should be produced for BOAC to fly on the North Atlantic run and elsewhere'. Even so, the announcement about the Boeing purchase was received with considerable criticism.

209. Immediately BOAC, in conjunction with the Ministry of Supply and the Ministry of Transport and Civil Aviation, started consultations with aircraft manufacturers in an endeavour to find a suitable British aircraft.

210. I need not here refer to the various proposals that were considered and dropped, but pass straight to the spring of 1957 when the VC10 project was under serious consideration.

211. Initially BOAC had intended to use the standard VC10 on Eastern and Southern routes and, according to the Ministry, there was a meeting on 23rd April, 1957, when the position was that:

(1) <u>Vickers</u> were not prepared to start the project unless they had firm orders for thirty-five aircraft at a price of £1.7m. each - the guaranteed performance resulting in an operating cost of 13. 7 pence per ctm on the Eastern route.
(2) <u>BOAC</u> wanted twenty aircraft at £1.6m. each to operate at 12 pence per ctm on the Eastern route.
(3) <u>HMG</u> was not prepared to contribute to the development of the aircraft or underwrite the project in any way.

212. Although the Ministry records put the BOAC stated requirement at 20 aircraft, it is right to say that the Board of the Corporation was in fact prepared to consider placing an order for 25 aircraft with an option on a further 10 provided both the price and performance were satisfactory.

213. On the 30th April, 1957, Sir Gerard d'Erlanger wrote to the minister seeking Government approval to the purchase, subject to detailed specification and contract, of 35 VC10s at a price which it was estimated would average £1,770,000 including escalation up to the date of delivery. The estimated cost of operation is not stated but the letter says 'the economic performance of the aircraft on the Corporation's route on which it would be flown is satisfactory at that price'.

214. Thus, within seven days of the previous meeting, BOAC reached the conclusion:-

(1) that it could take 35 aircraft against the 20 to 25 which was the previous assessed requirement;

(2) that a price estimated at £1.77m. was acceptable, whereas the earlier maximum price was £1.6m. and,

(3) that the operating cost estimated at 13.7 pence per ctm on the Eastern route was satisfactory, although quite materially above the 12 pence per ctm (the estimated operating cost of the Boeing) which had previously been demanded.

I should here interpose a note to the effect that although the estimated cost penalty of the VC10 against the Boeing on the Eastern route was 1.4 pence per ctm, it was higher on the Southern route and amounted to 4.4 pence per ctm. It is right to say that at that time there was no certainty that the Boeing would be able to operate with acceptable payloads throughout the Eastern and Southern Routes, although, according to the Ministry records, BOAC told them in October 1956 that 'contrary to earlier expectations the Boeing could operate with a reasonable payload into airfields on the Eastern and Southern routes.'

215. The Ministry advise me that when the proposition was examined in May 1957 the Economics Branch of the Department concluded that 'the traffic forecast on which the requirement for 35 aircraft depended could be seriously very optimistic and, if not realised, would result in the Corporation having up to 9 aircraft too many'.

216. Government approval was given on 22nd May, 1957, and Vickers were notified by BOAC on the same day.

217. In May an aircraft with 123 seats was envisaged but over the succeeding seven months many modification were introduced so that by the end of the year the aircraft, which was then known as the long-range VC10, was to have a seating capacity of between 135 and 141 and the cost, which included estimated escalation, had risen to £2,017,000 which was only £25,000 less than the estimated cost of the Boeing which had 25% more seating capacity. The comparable estimated direct operating costs per ctm were:

|  | VC10 | Boeing |
|---|---|---|
| Eastern routes | 13. 5 | 12. 1 |
| Southern routes | 20.0 | 15.6 |
| North Atlantic routes | 16.6 | 12.7 |

218. On 31st December, 1957, the Board of BOAC gave formal approval to the signing of a contract for 30 long-range VC10s for the Eastern and Southern routes but concluded that the VC10 would not be competitive with the Boeing on the North Atlantic. The number of aircraft was reduced from 35 considered previously because it was a larger and more expensive aircraft and had a larger seating capacity.

219. On 8th January, 1958, however, which was only eight days later, the managing director (Sir Basil Smallpeice) submitted to the Board Technical Committee a paper from which I take the following extract:

Since the end of December, the Royal Aircraft Establishment at Farnborough have carried out further work on the take-off characteristics and drag of the VC10 and the Boeing 707. The results more than confirm our expectation that the Vickers estimates would prove to be conservative relative to those of Boeing.

In regard to take-off characteristics, the RAE report that 'the VC10 should have a take-off field length of about 25% less than that for the Boeing 707/420 with 3B engines, and about 10% less if both aircraft have the 3C engine.

The effect of the revised estimate of drag is that the RAE calculate that 'the fuel for long range cruise should be at least 3% less than for the VC10 compared with the Boeing 707/420. If the Boeing 707 were fitted with 3C engines, the cruise fuel consumption would on this basis be at least 1% less for the VC10.

The effect on cost per ctm for the North Atlantic operation is to eliminate altogether the 31% higher cost of the VC10 and bring it down to the level of the developed Boeing 707, as follows:

|  | Pence |
|---|---|
| Direct operating cost per ctm for VC10 on North Atlantic quoted on Appendix 2 (page 1) | 16.6 |
| Benefit derived from field length revaluation | 2.2 |
|  | 14.4 |
| Benefit derived from estimated saving in cruise fuel consumption | 1.9 |
| Revised estimate of cost per ctm – VC10 on the North Atlantic | 12.5 |
| Estimated cost for Boeing 707 with 3C engines | 12. 7 |

These figures make it evident that the VC10 should be equally as good on the North Atlantic as the Boeing 707; even if the full benefit estimated by the RAE above is not achieved, there are other factors which should make up any shortfall.

I should therefore be grateful for the authority of the Board to enter into a contract with Vickers for the full number of 35 aircraft.

220. On the following day the Committee agreed to the purchase of 35 aircraft and the Board confirmed the decision.

221. As the adjustments to operating costs in the above paper appear to be based on investigations carried out by the RAE, it is fair to say that the RAE investigations did not deal with operating costs and in so far as these appear in the Board paper they are the result of BOAC's own calculations. In case this should be of importance in future discussions, I have embodied in Appendix XXI the results of a review carried out for me as to the relevance of the RAE investigation.

222. Although BOAC had already received in the previous May covering authority from the Government to enter into the VC10 contract (see paragraph 216), it no doubt advised the Government of the Board decision on the 9th January because the Minister appears to have been apprehensive as to the ability of the VC10 to compete with the Boeing on the North Atlantic. Sir George Cribbett wrote to the Minister on the 15th January, presumably to allay any fears there might have been. This letter, however, did not satisfy the Minister, who wrote to the Chairman, Sir Gerard d'Erlanger, on the 19th February, to which letter the Chairman replied on the 25th February, 1958.

223. This correspondence is so extraordinary that I set out all three letters below:

(1)   Sir George Cribbett's letter of 15th January, 1958, to the Minister:

Draper (Watkinson's private secretary) asked me on the telephone whether we were now satisfied that the VC10 we have ordered had a satisfactory North Atlantic performance. I explained the position to him on the telephone and promised to send you a copy of the short summary of the results of recent investigations by Farnborough into the take-off and drag performance of the VC10 compared with the Boeing 707.

I enclose this summary which I am sure you will find most interesting. We now have the assurance that the VC10, powered with the Conway IIIC engine will have an economic performance on the North Atlantic which will compare with the Boeing 707 performance on the assumption that this aircraft is re-engined with the IIIC.

(2)   Minister's letter of 19th February, 1958, to Sir Gerard d'Erlanger:

George Cribbett wrote to me on 15th January enclosing a copy of your Board Paper summarising the latest conclusions on the transatlantic capabilities of the VC10.

I am glad to know that you now feel that on this route the British aircraft can be expected to hold its own against the Boeing 707 even if the latter is equipped with the developed Conway engines.

If, however, I have correctly understood the Board Paper the apparent improvement of the VC10s operating costs over the North Atlantic from 16.6 to 12.5 pence per ctm results from a revaluation of the aircraft by Farnborough experts, who formed a more favourable view of its performance than the manufacturers themselves. Am I to take it that Vickers now accept this re-assessment, and that the assurance to which you refer in the second paragraph of your letter that the economic performance of the VC10 will match that of the Boeing, is one to which the manufacturers are committed?

I notice that the Board paper does not say anything about the effect of the increased weight and power on the economics of the VC10 on the Eastern routes for which it is primarily intended. I hope you can assure me that they have not been impaired. Such assurance would be welcome in itself and it would also help me in considering how to deal with the matter of the increased initial price about which you wrote to me on the 17th January.

(3)   Sir Gerard d'Erlanger's letter of 25th February, 1958, to the Minister:

Thank you for your letter of the 19th February about VC10 performance. At the time of our Board meeting in January events were moving very rapidly and it was possible for the Board to take into account some factors which were not reflected in the paper George Cribbett sent you.

Take-off performance is naturally a critical item in connection with jet performance generally and one view was taken by Vickers and a much more optimistic view taken by Boeings. The Farnborough experts established to their and to the Corporation's satisfaction that whether one applied the optimistic or the pessimistic view to both aircraft, the performance of each was broadly the same. What had happened previously was that the pessimistic Vickers views had been applied to VC10 performance, whilst the 707 was given the benefit of Boeings' optimism.

Vickers have not adopted Farnborough estimates of VC10 performance and their guarantees remain as they were. If Vickers' view of the take-off performance question is justified by events, then we cannot expect the VC10 to do better than guarantee. On the other hand we are satisfied that in those circumstances it should be mentioned that if the VC10 does not match the economics of the Boeing 707 the chances of worldwide sales of the VC10 will be remote. It seems, therefore, that having regard to the amount which is at stake and to the reputation of both Vickers and Rolls Royce, there will be every incentive for this to be achieved.

With regard to VC10 performance on eastern routes, I am advised that the increased weight and power of the version we have ordered as compared with the earlier version shows little, if any, economic penalty. We feel that such marginal penalty as there may be will be more than offset by the advantages flowing from the flexibility which we shall have as a result of being able to switch aircraft to the Atlantic run when necessary. An integrated fleet is likely to produce far greater economic benefits than any marginal improvements the so-called Eastern Hemisphere aircraft might have over the worldwide aircraft.

224. The extraordinary features about this correspondence are, first, that BOAC as the buyer should be prepared to rate the VC10 aircraft higher than Vickers as the seller were prepared to guarantee and, second, that the Chairman of BOAC, who is later on record as saying that he never wanted to buy the VC10 but always wanted a Boeing (paragraph. 236), should have confused himself into assuring the Minister that BOAC felt the VC10 would be as good as the Boeing, and that he should have so expressed himself at a time when it looked as though the Minister was uneasy about the matter. If Sir Gerard d'Erlanger did not want the VC10, here was a golden opportunity to lay before the Minister the very heavy annual burden that

would be placed on BOAC in flying it rather than the Boeing. If the Government could have been persuaded to drop the VC10 project there was plenty of time to order Boeings. In fact, if ordered at that time they could have been in service three or four years ahead of the VC10. At that time some people doubted whether the Boeing would be able to operate up to its guaranteed performance but any doubt could have been embodied in the submission to the Minister.

225. The order for the 35 long-range standard VC10s was signed on the 14th January, 1958, and it was a term of the contract that BOAC should have an option, exercisable up to August 1962, to purchase a further 20 aircraft at the same price.

226. In January 1960 Vickers told the Ministry and BOAC that they had seriously under-estimated the costs of making the 35 standard VC10s and the position was so serious that they might be unable to continue production of the aircraft unless a further order for at least 10 Super VC10s at a price of £2.7m. each was placed immediately.

227. Shortly before this BOAC had shown interest in a larger aeroplane, such as a Super VC10, provided the operating costs would match those of the Boeing 707. In November 1959 however, the Technical Committee had reviewed the Corporation's capacity needs up to 1966/67 and concluded that it should not at that time exercise the option for any of the 20 VC10s or Super VC10s.

228. I am assured that the Board of BOAC was at that time under very strong pressure from the Ministry to place a further order for VC10s. This is in some measure confirmed by the following minute of 7th January, 1960:

> We would still prefer, as in November, not to enter into any commitment until more experience had been gained as a basis for our requirements in the mid-1960s. This view was subject to the effect of Vickers ceasing to produce our VC.10 which was vital to our operations from 1964 onwards. Furthermore, the effect of such a situation on the Government policy for the aircraft manufacturing industry was also involved.
> It was agreed that the matter should be discussed by the chairman with the minister in the light of the minister's policy as to the future of the Corporation and the independent companies and that the attitude taken by the Board last November could be open for reconsideration.

229. Accordingly Sir Gerard d'Erlanger went to see the Minister (Mr Duncan Sandys) on the 13th January and within a fortnight BOAC was committed to buying ten Super VC10s in addition to the 35 standard VC10s already on order.

230. Although the many contemporary records which I have seen leave me in no doubt that BOAC was in fact under very strong pressure from the Ministry to place a further order for aircraft which at that time it was not satisfied it would need, the BOAC minute of 15th January, 1960, indicates that BOAC was leaning over backwards to meet the Minister's wishes. The extract from the minute is as follows:

Further to Board Minute 4316, the Chairman referred to discussions which he had with the Minister of Aviation on the question of our ordering Super VC10s, during which the chairman had stated that consideration was being given to an order for not more than ten Super VC10s at a price of £2.4m. each, but that this was subject to the approval of the Board.

The Minister's attitude was that, while he would not press the Corporation to undertake any such commitment, the order for Super VC10s would be helpful to Government policy for the aircraft manufacturing industry, and it was a matter for the Corporation to decide. The Minister had further stated that it was not the intention of the Government to prejudice the planned expansion of the Corporation.

The Chairman had subsequently informed Vickers of the outcome of his meeting with the Minister and Vickers had stated that they might not even be able to proceed with the manufacture of our 35 VC10s if the Corporation's order for Super VC10s at £2.4m. each was to be restricted to ten aircraft.

Vickers emphasised that they had underestimated their costs of production of our VC10s and that the aircraft would be superior in performance to that contemplated at the time the order was placed.

The Managing Director referred to forward traffic estimates, which had been the subject of consideration by the Management and the Chairman's Aircraft Requirements Committee, which showed that estimated traffic growth was such that from 1966 onwards there was a gap between capacity available and that required which would justify our ordering ten Super VC10s. Because of the greater economy of the Super VC10 on the transatlantic route, it was estimated that the financial result would be improved by £1.5m. per annum with the operation of a combined fleet of 35 standard VC10s and ten Super VC10s (at a price of £2.4m. each) as, compared with the operation of an augmented fleet of standard VC10s.

Against the above background the Board decided:

a) That the Corporation would be prepared to negotiate an order for ten Super VC10s at £2.4m. each, and if such an order was unacceptable to Vickers, then it was for them to have further discussions with the Minister of Aviation with the view to their obtaining financial assistance from the Government;

b) That the ten Super VC.10s are to be regarded as part of our option under the contract for the standard VC10s leaving a further ten aircraft of either standard or Super VC10s to be the subject of the option. Failing a satisfactory arrangement for financial assistance by the Government, the Corporation would consider a price for the Super VC10s of £2.55m. per aircraft on condition that:-

(i) Vickers deliver the 35 standard VC10s on the delivery dates provided by the Contract;

(ii) Vickers reimburse the Corporation with the whole or part of the difference between £2.4m. and £2.55m. in proportion to the number of Super VC10s sold by Vickers between 10 and 20.

231. The chairman advised the Minister by letter of the Board's decision to place a further contract and I quote the Minister's reply of 22nd January, 1960, because, contrary to what it says, I believe it, supports the Board's case of ministerial pressure:

You told me at our recent meeting that the Corporation had for various reasons decided to place an order for 10 of these aircraft subject to satisfactory arrangements on cost.

While I made it clear to you that I was not asking you to adopt this course there is no doubt that your decision will be most helpful to the aircraft industry. As I told you, I am equally interested in promoting the financial prosperity of the Corporations and of the manufacturing industry. I must, therefore, leave it to you and Vickers to settle the price between you.

232. Within a few days the price was agreed at £2.55m. subject to the provision (b) (ii) in paragraph 230 above and BOAC sought the approval of the Ministry to proceed. A note prepared for me by the Ministry says:

Reviewing the case of BOAC's proposed purchase of Super VC10s in February, 1960, the Ministry noted that the requirement assumed a 13% annual increase in traffic up to 1967 and continued growth thereafter. The Super VC.10 would be exclusively a trans-Atlantic aircraft but on these routes its direct operating costs per seat mile would be 15% less than those of the standard VC10. The runway facilities at London and New York would be adequate to accommodate Super VC10s. The developed Boeing might be economically superior to the Super VC10 but further purchases from the U. S. were precluded by the 'Fly British' policy and the Government's undertaking to assist Vickers with the development of the VC series of aircraft. It seemed preferable that BOAC should order the Super VC10 rather than exercise their option for more of the standard version which was economically inferior to the Boeing. The Ministry therefore endorsed the Corporation's case and the Government approval for the order was given on 7th March, 1960.

233. I pass now to May 1960 and to the first record I can find of any dissatisfaction being expressed by BOAC to the Ministry about the economic viability of the VC10 fleet.  ⁃

234. On 12th May Sir Gerard d'Erlanger wrote to the Minister in the following terms:

An airline operating 707 (or D. C. 8) type aircraft will be in a very favourable competitive and economic position if that type provides a substantial part of its capacity. Due to the buy–British policy, BOAC's 707 aircraft will provide no more than 50% of its total output in 1962. Nevertheless BOAC should at that time be in a reasonably strong economic position.

There is, however, some cause for concern from 1964 onwards, in that the VC.10 will be 3$d$ a ton mile more costly to operate than the 707; in 1966 the VC10 and the Comet IV between them will be providing 75% of our total output. Each penny per ton mile on 75% of our output means a difference in cost of £2.25m. a year. But the position ought not to be as difficult as those figures might indicate because, as you know, the VC10 should be a more flexible aircraft than the 707 or DC8 on our 'Empire' routes and carry better payloads off marginal airfields. We shall, of course, not know the actual position until we fly the aircraft in 1964.

Although in this letter there is an intimation that the burden on BOAC could be of the order of £7.5m. yearly, the fact is not emphasized; on the contrary there is at the conclusion a suggestion that the position ought not to be as difficult as the figures suggest because of flexibility in the aircraft and the opportunity of carrying better payloads off marginal airfields.

235. However, I am satisfied that the Department were alive to the problem and to the prospect that BOAC's total costs would be likely to be some 20% higher than those of its principal rivals and that, in addition, there would be introductory costs of the VC10 of between £5m. and £10m.

236 On the 12th July, 1960, which was shortly before his resignation took effect, Sir Gerard d'Erlanger told the Minister that if BOAC had been given a free choice it would not have ordered the VC10 but would have ordered American Boeings and it only went forward with the project because the Government had made it clear that fifteen Boeing 707s were the most it could purchase.

237. Between September 1960 and January 1961 BOAC reached the conclusion, with which Vickers agreed, that the Super VC10 with 187 seats as contemplated and ordered was 'over-stretched' and would not prove a satisfactory aircraft. It also concluded that an aeroplane slightly larger than the standard and slightly smaller than the Super, providing accommodation for 159 passengers would produce a better economic result and would be more flexible. The Corporation therefore sought Government approval to vary the orders, substituting for the 35 standard and 10 Super VC10s, 15 standard and 30 modified Super VC10s. This, however, would have had the effect of increasing the overall cost by 7.2m. and the Government was only prepared to approve a variation provided the overall cost was not increased. Accordingly the order for 3 standard VC10s was cancelled and the order became 12 standard VC10s and 30 modified Super VC10s, Government approval having been obtained at the end of October 1961.

238. As compensation for the cancellation of the order for 3 standard VC10s, BOAC paid Vickers approximately £600,000 which was charged in the accounts for the year to 31st March 1962.

239. Meanwhile on the 14th April, 1961, Sir Matthew Slattery, who had succeeded Sir Gerard d'Erlanger as chairman with effect from 29th July, 1960, wrote to the Minister, (now Mr Peter Thorneycroft) setting out the grave disadvantage to BOAC in flying VC10s in place of Boeings. He then put the estimated annual penalty at some £11m. for flying the same seating capacity and some £7m. for providing the same frequency of service. He conceded that the VC10 could have superior commercial attraction which could give an improved load factor but estimated that to eliminate even a penalty of £7m. a year it would be necessary to increase the load factor by six percentage points.

240. Subsequently BOAC sought to arrive at a more exact estimate of the additional annual cost of flying a fleet of 42 VC10s as against the cost of flying a similar fleet of Boeings. This difference was considerably higher than the earlier 1961 estimates but was not accepted by Vickers, who claimed that a fair assessment of the difference was much less.

241. BOAC therefore invited Mr Stephen Wheatcroft on 21st March, 1962, to review the matter as an independent expert and to advise it on the figure of penalty per annum in all the circumstances, including assumptions as to what he felt could reasonably be expected as regards

operational efficiency. He arrived at the figure for 1966/67 of £10.7m. which could come down to £7.5m. after the early years, when the operating costs for aircraft are always high.

242. Unfortunately the assumptions which have to be made affect the final figure to a very material extent. Mr Wheatcroft points out at the end of his report that his calculations of:

> The inherent and introductory penalties of BOAC's planned VC10 and Super VC10 programmes in 1966/67 are significantly lower than those estimated by BOAC. The BOAC estimates have concluded that the total penalty in 1966/67 is likely to be £17.3m. It may be helpful to give here an approximate explanation of the differences in penalty estimates. The most significant differences in assumptions used are:
>
> a) Calculation of equivalent Boeing 707 hours
> b) cost of engine overhauls
> c) purchase price of aircraft.
>
> If the calculation of penalties in the previous section of this report had been based on BOAC's assessment of equivalent Boeing 707 hours (i.e. based on equal seats and different seating ratios) the total penalty for 1966/67 would have been estimated at          £13.53m.
>
> If, in addition to using BOAC's assessment of equivalent Boeing 707 hours, the calculations in this report had also been based on the relative engine overhaul cost estimated by BOAC the total penalty for 1966/67 would have been estimated at          £14.60m.
>
> Finally, if in addition to the two foregoing changes in assumptions, the calculations in this report had adopted the relative purchase prices assumed by BOAC for the three aircraft, the penalty for 1966/67 would have been estimated at          £16m.
>
> The reconciliation of the estimates serves to underline the fundamental importance of the three assumptions listed above.

243. BOAC advises me that in its view Mr Wheatcroft should have allowed for higher crew costs during the introductory period and that the amount he has allowed for cost of fuel and engine overhauls is too low. There are at present so many unknown factors that I question whether it is possible to arrive at a figure that could be regarded as reliable. I gather the opinion of technicians at the Ministry is that in the early years the penalty of operating a fleet of 42 VC10s against Boeings is about £11m. to £12m. a year. Whatever the figures may eventually prove to be, present indications are that it is likely to be higher than anything BOAC can carry.

244. There are a number of references in the many documents that I have seen to the better 'consumer appeal' expected of the VC10 which should give a better load factor than in the case of the Boeing. It is suggested that the benefit which may flow from the better load factor should be treated as some offset to the higher operational costs in any assessment of the penalty of operating the VC10 rather than the Boeing. I do not agree.

245. I believe that any sound commercial board ordering aircraft in 1959, for delivery five or six years later, would have required considerably improved 'consumer appeal' as an offset to the heavy costs of developing and installing a new type of aircraft and the recurrent additional annual costs of

running two fleets instead of one, even if the warranted operating costs of the new aircraft, to be delivered in five or six years' time were on a par with those of the fleet shortly to be delivered.

246. In my view, if, when the VC10 fleet is fully operational, the annual costs of operating it, are higher than the costs of operating an appropriate fleet of Boeings, excluding in each case pre-operational or development costs, the difference is the true measure of the burden on BOAC which arises from the decision to buy British aircraft.

247. In this report I repeatedly use the phrase 'an appropriate fleet of Boeings'. As Boeings have a larger seating capacity than VC10s it makes a considerable difference to the penalty calculation whether it is desired to provide the same seat mile capacity or the same frequency of service. For the purpose of his original calculations Mr Wheatcroft worked on the assumption that where the aircraft is required to provide at least a daily service it was reasonable to base the comparison on an equal output of seat miles but on other routes on equal frequences (*sic*). I intend the phrase 'an appropriate fleet of Boeings' to mean the number arrived at by this formula or such other formula as may be advocated by the panel which I propose in Section XI should be set up.

248. The whole trend of the VC10 negotiations is very bewildering. There is no question that in the autumn of 1956 the Government insisted that BOAC should buy British. There is also, I think, no doubt that throughout the whole period of Sir Gerard d'Erlanger's chairmanship the Ministers wanted BOAC to buy British and to buy as many aircraft as it could. The negotiations about the VC10 were handled personally by Sir Gerard d'Erlanger and I think he genuinely felt that he was acting in the national interest if he met the Ministers' wishes.

249. By the end of 1959 the Boeing was flying and any doubts that may have existed earlier as to whether it could meet its guaranteed performance were no longer justified. Its operational costs were known. Moreover, it was proving to be a much more flexible aeroplane than had been generally expected.

250. Owing to the escalation clause it is not possible to assess accurately the ultimate cost of the 42 VC10s, including spare engines, spare tools and equipment, etc. The estimate as at 31st March, 1963, amounts to £148m. This is made up as follows:
Aircraft, including provision for change orders, escalation and customer furnished equipment £123m.; spare engines £9.5m.; spares, tools and equipment, etc. £15.5m.

251. A recent assessment as to future aircraft requirements in the light of anticipated traffic trends shows that BOAC needs only 29 VC10s instead of the 42 which it has on order.

## CORBETT'S SUMMARY AND RECOMMENDATIONS: THE VC10

351. I have devoted a separate section of the report to the VC10 story because this will so vitally affect BOAC in the future.

352. Doubts have been expressed as to whether Vickers can so modify the VC10 as to eliminate the 'drag' difficulty and bring it up to the performance guaranteed by the contract. My report

is written on the assumption that this will be done. The disturbing fact is that even if the guaranteed performance is achieved the direct annual operating cost of a fleet of 29 VC10s could still be £7.5m. to £10m. more than that of an appropriate fleet of Boeings.

353. The international airline business is now so competitive and the profit margins so slender that BOAC, no matter how skilfully organised, has no prospect of running other than at a loss if the operating costs of a material part of its fleet are significantly above those of the fleets of its competitors.

354. In January 1960 when Vickers said they were in trouble with the original VC10 contract and might be unable to complete it, I think the Board of BOAC was wrong to enter into a contract for further VC10 aircraft, when it looked as though the full VC10 fleet would cost some £10m. a year more than an appropriate fleet of Boeings. Any improved customer appeal should, I think, have been regarded as no more than a commercial 'set off' to the very heavy development and installation costs and the continuing cost of running a two-type fleet as against a one-type fleet.

355. Then was the time to set clearly before the Minister its estimate of the possible annual penalty and to say that BOAC could not itself afford to run the risk involved, unless indemnified by the Government or 'directed' by the Minister.

356. After enquiry the Government might have reached the conclusion that it was in the national interest to press on with the VC10 project but BOAC would then have been protected from the risk of having to operate aircraft at much greater cost than its competitors.

357. Today we face the hard practical facts:
(i) that BOAC has on order 13 more aircraft than it requires, each of which may cost between £250,000 and £350,000 more to run each year than a Boeing;
(ii) if, when fully operational, the VC10 fleet costs significantly more to operate than a Boeing fleet, BOAC will not be able to cover the cost, and will continue to run at a loss;
(iii) recurring and mounting losses will make it well nigh impossible to maintain morale in the organisation;
(iv) any losses which BOAC incurs can only be financed from public funds.

358. Although one must regard BOAC as legally responsible for the position in which it now finds itself, I think it must be in the national interest to face the realities of today and give the reconstituted Board, charged with much more specific obligations, a fair chance to meet the challenge from its competitors.

359. I do not believe it is really practicable to maintain, let alone create, a keen and efficient team in any organisation which is consistently operating at a loss. This applies particularly in a nationalised undertaking which must be subject to constant criticism in Parliament and the press so long as it continues to show losses.

360. Apart from the political considerations involved, and these it is not for me to take into account, I think that BOAC should be required to cancel the 13 VC10s which it does not need

and, with the idea of cutting compensation to the minimum, to cancel them as soon as possible. If, of course, the Government can arrange for these 13 aircraft to be transferred to the Royal Air Force, who I understand have expressed interest in the VC10, this should help Vickers and BOAC. I can form no opinion as to the amount of compensation which might have to be paid to Vickers. I understand that the material has not been cut on at least thirteen aircraft and I assume, maybe quite wrongly, that the compensation could be agreed at something less than £1m. per aircraft. There is no provision in the contract for any cancellation by BOAC, so it is a matter that would have to be negotiated. If, of course, the figure should be materially higher than £1m. an aircraft it may be better to sell Boeings and to take delivery of the VC10s. This is a particularly inconvenient moment to have to report on such a matter.

361. If BOAC is to be put on a sound commercial basis in the future, any problem of substantially higher operating costs for the VC10 can only be solved if the Government is prepared to recoup BOAC, either by waiver of interest or some other means, the amount of the annual penalty. I do not believe this is a figure that can today be fairly assessed and it would be best done by an expert panel comprising technicians and business men when the aircraft is fully operational.

362. I can see the difficulties of giving effect to this recommendation, as the Government would not wish to give the impression to the other international airlines that they were subsidising their own nationalised airline, so it would have to be made clear that the extent of the aid was limited to the difference in operating costs of the VC10 and the Boeing which most of the other airlines fly. Nevertheless it would be unfair to Vickers if it appeared to be a subsidy to the British aircraft industry, as it is at least possible that in January 1960, when Vickers were threatening to discontinue VC10 production, they might have regarded the difficulties ahead, even given the further order for the Super VC10s, as so great as not to make it worth while continuing production, if the announcement of a large Government subsidy involved any risk to their international goodwill.

363. The only other solution that I have been able to think of is for the Government to take over the VC10 contract and to hire the aircraft out to BOAC at such a rate that they would cost no more to fly than Boeings. Fundamentally it comes back to the same question of a Government subsidy but it may be a better way of presenting the matter. Both suggestions are fraught with difficulties for the Government and it is a great regret to me that I have been unable to think of any less unattractive advice.

364. In connection with the proposal that there should be recouped to BOAC the amount of any penalty on VC10 operations, it may be said that if blind landing equipment is in due course fitted to the VC10, the gap between the operating costs relative to the Boeing will be narrowed but the proposal I make for an annual assessment by a panel would take care of this factor. If, moreover, the percentage load factor on the VC10 should in practice turn out to be a good many points ahead of the percentage load factor on the Boeing, so that the increased revenue earned by the VC10 more than covered the development and introductory costs and resulted in a substantial surplus on BOAC's accounts, any such surplus would have to be dealt with in accordance with the Ministry's instructions.

# TABLE 1

## BEA Annual Accounts 1952/53 to 1964/65

| Year ended 31-Mar | Profit/ (- loss) | Deficit Grant | Employee Numbers |
|---|---|---|---|
| 1952/3 | -£1,459,131 | £1,250,000 | 8,603 |
| 1953/4 | -£1,773,797 | £1,500,000 | 9,064 |
| 1954/5 | £63,039 | £1,000,000 | 9,117 |
| 1955/6 | £603,614 | nil | 10,108 |
| 1956/7 | £205,725 | nil | 10,540 |
| 1957/8 | £1,054,807 | nil | 11,232 |
| 1958/9 | £232,695 | nil | 11,676 |
| 1959/60 | £2,086,078 | nil | 12,337 |
| 1960/61 | £1,545,321 | nil | 13,640 |
| 1961/62 | -£1,488,065 | nil | 15,175 |
| 1962/63 | -£265,301 | nil | 16,010 |
| 1963/64 | £3,030,007 | nil | 17,108 |
| 1964/65 | £1,316,876 | nil | 18,011 |

BEA Annual Reports and Accounts

# TABLE 2

## BOAC Annual Reports 1952/53 to 1964/65

| Year ended 31-Mar | Profit/ (- loss) | Accumulated Deficit | Employee Numbers |
|---|---|---|---|
| 1952/3 | -£838,669 | £1,778,171 | 17,798 |
| 1953/4 | £1,065,397 | £841,260 | 17,255 |
| 1954/5 | £261,687 | £861,974 | 17,062 |
| 1955/6 | £117,331 | (£17,881) | 18,411 |
| 1956/7 | £303,352 | (£440,199) | 19,046 |
| 1957/8 | -£2,839,350 | £3,045,388 | 19,591 |
| 1958/9 | -£5,179,420 | £14,681,167 | 19,010 |
| 1959/60 | -£833,795 | £15,237,819 | 19,131 |
| 1960/61 | -£2,544,280 | £17,221,686 | 20,787 |
| 1961/62 | -£20,850,201 | £67,293,838 | 21,889 |
| 1962/63 | -£12,178,452 | £80,154,282 | 21,686 |
| 1963/64 | £951,000 | £90,510,000 | 20,626 |
| 1964/65 | £7,573,000 | £82,521,000 | 19,641 |

BOAC Annual Reports and Accounts

## TABLE 3

### 1951-64 Passengers carried by BOAC, BEA and the Independents

|  | BOAC Total | BEA Total | Independent Total |
|---|---|---|---|
| 1951/2 | 250,173 | 1,135,579 | 207,683 |
| 1952/3 | 290,629 | 1,400,122 | 324,843 |
| 1953/4 | 304,980 | 1,656,779 | 475,334 |
| 1954/5 | 291,136 | 1,874,316 | 641,323 |
| 1955/6 | 377,070 | 2,224,747 | 1,015,739 |
| 1956/7 | 397,557 | 2,461,065 | 1,205,561 |
| 1957/8 | 469,035 | 2,765,591 | 1,348,940 |
| 1958/9 | 495,692 | 2,828,715 | 1,423,694 |
| 1959/60 | 626,072 | 3,289,606 | 1,571,746 |
| 1960/61 | 896,460 | 3,990,957 | 2,280,154 |
| 1961/2 | 983,027 | 4,393,378 | 2,697,626 |
| 1962/3 | 976,512 | 4,914,927 | 2,925,732 |
| 1963/4 | 1,083,004 | 5,604,812 | 3,531,221 |

Source: ATAC, BIATA reports (includes charter passengers)

## TABLE 4

### 1952-67 Charter passengers (BIATA members only)

|  | trooping | contract |
|---|---|---|
| 1952/3 | 88,285 | 87,299 |
| 1953/4 | 147,825 | 74,959 |
| 1954/5 | 214,594 | 66,043 |
| 1955/6 | 204,700 | 258,713 |
| 1956/7 | 157,035 | 322,538 |
| 1957/8 | 137,821 | 307,692 |
| 1958/9 | 142,085 | 331,717 |
| 1959/60 | 119,584 | 173,927 |
| 1960/1 | 171,138 | 395,595 |
| 1961/2 | 314,734 | 301,181 |
| 1962/3 | 396,540 | 131,171 |
| 1963/4 | 425,362 | 213,836 |

Source: BIATA

# TABLE 5

## Passengers carried on scheduled services
## (Independent airlines)

|         | IT      | Domestic  | International |
|---------|---------|-----------|--------------|
| 1952/3  |         | 68,000    | 58,000       |
| 1953/4  | 8,000   | 100,000   | 143,000      |
| 1954/5  | 23,000  | 148,000   | 187,000      |
| 1955/6  | 46,000  | 219,000   | 287,000      |
| 1956/7  | 96,000  | 298,000   | 349,000      |
| 1957/8  | 137,000 | 349,000   | 429,000      |
| 1958/9  | 180,000 | 299,000   | 471,000      |
| 1959/60 | 167,000 | 366,000   | 585,000      |
| 1960/1  | 199,000 | 545,000   | 775,000      |
| 1961/2  | 273,000 | 816,000   | 845,000      |
| 1962/3  | 387,000 | 929,000   | 1,082,000    |
| 1963/4  | 526,000 | 1,241,000 | 1,125,000    |

to end March

Domestic includes Channel Islands, Isle of Man and other domestic routes
International includes vehicle ferries and Colonial Coach Class

Source: BIATA

# TABLE 6

## 1963 and 1964: Passengers carried by individual airlines

|  | 1963 | 1964 |
|---|---|---|
| Air Ferry | 85,000 | 151,000 |
| BUA - Air Holdings Group | 1,066,633 | 969,658 |
| BUA Charter | 553,335 | 536,571 |
| (British United Airways | 83,139 | 127743) |
| (British United Air Ferries | 178,093 | 384524) |
| (British United (C.I.) | 366,832 | 441465) |
| (Morton | 8,848 | 7252) |
| (Silver City | 429,721 | 8674) |
| BKS | 247,738 | 339,840 |
| Euravia/Britannia | 67,512 | 131,296 |
| Caledonian | 46,781 | 110,730 |
| Cambrian | 256,081 | 303,438 |
| Cambrian charter | 13,421 | 45,613 |
| Channel | 285,532 | 369,890 |
| Dan-Air | 115,215 | 43,316 |
| British Midland | 99,761 | 78,385 |
| Eagle | 153,436 | 513,783 |
| Lloyd International | 28,513 | 25,734 |
| Skyways Coach-Air | 117,756 | 105,113 |
| Passenger Totals for the calendar year. | 3,136,714 | 3,724,367 |

Source: Board of Trade, BIATA, *Aeroplane*, *Flight*

# ENDNOTES

## INTRODUCTION

1 Lawrence James, *The Rise and Fall of the British Empire* (Little, Brown and Company,1994) p.438.
2 Quoted in *Flight*, 12 July 1962.
3 *Aeronautics*, January 1949.
4 *Aeronautics*, August 1949.
5 *The Aeroplane*, 28 May 1948.
6 TNA BT 245/103.
7 *Flight*, 27 May 1948.

## CHAPTER 1

1 *The Aeroplane*, 16 November 1951.
2 Navy, Army and Air Force Institutes.
3 Quoted in *Flight* magazine, 16 November 1951.
4 TNA AIR 8/1803.
5 Letter to *The Times* by Eric Rylands, chairman of BIATA, 1 July 1952.
6 Quoted in *Flight*, 6 June 1952.
7 TNA PREM 11/16.
8 *Flight*, 4 July 1952.
9 TNA BT 245/168.
10 *The Aeroplane*, 16 February 1951.
11 IATA had finally agreed to the introduction of transatlantic tourist fares, which were introduced on 1 May 1952, and offered an alternative to first-class only travel on long-haul services.
12 BKS, the initials of its original founders, Barnby, Keegan and Stevens.
13 Aircraft registration marks are the aviation equivalent of a number plate or licence tag. British aircraft carry registration marks beginning with G (for Great Britain), followed by

a hyphen and four capitalised letters; you will find registration marks used throughout the text and captions as aircraft identifiers.

14 Sir Miles Thomas, *Out on a Wing* (Michael Joseph, 1964), p.97.

15 Quoted in *The Aeroplane*, 10 November 1953.

16 Lancashire was the parent company of Skyways.

17 *The Aeroplane*, 7 November 1952.

18 Taffy Powell, *Ferryman, from Ferry Command to Silver City* (Airlife, 1982), pp.162-64.

19 Powell, p.167.

20 Some were indeed long haul; freight to Khartoum is understandable, but passenger charters to West Africa in a Freighter must have been an endurance test.

21 Powell, p.173.

22 *Aeronautics*, January 1953.

23 General Critchley, a former BOAC Director General, disputed this, claiming that the Corporation had made a profit in 1945 under his stewardship. This may be so, as BOAC survived on Treasury grants during the war years (and subsequently), so profit and loss figures are hard to reconcile. The Government acknowledged that in the period 1946 to 1951, BOAC received £32 million in grants from the Exchequer.

24 *Flight*, 3 October 1952.

25 The Tudor's reputation went before it; the Berlin Senat objected to its use on passenger flights.

# CHAPTER 2

1 *Flight*, 29 April 1955.

2 The ten included four Mk.1, the two VIP Mk.3 short-bodied versions, and four of the slightly longer Mk.4 variants. In addition some of the former BSAA aircraft were bought for dismantling and use as spares.

3 TNA AIR 8/1803.

4 *Ibid.*

5 John Gunn, *High Corridors* (University of Queensland Press, 1988), pp.34–35.

6 Thomas, p.329.

7 TNA BT 245/328

8 *Ibid.*

9 *Ibid.*

10 *The Aeroplane*, 16 April 1954

11 Whitney Straight.

12 TNA BT 245/328.

13 *Ibid.*

14 *Flight*, 26 March 1954.

15 *Ibid.*

16 Quoted in *Flight*, 23 April 1954.

17 John Boyd-Carpenter, *Way of Life* (Sidgwick & Jackson, 1980), p.117.

18 TNA T 228/528

19 Thomas, p.344.

20 *Flight*, 27 April 1956.

21 Sir Basil Smallpeice, *Of Comets and Queens* (Airlife, 1981), p.70.

22 *The Aeroplane*, 4 June 1954.

23 TNA AIR 8/1803.

24 TNA AIR 19/839.

25 Quoted in *Flight*, 22 February 1957.

26 Cyprus had been annexed by Britain in 1914 when the Ottoman Empire entered the war on the German side – although Britain had previously extracted strategic occupation rights following the Crimean War – Cyprus was just one in the chain of military bases that stretched out to the Far East, Gibraltar, Malta, Cyprus, the Canal Zone, Aden, Ceylon and Singapore.

# CHAPTER 3

1 TNA PREM 11/3680.

2 BOAC Annual Report 1957/8.

3 *The Aeroplane*, 20 September 1957.

4 *Flight*, 2 August 1957.

5 Quoted in *Flight*, 23 August 1957.

6 Quoted in *Flight*, 20 December 1957.

7 *Flight*, 20 February 1959.

8 Aeroflot, the Russian airline, controlled all aspects of civil aviation in the USSR, apart from manufacturing.

9 TNA T 228/528.

10 TNA T 228/529.

11 TNA AIR 8/1803.

12 Later Sir Alec Douglas-Home, who succeeded Macmillan as Prime Minister in 1963. He once self deprecatingly said he did not think he would ever be Prime Minister, 'because I do my sums with matchsticks.'

13 TNA PREM 11/2240

14 *Ibid*.

15 Quoted in *Flight*, 20 December 1957.

16 Cambrian had transferred its Cardiff operations from the convenient if small airport at Pengam Moors to the modern but somewhat more remote former RAF station at Rhoose in April 1954.

17 *Flight*, 11 December 1959.

18 George Behrend, *Jersey Airlines International*, Jersey Artists Ltd, 1968.

19 Tony Merton Jones, *British Independent Airlines*, Vol.2, p.227.

20 Letter from Harold Watkinson, Minister of Transport and Civil Aviation, to Lord Terrington, 5 June 1958.

21 Quoted in *Flight*, 21 November 1958.

22 Civil Aeronautics Board, which had been in existence since 1939, and had a reputation for being somewhat legalistic.

23 Quoted in *Flight*, 21 November 1958.

24 Quoted in *Flight*, 6 November 1959.

25 The Comet 4 was not designed for transatlantic routes but its introduction in advance of the Boeing 707 was something of a coup. Nor was the original 707-120 intended for long-haul over-water stages, but it was used on this route until the larger, longer range 707-320 versions became available nearly a year later.

26 HoC Debate, 27 January 1958.

27 Canadian Pacific Airlines 6, Aeronaves de Mexico 2, Cubana 2, El Al 3, Hunting-Clan 2, Northeast (USA) had just cancelled its order for 5.

28 TNA PREM 11/2241.

29 *Ibid.*

30 *Ibid.*

31 See Appendix 1 for more about the development of the Trident and BEA's baleful influence.

32 The design resembled Laker's own private venture offering, the Aviation Traders Accountant, which never went into production. Perhaps the name had something to do with it!

33 *Airlift*, September 1959.

34 *Ibid.*

# CHAPTER 4

1 TNA T 224/273.

2 Keith Hayward, *Government and British Civil Aerospace, a case study in post-war technology policy*, Manchester University Press, 1983, p.38.

3 These are flights in which a person or organisation charters an aircraft for their own sole use.

4 Quoted in *The Aeroplane*, 21 October 1960.

5 Fourteenth Barnard Memorial Lecture, Royal Aeronautical Society, 15 March 1967.

6 BIATA Annual report 1959-60. The Association's president that year, Cyril Stevens, was the 'S' in BKS.

7 BIATA *op.cit.*

8 *Aeronautics*, August 1960.

9 Quoted in *The Aeroplane*, 23 November 1961.

10 TNA T 224/273. Both this file and the subsequent T 224/274 chart the course of the Air Transport Licensing Bill through its various stages.

11 *Ibid.*

12 *Ibid.*

13 *Ibid.*

14 *Ibid.*

15 *Ibid.*

16 Hansard, 2 March 1960.

17 The subsidiary companies and companies in which BOAC had an interest included: Bahamas Airways, BWIA, Middle East Airlines (MEA), Turkish Airlines, Kuwait Airways, Gulf Aviation, Aden Airways, Ghana Airways, Nigeria Airways, Hong Kong Airways, Malayan Airways and Borneo Airways.

18 *Flight*, 11 October 1962.

19 *Flight*, 26 February 1960.

20 *Flight*, 19 February 1960.

21 *Ibid.*

22 Quoted in Francis Hyde, *Cunard and the North Atlantic 1840-1973*, Macmillan, 1975, p.279. Chapters 9 and 10 cover Cunard's involvement with air transport.

23 BUA's Britannias had water-injection Proteus 765s and were more suited to the hot and high operating conditions of the African services. They were replaced on trooping duties out of Stansted by the BOAC aircraft, which had lasted barely four years in the corporation's service.

24 TNA BT 245/254 suggests that the Ministry may have been influenced by the possibility that Eagle (Bermuda) would start operating from Bermuda to Luxembourg instead.

25 BG Cramp, *British Midland Airways*, Airlife, 1979, p.44.

26 *Flight*, 24 June 1960.

27 *Flight*, 11 November 1960.

28 Falcon had a classy chairman: Dr James Robertson-Justice, himself a falconer, and star of many British films; best remembered as Sir Lancelot Spratt in the *Doctors* comedy series.

29 *Flight*, 1 July 1960.

## CHAPTER 5

1 He was once asked by BEA's counsel, Henry Marking, if he would define 'material diversion', always a critical factor in licensing disputes: 'You are trying to put salt on my tail, Mr Marking,' the wily lord replied, 'and I am not going to be caught.'

2 *Flight*, 23 March 1961.

3 *Flight*, 10 August 1961.

4 Quoted in *Flight*, 27 July 1961.

5 Quoted in *Aeronautics*, August, 1961.

6 BEA Annual Report and Accounts 1960-61.

7 *Flight*, 29 June 1961.

8 Quoted in *The Aeroplane*, 5 October 1961.

9 *Flight*, 30 November 1961.

10 *Ibid.*

11 *The Aeroplane*, 30 November 1961.

12 *Journal of the Royal Aeronautical Society* – The Role of Private Enterprise in British Air Transportation, Vol.71, June 1967.

13 Smallpeice, p.146.

14 *The Aeroplane*, 24 March 1966.

15 *Flight*, in its 16 May 1963 issue, calculated that there were 600,000 IT passengers in 1962, 400,000 in 1961 and 250,000 in 1960, of which 200,000, 100,000 and 50,000 respectively were carried by foreign airlines.

16 Quoted in *Flight*, 7 February 1963.

17 Quoted in *Flight*, 15 November 1962.

18 It introduced British carriers to the concept of 'uplift ratio'. In order to reserve the United States market to its own carriers, the Americans obliged British carriers to carry a percentage of British originating traffic to balance traffic originating in the US, a much

larger and more prosperous market. For every four flights that Caledonian operated with United States-originating traffic, it had to operate three flights with UK originating passengers.

19 Aden Airways, a subsidiary of BOAC, held trooping contracts to carry forces personnel within the Arabian Peninsula, and between Aden, Mombasa and Nairobi.

20 When Airwork and Skyways had performed the trooping flights to Singapore, they had been paid £13,366 per flight on the 63-seat Hermes. Hunting-Clan had tendered the 110-seat Britannia at £10,540, reducing the cost per passenger by around 60 per cent. Under the new deal, the cost of the Britannia charters went up to approximately £12,500, determined by the number of hours flown under the contract. (TNA AIR 19/1102).

21 TNA AIR 19/1102.

22 *Ibid.*

23 *Ibid.*

24 Quoted in *Flight*, 11 July 1963.

## CHAPTER 6

1 Cramp, p.48.

2 Quoted in *The Aeroplane*, 20 December 1962.

3 Scottish Airways was jointly owned by Whitehall Securities, the LMS Railway and David Macbrayne, and developed a comprehensive route network covering Scotland's Highlands and Islands.

4 Smallpeice, p.159.

5 *Flight*, 14 June 1962.

6 Quoted in *Flight*, 27 September 1962.

7 Quoted in *Flight*, 20 June 1963.

8 Quoted in *Flight*, 18 April 1963.

9 Quoted in *Flight*, 11 July 1963.

10 TNA PREM 11/4126.

11 TNA PREM 11/3680. In a surreal moment, his comments were mistakenly transcribed so as to refer to Victors (a heavy bomber built for the RAF) instead of Vickers.

12 Smallpeice, pp.125-6.

13 Quoted in *Flight*, 14 November 1963.

14 Annual Report for 1962-63, The British Independent Air Transport Association.

15 Harald Penrose in *Wings across the world* says that the report was shown to Sir Giles Guthrie later.

16 TNA PREM 11/4126.

17 TNA T 319/126. All further references to the Report in this section are from these, and the two following Treasury files.

18 Professor Edwards, *British Air Transport in the Seventies* (HMSO, London) 1969, p.325.

19 In appendix 21, Corbett notes that: 'The RAE did <u>not</u> conclude that the take-off performance of the VC10, or the runway length required, would be substantially better than on Vickers' own assessment. They confirmed Vickers' own figures for intrinsic performance. They used less conservative assumptions to convert inherent performance to runway length

requirements. The RAE investigation did not deal with operating costs, and the conclusions on costs do not flow directly from the RAE findings.'

20 TNA PREM 11/4126.

21 *Ibid.*

22 TNA PREM 11/4674.

23 *Flight International*, 28 November 1963.

24 Quoted in *Flight*, 2 July 1964.

25 Many years later, as an interested observer in the 1970s I was curious as to why the Hong Kong airline, Cathay Pacific, had to apply to the British licensing authority, by then the Civil Aviation Authority, for a British scheduled-service licence to fly between Hong Kong and London. Now I know why. The ruling also affected Gibraltar Airways when it wanted to start flying to London.

26 *Flight*, 9 April 1964.

27 PRO AIR 19/1102.

28 TNA PREM 11/4676.

29 *Ibid.*

30 The 20th Brancker Memorial Lecture, 11 February 1963.

# APPENDIX 1

1 The sources for this appendix include *Jane's, British Civil Aviation* by D.G.T. Harvey; *British Commercial Aircraft* by Paul Ellis; *De Havilland Aircraft since 1909*, by A.J. Jackson; *The World's Airliners*, by Peter Brooks; the Putnam series *British Civil Aircraft*; John Stroud's articles over the years in *Aeroplane Monthly*.

2 Quoted in *Aircraft Illustrated*, September 1979, by Doug Birch.

3 *Ibid.*

4 Hayward, p.34.

5 The Hermes was briefly reintroduced into BOAC service in 1954, for six months, following the grounding of the Comet fleet.

# BIBLIOGRAPHY

Aldcroft, Derek H., *British Transport*, Leicester University Press, 1971

Aldcroft, Derek H., *Studies in British Transport History 1870-1970*, David & Charles, 1974

Aldcroft, Derek H., *British Transport since 1914*, David & Charles, 1975

Behrend, George, *Jersey Airlines International*, Jersey Artists, 1968

Behrend, George, *Channel Silver Wings*, Jersey Artists, 1972

Bonavia, Michael, *The Nationalisation of British Transport*, St Martin's Press, 1987

Boyd-Carpenter, John, *Way of Life*, Sidgwick & Jackson, London, 1980

Brabazon of Tara, Lord, *The Brabazon Story*, Heinemann London, 1956

Brooks, Peter, *The Modern Airliner*, Sunflower University Press KS, 1961

Brooks, Peter, *The World's Airliners*, Putnam, 1962

Church, Richard, *The One-Eleven Story*, Air-Britain (Historians), 1994

Cleife, Philip, *Airway to the Isles*, Hodder and Stoughton, London, 1966

Corbett, David, *Politics and the Airlines*, George Allen & Unwin, 1965

Cramp, B.G., *British Midland Airways*, Airlife, 1979

Davies, R.E.G., *History of the World's Airlines*, Oxford University Press, 1964

Davies, R.E.G., *Rebels and Reformers of the Airways*, Smithsonian, Washington, 1987

Davies, R.E.G., *De Havilland Comet*, Paladwr Press, 1999

Davies, R.E.G., *British Airways An Airline and its Aircraft Vol.1 1919-1939*, Paladwr Press, 2006

Davis, Peter W., *Vickers Viscount and Vanguard*, Air-Britain (Historians), 1981

de Havilland, Geoffrey, *Sky Fever*, Airlife, 1979

Dobson, Alan P., *Peaceful Air Warfare*, Clarendon Press Oxford, 1991

Doganis, Rigas, *Flying Off Course*, George Allen & Unwin, 1985

Doyle, Neville, *The Triple Alliance*, Air-Britain (Historians), 2002

Eastwood, A.B., *Piston Engine Airliner Production List*, TAHS, 1996

Eastwood, A.B., *Turbo Prop Airliner Production List*, TAHS, 1996

Eglin, Roger, *Fly Me, I'm Freddie*, Weidenfeld & Nicolson, London, 1980

Ellis, Paul, *British Commercial Aircraft*, Jane's Publishing, 1980

Gardner, Charles, *British Aircraft Corporation*, Batsford, London, 1981

Gradidge, J.M.G., *The Douglas DC-3 and its predecessors*, Air-Britain (Historians), 1984

Halford-MacLeod, Guy, *Britain's Airlines Vol.1, 1946-1951*, Tempus, 2006

Hardy,m.J., *BAC One-Eleven*, Ian Allan, 1985

Havighurst, Alfred F., *Britain in Transition, the 20th Century*, University of Chicago Press, 1979

Hayward, Keith, *Government and British civil aerospace*, Manchester University Press, 1983

Hedges, David, *The Eagle Years 1948-1968*, TAHS, 2002

Higham, Robin, *Britain's Imperial Air Routes 1918 to 1939*, G.T. Foulis , 1960

Hooks, Mike, *Croydon Airport*, Chalford, 1997

Hyde, Francis, *Cunard and the North Atlantic 1840-1973*, Humanities Press NJ, 1975

Jackson, A.J., *British Civil Aircraft 1919-1972, Vol.1*, Putnam, 1959

Jackson, A.J., *British Civil Aircraft 1919-1972, Vol.2*, Putnam, 1960

Jackson, A.J., *British Civil Aircraft 1919-1972, Vol.3*, Putnam, 1960

Jackson, A.J., *De Havilland Aircraft since 1909*, Putnam, 1962

Jackson, Peter, *The Sky Tramps*, Souvenir Press London, 1965

Jenkins, Gilmour, *The Ministry of Transport and Civil Aviation*, George Allen & Unwin, 1959

Kelf-Cohen, R., *Twenty Years of Nationalisation*, Macmillan, 1969

Kniveton, Gordon, *Manx Aviation in War and Peace*, The Manx Experience, 1985

Kniveton, Gordon, *Wings of Mann*, The Manx Experience, 1997

Lo Bao, Phil, *Bristol Britannia*, Aviation Data Centre, 1996

Lo Bao, Phil, *The de Havilland Comet*, Aviation Data Centre,

London, Peter, *Aviation in Cornwall*, Air-Britain (Historians), 1997

Longhurst, John, *Nationalisation in Practice*, Temple Press, 1950

Martin, Bernard, *The Viking, Valetta and Varsity*, Air-Britain (Historians), 1975

Merton Jones, Tony, *British Independent Airlines 1946-1976*, TAHS, 2000

Middleton, D.H., *Airspeed*, Terence Dalton Lavenham, 1982

Olley, Gordon, *A Million Miles in the Air*, Hodder and Stoughton London, 1934

Payne, L.G.S., *Air Dates*, Heinemann London, 1957

Penrose, Harald, *Wings across the world,* Cassell, London, 1980

Powell, Taffy, *Ferryman, from Ferry Command to Silver City*, Airlife, 1982

Pudney, John, *The Seven Skies*, Putnam, 1959

Raitz, Vladimir, *Flight to the Sun (with Roger Bray)*, Continuum, London and New York, 2001

Sampson, Anthony, *Empires of the Sky*, Hodder and Stoughton London, 1984

Seifert, Karl-Dieter, *Der deutsche Luftverkehr 1955-2000*, Bernard & Graefe Verlag, 2001

Simons, Graham, *The Spirit of Dan-Air*, GMS Enterprises, 1993

Simons, Graham, *Colours in the Sky*, GMS Enterprises, 1997

Smallpeice, Basil, *Of Comets and Queens*, Airlife, 1980

Smith, Myron J., *The Airline Bibliography – Salem College Guide to Sources*, Locust Hill Press, 1988

Standon, Tommy, *History of Cambrian Airways*, Airline Publications & Sales Ltd, 1979

Sterling, Chris, *Commercial Air Transport Books*, Paladwr Press, 1996

Sterling, Chris, *Commercial Air Transport Books*, Supplement, Paladwr Press, 1998

Stroud, John, *Annals of British & Commonwealth Air Transport*, Putnam, 1962

Stroud, John, *Railway Air Services*, Ian Allan, 1987

Stroud, John, *Jetliners in Service since 1952*, Putnam, 1994

Sykes, T., *The DH104 Dove and DH114 Heron*, Air-Britain (Historians), 1973

Taylor, J.W.R., *Civil Aircraft Markings*, Ian Allan (annual publication from 1950)

The Aeroplane, *Who's Who in British Aviation*, Temple Press, 1947

The Aeroplane, *Directory of British Aviation*, Temple Press (annual publication)

Thetford, Owen G., *ABC of Airports and Airliners*, Ian Allan, 1948

Thomas, Miles, *Out on a Wing*, Michael Joseph, 1964

Wheatcroft, Stephen, *The Economics of European Air Transport*, Harvard University Press, MA, 1956

Wheatcroft, Stephen, *Air Transport Policy*, Michael Joseph, 1964

Williams, J.E.D., *The Operation of Airliners*, Hutchinson, London, 1964

Wilson, Stewart, *Viscount Comet and Concorde*, Aerospace Publications Pty, 1996

Wilson, Stewart, *Boeing 707, Douglas DC-8 & Vickers VC10*, Aerospace Publications Pty, 1998

Wright, Alan J., *The British World Airlines Story*, Midland Publishing, 1996

# ARTICLES

ATAC, Report of the Air Transport Advisory Council (annual), HMSO

BEA, Report and Accounts (annual), HMSO

BIATA, Annual Reports British Independent Air Transport Association, 1951/52 – 1959/60

BOAC, Report and Accounts (annual), HMSO

Brooks, Peter W., 'The Development of Air Transport', Transport Economics and Policy, 1967

Brooks, Peter W., 'Problems of Short-Haul Air Transport', Royal Aeronautical Society, 1952

Humphreys, B.K., 'Nationalisation and the independent airlines', Journal of Transport History, 1976

Humphreys, B.K., 'Trooping and British independent airlines', Journal of Transport History, 1979

Laker, F.A., 'Private Enterprise in British Air Transport', Royal Aeronautical Society, 1966

Lyth, Peter J., 'A Multiplicity of Instruments', Journal of Transport History, 1990

Wheatcroft, Stephen, 'Licensing British Air Transport', Royal Aeronautical Society, 1964

Williams, J.E.D., 'The Role of Private Enterprise in British Air Transportation', Royal Aeronautical Society, 1967

Williams, J.E.D., 'Holiday Traffic by Air' – 25th Brancker Memorial Lecture, Institute of Transport Journal, 1968

Wyatt, Myles, 'British Independent Aviation – Past and Future', 20th Brancker Memorial Lecture, 1963

# PERIODICALS AND MAGAZINES

*Aeronautical Quarterly* (RAeS)

*Aeronautics*

*Aeroplane and Commercial Aviation News*

*Aeroplane Monthly*

*Aeroplane, The*

*Air BP*

*Air Enthusiast*

*Air Pictorial*

*Air-Britain Digest*
*Aircraft*
*Aircraft Illustrated*
*Airlift*
*de Havilland Gazette*
*Esso World*
*Flight*
*Flight International*
*Interavia*
*Journal of the Royal Aeronautical Society* (RAeS)
*Journal of Transport Economics and Policy*
*Journal of Transport History*
*Modern Transport*
*Propliner*
*Shell Aviation News*
*World Airline Record*

## THE NATIONAL ARCHIVES: FILE NUMBERS

AIR 8/1803, 19/839, 19/1102, 20/10924, 33/41

AVIA 63/27

BT 217/1418, 245/103, 245/168, 245/229, 245/237, 245/254, 245/328, 252/489

PREM 11/16, 11/2240, 11/2241, 11/2597, 11/3680, 11/3984, 11/4126, 11/4674, 11/4675, 11/4676

T 224/273, 224/274, 224/301, 224/302, 224/303, 224/304, 228/528, 228/529, 319/126, 319/127, 319/128

# INDEX

If you are interested in purchasing other books published by Tempus, or in case you have difficulty finding any
Tempus books in your local bookshop, you can also place orders directly through our website

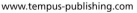
www.tempus-publishing.com

BC        1/08